A Prince *in a* Republic

The **Institute of Southeast Asian Studies (ISEAS)** was established as an autonomous organization in 1968. It is a regional centre dedicated to the study of socio-political, security and economic trends and developments in Southeast Asia and its wider geostrategic and economic environment. The Institute's research programmes are the Regional Economic Studies (RES, including ASEAN and APEC), Regional Strategic and Political Studies (RSPS), and Regional Social and Cultural Studies (RSCS).

ISEAS Publishing, an established academic press, has issued more than 2,000 books and journals. It is the largest scholarly publisher of research about Southeast Asia from within the region. ISEAS Publishing works with many other academic and trade publishers and distributors to disseminate important research and analyses from and about Southeast Asia to the rest of the world.

THE LIFE OF SULTAN HAMENGKU BUWONO IX
of YOGYAKARTA

A Prince *in a* Republic

JOHN MONFRIES

INSTITUTE OF SOUTHEAST ASIAN STUDIES
Singapore

First published in Singapore in 2015 by
ISEAS Publishing
Institute of Southeast Asian Studies
30 Heng Mui Keng Terrace
Pasir Panjang
Singapore 119614

E-mail: publish@iseas.edu.sg
Website: <http://bookshop.iseas.edu.sg>

All rights reserved. No part of this publication may be reproduced, stored in a retrieval system, or transmitted in any form or by any means, electronic, mechanical, photocopying, recording or otherwise, without the prior permission of the Institute of Southeast Asian Studies.

© 2015 Institute of Southeast Asian Studies

Every effort has been made to identify copyright holders; in case of oversight, and on notification to the publisher, corrections will be made in the next edition.

The responsibility for facts and opinions in this publication rests exclusively with the author and his interpretations do not necessarily reflect the views or the policy of the publishers or their supporters.

ISEAS Library Cataloguing-in-Publication Data

Monfries, John.
   A prince in a republic : the life of Sultan Hamengku Buwono IX of Yogyakarta.
   1. Hamengku Buwono IX, Sultan of Yogyakarta, 1912–1988.
   2. Sultans—Indonesia—Yogyakarta—Biography.
   3. Yogyakarta (Indonesia)—Kings and rulers—Biography.
   4. Politicians—Indonesia—Biography.
   5. Nationalists—Indonesia—Biography.
   I. Title.
   II. Title: Life of Sultan Hamengku Buwono IX of Yogyakarta
DS644.1 H2M27   2015

ISBN 978-981-4519-38-0 (soft cover)
ISBN 978-981-4519-39-7 (e-book, PDF)

Typeset by Superskill Graphics Pte Ltd
Printed in Singapore by Mainland Press Pte Ltd

CONTENTS

Foreword by Virginia Hooker — vii
Preface — xi
Glossary — xix
List of Abbreviations — xxiii
Editorial Points Including Notes on Referencing — xxvii

1. Introduction and Theoretical Considerations — 1
2. Early Days — 28
3. Dorojatun Becomes Sultan — 60
4. The Japanese Occupation — 95
5. Revolution — First Phase — 133
6. Revolution — The Dutch Attack and Aftermath — 173
7. The Problems of Independence — 213
8. The End of Guided Democracy and the Rise of the New Order — 239
9. Hamengku Buwono in the New Order — 269
10. Conclusions — 304

Bibliography — 331

FOREWORD

A FINE BALANCE: THE PROFESSIONAL LIFE OF SULTAN HAMENGKU BUWONO IX

This book is a political biography of Sultan Hamengku Buwono IX (1912–88), one of Indonesia's most respected founding fathers. Although revered and admired at home and abroad, this is his first biography in English. This is largely because the Sultan was an intensely private person who meticulously guarded his public persona, and information about his life is not readily accessible. In 1971, although he was one of Indonesia's best-known public figures, the Indonesian daily *Kompas* described him thus:

> The Sultan resembles a 'Sphinx'; he is usually quiet but has charisma. As a long-standing national-level leader, he has the affection of the public, but always maintains his integrity.[1]

Writing the biography of such a figure — a royal, an active member of the Suharto and Sukarno administrations, and ruler of his own principality — yet a person who revealed little of himself on the public record, presents any scholar, Indonesian or foreigner, with major challenges. It is hardly surprising, then, that a full critical examination of the Sultan's life has been long in coming. As his first and final chapters show, Dr Monfries has approached the Sultan's biography in the full knowledge of these challenges.

Dr Monfries brings to this enterprise an unusual, even unique, set of skills and experience. He graduated from The Australian National University in 1968 with an honours degree in Southeast Asian Studies, specializing in Indonesia and Indonesian language. In late 1967, he applied for entry to the Australian diplomatic service (the Department of Foreign Affairs and Trade) and was accepted in 1968. He had a long and distinguished career with postings in Indonesia, as Counsellor in the

Australian Embassy in the Netherlands, and as Australian Commissioner to Brunei. His first trip to Indonesia was in late 1967 when, as a newly graduated student, he witnessed the poverty and desperate condition of post-Sukarno Indonesia and the shock of a population which had experienced mass killings on a scale beyond comprehension.

He was posted to Indonesia as a diplomat between 1969 and 1971 and observed the early years of Suharto's New Order government, a vital period of transition towards economic development, increasing military influence, and enforced political stability. During this posting, Dr Monfries married the talented and vivacious Isti (as she is affectionately known), whose family was closely linked with the ruling line of Yogyakarta. During his diplomatic career, Dr Monfries and his wife returned often to Indonesia and now, in retirement, maintain their close ties with Yogyakarta. Soon after retirement, Dr Monfries returned to academia to start a second career as an active researcher and lecturer.

These experiences, his academic training as a historian, his linguistic skills (Dutch, Indonesian, and some Javanese), and an extensive personal network in Southeast Asia and Europe, have enabled Dr Monfries to access sources and weigh up evidence with admirable skill and judgment. In short, he knows what is needed and he knows where to seek the necessary materials.

Dr Monfries has taken seriously the particular challenge of doing justice to an individual whose culture and background are so different from his own. Conscious that this might be an issue of concern for some readers, he explains how he has responded to this difference.[2] He has, he tells readers, paid careful attention to facts and sources, "allowing them to lead where they may". As a reader I can say that Dr Monfries has been painstaking in his search for sources and that they have led in some intriguing directions. Materials such as war records in the Netherlands, interviews with prominent Indonesians who worked with the Sultan, diaries of his contemporaries as well as a wealth of public documentation have all contributed to a meticulously assembled analysis of the man and his times. An unexpected source of inside information about the period of transition between the Old and New Order was the unpublished personal observations of long-time Indonesia watcher, the late Professor Herb Feith, included among his personal papers in the National Library of Australia. However, where gaps or uncertainties in the evidence are important for an understanding of Hamengku Buwono's thinking, Dr Monfries acknowledges this and suggests a range of best guesses.

The wide array of sources provides the evidence which underpins the biography, but how has the evidence been used? The lifetime of Sultan Hamengku Buwono IX, father of the present Sultan of Yogyakarta, spans the most significant periods of Indonesian history — from Dutch colonial rule, through the Japanese Occupation of the then Netherlands East Indies, to the bitter struggle for independence, the intense nationalism and chaos of the Sukarno years, the removal of Sukarno and the establishment of Suharto's New Order. The Sultan was, in fact, appointed by Suharto to the long-vacant office of Vice President and served a five-year term between 1973 and 1977. As Dr Monfries notes, "If a list were made in 1940 of the top twenty Indonesian figures in official positions, followed by a similar list in 1975, the only name in common between the two would be Hamengku Buwono IX."[3] This continuity of public service at the highest level has given Dr Monfries the opportunity to use the Sultan's life as a window on to his times and, conversely, to situate the Sultan in a range of contexts which have been critical to the shaping of modern Indonesia.

Set against his historical and social context, Dr Monfries analyses the Sultan's public persona using a set of perspectives that together reveal the complexity of his actions and decisions. These perspectives include the concept of power, sacred and political; leadership, royal and political; identity, Javanese and Indonesian; nationalism and the principality of Yogyakarta; democracy working at the national and local levels. It becomes clear that the Sultan was committed to service to a degree that is rare and impressive, but distanced himself from political advancement. Not all his decisions were well founded, and the reasons for this are suggested in the study.

In his discussion of the range of historiographical possibilities on offer to a writer of biography, Dr Monfries mentions the approach of "subaltern" history and, in a lighter vein, adapts the concept to ask "can the Sultan speak?"[4] He invites readers to judge whether they consider he has been able to use the available sources to enable the Sultan's positions and views to be heard. It is indeed for the reader to make that call. For my own part, I felt that Dr Monfries has convincingly and persuasively used his sources to show how successfully the Sultan preserved his private life. Dr Monfries has read his sources against the grain in a way which reveals the subtle methods the Sultan used to present a particular public persona while maintaining the integrity of his private one. The recognition of the dichotomy, or perhaps better complementarity, between the outer and inner man, is one of the achievements of this biography.

The Sultan's public life, as recorded and analysed so professionally in this book, was finely balanced, deliberately so, in ways which enabled his reputation and his principality to survive intact despite serious challenges. Dr Monfries is to be warmly congratulated for revealing those balances and the means by which they were achieved. Along the way, readers also learn how the Republic of Indonesia came into being and began its journey from developing to developed nation status.

Notes

1. Quoted by Monfries in Chapter 9.
2. See Monfries Chapter 10.
3. See Monfries Chapter 10.
4. Also in Monfries Chapter 10.

Emeritus Professor Virginia Hooker
Department of Political and Social Change
School of International, Political and Strategic Studies
College of Asia & the Pacific
The Australian National University

PREFACE

This book is based on my doctoral thesis written at the Australian National University (ANU) several years ago, about the life of Hamengku Buwono IX of Yogyakarta, who was long prominent in Indonesian affairs but had not attracted much scholarly interest from foreigners.

I would like to thank the supervising panel for their care and attention, especially my supervisor Ann Kumar, and the other panel members Virginia Hooker and the late and much-missed Ian Proudfoot. At ANU, I am indebted to various colleagues for much useful advice and dialogue, including my fellow PhD students at the time, Mary Kilcline Cody, Peter Quinn and Mark Emmanuel. David MacRae provided me with a useful information statement for informants, which I used virtually verbatim.

I would also especially like to thank David Reeve, Shigeru Sato, David Jenkins, McComas Taylor, Liudmila Mangos, and Chris Manning and the Indonesia Project. I appreciate the help of Oliver Mann, then of the National Library, and others there, as well as Mrs Betty Feith for permission to examine her late husband's private papers in the Library. My thanks go to Monash University, especially Brenda Le Grand, for access to Herb Feith's public archives in the library there. Particularly warm thanks are due to my wife, Isti Monfries, who helped and supported me in a wide variety of ways.

In Yogyakarta, I have to thank H.H. Hamengku Buwono X for his help and reminiscences of his father, as well as that of several family members, especially G.B.P.H. Prabukusumo, Romo Noordi Pakuningrat and K.R.T. Jatiningrat, Pak Suwignyo and staffers at the Kraton Archives, as well as personnel of the Yogyakarta Special Region Archives, such as Bu Ikrar and Pak Hardo.

In Jakarta, the large numbers of necessary acknowledgements make it difficult to single anyone out, but I should particularly mention the late (and also much missed) Geoffrey Forrester and his partner Peter Kelly, Nono

Anwar Makarim, G.B.P.H. Pakuningrat, and Princess Nindyokirono. My research afforded me the unique opportunity to meet and converse with a number of distinguished older-generation Indonesians, some of whom are now alas deceased. It was a real privilege to meet and interview such figures as the late Sudarpo Sastrosatomo, Rosihan Anwar, Radius Prawiro, Frans Seda and Wijoyo Nitisastro. I also need to express appreciation to Pak D. Ashari, Pak Emil Salim, Pak Mashud Wisnasaputra, and Pak Muchlis Paeni (former Director of the Arsip Nasional). I hope I may be forgiven if some who helped have been overlooked.

I was fortunate enough to make two productive fieldwork visits to the Netherlands, the second on a fellowship from the National War Documentation Institute (NIOD), Amsterdam. I am especially grateful to the staff of the Dutch National Archives, notably Sierk Plantinga and Francine van Anrooy; and also to the NIOD and its Director Hans Blom, as well as several staff members there, such as Peter Post. Others in archive-related positions who helped were H. Verbruggen of the Central Archive Depot, Rijswijk of the Defence Ministry, and Hans Hollander of the Foreign Ministry Library. At KITLV Leiden, I especially wish to thank Rini Hogewoning, and in Haarlem, Florence Koorn of the local archives.

Others in the Netherlands who were most helpful included my former teacher Professor Heather Sutherland, as well as Madelon Djajadingrat-Nieuwenhuis, Mr and Mrs Fred Adam, Pim Westerkamp and Alois Gronert.

It is customary to add that any errors in this book are of course my own; but as and when errors appear, I'm sure I'll find a way to blame someone else.

EDITORIAL CONVENTIONS

Terms

In re-examining Javanese ideas of power and kingship and in using Hamengku Buwono IX as an intriguing example of these, I draw on work by Anderson, Geertz, Kumar, Mudjanto, Ricklefs, and Soemarsaid Moertono. As Anderson[1] and others point out, English words like "power", "kingship", "royalty", and "authority" are sometimes difficult to translate into Indonesian or Javanese, and equivalent terms in those languages are sometimes lacking or shift subtly in meaning. Nevertheless, if we are to review or illuminate the Indonesian and the Javanese political processes, we must attempt to tackle these concepts. In this book, terms commonly used about Indonesian history not surprisingly occur frequently. These include "revolution", "kingship", "power", "influence", "Gestapu", "democracy", "administrators", and "solidarity-makers". Some explanation about some of them, including their relationships with equivalent Indonesian terms, is in order. I have tried throughout for example to use the word "Revolution" as a time marker for the historical period 1945–49 — when the Indonesians were seeking political independence from the Dutch — and not to employ the word in any other sense. In Indonesian the equivalent term *"revolusi"* can have this meaning, but can also mean something akin to both "political revolution" and "social revolution", and terms commonly used for the period under discussion have changed in the interim, e.g., *perang kemerdekaan, revolusi kemerdekaan*.[2]

I prefer to describe the armed actions by the Dutch in 1947 and 1948 as the first and second "attacks". Indonesian sources commonly call them "Dutch military aggression no 1" and "Dutch military aggression no 2", while the Dutch government (and some modern scholars) used the phrase "police action".[3] Where available, a neutral term would seem preferable.

During the Revolution, two largely opposing streams of thought emerged among Republicans as to how to deal with the challenges they faced from the Dutch. These are usually described as *diplomasi* and *perjuangan*. I have normally used the Indonesian terms for both of these. It should be noted that *perjuangan* (literally "struggle") carries an important ambiguity, in that it can imply either violent conflict, or relatively peaceful revolutionary agitation such as demonstrations, posting of placards, holding of meetings, etc.[4]

During the Suharto period, the term "New Order" came into existence. I use this to designate the government of the time and have tried not to use it in other senses. I have avoided using the word "Gestapu", preferring "30 September Movement", because the New Order coinage of "Gestapu" carries a strong ideological and emotional charge. Finally, I have also tried to avoid sexist language (e.g., the use of "he" or "his" where a gender-neutral term is needed), but may have not always succeeded in this.

THE SOURCES

The scope, range, and availability of the sources vary according to the period of the subject's life. The inner workings of the Yogyakarta kraton in the 1920s when the young Dorojatun was growing up are especially obscure. In political terms, this may be of little moment because of the kraton's political impotence in the period, but it means no inside story about his early life is available. Sources on his period in the Netherlands are limited to the scanty official records and a few reminiscences long afterwards. Voluminous Dutch official reports on Hamengku Buwono's early period as Sultan are useful, but there are contradictions between these and Hamengku Buwono's later account. The brief memoir by Hamengku Buwono's doctor provides a chatty and informative additional perspective.

The Japanese period is especially poorly documented, a circumstance which perhaps helps to explain why some conventional accounts of the period have gone unchallenged and even unexamined. It is thus more than normally difficult to ascertain the exact relationship between Hamengku Buwono and the Japanese occupiers, although contemporary press accounts are useful in building a picture of Hamengku Buwono's activities in the period. By contrast, Hamengku Buwono's role during the Revolution is reasonably well documented, especially the crisis of 1948–49, although the weight of Dutch material, irreplaceable though it is, may be a distorting factor in some cases. The period as Defence Minister has generated much relevant material, especially the media reports, parliamentary records, eyewitness accounts by major players, and Feith's magisterial work, later qualified in some respects by Sundhaussen. Some judgments on these two periods could be made with a reasonable degree of confidence.

Hamengku Buwono's role in the 1960s and 1970s generated an extensive public record, but the inside story was harder to discern, particularly because many who knew him were reluctant to speak frankly about a figure of such eminence. Only three of the informants were of the same generation as Hamengku Buwono, who was thus very senior to nearly all of them, and this too seemed to intensify the constraints. On the period when Hamengku Buwono was Vice President, much remains unclear, because of the obscurity of the relationship with Suharto at the time and because of the paucity of official records, giving rise to suspicion that much material had been suppressed. Nevertheless, although his own family knew little about his early career, they had some information about the vice presidency period, and I was also able to obtain some fascinating details from various other informants.

Thus, several informants did speak frankly to me, and I have adopted the practice of referring to them anonymously; they are identified in the footnotes therefore as "Informant no 1", or similar. This awkward compromise is aimed at avoiding possible embarrassment to them, as some still sensitive issues were canvassed in their remarks.

I have consulted as many of the accessible primary sources as possible, in the Netherlands, Indonesia, and Australia. The latter included the holdings at the ANU, the National Archives of Australia, and the National Library. In Jakarta, I was able to visit the Arsip Nasional, my research assistants obtained further Indonesian-language material from the Indonesian National Library, and I interviewed over thirty Indonesians who had known Hamengku Buwono.

In Yogyakarta, I visited the palace archives and the Yogyakarta Special Region Archives, as well as conducting further interviews. A two-week visit to Cornell University in the United States enabled me to sample some of their extensive material. I visited the Netherlands twice and found invaluable material at the Haarlem Regional Archive, the Nationaal Archief (Dutch National Archives), the Central Archive Depot of the Ministry of Defence, the Military History Institute (IMG), and the War Documentation Institute (NIOD). My knowledge of Indonesian and Dutch eased the task of consulting the relevant archives. Access to sources in Javanese has been more limited, although I have in fact found only a few relevant Javanese-language documents. The bibliography provides a comprehensive list of sources.

Spelling

Except where today's usage retains the old form, I have changed Indonesian names to reflect the current system of Indonesian orthography; this complies with current trends in Indonesian usage, especially where the name is of a dead person (e.g., the spelling "Syahrir" is now commonly used rather than the old form). For example, Hamengku Buwono's early name is spelt "Dorojatun" throughout, rather than the former version "Dorodjatoen". I have also used the official spelling of "Yogyakarta", illogical though that spelling is (it does not reflect normal pronunciation), rather than "Jogjakarta". An exception, however, is in the spelling of the names of authors and book titles (in the footnotes and bibliography), where a change to modern orthography would inhibit ease of reference. The spelling of Dutch words will also reflect modern Dutch spelling, with the same exception. Similarly, where book or article titles use the old spelling of "Jogjakarta" or variants, I have retained that original spelling.

Permissions

The photographs presented here cover all periods in Hamengku Buwono's life, although coverage is spotty in some cases, especially his early years. I have used some photos that very commonly appear in accounts of his life, but have been fortunate enough to find some that have not previously been published, and in this context, I especially repeat my appreciation to K.R.T. Jatiningrat, and also to the Yogyakarta Regional Archives, for some of the rarer and more interesting images.

Every effort has been made to obtain appropriate permissions for reproduction of the photographs in this volume. In most cases, copyright holders have been approached, and permissions received; and suitable acknowledgements are made in the sections where images are presented. In a few cases, however, especially images from the 1950s or earlier, it has not always been possible to trace whether copyright still holds. In Indonesian law, copyright ceases after fifty years. Images attributed to the "Indonesian Government" are reproduced in accordance with the permission granted under Article 14 of the Indonesian Copyright Law (Law no. 22/2002). Unfortunately, some of the older images are of poor quality; I hope the reader will indulge this unavoidable defect.

A slightly changed version of Chapter 6 of this book, on Hamengku Buwono's role in the Indonesian Revolution, was published in 2008, as an article entitled "The Sultan and the Revolution", *Bijdragen tot de Taal- Land- en Volkenkunde*, 164–2/3, 2008, pp. 269–97. I wish to thank Koninklijke Brill N.V. for permission to republish this material.

Finally, I have to express my gratitude to my son Jeremy Monfries, for technical help and advice about the images used here.

Notes

1. Anderson, "The Idea of Power in Javanese Language and Culture", in *Language and Power*, p. 19.

2. On the various connotations of "revolution", see Reid's instructive discussion, *An Indonesian Frontier, Acehnese and Other Histories of Sumatra*, pp. 321–24.
3. Even the massive twenty-five-volume series of Dutch official documents, *Officiele Bescheiden Betreffende Nederlands — Indonesische Betrekkingen 1945–50* (cited throughout as "*NIB*") habitually uses the loaded term *politienele actie* — "police action". See Bibliography.
4. An ambiguity picked up by the editor (Mula Marbun) of Nasution's massive eleven-volume work *Sekitar Perang Kemerdekaan* (On the War of Independence), who preferred to use *bertempur* (= fighting), implying a sharper distinction with the *diplomasi* approach.

GLOSSARY

(Non-English words not otherwise identified are Indonesian; Jp = Japanese; Jav = Javanese; D = Dutch)

abdi dalem (Jav)	palace retainers
adat	customary law
aksi sefihak	unilateral action
Bale Agung	Supreme Council, colonial-era representative body in Solo
bapak	father, patron; also term of address, equivalent of "Mr", or "sir"
bhuta (Jav)	ogres
Budi Utomo (Jav)	Noble Endeavour, early semi-nationalist organization
Chuo Sangi-in (Jp)	Central Advisory Council
Dewan Penasihat	advisory council in the colonial era
diplomasi	diplomacy, used during the Revolution to connote negotiations with the Dutch
dukun	mystical adviser, soothsayer
garwo padmi (Jav)	queen, principal wife of a ruler
Gerinda	Jogjakarta regional political party in 1950s
Gestapu	**G**erakan **S**eptember **T**ig**a Pu**luh — 30 September Movement
Golkar	Golongan Karya — Functional Groups; presented as a government-sponsored alternative to political parties in the New

	Order; survives to the present as a major political party
gotong royong	cooperation
halus	refined
Hokokai (Jp), especially Jawa Hokokai	(Java) Service Association
Joyoboyo	a medieval Javanese prince who supposedly made a series of predictions about Java's future history; the Javanese equivalent of Nostradamus
kabinet ndelik (Jav)	secret cabinet
kabupaten	regency
kasar	coarse, rude
kawula-gusti (Jav)	lord and subject (refers to the bonds linking the Javanese king and his subjects)
kedaulatan rakyat	people's sovereignty
Keibodan (Jp)	auxiliary police
keistimewaan	special status
prinsip kekeluargaan	family principle
Kempeitai	Japanese secret police
kepatihan	vizier's office, i.e., kraton government
kesaktian	charisma
koo or ko (Jp)	prince
kooti or kochi (Jp)	principality
korte verklaring (D)	Short Declaration, document where minor local rulers acknowledged Dutch suzerainty in the colonial era
kraton (Jav)	palace
Kyai Joko Piturun	sacred kris, an important heirloom of the Jogjakarta kraton
Laskar Rakyat	People's Militia
merdeka	independent (kemerdekaan — independence)

Glossary

negara	state or nation
ngoko	low Javanese
nusa dan bangsa	homeland and people
Nyai Roro Kidul	goddess of the south seas
Pakempalan Kawula Ngayogyakarta (PKN)	Union of Subjects of Jogjakarta
Pakualam	Jogjakarta prince, junior to the Sultan
pamong praja (Jav)	Javanese civil service
Pancasila	Five Principles, Indonesian national ideology
panewu	sub-district head
Patih	colonial-era vizier or prime minister
pemuda	(radical) youth
Pejabat Presiden	Acting President
perang kemerdekaan	War of Independence
perang sabil	holy war (similar to jihad)
perjuangan	struggle
permaisuri (Jav)	queen
Peta	Japanese-era Indonesian army
priyayi	Javanese aristocracy
pusaka	sacred heirloom
Putera	early Japanese-era political organization
Raadsman voor Studeerenden (D)	Student Counsellor, senior official of the Ministry of Colonies
raseksa (Jav)	giant
revolusi	revolution
romusha (Jp)	Japanese-era labourers
sabda pandita ratu ora wola-wali (Jav)	a king's words cannot be taken back
sanyo (Jp)	Indonesian adviser to major government departments
Seinendan (Jp)	army youth auxiliary

Serangan Umum	general offensive
siap!	(literally) get ready! (denotes the period of a few months after the Proclamation of Independence in 1945)
Somutyokan (Jp)	vizier, equivalent to the Dutch-era Patih
Sunan or Susuhunan	traditional ruler of Solo
tanah sabrang (Jav)	lands across the sea
tapa (Jav)	meditation and self-abnegation
Tentara Pelajar	Student Army
Volksraad (D)	People's Council, the colonial-era representative assembly
Vorstenland (D)	princely state
wahyu (Jav)	divine inspiration, legitimacy
wisik (Jav)	mystical guidance

ABBREVIATIONS

(Note — Abbreviations of the names of some documents or document series commonly cited in the endnotes are provided in the main bibliography.)

ADB	Asian Development Bank
Bapekan	Badan Pengawas Kegiatan Aparatur Negara — State Apparatus Supervising Board
Bappenas	Badan Perencanaan Pembangunan Nasional — National Planning Board
BB	Barisan Banteng (Buffalo Legion)
BFO	Bijeenkomst voor Federale Overleg — Federal Consultative Assembly
BPI	Badan Pusat Intelijens– Central Intelligence Body
BPK	Badan Pemeriksa Keuangan — National Audit Board
BPUPKI	Committee to Investigate Preparations for Indonesian Independence
BULOG	Badan Urusan Logistik — Logistics Board
CAD	Centraal Archief Depot (Central Archives Depot), Dutch Ministry of Defence, Rijswijk
CMI	Centrale Militaire Inlichtingsdienst (Central Military Intelligence), the former NEFIS
EKUIN	Ekonomi, Keuangan dan Industri — Economy, Finance, and Industry (ministerial portfolio under the New Order)
GOC	United Nations Good Offices Committee
HBS	Hoogere Burger School — Dutch-era high school

IGGI	Inter-Governmental Group on Indonesia
IMF	International Monetary Fund
IMG	Instituut voor Militaire Geschiedenis (Institute of Military History), Ministry of Defence, The Hague
KAMI	Kesatuan Aksi Mahasiswa Indonesia — student action front of the 1960s
KNI or KNIP	Komite Nasional Indonesia, Indonesian National Committee (i.e., proto-parliament)
KNID	Komite Nasional Indonesia Daerah (Regional Indonesian National Committee)
KNIL	Netherlands Indies colonial army
KOTI	Komando Operasi Tertinggi — Supreme Operations Command
LBD	colonial-era air raid warning service
LKB	Lembaga Kesadaran Berkonstitusi — Institute of Constitutional Awareness
MPRS	Majelis Permusyawarahan Rakyat Sementara — Provisional People's Consultative Congress
NA	Nationaal Archief (National Archives), The Hague
NAA	National Archives of Australia, Canberra
Nasakom	**Nas**ionalis, **a**gama, **kom**unis — nationalist, religion, communist; a unifying slogan of Guided Democracy
NEFIS	Netherlands Forces Intelligence Service — later CMI
NICA	Netherlands Indies Civil Administration
NIGIS	Netherlands Indies Government Information Service, English-language radio service in Melbourne, monitoring radio reports from the Indies during the Japanese occupation
NIOD	Nationale Instituut voor Oorlogsdocumentatie (National Institute for War Documentation), Amsterdam
NMM	Netherlands Military Mission
NSB	Nationaal-Socialistische Beweging, National-Socialist Movement, the Dutch counterpart to the Nazis

ORI	Oeang Republik Indonesia, Republic of Indonesia currency
Parindra	1930s nationalist party
PI	Perhimpunan Indonesia, Indonesian Association, a 1930s organization of radical Indonesians in the Netherlands
PIR	Partai Indonesia Raya — Greater Indonesia Party
PKI	Communist Party of Indonesia
PKN	Pakempalan Kawula Ngayogyakarta — Union of Subjects of Jogjakarta
PKS	Pakempalan Kawula Surokarto — Union of Subjects of Surakarta (Solo)
PNI	Partai Nasionalis Indonesia — Indonesian Nationalist Party
POPDA	Panitia Oeroesan Pengangkoetan Djepang dan APWI — Committee for the Evacuation of Japanese and Allied Prisoners of War and Internees
PPKI	Committee for the Preparation of Indonesian Independence (Panitya Persiapan Kemerdekaan Indonesia)
PRN	Partai Rakyat Nasional — National People's Party
PRRI	Pemerintah Revolusioner Republik Indonesia — Revolutionary Government of the Republic of Indonesia
PSI	Partai Sosialis Indonesia — Indonesian Socialist Party
RAPWI	Organization for the Recovery of Allied Prisoners of War and Internees
RIS	Republik Indonesia Serikat — United States of Indonesia
RMS	Republik Maluku Selatan — Republic of the South Moluccas
Roepi	Rukun Pelajar Indonesia (Indonesian Students Association), a 1930s organization in the Netherlands
SPRI	Staf Pribadi Republik Indonesia — Republic of Indonesia Private Staff

SSKAD	Sekolah Staf dan Komando Angkatan Darat, army staff command college in Bandung (now with the same name, but different abbreviation — SESKOAD)
Supersemar	surat perintah sebelas Maret — 11 March Order, under which Sukarno ceded executive power to Suharto
SVIK	Student Organisation for the Advancement of Indonesian Culture, a 1930s organization in the Netherlands
TKR	Tentara Keamanan Rakyat (People's Security Army), later TRI — Tentara Rakyat Indonesia — Indonesian People's Army, later TNI q.v.
TNI	Tentara Nasional Indonesia — Indonesian National Army

EDITORIAL POINTS, INCLUDING NOTES ON REFERENCING

Footnotes will normally quote the author's name, the title of the work quoted, and the page number (only). Full details of referenced works, including publisher, place and date of publication, and edition number where applicable can be found in the Bibliography. Where websites are referenced, I have tried consistently to provide the website address, the author's name (if available), the date of the document (if available), and the date the website was accessed.

In the footnotes, in accordance with normal practice, the names of books and journals are italicized, while titles of journal articles are provided in double quotes. I have provided volume numbers and issue numbers for all journal references where available. Translations of the titles of foreign-language texts are also provided in the footnotes, as well as in the Bibliography. Some sources are so commonly cited that their names are abbreviated in the footnotes (e.g., *TUR* for *Tahta untuk Rakyat*); in these cases, the full title and author's name are given at the beginning of the chapter, with an indication of the abbreviation to be used thereafter. A list of these abbreviations is in the Bibliography.

Foreign-language words (e.g., *revolusi*, *kooti*, or *Vorstenland*) are italicized the first time they appear in each chapter, but not thereafter.

1

INTRODUCTION AND THEORETICAL CONSIDERATIONS

INTRODUCTION

Hamengku Buwono IX, although so prominent in Indonesian politics for so long, has not yet attracted a full-length study in English. He never had a prominent role in Indonesian foreign policy, except in foreign economic policy in the 1960s. Hamengku Buwono lacked the charisma and oratory of Sukarno, the engaging style of Malik, the administrative tenacity of Hatta, the intellectuality of Syahrir, or the direct command of troops of Nasution. Of the figures who came to notice in the Revolution, however, only Malik[1] had a longer career; but although Malik left no enduring political legacy, Hamengku Buwono bequeathed a thriving principality to his son and successor. When the Republican leaders could no longer bear the increasing dangers of Jakarta in 1945, they were constrained to move to Yogyakarta at the Sultan's invitation. When the Dutch had captured those leaders in 1948, the Sultan was able effectively to defy the invaders. When Sukarno's Guided Democracy failed, the untried General Suharto called on the Sultan to guide the country's economy. When the political leadership faltered, the country turned to the quiet, unassuming Sultan. One image in Indonesian writing about him is that of the goalkeeper, who saves the side when all else fails.² This of course, like many other assertions about him, is an oversimplification and has to be examined critically.

But there is also something elusive about Hamengku Buwono. As I remark in Chapter 7, he recalls A.J.P. Taylor's description of Lord Halifax — "He was always at the centre of events yet managed somehow to leave the impression that he was not connected with them."³ Historical accounts often mention the Sultan's presence at meetings or events without specifying exactly what his role was. Foreign accounts (e.g., the Australian official records) refer occasionally to meetings with him but rarely give details of the conversations. When the Dutch captured Yogyakarta in 1948, records of nine republican cabinet meetings fell into their hands. In only one of them is there any comment or statement by Hamengku Buwono, who was admittedly a junior minister of state at the time. Few of his public speeches or other records reveal the real man behind the myth. His formal speeches in any period — from the colonial period to the 1950s or 1960s — are usually very orthodox and only occasionally revealing; some may well have been written for him, and despite his good education, the speeches surprisingly contain no erudite literary or historical quotations or references. It is only in his fascinating letter to the Republican delegation after the dramatic meeting with the Dutch occupiers on 2 March 1949 that the emotionally committed, resolute nationalist seems to emerge. He carried almost to an extreme the Javanese tag, *Sabda pandita ratu ora wola-wali* — "a wise king cannot take back his words", with its corollary that the king must be sparing with them.

Hamengku Buwono's long and complex career features several paradoxes and even contradictions. He was "a prince in a republic",⁴ with all the constitutional conundrums this implies (discussed in Chapter 5); he had an important local and regional role in a country which spurned regionalism; he seems to have been a reluctant Sultan⁵ but behaved as a feudal lord in the palace; he moved easily between a traditional Javanese world and a modern Western milieu; he made relatively few public statements although he was so conspicuous in national politics; although representative of a feudal order, he received open hostility from the Indonesian Communist party (PKI) and other radicals only during the 17 October 1952 affair, where he was not the main target; and he was involved in politics for forty years while giving the impression of being apolitical. It could be added that he was widely known as a "democrat" but ended his career as deputy to a highly undemocratic President; whether

Introduction and Theoretical Considerations

intentionally or not, he left open the possibility of preserving his dynasty while allowing a public impression to arise that he intended to end it;[6] and he provided an example of the continuing strength of ascribed status in a very turbulent polity, in a nation (and a world) where most other royalty became out of date or even thoroughly discredited.

He attracted widely varying characterizations for such a quiet personality. He has been described as "the Napoleon of Indonesia",[7] "a political nonentity",[8] "not an intellectual but had a strong intuition",[9] "a patriot with a democratic spirit",[10] "the one Javanese leader who has consistently commanded the trust of non-Javanese",[11] and "a problem-solving icon".[12]

AIMS

The first, but by no means only, objective of this study is to outline the facts of Hamengku Buwono's political life. This is considerably easier than the accompanying need to describe from time to time what motivated his actions, because he rarely explained this in any detail. Nevertheless, inferences and deductions can be made. A further essential task is to set his life in the wider context of developments in Indonesia and elsewhere as his career progressed, and to outline how his actions were affected by the context. He was an actor in Indonesian history, and his life can only be understood in terms of the dramatic events of his time. He was a prince of Yogyakarta and part of the context is the cultural and social environment in which he operated. He was also a practising politician, and the national political firmament was his milieu for much of his career. Accordingly, his relationships with other important figures, especially Sukarno and Suharto, form an essential part of the story. The difficulty here is to strike the right balance between Hamengku Buwono's story and the context, and steer between the Scylla of concentrating entirely on him without adequately explaining the background, and the Charybdis of overwhelming the main story with background detail. Ultimately the aim must be to make sense of the life, through whatever evidence we can muster, and to reach judgments about the meaning of Hamengku Buwono's actions and his role in and influence on the historical events of his time.

This study would be incomplete without some judgments about Hamengku Buwono's ultimate effect and role in Indonesian history, even though it may still be too early for definitive assessments. What success did he have? What difference did he make? What, ultimately, did he stand for? How did he survive politically in such a volatile country and during such a turbulent period? How much power did he in fact have during his career? Was he predominantly a modern figure or a traditional one, and how important to his career was his identity as a Javanese feudal ruler? Finally, I will attempt to relate my conclusions about Hamengku Buwono to the theoretical considerations outlined below.

Although Hamengku Buwono died twenty-five years ago, some conclusions about his life may still need to be provisional and tentative, especially in the New Order phase. Many records of that period are not (or not yet) available, and key informants on the period remained sensitive about providing details about the period and the man, no doubt because some of the main actors including Suharto himself were still alive. In Hamengku Buwono's case, some were also clearly reluctant to speak frankly or critically about such an iconic figure.

BIOGRAPHICAL WRITING AND HISTORY

Any biographical writing has to be based on the assumption that the subject is interesting and instructive in some way. Usually a subject has achieved distinction in some field, often politics or literature, and the writer assumes that the reading public would want or need more comprehensive details about them. Royal subjects are different in that their position has arisen through birth rather than achievement, but if the subject is involved with dramatic events, a biography may still be worth writing, even where the subject is manifestly unfitted to his or her role in history, a proposition which does not apply in the present case.

Various subgenres of biography have been identified,[13] which are explored in more detail below. The genre is healthy, despite a variety of critical assaults upon it; more and more biographies and theoretical writings appear from year to year, the majority being by Westerners about Westerners, although a Western writer or scholar will produce an account of a prominent Asian from time to time.[14] Asian writers and scholars have of course written many biographies about their own leaders. In Indonesia, most well-known political leaders, including Hamengku Buwono, have been the subject of brief and entirely uncritical official biographies, as well as some unofficial but equally uncritical biographies. Hamengku Buwono has attracted only two biographies by individual Indonesian writers.[15]

It may be useful to describe briefly the current state of theory about "life-writing", examine how these theories may apply to what we might call the cross-cultural biography, and explore whether this poses certain questions and difficulties of its own. Ideas of power are also relevant, because Hamengku Buwono's career raises some questions of the typology of power. In discussion of the 1950s and 1960s, for example, I refer to Feith's useful distinction between the two different types of political actors in the period, namely "administrators" and "solidarity-makers".[16] Feith placed the Sultan firmly in the former group,[17] a judgment I would concur with.

Another perspective is to examine the influence on Hamengku Buwono of traditional Javanese ideas of power and of ideal conduct. Although the primary focus is on Hamengku Buwono as a political actor in Indonesian national politics, it will be useful to devote some space to examining Hamengku Buwono from a number of viewpoints, because each one may add to the total picture. Referring to Javanese ideas of power in Chapters 3 and 6, I conclude that Hamengku Buwono at times seemed to behave (or tried to behave) as a traditional and ideal Javanese prince should, but in most of his actual policies, he seemed indistinguishable from a Western-style politician. These issues will be revisited in the concluding chapter.

I have referred relatively briefly to Hamengku Buwono's role as a local ruler and administrator in Yogyakarta (and his impact on Yogyakarta after 1950, when he moved into national politics in Jakarta, is hard to identify). I give relatively light coverage to his private life because this never seemed to impinge on his political pursuits; to the extent that women, including his mother and the five wives he married, exerted political influence on him, this is not readily discernible from the available evidence. I have only occasionally adverted to his private economic and commercial interests.

There appears little to say on Hamengku Buwono's attitude to religion. All his life he was an orthodox Muslim, but he did not bring his faith directly into his political life. In his speeches or letters, references to Islam, Allah, or the Prophet Muhammad are surprisingly rare.[18] To the extent that his political ideology is evident (and this is a difficult subject, as I hope will emerge from this account), it seemed to be based more on secular nationalism than on religion. It is a matter for conjecture whether this attitude arose from his Western education or from other factors, notably of course his syncretic Javanese cultural background.

In Chapter 2, I introduce the early influences on him, including his Dutch-style education, and give some detail of the ideology of the Yogyakarta court; and I attempt to outline how this ideology may have influenced him. Chapter 3 provides an account of his first years as Sultan, from the negotiations with the Dutch which gave an early indication of his firmness of character, and Chapter 4 covers the Japanese years up to the proclamation of independence. I examine the various claims made about his relations with the Japanese.

The crucial period of the Revolution[19] is discussed in Chapters 5 and 6. I outline his actions during 1946–47 within the Yogyakarta principality which first identified him as a significant political reformer. I try to reach conclusions about why the young Sultan chose to join the Republic and his relations with other Republican leaders, the military and the Dutch. In particular, the question of how the Dutch came to misjudge Hamengku Buwono so disastrously right up to 1949 merits some attention.[20] I examine in some detail the Dutch attack in November 1948 and the subsequent nationalist resistance, including the much-debated *Serangan Umum* (General Offensive), which in some ways was his finest hour.

Hamengku Buwono's role in the 17 October 1952 affair is recounted in detail in Chapter 7, because of its effect on his career and also because of its consequences for military/civilian relations which have some resonance even today. One of his major allies at the time, Nasution, returned to important positions during the fifties, but the Sultan had no significant national role until the mid-1960s, when he made a conspicuous but ambiguous comeback.

Chapters 8 and 9 treat the crucial and turbulent period of the 1960s and the New Order. Hamengku Buwono's role in the formulation, presentation, and implementation of the New Order's economic policies is recounted, although the detail is sometimes sketchy. The record indicates that he played a greater role in the implementation and the presentation of the New Order's economic policies than in their formulation, although direct evidence of his role behind the scenes is deficient. His decision to join the Government owed something to his attitude towards the concept of service to the nation, but also, I believe, to a calculation that his political legacy, the Yogyakarta sultanate, would best be served by resuming a prominent role in the national government. He shared in the growing prestige and confidence of the new government as economic stability was established, aid subventions soared, and prosperity spread, although not without setbacks and controversies. Among political insiders, his reputation faded because of an alleged lack of dynamism, but his public reputation remained surprisingly high.

His relations with Suharto during the 1960s and 1970s are especially obscure. The natural reticence of both men, the growing sensitivity — especially during the 1970s — of personal relationships with the increasingly powerful President, and the rarity of firsthand accounts of their meetings, militate against an intimate understanding of this important relationship. What does seem clear is that Hamengku Buwono's period in the Vice Presidency, despite its appearance as the apex of his political career, was in many ways its nadir. His power and influence were circumscribed; Suharto needed him less except for his prestige; many of Suharto's military and even his business associates were much more influential than Hamengku Buwono, and he never found a real role for himself; to an extent he did not even seem to try.

I attempt to draw some general conclusions about Hamengku Buwono and his career in the final chapter, as well as re-examining and drawing conclusions about the various theoretical issues raised in this study.

BIOGRAPHICAL THEORY

The following discussion tries to provide an overview of current theories of biography, without being able to delve very deeply into the many complex questions the subject inevitably raises. On theoretical questions, much has been written about biography (or "life writing", thus including autobiography) in recent years, and the genre as a whole remains both a popular subject in itself and a cause of much debate and dissension. One commentator has even claimed that if charges of trivialization and distraction through side issues were not met, "biography may continue to lack a cogent scientific or imaginative justification".[21] Another described political biography baldly as "bad history".[22] Elton wrote many years ago, "even at its best biography is a poor way of writing history".[23] Qualifications and rebuttals of these negative views are discussed a little later in this chapter.

Biographical writing goes back at least to the classical Greeks, notably Plutarch's *Lives*.[24] Plutarch was regarded as a model in English biographies such as Boswell's *Life of Johnson*, and was still so regarded in the nineteenth century. During the twentieth century, many new trends and developments occurred in biography, which might be divided conveniently into several main types, occurring more or less seriatim but overlapping. The first was the traditional "Great Man" biography, common in the nineteenth century and lasting well into the twentieth and longer. In the nineteenth century, many would have agreed with Carlyle that "history is the biography of great men".[25] The biography of the time was usually long, hagiographic, often aimed at demonstrating that the subject was a great imperialist, leader, Christian, or adventurer. Either consciously or unconsciously, they implied justification of some ideology, often conservative, colonial or imperialist. They almost always presented the subjects as heroes.[26] In one sense, the Great Man biography has been superseded, because very few biographers now would consciously try to present a subject entirely uncritically as an exemplar of a particular ideology or movement. But in another sense, the Great Man (and now Great Woman) biography persists, although normally in more critical and realistic vein.

Lytton Strachey is taken as marking a major departure, because of his debunking and irreverent writing style. Strachey extolled brevity and economy and decried the earlier "tone of tedious panegyric" which characterized biographies of the Victorian period.[27] This style is presented as more dispassionate and clear-eyed, not attempting to deceive the reader by clothing didactic purpose in the presentation of a hero's life. The term "New Biography" came into use to describe this mode of writing. Unfortunately, Strachey is not a model of the factual biographer, because despite his care to research his subjects, he occasionally distorted the picture by inventing some of his "facts".[28]

Many early biographies can also be accused of distortion or at least omission, especially where the subject's private life is concerned. "Though some of the great classic biographies were written under this system [i.e., the traditional heroic biography], what went into them was severely censored."[29] By contrast, enormously detailed biographies (such as those by Ellmann, Edel or Holroyd) are again prevalent, but the second era of the monumental biography, after the brevity and wit of the Strachey "period", is different from the first in that nothing at all seems to be censored. Although a biographer may risk criticism as a hagiographer or apologist if the subject's sexual behaviour or personal crises are ignored,[30] monumentalism too has its drawbacks, because a biography may lose focus if nearly every available detail is included. Nevertheless, some of these modern biographies are beginning to be regarded as classics of the genre.[31]

The popularization of Freud's ideas and their development by other psychologists such as Jung and Adler led to a sub-genre of "psychobiography", using psychoanalytic techniques to illuminate the subjects' inner life and motivations. This approach attempts to psychoanalyse the subjects through using available psychoanalytical tools, using evidence about their state of mind through deductions from their writings, policies, or actions. As early as 1920, psychology began to influence biography.[32] Landmarks in the subgenre are said to include Erikson's *Young Man Luther* and his *Gandhi*, the latter apparently being the only biography of an Asian to be accorded theoretical importance.[33] The psychobiography approach is controversial, but Erikson claimed that "a clinician's training permits and in fact forces him to recognize major trends [in the subject's psychological development] even where the facts are not available".[34]

It is true that "the professional historian has always been an amateur psychologist".[35] In political biography, the analysis of a statesman's motives for his actions is an inevitable part of biographical writing, and this is a psychological matter, albeit contentious. It would be almost unimaginable to produce a biography without making some attempt to delve into the subject's motivations, values and ideology, which derive from and form part of their psychological inner self; in other words, the biographer usually seeks to discern at least some elements of the Jungian Shadow. Carr's call for the historian to have "an imaginative understanding for the minds of the people with whom he is dealing"[36] is really a plea for historians to attempt to penetrate the psychology of their subjects. A further useful point is made by Clendinnen who indicates that, although the basic personality changes little through life, a person's psychological make-up does not remain entirely static and may develop or even regress in unexpected ways depending on the challenges and stresses the person experiences.[37]

Although we may feel some confidence that "human beings could be subjected to almost scientific analysis",[38] psychology and biography remain in "uneasy alliance"[39] because of the many uncertainties involved, and the evident impossibility of one person ever gaining a complete understanding of another. But in the present work I unavoidably refer regularly to Hamengku Buwono's presumed or (at times) stated motivations for his actions, and endeavour to analyse the reasons for these, without any pretence at psychoanalysis.

Modern ideas about biography have branched out in many directions since the emergence of the New Biography in the 1920s, not least under the influence of postmodern theory. A vast number of subgenres have been identified, including literary biography, political biography, royal biography, feminist biography, and many others. The first two subcategories are the most numerous.[40] What is clear is that the whole genre is thriving, and theoretical study of it, although overshadowed by the greater attention given to autobiography, is also more active than it was.

Postmodern[41] approaches using the insights of thinkers like Foucault have cast doubt on earlier scholars' claims to empiricism in all the social sciences, whether in history, anthropology, politics, biography, or any form of written literature. The postmodernists say that biographers deceive themselves if they believe that an objective presentation of cold hard fact about a person is possible, or even desirable. All writers transform available information (records, interviews, photographs) into a narrative of figurative language, into which they inevitably obtrude their own discourse. Available historical facts are also already selected by chance or the biases of the earliest recorders of events (as E.H. Carr noted many years ago).[42] Applying this to biography, a postmodernist would argue that there will be as many widely differing biographies as there are biographers. Different strings of facts could be (and have been) selected by different writers to provide varying accounts of the same subject. Although this is plausible, a crucial question is whether one account is better than another, and what criteria can help us to decide this. On this issue, I do not find postmodern critiques of much practical assistance.

Critiques of traditional biography claim that it usually contains several features of which the biographer may be unaware. One is the extent to which biography can be self-description, as a form of conscious or unconscious autobiography.[43] In another sense, biography can be the appropriation of another person's life, in other words an assertion of power, and it can even consciously or (more often) unconsciously support and justify a particular ideology.

It is unclear how far biography can be described as self-description. It is true that — with varying degrees of self-revelation — biographers describe themselves in describing their subject. Any judgements they make, either negative or positive, about their subjects' actions or personalities invariably imply that they, the biographers, would have done something respectively different or similar. From this, one can deduce something about the writer's moral values and political standpoint. Even the selection of facts and episodes in a subject's life can subtly reveal what the biographer likes or thinks is important. But there has to be a limit to this. A biography necessarily relates to the subject at hand, and a different type of distortion will arise if the biographer's own identity obtrudes itself. Perhaps indeed, as asserted with increasing frequency in recent times, writers must be aware of their own biases and preoccupations and even honestly reveal them from the start, but ideally they should then step back. The further question is whether they can and do detach themselves, and it has to be conceded that complete detachment remains an ideal which by its nature may well be unattainable; it could also be argued that total detachment would be undesirable, in that the writer must also be engaged closely with the subject. There may be no definitive solution to this dilemma; the best a biographer may hope for is to find a suitable balance.

A great deal has also been written, in Foucauldian vein, about biography (or any history) as an assertion of power in some sense. In writing about another person, we are acquiring knowledge and expertise about them and about the period in which they lived. This also means to at least some extent asserting ownership of the subject's life, or what they represented. "The act of writing ... remakes the life."[44] But while we may value the reminder that all human relationships include an important power element, a criticism of the more extreme statements along these lines is that if power is everywhere, then such an explanation can lose its explanatory force.[45] The statement that a biography is an assertion of power where all relationships are assertions of power is a useful reminder, but does it add much to our knowledge?

The argument that a biography — or any writing — consciously or unconsciously supports an ideology is cognate with the previous claim, and we have already referred to it in discussing the Great Man genre. If the claim is true, it would presumably be best if writers were aware of what they were doing and therefore even stated what ideology they were advocating. In fact, while in self-reflexive vein many now state their background, attitudes and perspectives, few would concede that they are advocating a particular ideology.

Susan Tridgell[46] argues that we should welcome a variety of different versions of the same biographical subject, and not regard it as a problem or weakness of the genre. "One of the main conclusions which this dissertation comes to is that of the need for competing approaches to biography: something which, it is argued, the genre is well-qualified to fulfil. The proliferation of differing biographies of the same subject (often seen as a weakness of the genre) is instead seen as a strength."[47] This appears perfectly valid, but the question again arises as to whether one version is better than another and how to decide this. The issue is discussed a little later in this chapter.

Another way of analysing biography is as text. The debate about biography as text (i.e., language) forms part of the postmodernist challenge to history in the broad sense, leading to this style of critique being described as "the linguistic turn". Since history is written language, it can ultimately be analysed as literature. "The emphasis now is less on history as a process of objective discovery and report but, rather, [it] accepts its unavoidably fictive nature, that is, its literary constructedness."[48] The idea that language did not represent reality but in fact constructed it problematized historians' efforts to portray the past in any theoretically acceptable way. The thinking derived ultimately from a pioneer in the theory of language structure, Ferdinand de Saussure, whose work led on to both structuralism and semiotics, and influenced such well-known figures as Derrida and Foucault, although the latter were also critical of several of de Saussure's key assumptions.

These challenges to historiography have led to fierce debate which can only be covered in fairly brief terms here. With varying degrees of reluctance, most historians have accepted a much broader definition of history writing than before, partly as a result of the emergence of postmodern theories, including more attention to social groups and methods of representation which were previously overlooked. Postmodernist theory has helped to potentiate and inspire a variety of new modes of thinking and writing, such as the postcolonial school, subaltern studies, gender history, and new approaches to social and cultural history.

Nevertheless, traditionally minded historians have strongly disputed the more extreme assertions of some postmodernists, for example their claims that history is no different from fiction or poetry[49] or that history merely presents bourgeois ideology in disguised form.[50] They have continued to insist on the ultimate reality of what they are dealing with, and have accused the postmodernists of "hyper-relativism". Hobsbawm called for the maintenance of the "absolutely central distinction between establishable fact and fiction, between historical statements based on evidence and those which are not".[51] The debate about Richard J. Evans' 1997 book *In Defence of History* raised many of these questions in sharp form. While acknowledging the positive factors arising from postmodernism, including a much greater plurality of the discipline, Evans argued against

Jenkins' (and others') claims about the supposed impossibility of inferring past events, situations, beliefs and actions from documentary evidence. He concluded "the past ... really happened, and we really can, if we are very scrupulous and careful and self-critical, find out how it happened and reach some tenable though always less than final conclusions about what it all meant".[52] This may be an excessively simple credo, but it seems the more convincing line of thought, and I regard it as unacceptable to equate history (and biography) with fiction. It is true that literary theory and history theory are now much more entangled with each other than ever before; historical biography may share many features and conventions with literature; it may *be* — or aspire to be — literature; biographers may in some ways be likened to novelists, and often are;[53] but biography cannot be equated with literary fiction, if the word "fiction" is to retain any meaning at all.

In the context of the theory of biography, it is relevant to consider what a postmodern biography might be like. Lambert declared that postmodernism could allow "the possibility of breaking out of the traditional, totalising mode of inscribing a life and into new techniques of life-narration.... The postmodern 'decentred self' has been shaped ideologically by its relationships with important others".[54] Pointing to Simon Schama's work, she suggested that "postmodern biography could include techniques of fragmentation, echoes, variation of narrative perspectives, parodies and pastiches".[55] This suggests a number of imaginative, fresh and even adventurous approaches to biography through using literary devices more familiar in fiction, although it is not entirely clear what is meant by some of these categories. For example, what is meant in practice by "echoes" and "fragmentation"? A very few examples of postmodern biography seem to have appeared to date,[56] although few modern biographies would remain uninfluenced by the current theoretical climate.

An important related point is the extent to which a biographer can legitimately use his or her imagination, and even more contentiously, whether it is legitimate to invent material. Perhaps echoing Strachey, Ira Nadel asks provocatively "To what extent is fact necessary in a biography? To what extent does the biographer alter fact to fit his theme and pattern?"[57] Lambert notes that Schama admitted fabricating some material in his account of the death of General Wolfe in the work earlier referred to.[58]

The well-known biographer Holroyd, who refuses to subscribe to any theory, seems to take a middle position on the point, favouring the imaginative use of sources and arguing that while "the biographer may not invent dialogue" (or by implication anything else), "quotations from letters and diaries" may be used to simulate dialogue.[59] Yet it seems repugnant to the historian's normal approach to go so far as to fabricate material, even where the material arguably conveys a psychologically accurate picture of the reality under discussion.[60] It may be legitimate and even desirable to draw judiciously upon fictional accounts if they aptly reflect the mood or atmosphere of the scene which the biographer is describing, but I would argue that the biographer must keep faith with the reader by making clear what material is being drawn on, and how it is being used. "A biographer is a writer who is on oath",[61] and the biographer fails if readers have cause to believe they have been deliberately misled.

One claim made by the subaltern studies school and others is that biography is elitist,[62] concentrating too much on leaders and prominent figures, and that important historical insights can be gained by shifting the focus to lesser known personalities or groups. Thus, we have biographies of "the people", or of the poor, or of minor figures associated with major ones.[63] Some social scientists' dislike of explanations of history based on individuals is understandable, especially if they wish to emphasize the importance of the broad historical trends which seem to occur from time to time.[64] Did the hour produce the person, or did the person produce the hour? What *difference* did an individual make to history, and can an individual make a difference? If the leader — such as Napoleon, Julius Caesar, Catherine the Great — had not been there, would events have turned out much the same? The issue is in essence unsolvable because the leader *was* there, the events *did* happen as they did and not another way. We cannot know an alternative course of events, because it did not happen. But it is intuitively hard to believe that, for example, France would have been as important and powerful in Europe in the years 1800–15 without the presence of Napoleon, or Germany during 1932–45 without Hitler.[65]

One answer to the claim of elitism is that political biographies normally concentrate on leaders because — although we cannot be sure what difference they actually did make — their lives can usefully illuminate the great events through which they lived and can at times be used to make sense of broad historical trends. Biography provides one perspective through which wider events can be explained. In the present case, biographical treatments of modern Indonesian history have naturally concentrated on the two first presidents, but new insights may well be gained from an examination of the perspectives of lesser-known figures like Hamengku Buwono. This argument may be related to claims by Tridgell and others for the illumination provided by a diversity of perspectives.

Alexander[66] argues that biography's advantages outweigh the disadvantages. These include that biography, by isolating one element (a person) in a historical process, helps to illuminate the relationships surrounding it, and that biographies can be "centrally linking texts, uniting disparate elements in an increasingly fragmented world".[67] All good biographies will describe and illustrate the context of the subject's life.[68] At its best, biography can become "'sociography', speaking of entire societies through individuals".[69] Alexander quotes Boswell's boast of having "Johnsonised" his age, describing seventeenth-century London through his account of the great man's life.[70] It is presumably only the exceptional biography for which such a claim can be credibly made.

A number of problems have been identified in biography, although not definitively settled. One, paradoxically, is the danger of coherence.[71] A biography can give an artificial unity to a person's life when in fact it was merely a part of chaotic, unplanned, and fractured reality.[72] A person's life, even the life of people who are regarded as unusually successful, is often characterized by changing fortunes, serious challenges, and temporary or even long-lasting setbacks. A famous example of an apparently disappointing career, even to late in life, was Winston Churchill, who became Prime Minister in 1940 at the age of sixty-five. In the current case, around 1957, Hamengku Buwono might have been plausibly seen as a political failure, at least at the national level. The perhaps unavoidable danger is that the biographer will establish a spurious tone of order and even inevitability in describing a life which, when lived, may have seemed defective, chaotic and unfocused.[73] The biographer can point out the times of doubt and uncertainty in a subject's life, but it might be argued that a biography which tries to represent a life fully in all the detail of its vagaries and vicissitudes would be almost unreadable. Again, a balance must be struck.

A further risk is that sources may mislead the writer in some way, or even that "all sources can mislead".[74] Carr warned that the weight of the sources may push the historian in the wrong direction (or *a* wrong direction).[75] In this study, probably the most interesting period of Hamengku Buwono's career was the Indonesian Revolution. Within the available corpus of the sources for this period, the weight of Dutch sources, compared with Indonesian sources and others, is disproportionately large, and it imposes a certain bias which may or may not mislead. Dutch sources tended to exaggerate (the occasionally very real) disunity in the Republican camp, including the extent to which Hamengku Buwono had his own independent aims separate from the other leaders. As will appear, I have concluded that many Dutch accounts were misleading in this respect and that Hamengku Buwono stuck loyally to the Sukarno/Hatta leadership. But the lack of frank and critical inside accounts from the Indonesian side does leave the possibility that some episode occurred where Hamengku Buwono deviated from absolute loyalty, or where his supporters did; and that this was subsequently ignored in Indonesian sources. In such cases, the writer can only rely on what the sources reveal, while pointing out the ambiguities or lacunae.

ASIAN PERSPECTIVES

Comparatively little seems to have been written about the theoretical questions raised by what might loosely be called "cross-cultural biography", by contrast with biography in general. The type of questions which might be asked would include: to what extent, if at all, does a biography written by, say, a non-Indonesian about an Indonesian, necessarily differ from one written by a fellow Indonesian? Should there be any difference? Does the writing of cross-cultural biography raise any issues different from biography in general?

David Chandler,[76] the biographer of Pol Pot, put forward (while by implication disowning) what he called a possible Orientalist version of the man's life, depicting him as "an empowered warrior prince", emerging from the forest in 1975 to govern his kingdom. But are biographers "Orientalist" if they refer to the subject's mystical inclinations or cultural environment, which are surely part of their life-experience? Such an interpretation of a politician's life is not the only possible one, but it adds a dimension to the picture which may be valuable. In writing about Sukarno, for example, Dahm (and Legge to some extent) drew attention to the influence of Javanese mysticism in Sukarno's life, especially the wayang shadow play.[77] Javanese mysticism had a role in the life of Suharto, although Elson for one concluded that its role was not as significant as popularly believed.[78] In Hamengku Buwono's case, I refer at times to the ways in which his behaviour seemed to mirror ideal Javanese conduct. This aspect could be seen as another analytical tool; it is not to be over-used, but also should not be neglected in illuminating the subject's career.

David Hill, who wrote about the celebrated Indonesian journalist Mochtar Lubis, described his "puzzling, often tense relationship" with his subject.[79] Reacting to postmodernist critiques of biography and admitting the parallels with modes of literary fiction, Hill grappled with the "real Mochtar" and the "textual Mochtar", recognizing that his version of the textual Mochtar would inevitably differ from the real one and that the real one was — and always would be — ungraspable. "What I endeavoured to do was to present a detailed, reasoned and thoughtful view of Mochtar Lubis within the context of his society, having due regard to his achievements, but not shrinking from the responsibility of criticism."[80] This is an aspiration that any biographer might hold, although it represents something of a counsel of perfection.

Hill also referred to the problem of "explaining one culture in the language of another",[81] and the epistemological issues this raised. Although he did not go into detail on this crucial aspect, his account referred to the assumption by a group of prominent Indonesians that biography meant eulogy, though admittedly they were assembling a festschrift for Mochtar's seventieth birthday;[82] that his initial admiration of Mochtar had to be tempered by the criticism he heard from a variety of sources; and that the living subject "far from being passive, continually modifies his behaviour according to the behaviour of the observer".[83] Again, none of these points seem to differ from the problems faced by a non-cross-cultural biographer.

For the purposes of this study, one obvious difference is that the biographer cannot have a personal relationship with a dead subject, but the existence of the subject's family or associates poses its own potential problems and ambiguities, as well as constructive opportunities. A biographer who emphasizes (or merely uncovers) negative aspects of the subject's life runs the risk of offending the subject's family and friends, or even shocking them with family secrets of which they were unaware.[84] The sensitivities may become even greater where the subject is of royal status and regarded as a national hero. On the other hand, a biographer may be fortunate enough to reveal the true virtues and merits of the subject by stripping away myths and misunderstandings. It is at least arguable that a subject is all the more a hero if he or she overcomes mistakes or character flaws in registering great achievements.

In the same set of essays as the essay by Hill quoted above, Angus McIntyre identified two problems with biographical approaches to Indonesian — and especially Javanese — subjects. The first was cultural relativism in the sense of excessive reliance on cultural explanations for the subject's actions, and a failure to investigate the biographer–subject relationship in any depth.[85] He criticized Dahm for failing to carry through convincingly the culturally based explanations of Sukarno's motivations which he at first highlighted as having great explanatory power. On cultural relativism more generally, the biographer must indeed be wary both of uncritical acceptance of "exotic" social norms which might infringe universal social rights, but must also avoid the Orientalist idea that a "Western" normality exists against which the other is judged and found wanting, perhaps merely through being unfamiliar.

On the biographer–subject relationship, McIntyre found common ground with Hill in drawing attention to the perils of excessive identification with the subject on one hand and excessive negativism on the other. This would depend on the degree of objective sympathy, however dangerous or slippery such a term might be, which the biographer might feel towards a historical figure. It would be easier to identify with figures like Gandhi or William the Silent than with Hitler or Idi Amin. Perhaps the terminology needs to be refined, and we might say that the biographer has the task of finding some *empathy* with the subject, even a repellent subject, while maintaining also a degree of detachment.

More generally, a biographer who writes, especially debunkingly or even merely realistically, about a hero from another country will run the risk of being told "you do not understand our culture, our country or our people", or even facing allegations of slander or cultural contempt. As Hill found, it appears difficult or perhaps impossible to avoid this, because the foreigner will inevitably hold attitudes and make judgements, especially where these are negative, which some locals will dislike. This factor may be a deterrent, but it cannot become a pretext for non-action. Asian subjects are at least as deserving of biography and explication as Western ones, perhaps more so. The existence of a cultural gap calls out for mediation and explanation, rather than avoidance.

Some Asian writers admitted that biography in at least some parts of Asia, as in the premodern West or even nineteenth-century England, was synonymous with hagiography. A Thai writer linked this phenomenon to Buddhist beliefs.[86] On biography in China, Twitchett noted that "the purpose of biography was essentially commemorative … designed for a didactic purpose…".[87] Two Chinese writers said that "in Chinese society, writing about a person is tantamount to extolling that person and building up his [sic] image".[88] Similarly, the nationalist tone of much biographical writing in Indonesia looks excessively simplistic and hagiographic to an outsider, despite the evident importance of nationalism to the identity of many Indonesians.[89] Van Klinken criticized the "one-dimensional" biographies of historical figures too often produced in Indonesia,[90] whose sole objective seems to be to reinforce the Indonesian nationalist discourse.

Is the rejection of these "one-dimensional biographies" an Orientalist attitude? Is the nationalist discourse equally valid with that provided by a supposedly more realistic, sceptical, and dispassionate historian? Suhartoist versions of Indonesian history are now being increasingly contested within Indonesia,[91] but the new revisionism generally has a limited political focus and ignores wider theoretical and methodological questions. The probably overdue re-examination of conventional nationalist versions of Indonesian history may be starting, but there are only a few tentative signs of this as yet.[92] The main reasons for dissatisfaction with nationalist versions of history in general, and (of course) not just Indonesian ones, are that they are limited and often shallow, that they usually ignore alternative propositions and overlook minority and "loser" stories,[93] and that they characteristically portray local leaders in unrealistically heroic terms. "Getting history wrong is an essential part of being a nation."[94] Biographer/historians may well carry conscious or unconscious biases and ideologies into their writings, but they might hope to avoid any innate motivation to get the history wrong.

We might conclude from the rather scattered writings on this topic that the problems and issues of cross-cultural biography differ little from those of biography broadly, apart from the need to be sensitive to the subject's different (sometimes very different) cultural background. But the cultural differences do not seem to differ in kind, merely in degree, from differences which any biographer would have with any subject. A Westerner writing a biography of fellow-Westerner Goering might have more difficulty summoning up the necessary empathy for the subject than he or she would have in writing a biography of the culturally different Nelson Mandela or the Dalai Lama.

Finally, in this study, I have tried to bear in mind Pieter Geyl's dictum — "it is a historian's task to demolish myth".[95] Historians cannot escape the period in which they live, and this particular period in Indonesia, characterized by emerging democracy and thus reassessment of many unquestioned attitudes and judgements of the Suharto period, is an appropriate time to re-examine standard accounts of important political figures during the first half-century or so of Indonesia's existence.

I also tried to recall, and to avoid the dangers of, Edward Said's warning:

> Can one divide human reality, as indeed human reality seems to be genuinely divided, into clearly different cultures, histories, traditions, societies, even races, and survive the consequences humanly? By surviving the consequences humanly, I mean to ask whether there is any way of avoiding the hostility expressed by the division, say, of men into "us" (westerners) and "they" (Orientals).[96]

Any Westerner attempting to write about an Asian may be subject to the charge of "Orientalism", and such an effort should be accompanied by the necessary awareness of one's own perspectives and biases, to the extent possible. But Said's question seems unduly pessimistic, in that no hostility necessarily exists in attempts to identify and explain cultural differences. The Other is simply the Other, and not the Enemy. The difficulty — which surely can be avoided with care — is to refrain from treating the Other as inherently inferior, according to the biographer's normative, cultural or moral prejudices or ideology.

METHODOLOGY

From the available theories discussed earlier, we may conclude that different and even competing approaches to a particular subject can be equally informative. The issue is what versions can be ruled out and on what grounds, and, unfortunately, available literature tells us little about this. Theorists have been so concerned to combat and question traditional ideas of historical truth, objectivity, and empiricism that they have paid much less attention to that issue. But some notion of what a good biography might be, and some practical advice on life writing does emerge.

In discussing biographies of Bertrand Russell, Tridgell[97] contrasts one biography which presented the subject as "the autonomous, high-achieving, isolated and triumphant male self", with another more satisfactory "relational" approach. Her preferred approach was to identify and explain the self in the context of relations with other selves, rather than seeing the subject in isolation. Thus, Hamengku Buwono might most beneficially be seen in relation with other important Indonesian historical figures, especially Sukarno and Suharto, but also Nasution, Malik and the New Order technocrats. Nevertheless, this seems to be an argument about emphasis rather than an either/or choice. As noted earlier, a biography has to present both the individual self and its context. As always, the need is to balance the central story with due references to context (including relational aspects) and wider issues.

Lucy Townsend, referring to the biographer "as sleuth",[98] outlines what she calls the "concentric circles method", where the researcher studies first the subject's own origins, family and career, then the subject's milieu, then the larger context (in her case, the American education system in the nineteenth century), and then the wider American society of the period. Similarly, as a way of visualizing Hamengku Buwono's life, we could postulate a series of circles, not necessarily concentric but overlapping, which would be of fluctuating size and centrality as Hamengku Buwono's career advanced. We might see him first in the narrow context of the Yogyakarta kraton, then in colonial contexts (both Dutch and Japanese), and then in the wider context of Indonesian national politics. After 1950, the kraton circle, while in some ways central to his life during the Revolution, would move off-centre and be almost swallowed up by the "national politics" circle.[99] The New Order period would show a large national-politics circle, a fairly large international circle surrounding it, and a small overlapping kraton circle to one side. I have not directly adopted this methodology but it has been an influence in thinking about Hamengku Buwono's life.

The method adopted here is empirically based historical narrative, with attempts to place Hamengku Buwono in his historical and political context, and with the occasional digression to outline points of theoretical interest, to refer to different modes of observing him, to attempt to explain his actions or motivations, and to explore his interactions with other important figures. The chronology is the conventional one, proceeding from Hamengku Buwono's birth up to the end of his political career. Although this may be a banal and routine approach, and a few historians have preferred to smash "the chronological idol",[100] in this case, each period usefully underpins and helps to explain subsequent events in the subject's life. The chronological approach can also reveal "connections between activities, energies, and interests that might otherwise seem to have nothing to do with one another".[101]

Notes

1. Some might argue also for Roeslan Abdulgani, but the wily Roeslan, although incredibly adaptable and durable, did not serve at very senior levels for quite as long as the Sultan and Malik.
2. For example, Kutoyo, *Sri Sultan Hamengku Buwono*, p. 165, Moh Roem in *Tahta untuk Rakyat* (henceforth *TUR*), p. 141; and Mohammad Natsir in *TUR*, p. 197.
3. A.J.P. Taylor, *Origins of the Second World War*, 2nd ed., pp. 133–34.
4. *Tahta untuk Rakyat*, p. 152, in the brief commentary provided by T.K. Critchley.
5. See the Dutch Governor's note that the young Prince Dorojatun had told him that he accepted the position of Sultan "purely from a feeling of duty". Mail reports (Mailrapporten), MR 279 geh /40, Governor's letter of 18 February 1940.
6. The column by Herry Komar in *Tempo*, 15 October 1988, indicates it was a common opinion that he intended to be the last Sultan. The idea that he was "the last Sultan" was common among outside observers, e.g., Ivan Southall, *Indonesian Journey*, p. 75.
7. Westerling, *Challenge to Terror*, p. 226.
8. Woolcott, *The Hot Seat*, p. 132.
9. Sujatmoko, quoted in Nursam, *Pergumulan Seorang Intelektual* [The Struggle of an Intellectual], p. 193.
10. Adam Malik, *Mengabdi Republik* (Serving the Republic), vol. 1, p. 37.
11. Brackman, in *TUR*, p. 242.
12. Ruth McVey, "The Case of the Disappearing Decade". In Bourchier and Legge, eds., *Democracy in Indonesia, 1950s and 1990s*, p. 9.
13. See Jolly, *Encyclopedia of Life Writing*.
14. For example, several biographies of Mao Tse Tung have appeared, also several about Sukarno (by Legge, Dahm, et al.), scores on Gandhi and at least a dozen about Nehru. Other leaders like Lee Kuan Yew, Mahathir, and Marcos have attracted Western biographical attention. For Indonesia, biographies have appeared of figures like Hatta, Nasution, Syahrir, and Suharto.
15. Sutrisno Kutoyo (*Sri Sultan Hamengku Buwono IX, Riwayat Hidup dan Perjuangan*) and Sudarisman Purwokusumo (*Sultan Hamengku Buwono IX*). The latter work seems out of print and unobtainable.
16. Herbert Feith, *Decline of Constitutional Democracy*, p. 33.
17. Ibid.

Introduction and Theoretical Considerations

18. I have found only two references to "Allah", and two to "Tuhan" — his radio address on 15 August 1946, celebrating the first anniversary of the Proclamation, mentions Allah. *Patriot*, 14 September 1946. He refers to "Tuhan yang Rahman dan Rahim", in a message of 1 July 1944 (*SM* of that date); and a reference to "Tuhan" in a message about defence measures in Java in *SM* of 15 June 1944. I have found only one such reference (to Allah) in the New Order period, in his statement of 22 October 1965 — see Chapter 8 — and none at all after that.
19. I prefer the term Revolution to describe this period (*Revolusi* or even *Revolusi fisik* in Indonesian). During the Soeharto period, the term *perang kemerdekaan* was often used, which is an almost direct translation of the American term "War of Independence". The only discussion I have seen of these changes in terminology occurs in Reid's instructive treatment of the concept of "revolution" as it applies to Indonesia in *An Indonesian Frontier, Acehnese and Other Histories of Sumatra*, pp. 321–24.
20. Kahin, p. 176.
21. Eric Hornberger and John Charmley, eds., *The Troubled Face of Biography* (Macmillan, 1989), p. 14.
22. Philip Holden, "Lee Kuan Yew, A Man and an Island: Gender and Nation in Lee Kuan Yew's 'The Singapore Story'", *Biography* 24, no. 2 (Spring 2002): 401.
23. Elton, *The Practice of History*, p. 123.
24. I.B. Nadel, *Biography: Fact, Fiction and Form*, p. 17.
25. Quoted by Carr, *What is History?*, p. 43.
26. Examples include G.B. Smith, *General Gordon the Christian Soldier and Hero*, 1898, *The Life and Correspondence of Thomas Arnold*, by A.P. Stanley, 1846, and Samuel Smiles, *Lives of the Engineers*, 1861.
27. D.K. Merrill, *American Biography*, p 208.
28. "Strachey's influence was almost entirely pernicious" (because of his cavalier attitude to truth). P.F. Alexander, "Biography: A Case for the Defence". In *National Biographies and National Identity, a Critical Approach to Theory and Editorial Practice*, edited by McCalman et al., p. 79 and p. 81.
29. Glendinning, op. cit., p. 55.
30. Ibid.
31. Such as Janet Browne's two volumes on Darwin.
32. Nadel, op cit., p. 111.
33. The American biographer and theorist Leon Edel was influential in advocating the virtues of psycho-biography. See the anonymous obituary in *Biography* 21, no. 2 (Spring 1997): 151.
34. Quoted by Weiland in Epstein, ed., *Contesting the Subject, Essays in the Postmodern Theory and Practice of Biography and Biographical Criticism*, p. 205.

35. Peter Gay quoted by Walter Phillips, "Historians, Biography and History", in *Tracing Past Lives*, p. 7.
36. Carr, op. cit., p. 18.
37. Clendinnen, Inga, "In Search of the Actual Man Underneath", public lecture, ANU, 4 May 2004.
38. Alexander, op. cit., p. 89.
39. A. Lieblich, op. cit., pp. 264–65.
40. Jolly, *Encyclopedia of Life Writing*.
41. Even the use of the term "postmodern" is of course an oversimplification; I use it here to denote the (very) broad school of thought which can be broken down into "postmodernism", post-structuralism", "deconstructionism", etc.
42. Carr, op. cit., p. 4. Carr noted that every known historical fact was already the result of a process of selection and interpretation before the historian gathered it.
43. "Biographers are all autobiographers, although the pretensions of their profession won't allow them to recognise it or even see it." Fish, quoted by Susan Tridgell, p. 156, PhD thesis ANU, *Understanding Selves through Modern Western Biography: Insight, Illusion or Particularity?*, 2002.
44. Nadel, op. cit., p. 207.
45. See Champion's review ("A Humanistic Response to High Theory in Literature", nd) of Miller and Freadman, *Rethinking Theory*, where he quotes "The result of this undifferentiated and ubiquitous conception is that the notion of power loses all explanatory force since on this account there is nothing that is not power", p. 173 <http://www.the-rathouse.com/RC_FreadmanMiller.html> (accessed 12 July 2005).
46. Tridgell, op. cit., p. vi.
47. Ibid.
48. Alan Munslow, "What History Is", *History in Focus: The Nature of History*, October 2001.
49. Berkhofer "fails to see much, if anything, in the distinction drawn between fact and fiction". Quoted by Keith Jenkins in his introduction, Jenkins, ed., *The Postmodernist History Reader*, p. 16.
50. Jenkins, ibid., p. 7, "on my reading, lower case history … is bourgeois ideology".
51. Hobsbawm, *On History*, p. viii. Note also "… most sociologists make bad historians: they don't want to take the time to find out", p. 278.
52. R.J. Evans, *In Defence of History*, p. 154. The main targets of Evans' criticisms were postmodernist theorists of history like Hayden White, Keith Jenkins, Ankersmit, and Munslow. He said his main target was "postmodernist literary theorists who adopt jargon in order to seem scientific".
53. O'Connor, *Biographers and the Art of Biography*, p. 17.

54. C.J. Lambert, "Post-Modern Biography", *Biography* 18, no. 4 (Fall 1994): 305.
55. Ibid., p. 310.
56. We have mentioned Schama's work (*Dead Certainties*) as described by Lambert. For a broad outline of postmodern historiography, see Evans' *In Defence of History*, pp. 244–48.
57. Nadel, op. cit., p. 5.
58. Lambert, p. 308.
59. Holroyd, loc. cit.
60. Hobsbawm, *On History*, "we cannot invent our facts", p. 7.
61. Desmond McCarthy, quoted by Ulick O'Connor, op. cit., p. 34.
62. Philips in Broome, ed., *Tracing Past Lives, the Writing of Historical Biography*, p. 3.
63. Alexander, op. cit., p. 92, instancing biographies of Nora Barnacle, James Joyce's wife, and the mother of Henry Lawson.
64. See for example Hobsbawm's reference to "Kondratieff waves", op. cit., pp. 66–67.
65. Hobsbawm takes a middle view on the question — "individuals do not always make all that much difference in history" but "sometimes they do make a difference", p. 324. Many historians have ruminated on these questions — Benda referred to "the irreducible importance of the individual actor in history". Quoted by McIntyre in McIntyre, ed., *Indonesian Political Biography: In Search of Cross-Cultural Understanding*, p. 292.
66. Alexander, op. cit., p. 88.
67. Ibid., p. 91.
68. Ibid.
69. Ibid., p. 92. The word "sociography" is Donald Horne's.
70. Ibid.
71. Nadel, op. cit., p. 155. "Elemental to biography is the sense of coherence".
72. Lambert, ibid., p. 311.
73. "The imposition of order on life is untruthful and a distortion." Alexander, op. cit., p. 80.
74. Victoria Glendinning, "Lies and Silences", in Hornberger and Charmley, eds., op. cit., p. 51. See also Kenneth Silverman, review of Mark Kinkaid–Weekes' contribution ("Writing Lives Forwards") to *Mapping Lives: The Uses of Biography*, in *Biography* 27, no. 3 (Summer 2004): 597. Kinkead-Weekes was the author of volume two of the Cambridge biography of D.H. Lawrence.
75. Carr, p. 8.
76. David Chandler, "Writing a Biography of Pol Pot", in *Tracing Past Lives, the Writing of Historical Biography*, edited by Broome, p. 78.
77. Legge, *Sukarno*, pp. 22–24, 43–44, 47–48. Dahm, pp. 24–29 and passim.

78. Elson, *Suharto*, p. 302.
79. David Hill, "Objectifying Mochtar Lubis: Personalising the Process of Biography", edited by McIntyre, op. cit., pp. 265–85. This is not a feature peculiar to biographies of living Asian subjects.
80. Hill, ibid., p. 273.
81. Ibid., p. 278.
82. Ibid., p. 282.
83. Ferrarrotti, quoted by Hill, ibid., p. 275.
84. One example is the many (almost all negative) revelations in J.D.F. Jones' biography of Lauren van der Post, *Storyteller, The Many Lives of Laurens van der Post*.
85. Angus McIntyre, "Foreign Biographical Studies of Indonesian Subjects: Obstacles and Shortcomings" (pp. 291–315) edited by McIntyre, ibid., p. 294 and p. 307.
86. Sulak, "Biography and Buddhism in Thailand", *Biography* 17 (Winter 1994): 11.
87. Quoted by Wang Gungwu, "The Rebel-Reformer and Modern Chinese Biography". In *Self and Biography, Essays on the Individual and Society in Asia*, edited by Wang Gungwu, p. 186.
88. Di Feng and Shao Dang Fang, "Life Writing in China", *Biography* 17 (Winter 1994).
89. See Watson, *Of Self and Nation*.
90. G. Van Klinken, "The Battle for History after Suharto", *Critical Asian Studies* 33, no. 3 (2001): 323–50.
91. See van Klinken, ibid.
92. See the illuminating article by Rommel Curaming, "Towards Reinventing Indonesian Nationalist Historiography", *Kyoto Review*, March 2003 <http://kyotoreview.cseas.kyoto-u.ac.jp/issue> (accessed 15 June 2005).
93. "Elton was right in demanding ... a full and fair dealing with history's losers". Evans, *In Defence of History*, p. 230.
94. Renan quoted by Hobsbawm, op. cit., p. 35.
95. Pieter Geyl, *Encounters in History*, p. 413.
96. Said, *Orientalism* (London: Penguin, 1995), p. 45.
97. Tridgell, "Doing Justice to the Generations: Ray Monk's *Bertrand Russell*", Paper at International Conference on Life-Writing, 15–19 July, 2002, La Trobe University, Melbourne.
98. Lucy Townsend, "The Biographer as Sleuth: Using the Concentric Circle Method", *Biography* 16, no. 1 (1993): 19 et seq. In the writings I have explored on these subjects, especially in *Biography* magazine, this is the only article which actually highlighted the word "method".
99. Some biographers have looked at their subjects through geometrical metaphors,

cf. the circles metaphor quoted above. J.D.F. Jones, the biographer of the writer Laurens van der Post, noted the various "boxes" in which the subject kept different parts of his life (and different friends). J.D.F. Jones, op. cit., p. 378.
100. Evans, op. cit., p. 153.
101. Kinkead–Weekes, loc. cit.

2

EARLY DAYS

Dorojatun[1] was born on 12 April 1912 in Yogyakarta. His father was Prince Haryo Puruboyo,[2] a son of the reigning Sultan, and his mother was Raden Ayu Kustilah, who received the title of Kangjeng Raden Ayu Adipati Anom in 1915. She was the daughter of Prince Mangkubumi,[3] who was a brother of, and an influential adviser to, the Sultan, Hamengku Buwono VII. The Sultan paid a formal visit to congratulate Puruboyo, and paid him a special allowance in honour of the event.[4]

Dorojatun's mother was Puruboyo's official wife, and they had been married for four years.[5] When her husband unexpectedly became next in line to become Sultan not long after Dorojatun's birth, she had good prospects of becoming *permaisuri* (queen) in due course. But at the time this was in the future. Hamengku Buwono VII, although already in his seventies, seemed perfectly healthy and might live some years yet.

Prince Puruboyo became Sultan by accident. He was the fourth son of the monarch, but two of his elder brothers died relatively young and one was mentally unfit.[6] One of the first two, Hamengkunagoro, had lived long enough to marry and be named crown prince, but he died in 1913 at the age of 35 before he could become Sultan.[7] Puruboyo consequently became crown prince in his turn on 21 July 1914,[8] when Dorojatun was two years old.[9] From this time on, as the first and only son born to Puruboyo and his official wife, he was regarded as a likely future Sultan. His four[10] elder brothers were not expected to succeed to the throne because their mothers were minor wives of Prince Puruboyo.

When an important ruler is born in Java, a sign from heaven is usually expected, such as lightning, earthquakes, or volcanic eruptions. But the senior retainers of the palace[11] admitted in later years that no extraordinary events accompanied Dorojatun's birth. This did not prevent stories emerging much later that such omens had occurred, especially from those who believed that Hamengku Buwono IX had something of the Ratu Adil (Just King) about him.[12]

He was known formally as Gusti Raden Mas Dorojatun, although he carried the Dutch-style nickname of Henkie in his early years, after the husband of the reigning Dutch Queen Wilhelmina.[13] Javanese princes often bore European nicknames at the time.[14]

His father was regarded as a cold and distant parent, judging by the reactions in Yogyakarta to his decision to place the young prince with a series of Dutch families during his school years.[15] Of his first eighteen years, Dorojatun lived as much as thirteen years with Dutch families, after which he left for the Netherlands where he spent nine years away from Java. The phenomenon of being sent away for schooling is not unusual in Anglo-Saxon cultures, but it seemed strange in the Javanese context.[16] However, Dorojatun spent school holidays and other special occasions with his family in the kraton. Most of his brothers also boarded with Dutch families.[17]

His father's order to move to a Dutch home occurred when Dorojatun was only four, and local accounts have it that, crying bitterly, he had to be prised loose from one of the heavy pillars which are a feature of the kraton.[18] It is tempting to speculate that this prolonged isolation from his own family had profound effects on his personality and behaviour; that during his childhood, he learnt habits of keeping his own counsel, of learning to cope with being the odd one out, and of speaking and thinking in a foreign language. But this can only remain speculation. He was certainly no recluse, nor was he unsociable or aloof. By his own account, he was active and rather naughty as a child.[19] Nevertheless, the Javanese custom of restraining one's passions and concealing one's innermost thoughts can only have been reinforced by this early experience.

Puruboyo became Sultan Hamengku Buwono VIII in February 1921, following the abdication of his father.[20] He was regarded as a relatively progressive monarch, certainly compared with his father, who despite a reputation for generosity[21] was notorious for his dislike of modern technology, to the extent that he never travelled in a motor car and forbade his son from owning one.[22] Dutch was apparently never spoken in the palace until Hamengku Buwono VIII came to the throne. Hamengku Buwono VIII also favoured modern education for his children. In the 1930s he was described by a visiting prince from Sumatra[23] as "less old-fashioned" than the Sunan of Solo. His obituaries in 1939[24] noted that he had restricted forced labour for peasants and had undertaken various other agrarian reforms.[25] The founder of the Taman Siswa educational organization, Ki Hajar Dewantoro, spoke of the cordial relations between the Sultan and his organization.[26]

His photographs show a dignified but wary figure, less stiff and formal than his imposing white-moustached father. A Dutch governor described him as a "loyal, upright and charming person".[27] He was careful to avoid political trouble and any contact with movements or organizations which the colonial government disliked.[28] On the negative side, just after he became crown prince, an irreverent Dutch official described him as "having a startled look, and military uniform does not suit him".[29] He had a propensity for lavish expenditure[30] and showed occasional bad temper in private, leading to hasty decisions which he had to be talked out of.[31] He could apparently be jealous of other family members, notably his half-brother Suryodiningrat.[32] He won a major dispute with Dutch officials over financial matters in 1930, after which colonial officials did not enquire closely into palace finances, leading to the "budget chaos" which Dorojatun and the Dutch Governor had to clear up in 1940.[33]

On Hamengku Buwono VIII's death, his former Dutch schoolteachers testified to his quick understanding of their lessons, although due allowance has to be made for politeness in such circumstances.[34] What they did not say was that the Java princes had no political power and that their main function was to legitimize Dutch rule by providing an appearance of authority, and to preside over the cultural and social activities of the kraton. "The courts had degenerated into an effete formalism, an elaborate and antiquated artificiality."[35] The fresh challenges which emerged over the next two decades would bring into question once again the continuing relevance of the Javanese principalities.

Little is known of Dorojatun's mother. As a daughter of a prominent prince, she had been familiar with court life before she married her cousin Puruboyo, but in those days, women, even princesses, usually kept in the background. Dorojatun's mother was central to the main mystery of his childhood, the serious rift between his parents which led to her banishment from the palace around 1918 or 1919.[36] Family traditions speak darkly of palace rivalries and black magic, but no clear account is available.[37] Dorojatun's mother thus never became the official queen, but this did not prejudice his claims to the succession. The parents seem to have divorced about 1920.[38]

Dorojatun's first years were spent under the grim shadow of the First World War. Although the Netherlands remained neutral, Indies trade was severely disrupted and the economy suffered.[39] The period in which he grew up was characterized by considerable political ferment in Java. Organizations which are usually regarded as the first signs of Indonesian nationalism emerged, such as Budi Utomo, formed in Yogyakarta in 1908, and also Sarekat Islam and the Muhammadiyah in 1912. The Communist Party of Indonesia, the PKI, was founded in 1921.[40] In 1915 and again in 1920, dangerous outbreaks of plague in Central Java and the medical measures taken to combat them — which were highly offensive to traditional cultural mores — provided further reason for radicals to criticize the kratons' cooperation with the Dutch, however right and necessary such cooperation might have seemed to colonial administrators.[41]

Political reform by the authorities was too slow to satisfy the radicals of every stamp who were now emerging. In 1918 the prominent nationalist Dr Cipto Mangunkusumo called for all the Javanese princes to be "pensioned off".[42] Radicals like Haji Misbach of Solo blamed the current problems on three main oppressors, namely the colonial administration, capitalists and local rulers. Apart from their analysis of Javanese backwardness as a necessary condition of capitalism, the radicals accused the princes of conspiring with the Dutch to keep their own people in poverty. "The Javanese rulers were depicted as the impotent allies of the Dutch.... In the ideal society of the future there was no place for a Sultan or a Susuhunan."[43]

The glacial pace of political reform speeded up temporarily after the war. The formation in 1918 of the Volksraad (People's Council) promised the formation of representative political institutions, but, although the Volksraad remained in existence until the Japanese occupation, hope of progress soon faded. "The Volksraad had few powers, it was consulted on the budget, it could advise and propose, but it could not decide."[44] Similar disappointment attended the creation of regency councils in several provinces, but not the principalities, in the 1920s.[45]

The extreme radicals, the communists, launched ill-planned revolts in Java in November 1926 and in West Sumatra in early 1927, which were quickly defeated. The principalities were largely untouched by these incidents, although they too were affected by the more repressive attitudes of the colonial government which emerged afterwards.

Throughout the 1920s the nationalist press ran regular articles lamenting the powerlessness of the Java princes, their limited links with the people, and — occasionally — their lack of sympathy with struggling workers.[46] The Sunan of Solo was criticized for lavish expenditure and expensive travels with an enormous entourage.[47] Few signs of mutual understanding between the kratons and the nationalists were apparent in these years, although in contrast to Yogyakarta, from about 1927 some elements in the Solo kraton became increasingly nationalistic, as we will see.[48]

Much attention was given to the need for a representative body (known as a Bale Agung — Supreme Council) in both Yogyakarta and Solo, but the pace was agonizingly slow in even considering the proposal, let alone actually forming the councils.[49] This was an important demand both by Budi Utomo and, in Yogyakarta, by the increasingly influential Pakempalan Kawulo Ngayogyakarta (PKN — Union of Subjects of Yogyakarta), which had been formed in mid-1930.

In 1932, the Governor General pushed hard for the Bale Agungs to be formed; but he failed to meet the main demand of the princes and the nationalist organizations, that Bale Agung members should have immunity from the speech laws which greatly circumscribed what local political leaders could say in public.[50] Eventually the Sunan grudgingly accepted the unsatisfactory Bale which was offered, and it was officially formed in Solo in March 1935.[51] A possible Bale Agung for Yogyakarta remained on the agenda through the early 1930s, but no such body was ever formed in the colonial period.[52] For his part, Hamengku Buwono VIII was said to be averse to excessive democratization.[53]

Another notion which was current in these years was the proposal, pushed largely by Mangkunegoro VII, for a federation of the four principalities. The Solo kraton took this up while Yogyakarta remained aloof, but the adoption of the idea by the unpopular Governor of Solo[54] and consequently ebbing interest among the rulers meant that the proposal led to nothing.

Hamengku Buwono VIII occasionally appeared in public to open construction projects or attend formal ceremonies, but he made no speeches or other efforts to enable the people to know him better,[55] and he was occasionally reproached in the press for his conservatism.[56] With the important exception of the PKN which was his brother's initiative, the Sultan made little direct attempt to foster his relationship with the ordinary people.

With the one exception of the PKN therefore, the political picture in Yogyakarta in 1930 as the young Dorojatun left for nine years of education abroad, was one of growing economic gloom and political repression, even more so when the harsh Governor General de Jonge arrived in 1931, supported by the ultraconservative Colonies Minister (1933–37) Hendrikus Colijn.[57] Their rigid colonial policy would have convinced the seventeen-year-old student of the wisdom of his father's political caution, and also of his own avoidance of political activities during his student years. This caution was reinforced by the arrest of Sukarno at the end of 1929 and the suppression of his party, the PNI.[58] The Yogyakarta kraton gave no sign of disapprobation at these events, and it is not surprising that nationalists were suspicious of the political timidity and entrenched privileges of the Javanese nobility. This was an unpromising environment for the early years of a nationalist Sultan.

Ideas of the future political shape of an independent or autonomous state were taking various forms. Some Javanese thinkers dreamed of a future independent Java (only), and ideas ranged from the "aristo-democracy" of Noto Suroto (scorned by the younger generation but attractive to Javanese priyayi)[59] to concepts of a Javanese renaissance advocated by the Catholic leader Kasimo and others. By this time, however, perhaps a majority of politically conscious Indonesians favoured a unified Indonesian state, as typified in the famous Youth Pledge (one fatherland — Indonesia; one nation — Indonesia; one language — Indonesian) in 1928.[60] Nevertheless, for a young Yogyakarta prince at the end of the 1920s, a range of possible political futures for Java (or Indonesia) would still have appeared possible, and in any case, a postcolonial state of any kind was imaginable only in theory at the time.

The 1930s

We will complete this summary of pre-war political developments in Yogyakarta by following the story up to the early 1940s, although Dorojatun was a distant spectator for most of the period, and these developments only became of direct moment to him on his return to Java in October

1939. As mentioned, the sole exception to the growing political gloom in the year of Dorojatun's departure was the formation of the PKN by the Sultan's half-brother, Suryodiningrat. At the founding meeting in 1930, Suryodiningrat specifically stated PKN's political aim of enhancing the self-government of the Yogyakarta principality.[61] In another speech he reversed the normal Javanese concept of power relations by saying "The Javanese aristocracy has a certain debt of honour to settle in regard to the people. The people do not exist in order to serve the King. The King exists in order to serve the people."[62]

The PKN's scope was geographically limited to the principality, and the governing board was dominated by Yogyakarta princes. This implicit challenge to the all-Indonesia approach of the nationalist movement was an unwelcome development for the nationalists.[63] However, Suryodiningrat argued, not very convincingly, that the PKN, being purely local in nature, "would not impede the work of other parties".[64]

The new organization aroused much popular fervour, and by 1932 the membership had risen to 180,000 and later to a quarter of a million, testifying to the innate drawing power of the Yogyakarta monarchy.[65] The Sultan had endorsed the formation of the PKN,[66] but — at least according to Dutch official reports — its rapid growth and the consequent enormous popularity of Suryodiningrat sparked his increasing resentment. The Dutch government too was alarmed by the growth of the PKN, which it increasingly viewed as a political threat, disliking its calls for lower taxation and its criticisms of the Dutch-dominated sugar industry.[67] Thus, the Dutch authorities found common cause with the Sultan. The latter's alarm supposedly turned to anger when unsubstantiated reports emerged in 1933 that Suryodiningrat had claimed to be the king of all Muslims, a report which Suryodiningrat denied.[68] The Sultan apparently had to be talked out of dismissing Suryodiningrat from all his posts and exiling him.[69]

The PKN prudently softened its more overtly political activities, but it remained prominent in social and economic fields in Yogyakarta up to the Japanese period.[70] Some observers attribute the comparative resilience of the Yogyakarta kraton in the face of the nationalist challenge during the Revolution at least partly to the popularity of the PKN.[71] The PKN re-emerged as the regional party Gerinda after the Revolution, and attracted 150,000 votes in the 1955 elections.[72]

During the 1930s the Solo kraton flirted with the nationalist movement much more actively than Yogyakarta did.[73] Larson described the opposition in the Solo kraton to Dutch reform plans, the unsuccessful attempts by the Solo kraton to dominate the Mangkunegaran, the formation of a *Pakempalan Kawula Surokarto* (PKS — Union of Subjects of Surakarta) on the model of the PKN, and the links between factions in the Solo court and the nationalists. The story is one of intense factionalism and rivalry between the two courts in Solo, a struggle for the allegiance of the common people in the region, and a consequent preoccupation with their own affairs. Paradoxically, the Mangkunegaran was generally more favourably disposed to Dutch reform plans, leading to weaker popular support and a general reputation — which served the Mangkunegaran very ill during the Revolution — for being pro-Dutch.[74]

PKS meetings were even more provocative to the Dutch than PKN meetings, as the PKS leader came to be regarded by some as the Ratu Adil (Just King), and speeches were made predicting that soon "the kingdom would be reconquered".[75] Although the PKS later fell away because of internal dissensions, it continued to irritate the Dutch and the Mangkunegaran.[76]

The Dutch were also becoming apprehensive of the Solo kraton's contacts with the Japanese.[77] Colonial officials worried about Japanese interest in local mining ventures, which they thought hid an ulterior motive, and according to one Dutch intelligence report, secret Japanese plans had designated Prince Suryoamijoyo of Solo as their planned future "King of Indonesia".[78] Although opinions differ about the true extent of Japanese "burrowing" in the Indies during the 1930s, it does appear that they had some kind of intelligence network and useful contacts in the period.[79]

An alliance emerged between several kraton figures and the moderate nationalist party Parindra, which also had Japanese links,[80] in which three princes, including the high-ranking Leiden law graduate Prince Kartodipuro (later Sumodiningrat), joined Parindra.[81] Kartodipuro was the eldest son of Prince Kusumoyudo, the more promising of the two main claimants to succeed the Sunan, but the Dutch were determined that a "radical" like Kartodipuro must never become Sunan. His association with Parindra was an additional count against him, as the colonial authorities were increasingly suspicious even of moderate nationalism.[82] Solo at the end of the thirties has been described as "once again the centre of Javanese political nationalism".[83]

The Dutch accordingly turned to the more pliant prince Hangabehi when Pakubuwono X died in February 1939.[84] Larson indicates that the choice of Hangabehi led to a serious loss of prestige for the Solo kraton[85] and implies that the Solo principality would have had much better chances of surviving the Japanese occupation and the Revolution if Kusumoyudo had become Sunan.[86] But this is one of many historical "might-have-beens".

As war approached, Dutch observers doubted whether any understanding would be possible between the princely houses and the nationalist movement. One wrote in 1940:

> The nationalists ... may for the moment support the [princely] states against the Dutch-controlled Central Government, but there can be little comfort in this for the native princes, for the nationalist movement is fundamentally opposed to them.[87]

Hamengku Buwono IX's achievement was his ability to confound these gloomy but entirely reasonable expectations.

EDUCATION OF A JAVANESE PRINCE

Three of the princely houses, the Sunanate of Solo, the Mangkunegaran, and the Pakualaman, sent their sons to the Netherlands for education from around 1900 onwards. The Pakualam house was the most progressive of all, because as the smallest Vorstenland, its scions needed any advantage they could obtain.[88] Yogyakarta however was the most conservative of the four royal houses in its attitude to princely education, reflecting the stance of Hamengku Buwono VII.

The policy changed when Hamengku Buwono VIII came to the throne. He had travelled in Europe as crown prince,[89] and as early as 1919 he had sent one of his sons for schooling in the Netherlands.[90] In the 1920s and 1930s he sent more and more Yogyakarta princes there. The dispatch of Dorojatun and his brother Tinggarto to the Netherlands in early 1930 was part of Hamengku Buwono VIII's strategy to familiarize his sons with Western society, culture and intellectual life.[91]

Dorojatun first entered kindergarten at the Frobel school in Bintaran Kidul,[92] Gondomanan, across the Code river from the kraton suburb. He then moved to the Eerste Europese Lagere School B (Lower European Primary) in Kampementstraat (now Jalan Panembahan Senopati), followed by the Neutrale Europese Lagere School (Upper European Primary) in Pakemweg (now Jalan Kaliurang),[93] completing primary school in mid-1925.[94] A feature of his primary school years was the presence in his class of Mozes,[95] the son of the Sultan of Pontianak, who was to play a dramatic role in Dorojatun's life during the Revolution and after. But at this stage the two sultans' sons were probably little distinguishable.

In primary school, Dorojatun first entered the Indonesian scouting movement, with which he was ever after identified.[96] The choice of scouting as one of the main "extra-curricular" interests of his life perhaps provides further evidence of his personality and even ideological attitudes. Scouting's emphasis on healthy masculine outdoor activities, and its insistence on hierarchy, discipline and practical knowledge usually appeals to those who respond to rules, admire physical fitness and like to follow set procedures.

Dorojatun moved to the Hoogere Burger School (HBS) in Semarang in July 1925,[97] but the climate proved oppressively hot, so that he moved in 1928 to the corresponding HBS in Bandung. He lodged successively with a series of Dutch families, mostly teachers. After the Mulder family in early primary school, he lodged with the Cock family, then in Semarang with the family of the warden of Semarang prison, Voskuil.[98] In Bandung a break occurred in the pattern as he lodged (accompanied by Tinggarto) with a Dutch military man, Lt Col de Boer.[99] His father's instructions to all the Dutch families were to treat them as ordinary children,[100] as he wanted Dorojatun to learn discipline and simplicity.[101] Dorojatun and his brothers were never accompanied by palace servants during their sojourns with Dutch families.[102]

At some stage his father decided to send Dorojatun and his brother Tinggarto to the Netherlands for further education. Therefore, in March 1930, the seventeen-year-old Dorojatun and Tinggarto left by sea escorted by the Hofland family, the head of which was a director of the sugar mill at Gesikan, near Yogyakarta.[103]

THE NETHERLANDS

The economic background in the Netherlands became increasingly grim in Dorojatun's first years there. National income per capita dropped in real terms by 17 per cent between 1929, the year before Dorojatun's arrival, and 1934, the year in which he moved to Leiden.[104] Enrolments in the Indology faculty of Leiden University even ceased altogether for a few years.[105] Numbers of Indonesian students in the Netherlands tracked the economic trends, reaching 175 in 1931 but falling back to about one hundred in 1936 before recovering to about 140 in 1940.[106] This was a tiny elite, comprising sons (and a few daughters) of aristocratic or otherwise distinguished families from all over the Indies, including wealthy Chinese and Arab families.

Despite the unpromising external circumstances, Dorojatun seems to have been sheltered by his school and university life and was able to live reasonably well, although not lavishly. His allowance from his father does not seem to have been unduly large, judging by his need to take vacation jobs. He was also active in a variety of campus activities when he reached Leiden University.

Haarlem

Dorojatun's first four years in the Netherlands were spent at Haarlem, a small town to the south of Amsterdam, where he and his brother lodged with the school headmaster, Mourik Broekman,[107] a respected educator in a town with a reputation for high educational standards.[108] The school was the Haarlem Lyceum, in the next street from Mourik Broekman's dwelling.[109] The Lyceum was the product of a merger in 1925 between the Hoogere Burger School B (HBS-B)[110] and the Stedelijk Gymnasium. (The two schools were again split in 1933.) Dorojatun followed the HBS-B curriculum, which was the channel through which students who did not study classics could proceed to university. Many prospective colonial officials came through the HBS-B schools, and young men and women from the Dutch Indies community also attended. Indonesians from princely or wealthy families from the archipelago regularly undertook these studies during this period.

Dorojatun studied a variety of subjects, generally biased towards the physical sciences and languages. These included science, mathematics, history, commerce, geography, and several European languages (Dutch, English, French, and German). Dorojatun was an undistinguished student at Haarlem, perhaps because he had difficulty in adjusting to the change in milieu or the change of climate. Perhaps he was too involved in outside activities (he remained a keen footballer in his Haarlem years).[111] Whatever the reasons, in fourth grade his respectable but not high marks in most subjects were pulled down by failures in geometry, trigonometry, mechanics, and French. In mid-1932 he moved on to fifth grade, but the same pattern recurred the next year. Once again, good marks in languages (except French) and other subjects such as commerce, political science, and history were outweighed by failures in geometry, trigonometry and physics, and he was again forced to repeat. In mid-1934 he passed his exams and moved on to the Indology faculty of Leiden University. Tinggarto, who also had academic difficulties at Haarlem, unexpectedly passed his final examinations,[112] and the two brothers entered Leiden together. In keeping with his modest (and perhaps democratic) style, Dorojatun enrolled at Leiden simply as "Dorodjatoen" without any titles.[113]

The Indonesian students were supervised by the Raadsman voor Studeerenden (Student Counsellor), a senior official of the Ministry of Colonies.[114] He stood in *loco parentis*, ensuring that the students avoided trouble, especially political trouble. He had considerable personal contact with individual students, as when Syarif Hamid Alkadri (or Algadrie;[115] Dorojatun's former classmate Mozes, the future Sultan Hamid II of Pontianak) spent a summer vacation with the Raadsman and his family.[116] The Raadsman might be seen as a kind of spy reporting on the students, but he was also sensitive to their reactions. In 1931 he reported that the students came into contact only with "those elements of the Dutch community who liked to emphasise the repressive side of Dutch rule in the Indies". Consequently, the Indonesian students saw the rest of the Dutch community as hostile to them, and "they are full of mistrust and bitterness".[117]

The Raadsman's 1931 and 1932 reports record Dorojatun's arrival in Haarlem and note that his fourth grade studies were not proceeding well.[118] Later his move to the fifth grade is mentioned, with the comment that he is a "nice alert young man".[119] During the Leiden years, the Raadsman noted Dorojatun's "quiet personality", and each year repeated that he "keeps clear of all political activities".[120] He described Tinggarto as "a very diligent young man, whose conduct is exemplary".[121]

Another favoured student was the aforementioned Syarif Hamid Algadrie, who had arrived in August 1933 to train as an infantry officer in the Breda Military Academy. He had passed fourth in a class of twenty-nine and was moving on to the third year. The Student Counsellor described him as "a congenial young man of outstanding conduct".[122] He finished his military training in July 1936 and returned to the Indies.[123] If anything, based on academic results, Hamid Algadrie might have seemed destined for an even more illustrious career than Dorojatun, but there would have been little to distinguish the two in the 1930s, as promising sons of the

Indies nobility. No one would have imagined that in due course one would plot to assassinate the other.

Other students attracted more official attention and disfavour. A cousin of Dorojatun's, Sukadari, is accused of unsatisfactory conduct, moves in "extremist circles" but possesses "no talent for leadership".[124] The 1933 report devotes a full page to the activities of one Mohammad Hatta, recounting his involvement with the nationalist Perhimpunan Indonesia (PI), his arrest and subsequent acquittal on sedition charges, his graduation as a doctorandus in commerce, and his departure for the Indies in July 1932.[125]

Leiden

The student could choose between two courses of study in the Indology faculty. The first course took four years[126] and was a predominantly legal course leading to a law degree (Meester in de Rechten). Besides studies of general law, the degree included:

- the comparative ethnology of the East Indies
- tropical economics
- statistics
- Malay or Javanese language
- the institutions of Islam
- archaeology and history of the Indies
- comparative colonial history

The other course, Indology, overlapped with the law course, but took five years.[127] It offered a choice between a major in economics and a minor in languages or the reverse. Other available subjects were:

- political science
- constitutional and administrative law
- tropical economics
- customary law (*adat*)
- archaeology[128]

Dorojatun took the Indology course, with a major in economics,[129] although Indology was the choice of few ethnic Indonesian students.[130] Tinggarto opted for the more popular choice of law.[131] In later years Dorojatun recalled enjoying his studies of constitutional and administrative law,[132] taught by his favourite teacher Dr J.J. Schrieke.[133]

Leiden University was by far the most distinguished tertiary institution in the world specializing in academic study and instruction about the East Indies. Its only rival was the new Indology Faculty at Utrecht University, which had been established at the instigation of the oil industry to counter Leiden's supposed excessive liberalism.[134] The Indology faculty was a cooperative venture between the Faculty of Law on the one hand and the Faculty of Letters and Philosophy on the other, and thus was officially known in full as the "Combined Faculties of Law, and Letters and Philosophy". It had little institutional or administrative identity of its own, but the two faculties collaborated in providing staff, administrative support and funding. The Combined Faculties boasted virtually every renowned academic expert on the Indies, and included names which are still quoted in scholarly works on Indonesian history up to the present day. The toweringly eminent Professor Emeritus Snouck Hurgronje, the expert on Islam who had advised the colonial government thirty years before on methods of winning the Aceh War and had been involved in establishing Indology as an academic discipline,[135] was still active at Leiden when Dorojatun arrived, although he died in 1936.[136] The expert on adat law, C. von Vollenhoven, had died the year before Dorojatun's arrival,[137] but still cast a long shadow on adat studies. Other professors included N.J. Krom, the expert on ancient Javanese history, ethnography, and archaeology, who was the Dean of the Combined Faculties in 1934;[138] the economist J.H. Boeke who was the Secretary of the Combined Faculties that year;[139] lecturer on colonial law J.J. Schrieke, the ethnologist Josselin de Jong and the historian and Javanese linguist C.C. Berg.[140]

Doctoral theses submitted on Indies subjects in these years often related to ethnographic or cultural matters, such as P.J. Zoetmulder's thesis on "Pantheism and Monism in Javanese Suluk literature", or G.J. Held's thesis on "The Mahabharata".[141] There were theses on colonial history, such as H.J. de Graaf on "The Murder of Captain Francois Tack on 18 February 1686".[142] Few seemed interested in the Indonesian nationalist movement or even modern colonial history.

Rather out of the usual run was the seminal thesis delivered in 1934 by J.C. van Leur on "Eenige Beschouwingen betreffende de ouden Aziatische handel" or "Some Observations on Early Asian Trade"[143] (the basis for the well-known *Indonesian Trade and Society*),[144] which is credited with beginning a crucial change in Western scholarly thinking about Indonesian, and even Asian, historiography. Van Leur defended his revolutionary thesis in October 1934[145] (a month after Dorojatun enrolled at Leiden), and the thesis was published shortly thereafter.

Broadly, it argues for greater acknowledgement of the essential autonomy of Indonesian polities and of Indonesian traders in the early colonial period. Van Leur criticizes the tendency of colonial historians to apply mechanically Western historical methods[146] and periodizations to Asian societies without considering their uniqueness. Another sub-theme is his preoccupation with the need to respect and study Asian/Pacific societies on their own terms.

A related substantial theme — probably van Leur's main contribution to Indonesian historiography — is present in his thesis but emerges more clearly in his later writings (e.g., *On the Study of Indonesian History* of 1937). He argues that once colonial historians' narratives reached the period of the emergence of Europeans on the scene, they shift perspective abruptly and concentrate on the doings of the newcomers, as if Asian societies had become passive recipients of their actions. From about the eighteenth century, traditional histories of Indonesia became a story of European colonizers' journeys, conflicts with local rulers or with each other, and only secondarily (or not at all) a story of events and trends in the societies ostensibly under study. Van Leur says: "But with the arrival of ships from western Europe, the point of view is turned a hundred and eighty degrees and from then on the Indies are observed from the deck of the ship, the ramparts of the fortress, and the high gallery of the trading house."[147] Van Leur's criticisms eventually led to the widespread realization of the existence, or potential existence, of a series of indigenous discourses which were ignored by conventional histories.[148]

Van Leur foreshadows Edward Said in criticising "the irritating use of the fallacy 'Oriental' — a fallacy, because only dilettanti with a very vague notion and a few ideological simplifications push such divisions ('Oriental' and 'Occidental') to the forefront as dominant, thereby overlooking the richness, the complexity and the equal worth of organisational forms of culture and life which have reached maturity along 'autonomous' routes".[149] Such arguments would have been welcome to most Indonesian students, even those who avoided involvement in politics.

A better known set of ideas at Leiden was represented by the economics lecturer J.H. Boeke, whose doctrine of economic dualism was gaining currency. In view of Hamengku Buwono's later responsibility for the Indonesian economy, it may be worthwhile to outline briefly the substance of Boeke's arguments. Boeke believed that dualism arose from "the clash of an imported social system with an indigenous social system of another style. Most frequently the imported system is high capitalism".[150] Boeke was reluctant to ascribe to colonialism the problems arising from this situation, preferring to give the blame to capitalism.[151] He posits a series of dichotomies between the two clashing systems, (external) capitalism and (home-grown) pre-capitalism. The latter he describes as characterized by "communalism, originalism, original class distinctions — a man is born into a status and never dreams of trying to get into another; little or no exchange; production is in and for the household".[152]

Boeke theorized about the "limited needs" of the villager whereby he would respond to price incentives in a supposedly different way from the Westerner, producing fewer commodities when the price was high, doing less work when wages increased, and cultivating only the amount of land needed for subsistence and no more.[153] Mackie indicates that Boeke's analysis led to a "despairing pessimism" that any rural economic development would be possible, and that he could only prescribe some vague form of "village restoration" of an indigenous nature appropriate to Eastern culture.[154]

These ideas owed something to the broad East–West distinctions which informed much colonial thinking about Asia in those years, including the stereotyping of Asia as passive, feminine, receptive, static, and traditional, while the West was characterized as aggressive, masculine, active, dynamic and progressive. This was just the kind of stereotyping which van Leur was questioning.[155] Although it would be simplistic to dismiss Boeke's writings as merely stereotyping Asian societies, some such thinking does appear to influence them.

Other Dutch scholars disputed Boeke's ideas at the time,[156] but his theories remained popular up to Boeke's death in 1956. Nowadays very few scholars would accept ideas of dualism without considerable modification. Mackie notes the "near-racist" overtones of Boeke's thinking,[157] and the evidence that the actual economic behaviour of Indonesian peasants could be explained by conventional economic theory without the need for any special theorizing.[158]

In the late 1930s, the revolutionary economic ideas of John Maynard Keynes were becoming known in England, but were far from the orthodoxy which they later achieved, and would have been almost unknown in the Netherlands. Keynesianism only emerged into true prominence during the war and post-war years.[159] By the time Dorojatun, as Hamengku Buwono IX, joined the New Order as Chief Economic Minister in the 1960s, the economics he had learned long before had been overtaken not only by the Keynesian revolution but also by the challenges to Keynesianism (especially monetarism) which were already emerging. Nevertheless, when Dorojatun became Sultan, and — much later — when he became Indonesia's leading economic minister, he must have recalled Boeke's theories, although the lack of clear prescriptions for action in Boeke's teachings would limit any attempt to give practical application to them.

Life in Leiden

Dorojatun, together with Tinggarto, lived first at Zoeterwoudse Singel 79,[160] moving in 1935 (apparently without Tinggarto) to Kloksteeg 7A,[161] behind the enormous Protestant church, across the canal from the main university buildings and about a hundred metres from the main library building on the Rapenburg canal. By 1939, he was lodging at Vreewijkstraat 13, a little further from the city centre.[162] All these addresses were within easy walking distance of the main university buildings and the library.

In 1935, he and Tinggarto were joined in Leiden by their younger brother Raisulngaskari (later Prince Bintoro).[163] The relationship between these three was Dorojatun's closest family relationship in his student years, and his confidence in his two brothers seemed to grow stronger in later life. Tinggarto (as Prabuningrat) became a trusted lieutenant during the Revolution and later, and Bintoro performed a variety of services for him, including representing Yogyakarta on the constitutional committee, the BPUPKI, in 1945.[164]

Again, Dorojatun was not a distinguished student at Leiden. He failed his first attempt at the candidates' examination in economics in March 1937,[165] but he passed at the second try in December[166] and moved on to the doctorandus programme.[167] Tinggarto had passed his candidates' examination in law five months earlier.[168] Success in December 1937 perhaps confirmed to Dorojatun that his many extracurricular activities were not distracting too much from his studies.

Other Activities

At one stage during his time in Europe, Dorojatun perfected his English for two months at a "tutoring establishment in Rottingdean" in Sussex and also accompanied an Indonesian dance group on a visit to London in 1936, raising funds for the Chinese Red Cross.[169] He plunged enthusiastically into campus activities in his Leiden years. He joined the student society "Minerva" and the student militia (the Leidsche Corps),[170] he was a leading member of the "Krishna" debating club under Professor J.J. Schrieke,[171] and he even went skiing during vacations as well as taking vacation jobs.[172] He became Secretary of the Indies Association in 1938.[173] As well as being active in sport, he and Prabuningrat were apparently also keen ballroom dancers.[174] Not surprisingly, he also apparently had at least one Dutch girlfriend during these years.[175]

His most prominent involvement related to the student council of the Indology Faculty. He became a council member in 1937,[176] and was elected President in 1938.[177] The elections to the council were not particularly democratic. The normal pattern was the announcement in February in the Leiden University journal of the official slate of candidates for the next year, adding that if any rival candidate or slate of candidates was standing, they should advise the Board Secretary before a certain date.[178] No rival candidates seem to have offered themselves in those years.

Although the elections may have been prearranged, it may seem extraordinary that a Javanese could be elected to the presidency of the faculty association of a Dutch university when over ninety per cent of the students were Dutch, and this achievement shows the level of confidence in Dorojatun on the part of other leading students. It was from this period that we can date Dorojatun's ability to organize and run meetings, to follow through agendas and seek consensus, which stood him in good stead in later years, as he chaired or attended hundreds of meetings of the Indonesian cabinet and the other organizations with which he was involved, such as tourism organizations, sports bodies, and the scouting movement.

Dorojatun's presidential report for 1937/38,[179] the first published document associated with his name, is a brief factual account of the year's doings. He refers to preparations for the tenth anniversary celebrations of the Indology faculty on 10 May 1938, rejoices in the larger numbers of faculty students who attended the recent Indies Conference,[180] and lists a series of lectures, film evenings and other events. The annual report betrays few individual quirks of personality or any of his current preoccupations. Unlike his predecessor and successor as President, he did not find it necessary to express concern about the faculty's budget[181] or to chide the membership and other students for their alleged lack of a wide-ranging knowledge of the Indies.[182]

Dorojatun reported that the best attended event of the year was a lecture in February 1938 by former Governor General de Jonge.[183] The report does not specify whether he himself attended the meeting, but it is unlikely that as President he would have missed such an important event. If any nationalist feelings were lurking in his breast at this stage, he might have felt some ambiguity in meeting the Governor General who had said "We have ruled the Indies for three hundred years with the whip and the club, and we will rule it for three hundred more with the whip and the club." De Jonge probably caused unease more generally at Leiden especially in the Indology Faculty, bearing in mind that his repressive policies contradicted the thrust of the Ethical Policy which the relatively liberal Leiden University favoured.[184] For his part, de Jonge, former Minister of War and Director of Royal Dutch Shell,[185] may have regarded Leiden as a hotbed of the Ethical Policy liberalism so detested by Indies conservatives.

Another report with which Dorojatun was associated, the annual report of the Indies Association of which he was Secretary, takes a more aggressive tone. While indicating the growing interest in the Indies among students, the report laments that too few of the student body attended the lectures arranged by the Association. This ignorance could lead to "naiveté about complicated matters and the formation of an idiosyncratic picture of the Indies". Students should "not be misled by stories (of the Indies) which are now bandied about, which are at times grim, and can only damage Dutch–Indies relations".[186] The strongly minatory tone suggests that Dorojatun himself did not write the report, but as Secretary he must have approved it.

Dorojatun's brothers and cousins were also involved in various student bodies. Tinggarto became Vice President of the newly formed Roekoen Pelajar Indonesia (or Roepi — Indonesian Students Association), and "Technical Adviser" of the Student Organisation for the Advancement of Indonesian Culture, the SVIK.[187] Raisulngaskari was a board member of both organizations,[188] as well as one of the debating clubs.[189] Their older cousin Hertog was probably the most active, as a board member of the

SVIK,[190] President of the WDO ethnology discussion group in 1938,[191] and first President of Roepi,[192] which attempted to cover a wide range of Indies-related activities.[193]

The princes avoided organizations with a more political or radical stamp, such as the PI of which Hatta had been a member, now led by the more left wing students who campaigned actively in the Netherlands for acceptance of the Sutarjo petition.[194] By his own account, Dorojatun never discussed nationalism or the nationalist movement with anyone, although he did occasionally meet nationalist students.[195] He could have kept in touch indirectly with the developments through mutual acquaintances and relatives such as Hertog; but if he ever showed any interest in this, it was well hidden.[196]

Evidence of intelligence surveillance emerged in 1936 when Dorojatun attended a meeting of the semi-fascist NSB. He was called to the Ministry of Colonies the next morning (by the Raadsman?) and warned off doing any such thing again.[197] One would be intrigued to know what he thought of the NSB, or indeed the reaction of NSB members to the presence of an Asian at their meeting; but further details are unavailable. Dorojatun could normally live with some police invigilation, but at times it became irritating. One account indicates that he sometimes "enjoyed playing cat and mouse games" with the agents following him.[198]

Contacts with the Dutch Elite

Dorojatun and his relatives had occasional contact with the highest elite of Dutch society. He apparently met the future queen Juliana, who was studying at Leiden at this time.[199] He met the Minister of Colonies, Welter, who was favourably impressed with him.[200] As noted earlier, he probably also met the former Governor General de Jonge[201] and the senior colonial official Meyer Ranneft.[202] Yogyakarta Governor Bijleveld visited him and his brothers during a visit to Leiden in March 1939.[203] Sometime the same year a more junior colonial official, E.M. Stok — later the Dutch Resident of Yogyakarta in 1949 in less peaceful times — visited Dorojatun at Hamengku Buwono VIII's request.[204]

Dorojatun attended the funeral of the man from whom he acquired his nickname, Prince Hendrik, the husband of the ruling queen, where he again met his former classmate Hamid Algadrie, now known as "Max".[205] In February 1937, he attended Princess Juliana's wedding, where his father was officially represented by his eldest sister the Ratu Pembayun and his elder brother Puruboyo.[206] There he met his later ally Prince Suryodilogo, the future Pakualam VIII, and it was during this visit that Suryodilogo's father, Pakualam VII, died and Suryodilogo returned abruptly to Yogyakarta to succeed his father.[207] Dorojatun and his brother Hangabehi, who had travelled from Java for the occasion, were their father's official representatives at Queen Wilhelmina's 40th jubilee celebrations late in 1938.[208]

Dorojatun therefore had several opportunities to meet and scrutinize the Dutch elite from close up. He kept abreast of local developments through reading the Dutch press,[209] and was able to obtain an appreciation of the strengths and weaknesses of a Western European democracy. When ideas and ideals of democracy were debated in Indonesia in later years, it was — for him — the Netherlands which first came to mind.

Indeed, it was said to be the contrast between Dutch democracy in theory and practice in Europe, and the reality of Dutch repression in the Indies, which turned him into a nationalist.[210] Sartono quotes a press interview (not further identified) where Hamengku Buwono mentions (1) that the treatment of their Indonesian servants by the family with whom he stayed in Bandung (de Boer) reinforced his resentment of the Dutch overlords; and (2) that he was conscious of nationalist scorn for the Javanese nobility which they regarded as Dutch puppets.[211]

In later years, Hamengku Buwono IX was often described as a democrat,[212] and it is pertinent to enquire what he understood as democracy. The Netherlands provided examples of representative institutions, coalition governments accommodating a range of viewpoints, freedom of speech and assembly, a constitutional monarchy with widespread respect for the royal family, and a society based on law. A few years before his period in the Netherlands, Hatta and his comrades had been acquitted on charges of sedition,[213] a remarkable example of the constitutional limitations on government power in a European democracy. Dorojatun also saw the election of an ethnic Indonesian, Roestam Effendi, to the Dutch parliament as a Communist Party representative,[214] indicating the level of pluralism possible in a democracy.

But he may not have been impressed by all features of Dutch democracy. He might well have thought that certain aspects of Western democracy were undesirable or inapplicable in the Indies (a view still held in some circles in modern Indonesia); given his later hostility to communism, even the election of Roestam may have appeared an excessive degree of liberty. The levels of free speech could have been distasteful to a Javanese accustomed to greater respect for authority. But it is indeed plausible that his attitude was much affected by the contrast between Dutch liberalism in the Netherlands and repression in the Indies, including the attitudes of colonial officials like Colijn and de Jonge, the denial by conservatives that even moderate nationalists had any popular support,[215] and the often contemptuous and sometimes brutal behaviour of many colonial Dutchmen towards the "natives", a phenomenon of which he was aware even if he did not suffer personally from it.[216] Years later indeed, he instanced Dutch mistreatment of the "natives" as a reason for his support for Indonesian nationalism.[217]

DEPARTURE

Even in the cloistered world of Leiden, alarming events in the wider environment intruded as the 1930s advanced. One wonders for example what happened to Jewish students like A.E. Cohen, President of the student union of the Faculty of Letters in 1936,[218] or J. Goldman, a board member of the Indology association in 1937.[219] Dorojatun would certainly have known Goldman. Radical students were sounding increasingly strident warnings about events in neighbouring Germany and about the dangers of fascism in general, including Japanese fascism.[220] The Indology faculty journal announced the publication by a group of concerned university and school teachers of a series of anti-fascist writings.[221] Fears of war led to the formation of an Indonesian peace organization chaired by Sujarwo Condronegoro.[222] None of the princes was involved in these organizations.

Although war was declared in September 1939, the Netherlands was neutral and had hopes of remaining out of a general European conflict as it had during the First World War. Nevertheless, on hearing the news, Hamengku Buwono VIII urgently ordered his sons to return to Java.[223] Dorojatun, who was absent on vacation,[224] received his father's cable after a delay of some weeks, and sought passage on the first available boat.[225] The first transport could take only one of the princes, so that Dorojatun boarded the vessel alone, leaving his brothers to follow as best they could.

Because of his sudden departure, Dorojatun's nearly complete thesis for the degree of doctorandus was taken in manuscript back to Java and was never submitted. It was lost, and only the title survives — *The Political Contract between the Sunan of Solo and the Dutch Government*.²²⁶

SUMMARY

At the end of his long student years, Dorojatun at twenty-seven could be seen as a typical "native" product of the Dutch colonial system, reasonably successful in his studies, and well prepared for his future role as Sultan of Yogyakarta through his studies of colonial law, economics, public administration and other Indology subjects, and familiar with many members of the Dutch elite, as well as with the Dutch system as a whole, and with the Dutch language. Dutch officials could feel confident that Dorojatun would become a competent and tractable Sultan in due course, deeply imbued with Dutch values and appropriately respectful of Dutch power and cultural achievements, well aware of his duties to the East Indies government and to his own people, and able to reconcile the two in a satisfactory manner like his father and grandfather before him. It could be imagined, at least by the Dutch, that a future Dutch Governor could write, as the current Governor had written of his father, that he was a "loyal vassal" dedicated to the Dutch crown.²²⁷ If Dorojatun had any rebellious thoughts, he kept them to himself. It is not surprising that Dutch officials failed to see the innate obstinacy and nationalistic pride in this reserved young man.

Indonesian nationalists in the Netherlands would have found it difficult to discriminate between Dorojatun and any other elite aristocratic student. If, as he later said, he avoided talking politics with other Indonesian students, they may not have sensed any sympathy in him for the nationalist cause, and may well have put him down as just another spoiled Indies princeling. If Dorojatun appeared reliable to Dutch officials (certainly compared with his fellow Leiden graduate, the Solonese Kartodipuro), for the nationalists he was an unknown quantity.

For his part, as he contemplated the return of his sons from the Netherlands, Hamengku Buwono VIII could feel satisfied with the results of his strategy of immersing them in Dutch society and culture. He could believe that Dorojatun and his brothers were already well equipped — in language proficiency, familiarity with Dutch mores, and academic attainment — to promote the interests of the Yogyakarta principality, and in due course to handle relations and negotiations with the Dutch colonial government. What must have been doubtful was the extent of Dorojatun's understanding of his own society and people, after a nine-year absence.[228] But Hamengku Buwono VIII could hope that over the next few years, under his guidance and encouragement, the young prince would regain his knowledge of the principality and acquire an ability to operate effectively within the kraton environment and within Yogyakarta society generally.

Dorojatun probably already had reservations about Dutch colonialism, but in accordance with the cautious approach taken by his father, he remained discreet, a habit which he followed all his life. Even if Dorojatun guessed that Dutch rule might be ending (and the stories of his father's prescience on the point have to be taken with some reserve), it was far from clear what should replace it, whether the pan-Indonesian nationalism of a Sukarno or a Hatta, a militarist monarchy like Japan, or a congeries of small aristocratic states, each of which might reflect the kind of polity envisaged by his uncle Suryodiningrat. Accordingly, if thoughts of freedom from Dutch rule were in his mind as he returned to Java, he would not necessarily have cast this in terms wider than his own milieu. His attention and his priorities would most likely have been limited to his family and to the principality of Yogyakarta.

Notes

1. He will be referred to by this name until we reach his coronation in 1940, when he took the style and titles of Sultan Hamengku Buwono IX.
2. Puruboyo (original name Suyadi) was born on 3 March 1880 and died (as Sultan Hamengku Buwono VIII) on 22 October 1939. Purwokusumo, *Kasultanan Yogyakarta* (The Sultanate of Yogyakarta), p. 50.
3. Princely titles were "recycled" from generation to generation. This Mangkubumi bore the same name as the founder of the Yogyakarta dynasty, the Mangkubumi who later became Hamengku Buwono I. Another later Mangkubumi became the current Sultan of Yogyakarta, Hamengku Buwono X.
4. *De Locomotief*, 28 April 1912.
5. *Pemandangan*, no. 56 (3 March 1940), which gives the date of the wedding as 1 January 1908 (KPC).
6. *Budi Utomo* (Dutch edition), 10–15 January 1921 (article by "John Top"), in IPO 1/1921, p. 35.
7. Pangeran Adipati Anom Hamengkunagoro died of an unspecified illness on 21 February 1913 — *De Locomotief*, 22 February 1913.
8. Anonymous, "Het Djokjasche Sultansgeslacht" [The Yogyakarta Sultan's Family], *Indische Gids* 43, no. 1 (1921): 332 [fiche 893].

9. *TUR*, p. 22, and Yogyakarta kraton website, 10 October 2002, <joglosemar/ygy_info2.html>.
10. Mailrapport MR 1283/39 of 26 October 1939 (fiche 1752).
11. *Seri Sultan, Hari 2 Hamengku Buwono IX*, p. 16.
12. For example, Rahardjo Suwandi, *A Quest for Justice*, pp. 103–6.
13. *TUR*, p. 23.
14. Prince Hangabehi of Solo, later Pakubuwono XII, was known as "Bobby" Hangabehi in the 1930s (*Moesson* magazine, 15 October 1985, p. 23).
15. *TUR*, p. 24.
16. Ibid.
17. *Hari 2 Hamengku Buwono IX*, p. 17.
18. Romo Noordi Pakuningrat, interview, 20 August 2002.
19. *TUR*, p. 27.
20. "Het Aftreden van de Sultan van Djocja" [The Abdication of the Sultan of Yogyakarta], *Indische Gids* 43, no. 1 (1921): 373 [fiche 893]. The abdication appears to have been instigated by the Dutch authorities because Hamengku Buwono VII was suffering dementia (Westerkamp, p. 4).
21. *Sri Mataram* (Yogyakarta, 21 January 1919) — IPO reports for 1919, fiche 114.
22. *De Locomotief*, 23 October 1940.
23. Tengku Othman of Deli, reported in *Pewarta Deli* of 17–21 December 1929, in IPO 1930, p. 33 (Fiche 629).
24. Ibid.
25. Suwarno, *Hamengku Buwono IX dan Sistem Birokrasi Pemerintahan Yogyakarta 1942-74* [Hamengku Buwono IX and the Bureaucratic System of the Yogyakarta Government 1942–74], p 68.
26. *Sedya Tama*, special memorial issue, 23 October 1939, p. 1.
27. Governor de Cock, 1934 *Memorie van Overgave* [Handover Report], p. 29.
28. Ibid., p. 32.
29. C.L.M. Bijl de Vroe, *Rondom de Buitenzorgse Troon* [Around the Buitenzorg Throne], p. 79.
30. MR 13 geh/40, letter of Governor Adam of 29 November 1940, p. 6. See following chapter.
31. Governor de Cock, *Memorie van Overgave* (1934), op. cit., p. 32.
32. Ibid.
33. The conflict was aired in the press, especially *Surabaiasch Handelsblad* (article reprinted in *Timboel Magazine* 4, nos. 21–22 (November 1930): 294.
34. *De Locomotief*, op. cit., 24 October 1940.
35. Ignace Kleden, "The Changing Political Leadership of Java", in *State and Civil Society in Indonesia*, edited by Budiman, p. 350.
36. The rupture clearly predated Puruboyo's becoming Sultan and probably predates his travel in Europe during 1919–20.

Early Days

37. Romo Noordi Pakuningrat, interview, op. cit.
38. Purwokusumo (op. cit., p. 66) indicates that they were divorced while Puruboyo was still Crown Prince.
39. Ricklefs, *History of Modern Indonesia*, p. 163.
40. Ibid., pp. 158–63.
41. Larson, *Prelude to Revolution*, p. 464.
42. *IPO*, 1919 passim. The debate about Cipto's effrontery went on for months in the local press during 1919.
43. Kees van Dijk, "The Threefold Suppression of the Javanese", in *The Late Colonial State in Indonesia*, edited by Robert Cribb, pp. 272–73.
44. Sutherland, *Making of a Bureaucratic Elite*, p. 64.
45. Ibid., pp. 106–9.
46. See for example, *Medan Bergerak* of 6 February 1919, in IPO reports of 1919 (Fiche 100), and *Sedya Tama* of 1 October 1929 (IPO 1929, p. 91), Fiche 622.
47. Larson, op. cit., p. 161.
48. Larson, p. 272.
49. Ibid., p. 304 et seq.
50. Ibid., p. 332.
51. Ibid., p. 333.
52. See the account of the PKN later in this chapter.
53. L. Adam, Governor of Yogyakarta, "In Memoriam Hamengkoe Boewono VIII", 4 November 1939, *Koloniaal Tijdschrift*, no. 24 (1940): 2.
54. Larson, op. cit., pp. 320–28.
55. No public statements by Hamengku Buwono VIII can be found in the IPO reports during the 1920s and 1930s. Nor apparently did Hamengku Buwono VIII make a speech on his enthronement in 1921 — "Het Aftreden van de Sultan van Djocja", *Indische Gids 1921* 1, no. 43 (1921): 374–76.
56. "The kraton fails to keep up with modern developments…. This is not to be wondered at, because the Sultan … has no advisers who are aware of the need to move with the times." *Sedya Tama*, 3–8 September 1928, in IPO 21/1928, p. 517.
57. Ricklefs, op. cit., p. 177.
58. Ibid., p. 176.
59. Van Klinken, *Migrant Moralities*, p. 76. On Noto Suroto, see Madelon Djajadiningrat — Nieuwenhuis, *Noto Soeroto — His Ideas and the Late Colonial Intellectual Climate*, Indonesia, no. 5 (October 1993).
60. Ricklefs, op. cit., pp. 176–77.
61. Larson, op. cit., p. 377.
62. Ibid., p. 389.
63. Ibid., p. 378. Larson indicates that the strength of the PKN also disturbed Sukarno.
64. *Sedya Tama* of 22 July 1930, in IPO 1930, p. 184 (Fiche 650).

65. Larson, p. 377. It was apparently still at the amazingly high level of 262,852 in July 1941 — ibid., p. 381.
66. Ibid.
67. O'Malley, *Second Thoughts*, p. 609.
68. Larson, p. 380.
69. De Cock, *Memorie van Overgave* (1934): 32. O'Malley — *Indonesia in the Great Depression*, pp. 332–35 — makes the valid point that the Sultan's reactions are reflected in reports written by officials with an interest in exaggerating the Sultan's antipathy to the PKN.
70. O'Malley, *Second Thoughts*, op. cit., p. 609.
71. Larson, p. 472.
72. O'Malley, *PKN*, op. cit., p. 113. The 1955 vote might be seen as a vote for the kraton.
73. Larson, p. 470.
74. Ibid., p. 461.
75. Ibid., p. 390.
76. Ibid., pp. 410–13.
77. Ibid., p. 415 et seq. and p. 423.
78. Ibid., p. 421.
79. For the term "burrowing", see P. Idenburg, ed., *Ten Years of Japanese Burrowing in the Netherlands East Indies* (Netherlands Information Bureau, 1942?).
80. R.C. Kwantes, *De Ontwikkeling van de Nationalistische Beweging* [The Development of the Nationalist Movement], vol. 4, p. 751.
81. Larson, p. 424.
82. Ricklefs, op. cit., p. 180.
83. Van Bruggen et al., eds., *Djokja Solo, Beeld van de Vorstensteden* [Jogja Solo, A Picture of the Princely Cities], p. 48. Henceforth cited as *Djokja Solo*.
84. Larson, p. 425. Pakubuwono X's reign was the longest of any Solo ruler up to that time.
85. Ibid., p. 472.
86. Ibid., p. 440.
87. Vandenbosch, *The Dutch East Indies*, p. 157.
88. Shiraishi, *An Age in Motion*, p. 38.
89. *Neraca* of 2 August 1919, in IPO 31/1919.
90. Poeze, *In het Land van de Overheerser* (In the Land of the Overlord), p. 280.
91. This was a deliberate strategy, expressed in Hamengku Buwono VIII's letters to his sons in the Netherlands in the 1930s. Informant no. 8, interview, 31 July 2002.
92. Yogyakarta kraton website <http://www.joglosemar.co.id> (accessed on 19 September 2002).
93. Sudarmanto, *Jejak-jejak Pahlawan* [Footsteps of the Heroes], p. 154.

94. *Merdeka Mingguan* 12 February 1949.
95. *TUR*, p. 27.
96. *Tempo*, 8 October 1988, "Lebih Besar dari Takhtanya" [Greater than his Throne], p. 4.
97. *Patriot*, 25 March 1947.
98. A copy survives of a brief letter of thanks from Hamengku Buwono VIII to Voskuil for looking after his son — letter of 28 September 1927, Hamengku Buwono X private library.
99. *TUR*, p. 167.
100. Ibid., p. 22.
101. Ibid., p. 28.
102. Ibid.
103. *TUR*, p. 29. Also Sudarmanto, op. cit., p. 155.
104. Boomgard, *Weathering the Storm*, pp. 27–28.
105. *Almanak Leidsch Studentencorps 1937* [Leiden Student Almanac 1937], p. 211.
106. Poeze, op. cit., p. 278.
107. Haarlem Archives (Archief Kennemerland), Haarlem population register, Fiche 934, drawer 21.
108. F. Koorn, "Herinneringen aan de Eerste HBS-B in de jaren dertig and veertig" [Memories of the First HBS-B in the Thirties and Forties], in *Haarlem Jaarboek 1997* [Haarlem Yearbook 1997], edited by F. Koorn (Archief Kennemerland, 1997), p. 121.
109. Dorojatun's elder brother Puruboyo (originally B.R.M. Sungangus Samsi) had studied at the HBS-B in the 1920s before going on to the Delft Technical School — *Sinar Matahari*, 8 October 1943.
110. Ir Mourik Broekman's address was Wilhelminastraat 7.
111. *Haarlems Dagblad* [Haarlem Daily], September 1988 (exact date uncertain).
112. Raadsman voor Studeerenden Annual Report 1934 [Jaarverslag Raadsman voor Studeerende], NA 2.10.49, part 78, p. 19.
113. *Archief inzake de Studentinschrijvingen van de Rijksuniversiteit Leiden 1934–35* [Student Enrolment Archive of Leiden University] 1934–35, inventory no. 58, student no. 82.
114. His name is given as O.M. Goedhart in the Leiden University Guides for 1937/38 (*Gids der Rijksuniversiteit Leiden 1937/38*, p. 222) and 1938/39.
115. Spelt "Algadrie" in other sources.
116. Raadsman voor Studeerende Annual Report 1932, NA 2.10.49, part 78, p. 2.
117. Raadsman Annual Report 1931, p. 3.
118. Raadsman Annual Report 1932, p. 7.
119. Raadsman Annual Report 1933, NA 2.10.49, part 78, p. 5.
120. E.g., Raadsman Annual Report for 1934, p 4.
121. Raadsman Annual Report 1932, NA 2.10.49, part 78, p. 37.

122. Raadsman Annual Report 1934, NA 2.10.49, part 78, p. 2.
123. Raadsman Annual Report 1937, NA 2.10.49, part 78, p. 3.
124. Raadsman Annual Report 1932, p. 25.
125. Raadsman Annual Report 1933, p. 37.
126. Fasseur, *De Indologen* [The Indologists], p. 448.
127. Ibid.
128. Vandenbosch, *The Dutch East Indies*, p. 164.
129. Leiden University, *Archief inzake de Studentinschrijvingen* [Student Enrolment Archive 1939], Student no. 840.
130. Poeze, op. cit., p. 279.
131. Ibid.
132. *TUR*, p. 31.
133. Ibid. J.J. Schrieke, the brother of the renowned sociologist and one-time Minister of Education Professor B.J.O. Schrieke, was a member of the NSB (*Nationaal Socialistische Beweging* — National Socialist Movement), the Dutch counterpart to the Nazis. He became a notorious head of the Ministry of Justice in the German occupation.
134. Vandenbosch, *Dutch East Indies*, p. 70.
135. Fasseur, op. cit., p. 401.
136. Obituary in *Almanak 1937*, p. 105.
137. Obituary in *Almanak Leidsch Studenten Corps* [Leiden Student Body Almanac] for 1934, p. 86.
138. Booth, ibid., p 63.
139. Ibid.
140. See the staff lists in ibid., pp. 51–52 and pp. 59–60.
141. *Almanak Leidsch Studenten Corps 1935*, p. 104.
142. Ibid.
143. Reviewed anonymously in *Leidsch Universiteitsblad* of 14 December 1934, pp. 11–12.
144. J.C. van Leur, *Indonesian Trade and Society, Essays in Asian Social and Economic History*, W. van Hoeve, 1955.
145. Ibid., p. 2.
146. Ibid., p. 25.
147. Ibid., p. 261. Van Leur adds rhetorically, "Is it possible to write the history of Indonesia in the eighteenth century as the History of the (Dutch East India) Company?" Ibid., p. 270.
148. J.R.W. Smail pursued, qualified and expanded van Leur's thesis in the 1960s in his influential article, "On the Possibility of an Autonomous History in Southeast Asia", *Journal of Southeast Asian History* 2, no. 2 (July 1961): 72–102.
149. Van Leur, ibid., pp. 24–25.
150. Boeke, quoted in Mackie, "The Concept of Dualism", p. 297, in Fox et al., eds., *Indonesia: Australian Perspectives*.

151. Ibid., p. 298.
152. Ibid., p. 299.
153. Ibid., p. 300.
154. Ibid., p. 301.
155. Van Leur's only direct comment about Boeke appears in a footnote (p. 309, n. 121): "thus, a separate field of ... the 'dualistic economy' (Boeke, *Ekonomie* and other works) seems to me to be out of the question".
156. Mackie, ibid., p. 298.
157. Ibid.
158. Ibid., p. 301.
159. For example, H.W. Arndt's *The Economic Lessons of the 1930s*, published as late as 1943, contains only two brief references to Keynes — p. 296 and p. 297.
160. *Almanak Leidsch Studentencorps 1935*, p. 276.
161. *Rijksuniversiteit Leiden Studentinschrijvingen 1935–36* [Leiden University Student Enrolments 1935–36], Inventory no. 235.
162. *Rijksuniversiteit Leiden Studentinschrijvingen, 1938–39* [Leiden University Student Enrolments 1938–39], Inventory no. 272.
163. Raisulngaskari lodged with his cousin Hertog at Teilingerhorstlaan 7, Wassen, just outside Leiden.
164. Another younger brother, Kirami (later Prince Murdoningrat), joined them in 1937, but his studies were cut short by the war. Poeze, op. cit., p. 281.
165. *Archief Inzake de Studentinschrijvingen*, 1938.
166. *Indologenblad* [Indology Journal], February 1938, vol. 9, no. 2, p. 7.
167. The doctorandus degree has no exact equivalent in English-speaking universities; the MA would probably be closest.
168. Ibid., 30 September 1937, vol. 8, no. 7, p. 5.
169. Forster, *Flowering Lotus*, p. 122. The best guess for the timing of the Rottingdean episode would be early to mid-1934, just before the move to Leiden.
170. Poeze, op. cit., p. 281.
171. *TUR*, p. 43, claims that Dorojatun used the debating skills he had learned at this club when negotiating the political contract with the Dutch Governor in 1939. Also *Almanak Leidsch Studentencorps 1939*, p. 193.
172. Romo Noordi Pakuningrat, interview, 20 August 2002.
173. *Almanak Leidsch Studentencorps 1938*, p. 179.
174. Epton, *Magic and Mystics in Java*, p. 130.
175. Informant 8, interview, 2 August 2002.
176. *Leidsch Universiteitsblad*, 5 March 1937, vol. 6, no. 11, p. 8. The Dutch name is *Bestuur der Studentfaculteit*.
177. *Almanak Leidsch Studentencorps 1939*, p. 89.
178. E.g., *Leidsch Universiteitsblad* of 5 February 1937, vol. 6, no. 9, p. 10, announcing candidates for the 1937/38 year.

179. *Gids der Rijksuniversiteit te Leiden voor 1938/39* [Guide to the University of Leiden 1938/39], pp. 223–24.
180. *Indische Conferentie* was the Dutch title.
181. Report by P.V. Putman Cramer in *Gids 1937/38*, p. 220.
182. Report by J.M. van Rijckevorsel in *Gids 1939/40*, p. 228.
183. *Gids*, op. cit., p. 223.
184. See Fasseur on the "White Man's Burden" tone of the Indology faculty from the 1910s onwards. Fasseur, op. cit., p. 384 et seq.
185. Ricklefs, op. cit., p. 177.
186. *Almanak Leidsche Studentencorps 1938*, pp. 178–79.
187. Raadsman Annual Report 1934, p. 19.
188. Ibid., p. 13. See also Poeze, op. cit., p. 262.
189. *Gids* 1939/40, p. 231.
190. Poeze, op. cit., p. 262.
191. *Almanak Leidsche Studentencorps 1938*, p. 203.
192. Poeze, op. cit., p. 266.
193. Ibid., p. 267.
194. Ibid., p. 265. For a description of the Sutarjo petition, see next chapter.
195. *TUR*, p. 32.
196. Poeze reports (p. 281) that "Prabuningrat (Tinggarto) said years later that the families with whom he and Dorojatun stayed were told: "These sons of the Sultan must not become too intimate with the nationalist movement." Van Kaam article in *Vu* magazine, loc. cit.
197. *TUR*, p. 208, containing an account by Hamengku Buwono himself in an interview.
198. Selosumarjan, "In Memoriam: Hamengkubuwono IX, Sultan of Yogyakarta", *Indonesia*, no. 47 (1989): 115–17. Attempts to trace Dutch intelligence reports of the period fail because very few such archives survived the war.
199. *Moesson* (no. 33/6, 15 October 1988), obituary by F.M.J. van Maanen.
200. Governor Bijleveld, MR 1283 geh/39, letter of 26 October 1939 from Bijleveld to Governor General, p. 1.
201. *Gids der Rijksuniversiteit Leiden 1938/39* [Royal Leiden University Guide 1938/39], op. cit., p. 223.
202. *Almanak LSC 1938*, p. 179. Meyer Ranneft lectured to the Indies Association in 1938.
203. MR 1283 geh/39, letter of 26 October 1939 from Bijleveld to Governor General, p 2.
204. Jaquet, *Minister Stikker en de Souvereiniteitsoverdracht aan Indonesie* [Minister Stikker and the Transfer of Sovereignty to Indonesia], p. 233.
205. *TUR*, p. 30.

Early Days

206. Governor Bijleveld, *Memorie van Overgave* 1937 [Handover Report 1937], NA 2.10.39 (Fiche 1), p. 52.
207. Ibid., p. 51.
208. Ibid., p. 52.
209. *TUR*, p. 31, where he mentions regularly reading the *Leidsche Courant*, Leiden's daily newspaper at that time.
210. Selosumarjan, interview, 31 July 2002.
211. Sartono, "Seputar Yogyakarta dan Beberapa Tokoh Kepemimpinannya" [Yogyakarta and Several of its Leading Personalities], p. 11.
212. Many descriptions of him use the word "democratic", e.g., *TUR*, pp. 17, 153, 209, 212; Selosoemarjan, *Indonesia* magazine (1989): 117.
213. Ricklefs, op. cit., p. 175.
214. Poeze, op. cit., p. 273 et seq.
215. Drooglever, *De Vaderlandse Club*, p. 41.
216. Note Selosumarjan's deeply felt comments on the subject, in *Social Change in Yogyakarta*, p. 43.
217. *Tempo* magazine 16, no. 26, 23 August 1986, "Sultan di Panggung Terbuka" [Sultan on the Public Stage], p. 14.
218. *Almanak Leidsche Studentencorps 1937*, p. 86.
219. *Gids der Rijksuniversiteit te Leiden voor 1937/38*, p. 220.
220. Poeze, op. cit., p. 263 and p. 270.
221. *Indologenblad*, Leiden, December 1936, p. 2.
222. Ibid., p. 263.
223. One account indicates that Hamengku Buwono, worried by his declining health, had asked the Dutch authorities to recall his sons, but they had refused. Then the outbreak of war had strengthened his resolve to bring them home, and the Netherlands East Indies Government had this time agreed. "Sultan van Yogyakarta Overleden" [Sultan of Yogyakarta Dies], *Indische Gids* 61, no. 2 (1939): 1057 [fiche 1155].
224. According to one source, he was actually on a trip to Berlin when Hitler invaded Poland, and only found his father's message when he returned "on the last train". Van Kaam, loc. cit.
225. Westerkamp, p. 6.
226. Ibid., p. 5. This is the only source for the topic of Dorojatun's thesis.
227. Bijleveld *Memorie van Overgave* 1937 [Handover Report 1937], NA 2.10.39 (Fiche 1), p. 36.
228. Dutch officials privately raised this question among themselves as negotiations on the political contract were commencing — MR 13/40, letter of 19 December 1939 to Governor General from the Director of the Binnenlandsch Bestuur, Drossaers, p. 14, reacting to comments on the point by Governor Adam of Yogyakarta.

3

DOROJATUN BECOMES SULTAN

On 18 October 1939, Dorojatun's father and other family members met him on arrival in Batavia.[1] Hamengku Buwono IX later recalled that an uncle had greeted him in high Javanese when he left the ship and that he knew at once that his father had named him as the successor, because his uncles had previously addressed him in low Javanese (*ngoko*).[2]

During the journey home to Yogyakarta, Hamengku Buwono VIII, already in rather poor health,[3] fell ill on the train,[4] and died in hospital shortly after reaching Yogyakarta. In Batavia he had already handed to Dorojatun the sacred kris Kyai Joko Piturun, an important heirloom of the Yogyakarta kraton, thereby reaffirming that Dorojatun was his chosen successor. Hamengku Buwono VIII's failure to take another principal wife after his divorce from Dorojatun's mother was taken in Yogyakarta to indicate his intention that Dorojatun should be the successor.[5] The naming of a crown prince was the prerogative of the reigning Sultan in consultation with the Dutch authorities, and Hamengku Buwono VIII had never taken a decision on the point.[6]

Dorojatun must have been unfamiliar even to most of his relatives. His father had sent him away while still a teenager in 1930, and apart from contacts with family members during rare visits to the Netherlands, and the occasional letter, few of which survive,[7] the family would have known little about his early manhood.

Nevertheless, it appeared likely that Dorojatun would become the next Sultan of Yogyakarta; so before examining the process of his accession, it will be useful to explore the nature, historical background, and ideology of his father's legacy, as it stood in 1940 and thereafter.

YOGYAKARTA — ECONOMIC AND SOCIAL SITUATION

The kingdom comprised five regencies and one city covering 3,168 square kilometres, compared with 132,187 square kilometres for the whole of Java.[8] As this comparison indicates, the significance of the tiny principality, and indeed of the other principalities, derived far more from their role as exemplars of traditional Javanese culture, than from any direct political power over the population of Central or East Java as a whole. Despite the lack of political power, however, they remained important across the Javanese cultural sphere as influences on manners and social interaction, language, fashion, art and even architecture.

During the nineteenth century the principalities, and especially Yogyakarta, had already become the most densely populated areas of Java.[9] In 1912, the year of Dorojatun's birth, the indigenous population of Yogyakarta was estimated at 1,178,051. (The population of other racial groups was never more than a few thousand then.)[10] By the time of the 1930 census, the population of the principality was recorded at 1,538,868,[11] an increase of over 30 per cent.

The entire population was estimated at 1,848,814 when the Japanese invaded in 1942,[12] including 1,821,542 indigenes.[13] By way of further contrast, the total population was nearly 3 million in 1989, the year after Hamengku Buwono's death.[14] In his lifetime, therefore, the population had increased by over 250 per cent. Even without war, revolution, economic decline, mass killings, and instability, such a huge increase over one generation would have posed a multitude of political, social and economic problems for any government.

Not long after Dorojatun's birth in 1912, the population of the Yogyakarta city was estimated at nearly 100,000, of whom 90 per cent were indigenous.[15] Later developments in the population of the city of Yogyakarta showed the following pattern:

1920	104,000
1930	137,000
1941	162,000[16]
1989	435,061[17]

Thus, in his lifetime, the population of the city increased by over 300 per cent.

Yogyakarta city was smaller than Solo, but it grew rather more strongly. The population in Yogyakarta and Solo was 104,000 and 134,000 in 1920, whereas it was 162,000 to 196,000 in 1941[18] respectively, so that Yogyakarta had grown from 78 per cent of Solo's size to 82 per cent. The number of Europeans in the city by 1940 had grown to exceed the numbers in Solo by a large margin (7,800 compared to 4,200), apparently reflecting the Solo kraton's relative unwillingness to encourage Europeans to settle in Solo,[19] and reinforcing the impression of Solo's coolness towards the Dutch colonial regime.[20]

Economically, Yogyakarta was a relatively poor area, where continued population growth combined with the 1930s Depression to cause or intensify much poverty and suffering. Yogyakarta was notoriously a food-deficit area, a situation which changed little until the New Order period. Even in 1968, Yogyakarta could be described as "a rice deficit area, known for chronic and sometimes serious food shortages".[21] The effects of the Depression were not uniform across all sectors, and most of the modern capitalist industries had declined proportionately more than the traditional village agriculture. But the lot of the average Yogyakarta peasant remained a grim one, and incomes in the principalities were said to be one quarter lower than in other parts of Java.[22]

The principalities' levels of education were weak by Indies standards. Whereas 94.1 per cent of the "natives" of the Netherlands East Indies were illiterate according to the 1930 census, the corresponding figures for Yogyakarta and Solo were 95.6 and 96.4 per cent, respectively. The state of infrastructure in the Vorstenlanden was said to be embarrassingly poor by comparison with the parts of Java under direct rule.[23] However, it is doubtful whether the Yogyakarta populace suffered disproportionately more than other peasants in Java during this period. Yogyakarta may have suffered a milder decline because of its comparative lack of significant export industries.

Yogyakarta was still mainly an agricultural economy, based on subsistence rice production, as well as sugar and vegetables. The limited industry included rice milling, sugar processing, silverwork and batik textiles. Tourism had made little mark as yet, despite the attractions of the ancient temples, the palace complex, and the nearby mountain scenery. The sugar industry had achieved a planting area of 7,658 hectares in 1938/39, recovering from the exiguous plantings of between 1,100 and 2,200 hectares in the grim years between 1933/34 and 1935/36, but still less than half the pre-Depression level of 17,329 hectares in 1930/31.[24] The silver industry was also recovering from the worst of the Depression, but it was shortly to slump once again after the outbreak of the war in Europe.[25]

History

During the disastrous reigns of Sunan Pakubuwono II (1726–49) and his son Pakubuwono III, a complicated and ever-changing four-sided conflict resulted in the three-way split of the kingdom of Mataram, and a major advance in Dutch political claims on the kingdom. The four sides (originally) were Pakubuwono II, his brother Prince Mangkubumi, his nephew Raden Mas Said, and the Dutch East Indies company, the VOC. After the succession of Pakubuwono III, the Giyanti Agreement of 1755 split the kingdom in two and Mangkubumi became Sultan Hamengku Buwono, with his own separate territory.[26]

It is unclear why Mangkubumi chose the title of Sultan for himself, a Muslim title rather than the Javanese title Sunan (or Susuhunan), but outside Java and even inside it in some quarters, the title of Sultan looks more important, echoing the title of the greatest Javanese ruler, Sultan Agung.[27] In this way, Mangkubumi subtly enhanced his own standing and that of his successors.

After further conflict, Hamengku Buwono's former ally and now bitter rival, Raden Mas Said, submitted to the Sunan and became Prince Mangkunegoro, also with his own small territory, which in its turn eventually became more and more independent of the Sunan.[28] Among the results of the incessant conflicts was confusion about the true succession to Mataram and a grudging acceptance by Javanese leaders of some measure of Dutch influence. However, this was not fully consolidated for some years, because of the VOC's collapse at the end of the century, and subsequent reimposition of varying levels of colonial control under Governor General Daendels, and the British interregnum (1812–17) under Raffles.

A lasting adverse development for the Yogyakarta dynasty occurred at the hands of the British. In the confusion following the takeover of Java by the British in 1812, Hamengku Buwono II, who had been cast aside by the Dutch, reasserted himself and clashed bitterly with Raffles. The British stormed Yogyakarta, exiled Hamengku Buwono II, and rewarded their local ally, Notokusumo, by splitting the Yogyakarta principality and naming Notokusumo as head of the new independent Pakualaman House, which comprised a small part of Yogyakarta city and a tiny enclave outside it in Kulon Progo in the west. The Dutch preserved this arrangement when they returned to Java in 1817.

The Pakualaman was far the smallest of the four principalities, but its creation was aimed at balancing the power and influence of the Sultan, as the Mangkunegaran balanced the Sunanate in Solo. These arrangements are usually taken as colonial divide-and-rule tactics, but the local divisions were real enough. In the period covered by this study, however, the relationship between the Sultanate and the Pakualaman was always much better than the relations between their counterparts in Solo.

Because of the origins of the Yogyakarta Sultanate, there remains an enduring rivalry (or even "cultural animosity")[29] with Solo. Each kingdom claims descent from the original kingdom of Mataram, and both the Sultan and the Sunan claim a mystical conjugal relationship with the Goddess of the South Seas, Nyai Roro Kidul. Both assiduously cultivate different versions of traditional Javanese culture. Even the princes and princesses of the Javanese houses were supposed to have intimate knowledge of cultural matters, and it is a source of pride in Yogyakarta that Dorojatun himself devised a new classically based dance.[30] The period of the revolution provided another stage for the Yogyakarta/Solo rivalry.

IDEOLOGY OF THE YOGYAKARTA PRINCIPALITY

Much has been written in recent years about Javanese ideas of power and ideal Javanese kingship, greatly influenced by Javanese, Indic and Muslim mystical traditions. We are concerned here to explore the ideas of kingship with which the young Sultan would have been familiar and with which he may have identified himself. I discuss later the difficult question of the extent to which we can deduce his actual adherence to these ideas, in the absence of explicit statements by him of his own political thinking.

Scholars have explored Javanese conceptions of power and kingship in some detail.[31] A necessarily oversimplified account of the nature of an ideal Javanese king would include the following elements:

- He possesses the *wahyu* ("godly spirit", but meaning something like "divine monarchic legitimacy" in this context);[32]

- He commands the seen and unseen worlds,[33] his power is unlimited, "but within himself is a force reflecting the Divine Soul" which provides mystic guidance (and thus some measure of control);[34]
- He must battle his base self and the temptation surrounding him,[35] and exercise restraint;[36]
- He gains strength and curbs his desires by practising asceticism and self-abnegation;[37]
- He is benevolent, maintains justice,[38] is generous, takes pity on the poor, and forgives the transgressions of his subordinates;[39]
- He is "a pious and ascetic Sufi king whose purpose is to trust and love God"[40] because "Just kings are the shadow of God";[41]
- He (the *gusti*, or prince/master) has a mutually dependent and empathetic relationship with his subjects (the *kawula*, a word which also means "servant"), "distinct but inseparable";[42]
- He is sparing in his words, because what a king says cannot be unsaid;[43]
- His victories are won with the minimum effort and loss;[44]
- He is descended from a line of renowned kings and princes (sometimes through a partly or wholly fictitious genealogy).[45]

The Sultan himself told an interviewer[46] of the concept of *wisik*, which does not seem to be mentioned specifically in the literature. This means something like the guidance from the Divine Soul mentioned above; but it seems to be broader because it can include guidance from ancestors like Sultan Agung or Hamengku Buwono's own father, through dreams or visions (unless it is argued that the Divine Soul speaks through the ancestors). Hamengku Buwono said: "*Wisik* is an important source (of guidance) for me! I am totally convinced that guidance from my ancestors is correct and I have to follow it. So because of that, people can understand my attitude during the Japanese period and the inception of the Indonesian Republic."[47] As we will hear, Hamengku Buwono claimed to have received *wisik* from his late father, leading to a sudden end to the negotiations on the political contract in 1940.

The King and Religion

Kings have always been preoccupied with demonstrating their closeness to the gods, as a means of reinforcing their legitimacy. According to Ricklefs the pre-Islamic king Hayam Wuruk was regarded as "a god, or more accurately, he was regarded as all gods to all people".[48] Javanese kings in more recent times have not claimed divinity, because such a claim would be contrary to Islam, for which the only divinity is Allah. Although they do not claim to be gods, Javanese kings need to give due regard to religious requirements, as an essential feature of the Javanese concept of the ideal ruler; and it is notable that one of the Yogyakarta Sultan's titles is Panatagama, meaning something like "Defender of the Faith". We quoted above the description of the ideal ruler as "a pious and ascetic Sufi king". Mudjanto[49] quotes from the Javanese text *Wulangreh*: "The king is a projection of God" and Ricklefs writes that "royal authority was seen as God's shadow upon the earth."[50] Kumar refers to the reputation for piety of Prince Mangkunegoro.[51] She also quotes a Javanese text which claims that the noble Pandawa brothers in the Indic epic the *Mahabharata* won the great war against their cousins "because they always remembered God and were patient and did not do evil".[52]

The most important historical role model for Javanese kings was the seventeenth-century king of Mataram, Sultan Agung, who is regarded as a hero of modern Indonesia because of his fierce resistance to the Dutch,[53] but was also regarded as a role model because of his claimed piety. Ricklefs notes "The surviving evidence from the 17th century is inadequate to describe Agung's religious life with any confidence, but … VOC records tell of holy men surrounding the Sultan at court, of his regular visits to the mosque, and of his insistence that European prisoners be converted through circumcision."[54]

Like many broad ideals, the concepts surrounding the ideal Javanese king are so demanding and all-encompassing that no human being could possibly attain all of them, and many Javanese texts relate to the failures of Javanese princes to live up to the ideal. Only Sultan Agung and perhaps the earlier Airlangga and Hayam Wuruk are regarded as examples of successful Javanese rulers.[55]

Succession in Java

The history of Java is dotted with bitter and often violent succession struggles, reflecting both dynastic factionalism and also some imprecision in the rules of succession. Succession in Java has usually been from one male ruler to the next (although not necessarily always through primogeniture); Java has had no Catherine the Great or Hatshepsut. This is reflected in the 1940 contract which specifies that a Sultan is succeeded by his male issue, with preference given to sons of the official wife.[56]

Hamengku Buwono IX never made any verified statement about his attitude to the succession, and few extant accounts make any clear reference to the issue. For many years after independence, unsubstantiated stories circulated that as a good Republican he intended to be the last Sultan of Yogyakarta,[57] the chief evidence for which was his failure to designate any of his wives formally as queen (*garwo padmi*). Nevertheless, he himself never made his position clear. But it is particularly hard to believe that the possibility of preserving his dynasty in some way never occurred to him; and we will see in a later chapter that he did make definite plans at a late stage.

GENERAL CONCEPTS OF GOVERNMENT

Apart from the traditional concepts of government, more modern ones included the theories of government purveyed in Dutch education, including the Ethical Policy, battered though that may have been by the repression and conservatism of de Jonge's period as Governor. Theories of colonial government promoted by Dutch administrators and scholars tacitly or explicitly assumed that the Dutch would rule the Indies into the indefinite future. Revealing an attitude directly antithetical to that of van Leur, Snouck Hurgronje argued that because Indonesians had "lost" their own political and cultural autonomy, the Netherlands should accept the moral obligation of preparing Indonesians for full participation in Dutch political and national life.[58] B.J.O. Schrieke advocated a political union of the Netherlands and the Indies. In his influential work published in the late 1920s,[59] de Kat Angelino saw the colonial government as serving the need to reconcile East and West: "Unless the inevitable and not undesirable meeting of East and West takes place under conditions of wise leadership and thoughtful protection, the result will be an impoverishing instead of an enriching of human culture … and may cause the disintegration of Eastern society."[60] Conservatives like Colijn opposed a unitary government for the Indies and argued for as much regional autonomy as possible.[61]

As we have seen, most Indonesian nationalists had moved far beyond this point. They would normally respond that all this was merely a cloak for Dutch political and economic self-interest, and that the well-being of the Indonesians was a secondary consideration in Dutch thinking.[62]

The emphasis placed by Colijn and others upon regional autonomy was regarded as a divide-and-rule tactic. Nevertheless, the climate of thinking set by such colonial experts continued to influence Dutch policy well into the Indonesian Revolution period.

Dorojatun had been away from Java for nine years and the Dutch wanted to isolate Javanese princes from nationalist political thought. He must however have been aware of Indonesian nationalist ideas, especially those of Ki Hajar Dewantoro, who was a scion of the Pakualaman house, who had cordial though not close relations with his father, and had regular contact with some members of his family through such organizations as the new Sonobudoyo museum.[63] During the Japanese period, if not before,[64] he became acquainted with Dewantoro, who remained a focus of attention in the nationalist press.[65]

Reeve[66] describes Dewantoro as an important influence on Sukarno's political thinking; and he traces the influence of Dewantoro's ideas right through the period of Guided Democracy into the Suharto period, with its notions of the family principle, the integralistic state, its strong suspicion of "fifty per cent plus one" Western-style liberal democracy, and the need for political representation of functional groups. Dewantoro argued for *kekeluargaan*, usually translated as the "family principle", a collectivist concept which likened the Indonesian nation to a family which had "a unity of interests, a unity of strengths, and a unity of soul".[67] He sought a fruitful blending of Eastern and Western elements while rejecting Western "individualism, egotism and materialism".[68] Dewantoro cast the state in the role of a benevolent father, and — by implication — all its citizens as dependent children, a concept which provided little scope for social disunity, a constitutional division of powers, or a loyal opposition. He envisaged a paternalistic polity in which competing interests could be reconciled, and even referred to the possible achievement of "socialism without class struggle",[69] a concept anathema to true Marxists. Some elements of Javanese mystical thought seemed to influence these formulations, especially the emphasis on harmony. Reeve has pointed to Dewantoro's use of the concept of the ideal relationship between the Javanese ruler (*gusti*) and subject (*kawula*), to illustrate the family principle.

This peculiarly Javanese formulation had elements in common with organicist conceptions of the state proposed by theorists like Hobbes or Hegel, for whom the state was omnipotent and its interests far above those of any individual.[70] The Japanese too had developed a kind of family (*ie*) principle,⁷¹ although it is not clear whether this had any influence on Dewantoro's thinking.⁷² Dewantoro conceded that "in certain cases the Great Leader may act as a dictator, in which capacity he need no longer abide by the existing rules and regulations but only by their main principles".⁷³ Dewantoro thus left much to the innate benignity and sense of restraint of whichever Great Leader eventually came to power.

During this period Sukarno's ideas had much in common with Dewantoro's, although with a more Marxist slant, expressing much hostility to capitalism and occasional sympathy for ideas of class struggle. But Sukarno remained ambiguous about whether class struggle and a social revolution were entirely necessary, and he argued that Marxism needed to be adapted to Indonesian circumstances.⁷⁴

The extent to which nationalist thinking in general had impinged on the world view of Javanese princes is quite obscure. Sukarno, Hatta and Syahrir were all in exile, and those nationalists still at large had to be circumspect in their public statements. But Dewantoro's ideas, especially the family principle, were mentioned regularly in the constitutional debates in 1945, attended by Hamengku Buwono's brothers Puruboyo and Bintoro, and of course Sukarno was a prominent and active participant. As eventually became clear, however, Hamengku Buwono, with his European education and despite his leanings towards mysticism, came to reject much of Sukarno's thinking, especially his sympathy for Marxism. His own princely status and the later attraction of the New Order Government to the idea of the family principle nevertheless lend support to the notion that the latter principle was not entirely anathema to him; and the kawula-gusti concept was one basis of Javanese ideas of kingship.

NEGOTIATIONS WITH GOVERNOR ADAM

Every prospective local ruler in the Dutch East Indies had to negotiate a new political contract. In most cases, the Dutch contented themselves with a Short Declaration (*korte verklaring*), but where important rulers were involved, a long political contract was negotiated. The number of native states requiring the long contracts had been reduced to sixteen (out of 282) by the late 1930s.⁷⁵ Needless to say, the two main Javanese principalities were regarded as very important and long contracts were the norm. As contracts changed over the years, the usual process was a diminution in the power of local rulers and an increase in the power of the

Dutch governors and residents. Indeed, the contract which was eventually concluded seems to contain more references to limitations on the Sultan's "right of self-rule" than to his actual powers.[76] "The so-called contracts had become mere acts of investiture, whereby the Government invested the vassal in his office only under certain conditions."[77] This trend did not go unnoticed in the Indonesian press.[78] Nevertheless, the length of the negotiations in Dorojatun's case gives rise to doubt whether the contracts were always regarded so lightly by Dutch officials as these judgements may indicate; and as an expert on political contracts, Dorojatun was well equipped to argue the finer points.

For Yogyakarta in 1939, the distinctive element was the existence of a fresh political contract with the new Sunan of Solo, signed earlier that year. Apart perhaps from the clauses on the budget, the Solo contract became the precedent to which Dutch officials looked, rather than the contract with Dorojatun's father which had been concluded nearly twenty years before. In early 1939, before Hamengku Buwono VIII's unexpected death, Dutch officials feared that he might demand a new contract once he had seen the agreement signed with the Sunan.[79] (This expectation may seem incongruous in view of the adverse reaction in Solo to the new contract there,[80] but it had some features which may have been attractive to Hamengku Buwono VIII.)

The young claimant was in a weak bargaining position as he faced up to the negotiations. He was dealing with experienced colonial officials who would be unwilling to make any great changes, even on paper, to the Sultanate's power structure. On the other hand, as Purwokusumo[81] points out, he was the first Sultan who was educated for his high position and he was also the first to speak fluent Dutch,[82] so that he would fully understand the contents of the contract, removing the possibility that — as had happened with other rulers in the past — he would sign a contract without knowing what it committed him to. Moreover, in some ways, the Governor was an ally of Dorojatun in the bargaining with Batavia, rather than an opponent, at least on budget issues.

The forty-nine-year-old[83] Governor Lucien Adam was a senior colonial official and an expert on Java. Like Dorojatun, he had studied at Leiden University and had received his doctorate in Law[84] there in 1924, on the subject of "The Autonomy of the Indonesian Village".[85] Adam had served in Yogyakarta previously[86] and also in Menado, and had many other postings on Java.[87] His academic interests seemed to be largely anthropological/ethnographical, as shown by a seventy-page article on adat law in Minahasa in 1925,[88] various articles in *Jawa* magazine, and elsewhere.[89] He was regarded as one of the most important colonial officials in the Indies, because only the most trusted and reputable officials were appointed to the governorships of the Vorstenlanden.[90] As he entered his fifties, he may well have expected to reach even more senior positions in Batavia later.

We might deduce that Adam was a relatively liberal figure in Indies terms, given his absorption of Ethical Policy ideas at Leiden in the 1920s, his intense interest in local culture, and his friendship with Hubertus van Mook[91] who had earlier served with him in Yogyakarta. In his academic interests, he seemed to echo the common Dutch preoccupation with Indonesian "sociological exoticism",[92] combined with (we might speculate further) the usual wariness about granting Indonesians anything but limited political rights.

Judging by the tone of Adam's reports, it appears that he soon established cordial relations with the young Dorojatun. Despite the generational difference, they had some experiences in common, not least their studies at Leiden University at different periods. Adam evidently saw Dorojatun as a promising young man with whom he could work productively, and his reports refer to the need to foster the good relationship between them.

In the custom of colonial suzerainty, the ruler of a Vorstenland always described the local Dutch Governor as his "father", and Governors referred to the rulers as their "son", neatly revealing the paternalism of Dutch rule.[93] In posed official photographs of governors and rulers, the two are usually shown with the Governor on the right (looking from the camera's viewpoint), and the ruler clasping the right arm of the Governor in an apparent gesture of dependence, like a bizarre wedding photograph.[94] This derived from long-standing custom; but the absence of any such photographs of Hamengku Buwono IX and Adam might indicate that at least the custom of linking arms had been abandoned, perhaps at the new ruler's insistence.[95]

Given the affectionate tone of his obituary of Hamengku Buwono VIII,[96] Adam probably regarded himself as a family friend and even a father figure for the young claimant. He felt that he was in charge of Dorojatun, even to the extent of recommending his reading.[97] As fellow Leiden intellectuals, he and the Sultan lent each other books.[98] He also shared the delusion that protestations of loyalty by Javanese princes indicated a principled devotion to the Dutch crown.[99] A Dutch woman who as a teenager had stayed at the Governor's palace described Adam as personally kindly and helpful, "with the inner directed gaze of an intellectual".[100]

Succession

Before commencing the negotiations, Dutch officials had to settle the succession formally. Retiring Governor Bijleveld advised Batavia that the succession presented no difficulties, because the late Sultan had left only one son from his official wife, namely Prince Dorojatun. Since his older brothers were all from minor wives, they had no claim.[101] The late Sultan had told Bijleveld of his intention to name Dorojatun as his successor, and the whole kraton community clearly assumed this would happen.[102] Bijleveld added happily: "During my latest leave in Holland I received from several quarters … the most favourable information about this son of a Sultan. He was active in the Leiden student corps. Also His Excellency Minister Welter … was full of praise for R M Dorojatun. And during my visit to the Sultan's sons in Leiden in March of this year, I gained the most excellent impression of him."[103]

The existence of these favourable opinions perhaps helps to explain the disappointment felt by Dutch officials during the Indonesian Revolution when they realized Hamengku Buwono's commitment to the nationalist cause. To the highly conservative[104] Welter in 1939, the quiet young Dorojatun must have seemed the kind of Western-oriented and pliant prince who would cooperate productively with the Dutch. To the limited extent that Ethical Policy ideals or hopes were still current in Dutch thinking, among them was the belief that a Western-educated elite would be so impressed with Dutch civilization that it would support Dutch rule.[105]

Bijleveld recommended that Dorojatun should not be named immediately as Crown Prince, so that he could familiarize himself with his realm without being too burdened by official duties.[106] He accordingly requested the Governor General for authority to enter into negotiations on the political contract, with the intention, once negotiations were completed, of naming Dorojatun as Crown Prince and then as Sultan immediately thereafter.[107] After obtaining the concurrence of the Council of the Indies (Raad van Indie),[108] the Governor General approved the proposal.[109]

Nevertheless, conforming with custom, a kraton family meeting was held at which all members agreed, not without some factional infighting,[110] that Dorojatun should be the successor.[111] Dorojatun asked at the meeting whether any other family members felt they should be Sultan, and no one spoke up.[112] Some Indonesian accounts of his life claim that his term as Sultan should actually be dated from this time ("around 26 October 1939").[113] After Indonesian independence, Hamengku Buwono was always reluctant to celebrate the anniversary of his accession, because it occurred under the aegis of the Dutch.[114]

Public reaction to the arrival of the new claimant was cordial, although most reports mentioned the length of his absence. The extent of his activities and interests in the Netherlands, and his education in Leiden were favourably noted.[115] The Sultan's physician recorded that the new Sultan was "much more business-like than his father".[116]

The Issues

The protracted negotiations between Dorojatun and the Governor pose a historical difficulty which will emerge in the next few paragraphs. But first some background is required. In the past, Javanese rulers had made little or no distinction between their private finances and those of their government, but in the 1930s Dutch officials attempted to inculcate this distinction in the native states, with varying degrees of success. Their efforts were not assisted by the complexity of the financial relations between the centre and the states, nor by the propensity of some rulers to indulge in extravagant expenditure.[117]

The main theme of the Governor's many reports about the negotiations, which lasted more than four months, the longest ever negotiations over a political contract,[118] was the need to impose gradual but substantial reductions in payments to the Sultan. Indeed, these annual payments were equivalent to about one-quarter of the entire budget of the Sultanate government. Adam identified four important issues — the civil list budget, the police, the forests and the Sultan's legal authority over his subjects. The most difficult issue was the civil list budget, and much argument occurred between the Governor and Batavia about the best way of reducing it, finally agreeing that no immediate reduction be made in 1940 and 1941, but that the amounts should decline progressively in later years.

The Governor reported favourably on Dorojatun's attitude, adding that he had quickly reformed kraton purchasing systems, had "set his family members to work in a most exemplary manner", and had displayed "a remarkable sense of responsibility".[119] He mentions requests and comments by Dorojatun about his extensive reform plans in the kraton, the extent of his powers over his subjects, the need for a clear division between kraton property and sultanate property, and the need to regularize payments to family members.[120] Dorojatun's plans included reducing the numbers of kraton civil servants; a reduction in the numbers of the kraton army (then numbering 813 men) and an offsetting increase in the salaries paid to them; a change in the role of the army to include guard duties. He also wanted to reduce the number of low-ranking civil servants in the subdistricts, but pay them better.[121]

The Governor's reports referred almost exclusively to the expenditure side of the kraton budget and hardly mentioned its sources of income apart from the official subventions from the Government budget. Both the Governor and the relevant officials in Batavia seemed to take for granted that serious economies in the kraton budget were necessary, although providing no direct explanation of the reasons for the assumption. Judging by the tone of the documents as a whole, however, it appears that the Yogyakarta government had for years been making enormous payments to the kraton without knowing what the sums were used for, and with no control over the extent of the private debts incurred by the Sultan, which the government might be forced to bail out if the debts became too large. A contemporary source noted, "The personal incomes of many rulers are still too great, but reductions cannot easily be made during the lifetime of the present rulers."[122]

One illustration of the limited extent of the Sultan's power was a matter which was *not* negotiated. The Governor's reports contained no reference to the budget of the principality as a whole. It appears that the budget of the Sultanate, as distinct from that of the kraton, was by this time the responsibility of the Governor assisted by the Patih (vizier), and the Sultan had no direct influence over it.

In February 1940, after months of negotiations, the Governor reported that the final contract should be drawn up in time for the Garebeg celebrations in April, implying that the process was at last at an end. His reports indicated that Dorojatun had read the draft contract with close attention, including the clauses on the judiciary, water supply, and police.[123]

The central conundrum about the negotiations, however, is that Hamengku Buwono's version of them — delivered many years later — bears no resemblance to the content of Governor Adam's reports. The Sultan, speaking in 1980, said that the talks began almost immediately and involved only himself and the Governor. He described three main points of contention — the position of the Patih, the advisory council, and the small kraton army.[124] He wanted to abolish the position of Patih, to create a more democratic advisory council, and to gain direct control over the army.[125] After months of argument, Hamengku Buwono's father appeared to him in a dream and advised him to sign the contract, "because the Dutch will not be here much longer". The latter story looks to foreigners like an obvious rationalization of his powerlessness, but such stories had been common in Yogyakarta even before the Sultan's statement in 1980.

The discrepancies between this account and the Dutch archives are many, and the difficulties in analysing the evidence only start with the obvious consideration that human memory cannot always be trusted after a gap of forty years.[126] The substantive points of difference are particularly hard to explain, especially the lack of references in Dutch reports to the putative main point of contention, the role of the Patih. Apart from one glancing reference,[127] the Patih and his role are not mentioned in any available report by Governor Adam. A prospective Sultan could well object to the role of the Patih, who was designated by the Governor and not by the Sultan, although the latter had to be consulted.[128] The role of the Patih was even more objectionable because the Patih had to support the Governor in the event of a disagreement between the Governor and the Sultan about any matter.[129]

The issue of the advisory council (*Dewan Penasihat*) is also somewhat confusing. An advisory council of some kind existed in the Sultanate well into the Japanese period,[130] and this seems to be what Hamengku Buwono was referring to in his 1980 interview. The Dutch-era advisory body comprised equal numbers of Dutch officials and nominees of the Sultan; Dorojatun apparently disliked the requirement that his nominees had to be cleared with the Dutch authorities, and had argued that the council members should be allowed to speak freely about any matter.[131] Selosumarjan indicates that Dorojatun wanted a major reform, including a general election through universal suffrage and a secret ballot.[132]

In the 1980 interview he was probably not referring to Article 16 of the contract, which specifies that the proposed formation of any representative council must gain the prior approval of the Governor General. (This may mean the Bale Agung, although that term is not used.) The term used in the Dutch-language version of the contract is *vertegenwoordigend lichaam*, i.e., "representative body", echoed in the Indonesian translation as *badan perwakilan* (also "representative body") rather than "Bale Agung" or "advisory council".[133] The Governor's reports made no reference to Article 16 or to an "advisory council", so if the matter was raised with him, he cannot have regarded it as significant.

The final point, the army, was indeed discussed, relating however only to the size of the force, its wage levels and the plan to use it for guard duties. The Governor does not refer to any demands by Dorojatun for direct control.[134]

If these points were so important to Dorojatun, why did the Governor not advise Batavia about them? Adam's approach was to explain to Batavia the chaotic state of the kraton finances, explore options to rectify the situation, and then progress through the various clauses of the contract, occasionally mentioning comments and requests made by the claimant. Nevertheless, the Governor's four main points (expenditures under the civil list, the article on the Sultan's legal authority over his subjects, the police, and forest management) bear no resemblance to Hamengku Buwono's three (the Patih, the advisory council, and the army). This considerable divergence begs for explanations, which are not easily forthcoming on the basis of the available evidence.

If we assume that Dorojatun did make the demands claimed, the Governor may have been reluctant to report contentious political demands by the successor. It might be embarrassing for the Governor to confess that he was having trouble with this neophyte Sultan-elect. Such demands were also the sort of claim which an unsophisticated successor might make if he was unaware of the extent to which his dynasty had lost any real power. As he realized his limited room to manoeuvre, he would come to a more realistic position.

But this explanation is unconvincing. Although the Governor gave little detail about his talks with Dorojatun, would he really avoid telling Batavia about important and highly political demands by the new prince? He would at least mention them, if only to cover himself if Batavia learnt of them through other channels.

The only similarity in his reports to the demands claimed by Hamengku Buwono is the reference to the police. Adam argued that the relevant clause in the contract should be altered to reflect the "reality" that the Governor

Dorojatun Becomes Sultan

and the Sultan, and not the vizier, jointly controlled the police.[135] Had this discussion led Hamengku Buwono forty years later to confuse this with argument about the kraton army? The reference to control of the police might also be a sop to Dorojatun by the Governor after rejecting his demands on other matters. (On this point, the Governor did not get his way, and the relevant clause retains the reference to the Patih exercising control over the police in the name of the Sultan.)[136]

Another possibility is that Hamengku Buwono was exaggerating his disagreements with the Dutch Governor. Much had changed in the forty years since his accession, and in Indonesia the ruling version of colonial history was the nationalist-Republican one. He would naturally portray himself as a true nationalist, bargaining hard with the arrogant Dutch Governor for more power, more democracy in his realm, and more direct involvement with his soldiers. Moreover, his 1980 account mentioned an exchange where the Governor sought his attitude to his ancestor Diponegoro, to which he replied that he admired the rebel prince. This reference placed Dorojatun and his family firmly in the direct line of Indonesian national heroes. Stories of sharp exchanges with Adam remain current in Indonesian versions of the negotiations,[137] although not in Dutch sources.

This explanation is also unsatisfactory. Hamengku Buwono's nationalist credentials were unquestionable in 1980. He would have no reason to seek to enhance his standing by making exaggerated claims about the past. Indeed, his normal approach was to say little about the past,[138] although he did make some statements near the end of his life.

None of the references to the young Dorojatun in the Governor's reports is particularly surprising. Dorojatun's queries and comments related to budget problems, questions of succession, current and future reform plans, a request for minor changes in the judiciary clauses, and his plans to pay his public servants and soldiers better, and these might all be expected from a new Western-educated Sultan. His most important, and successful, request was for inclusion of a formal stipulation in the contract that the son of an official wife has precedence in the succession over the son of a minor wife.[139] This request would have been aimed at reinforcing his position, which was strong but not unchallengeable. The family of the late Crown Prince (Hamengkunagoro) may never have been totally reconciled to losing the succession.[140] One of his brothers was later said to have felt that he could manage things better.[141] One story about the negotiations has Dorojatun replying to enquiries by anxious relatives, "If you don't agree with my approach, please choose another Sultan."[142]

Nevertheless, the contradictions between the Governor's reports and the version of events given by the Sultan appear susceptible of no simple explanation, and in the absence of further evidence we may reluctantly leave this as a minor historical mystery. The political contract exerted little effect on Hamengku Buwono's life after the Dutch defeat, except when the Dutch vainly attempted to reinvoke it during the Revolution.[143]

The negotiations provided early evidence that Dorojatun had a firmer cast of mind than his modest manner would indicate. He wanted to be Sultan but he did not rush to assume the position. Although the exact content of the negotiations may be in question, it is clear that he was prepared to spend time arguing for a better political contract, even though Dorojatun did not know what Adam was reporting to Batavia; if the stories about occasional heated exchanges are correct, he risked the possibility that Adam might begin looking for other candidates.[144]

Despite the debts left by his father, the relatively generous financial provisions during 1940 and 1941 seem to have left Hamengku Buwono with substantial reserves of Dutch guilders when the Japanese invaded, at least some of which he preserved during the occupation, apparently contrary to Japanese occupation law.[145] According to many Indonesian accounts, he was able to use these to benefit the Indonesian Republic during the Revolution.[146]

In late February came good news. The Governor had won the day and Batavia had accepted his proposals, especially the budget arrangements.[147] The final contract thus provided for initial payments to the Sultan of 1,230,000 guilders in both 1940 and 1941,[148] then reducing steadily to the targeted amount of a million guilders by 1960.[149] Although the budget would be tighter, the downward pressure on payments to the kraton would not be too oppressive, and indeed the records show that Hamengku Buwono received the payments for 1940 and 1941. And as matters turned out, Dutch control of the budget had only two more years to run.

The Contract in Perspective

The contract, in force for only the next two years, was more detailed than the 1921 contract with Hamengku Buwono VIII or the 1877 contract with

Hamengku Buwono VII.[150] Apart from the ultimately nugatory Article 16 on the establishment of a representative body discussed above, an important constitutional change was the clear statement in the contract that the Sultanate was a legal entity (*rechtspersoon*), a statement which was unprecedented in contracts with previous sultans. The effect of the change was apparently to incorporate the Sultanate formally into the territory of the Indies, rather than its previous status as a semi-separate "fiefdom".[151] It was the corresponding clause in the recent Solo contract which inter alia had helped to damage the prestige of the new Sunan.[152]

Nevertheless, Dutch observers disputed whether this development was unfavourable to the ruler. One pointed out that under the previous legal status of "fiefdom", the realm would automatically return to the sovereignty of the Indies Government on the death of a ruler. The new status left the implication that the realm remained a legal entity with its own character whether or not the ruler had just passed away.[153] The dynastic rights of the ruling family were acknowledged in the new Solo contract, rights which had not been mentioned in the previous contracts.[154] The same point could be made for the 1940 Yogyakarta contract, which had not yet been made public.

The clause on the legal status of the Sunanate had caused difficulty with the home government in early 1939, a bureaucratic dispute which was carefully kept from the public. When the Solo contract reached The Hague in April 1939, Colonies Minister Welter took strong exception to the change, arguing that it reversed 200 years of precedents and expressing the fear that the change would be used against the Dutch.[155] Larson concluded that Welter feared an adverse political reaction from the Solo court.[156] The Governor General's rather defensive response quoted Governor Orie of Solo as saying that earlier official correspondence had already foreshadowed such a change in the legal status of the principalities.[157] After Hamengku Buwono VIII's death, Minister Welter requested the Governor General to consult him if the new Yogyakarta contract were to diverge from the Solo contract.[158] Adam may thus have had little room to manoeuvre in the negotiations as a result of Welter's edict, and this may explain his obduracy as reported by Hamengku Buwono.

Available accounts lack any reference to consultation between the palaces about the negotiations. Dorojatun could conceivably have compared notes with the new Sunan about the political contract, but no indication of such consultation occurs in the sources. As will appear later, some consultation (on other matters) between the rulers did apparently take place during the early Revolution.

CORONATION

The coronation took place on 18 March 1940, and thus preceded the Garebeg celebration by over one month. This suggests some acceleration of events compared with the timetable envisaged in Adam's report of 18 February.[159] Local press reports indicated surprise at the announcement on 1 March that the coronation would occur that month rather than April.[160] This tends to confirm that Dorojatun had suddenly agreed to the draft contract, as he later claimed.

The ceremony occurred in the Mangunturtangkil pavilion in the Sitihinggil area of the kraton, attended by the Pakualam, the Mangkunegoro, two prominent princes from Solo (Kusumoyudo and Hario Mangkubumi),[161] senior Dutch officials like H.J. van Mook, and the governors of Semarang and Solo.[162] As always when he appeared with the large and florid-faced Governor, Dorojatun looked diminutive and dapper in his traditional Javanese costume. He was handsome in a way, with a well-known charming smile, but with a heavy jaw which grew more prognathous as he aged.

The political contract was signed[163] and the Governor gave a brief and high-flown speech, welcoming the new Sultan, referring to theories of government, including those of van Vollenhoven, and the need for the practical qualities of political leadership — intuition, knowledge of human nature, practical insight, and broad understanding. In words which might have been directed at the Governor General, he added "Narrowness of vision was the enemy of the administrator." The Governor pinned on the Sultan's chest the star of office[164] "as symbol of the bond between you, your father and your forefathers, but also between you and the Government".[165] In an intriguing hint of the nature of the negotiations, Adam added, "You have had, I believe, no reason to complain about my good faith."[166] That the Governor would make this remark could well imply that the negotiations had involved substantive disagreements or at least substantive issues.

All accounts[167] of the new Sultan's coronation address quote his statement: "*Al heb ik een uitgesproken Westerse opvoeding gehad, toch ben ik en blijf ik in de allereerste plaats Javaan.*" In other words, "I have had an extensive Western upbringing, yet I am and remain above all a Javanese."

Differing interpretations of this statement are possible. Several Indonesian observers take this as a more or less covert statement of (Indonesian) nationalism, an indication that despite his Dutch upbringing, he was indirectly expressing defiance of the colonial regime; and that he would have been franker about his Indonesian nationalism if he had been free to do so. For example, one observer claims that the word "Javanese" means "Javanese meaning 'Indonesian', not meaning of a feudal Javanese nature. He was a democratic figure."[168] Another commentator[169] also interprets the word "Javanese" as really meaning " 'Indonesian', because the terminology of 'Indonesia' was not as common then as it is now."[170]

This is an important point, because it raises again the question of Hamengku Buwono's concept of his own identity at this time. Little direct evidence can be adduced that he thought of himself as anything but a Javanese prince. He had been brought up as a Westernized Javanese and had never been encouraged to think of himself as an Indonesian. This would not prevent him resenting Dutch rule and wishing it to end, but it is assuming too much to believe that at this stage Indonesian nationalism was the focus of his thinking.

A related point arises elsewhere in the speech, where he says "may I conclude with the promise that I will work for the interests of the Land and People, to the limit of my knowledge and ability". The words "Land and People" are *Land en Volk* in the original Dutch and are translated in modern Indonesian versions of the speech as "nusa dan bangsa",[171] a standard Indonesian phrase rendered as "homeland" in the dictionary,[172] but now carrying a very modern "Indonesian" connotation — which *Land en Volk* does not. To Indonesians nowadays, the words "nusa dan bangsa" have only one meaning, namely the entire country of Indonesia. In 1940, however, the Dutch phrase *Land en Volk* would have meant the Yogyakarta principality or at most the island of Java, rather than the entire archipelago. In the mind of a Javanese prince of that time, he had little claim to represent citizens of the Indies outside his principality, and it would have been presumptuous to pretend otherwise.

Again, this is not to say that he did not feel alienation and dislike of the Dutch yoke. The long negotiations of the political agreement already indicated his desire for more freedom of movement. But we should be careful not to read too much of the future in events during this period. The evidence is too slight for a definite conclusion that Hamengku Buwono was already at this stage a firmly committed Indonesian nationalist.[173]

The point will be followed up when we discuss his attitudes during the Japanese occupation.

What may have been equally important in his thinking at this point was adverted to in his coronation speech — the double identity he had to assume: "I am fully aware that the task which now rests upon me is difficult and heavy, above all the requirement to bring the Western and Eastern spirits into a harmonious cooperation, without causing the latter to lose its essential character."[174] This description of his task in the Yogyakarta principality also reflected his need to harmonize the Western and Eastern aspects of his own character and within his own life.

SULTAN UNDER THE DUTCH

As part of the changes foreshadowed in the contract negotiations, Hamengku Buwono decreed that the kraton treasurer should henceforth handle all financial affairs, and that all sections must draw up detailed budgets.[175] He imposed various economies in the kraton,[176] and changed the mode of payment of the abdi dalems' salaries and their modes of dress, although the extent of changes did not satisfy some commentators.[177] He was also supposed to have made several incognito visits to villages and markets shortly after becoming Sultan.[178] It is not entirely clear, however, whether he was able to institute all the changes discussed in his talks with the Governor. In promoting reforms outside the kraton, Hamengku Buwono was constrained both by Dutch power and by the need to manage the budget carefully. Further reforms had to await the late Japanese period and the Revolution.

As war broke out in Europe and tensions grew over the role of Japan in the Pacific, nationalists in the Indies argued for closer cooperation between the Indies Government and the Indonesian people. The notion of a people's militia, which had been first raised as long ago as 1912 and even more strongly when the First World War erupted,[179] again became a hot issue. In the Volksraad in October 1939, however, leaders such as Sutarjo, Thamrin, and Oto Iskandar Dinata were unable to dent official complacency. Sutarjo complained that official policy provided no encouragement for Indonesian intellectuals to take an interest in national defence, and Iskandar Dinata added that only Dutchmen were invited to defend the Indies; but the government denied these claims, referring to recent efforts by local princes and officials in the defence field.[180] Complaints about continued restrictions on organizations, public meetings and press freedom were also dismissed.[181]

Brown has described the nationalists' efforts to win over the colonial authorities as "showing optimism bordering on the unbelievable".[182]

Even the German occupation of the Netherlands and the flight of the royal family and government to London led to no change in policy by Governor General Tjarda van Starkenborgh Stachouwer.[183] The government could not even bring itself to move any distance towards moderates like Sutarjo.[184] A crucial moment arrived in June 1940 with the opening speech by the Governor General to the Volksraad. Abeyasekere says: "As the audience waited with bated breath, the Governor General blandly observed that the Government was touched by the people's widespread wish to help, and … that discussions concerning changes in state and society should wait until the war was over."[185]

Nationalist opinion was outraged at this official short-sightedness. The main nationalist organization Gapi urged democratic reforms, arguing that "the Indies constitution should now be democratic so as to inspire greater enthusiasm for defence among the population".[186] Throughout late 1939 and 1940, nationalists had been campaigning for an Indonesian parliament,[187] but this demand too was rejected in August 1940.[188]

Efforts were made across Java to raise funds for the war. In Yogyakarta, Governor Adam chaired the Support Committee, and the Sultan contributed 2,000 guilders personally, the Sultanate 3,000 guilders, and the Pakualaman 1,500 guilders.[189] But reactions to the Indies Government's defence measures in the principalities were often complicated by political considerations. Government proposals for an air raid warning service (Luchtbeschermingsdienst [LBD]) were welcomed by the more leftwing elements such as Gerindo, whereas the supposedly more conservative Parindra argued that cooperation in this area should be matched by political concessions from the government. Unlike the Mangkunegoro, the Sunan resisted the formation of an LBD until the government forced one on him in November 1940.[190] An LBD was formed without controversy in Yogyakarta about the same time.[191]

The Pakualam was outspoken in his support of the Dutch government. In April 1940 his Pakualam Legion had been re-formed with a strength of two companies, and in May 1940, following the invasion of the Netherlands, he publicly assured Governor Adam of the continued support of the Pakualam House. The Sultan was said to be more reserved, rather to the disappointment of the Dutch authorities.[192]

Welter visited the Indies during April–May 1941 from his base in wartime London.[193] The nationalist press still hoped for more positive responses than had been given to the Sutarjo petition of July 1936, which had requested a conference to discuss Indies autonomy,[194] but which had been humiliatingly rejected after a delay of two years.[195] But Welter refused to meet any nationalist leaders and gave no further response to the request for an Indonesian parliament.[196] Despite calls in the local press for Welter's party to meet the four Javanese rulers, they did not visit the Vorstenlanden.[197] On return to London Welter reported, with astonishing complacency in the circumstances, that the natives well understood his reasons for refusing political reforms.[198]

During the last years of Dutch rule and into the Japanese period, great changes happened in the new Sultan's private life. He took his first wife, Pintokopurnomo, in 1940, and married the next three over the next 6–7 years. They were all well-connected aristocratic Javanese women, and the marriages might be regarded as typically dynastic. Perhaps surprisingly, it was not until 1943 that the first child (a girl) was born, and the first son — the future Hamengku Buwono X — arrived in 1946. Over the next two decades, Hamengku Buwono acquired a total of twenty-one children by his four wives, six of them male, thus apparently consolidating the succession. As well as the future Hamengku Buwono X himself, several of the children made solid careers for themselves, such as Prabukusumo, who led the local branch of Susilo Bambang Yudhoyono's party to a victory in the elections of 2009, before breaking with SBY over the Yogyakarta specialness issue. None of the children (unlike the royal family in Solo, or indeed the Pakualaman) involved themselves in scandals likely to embarrass their father. Nevertheless, in less-guarded moments some of the children admitted some feeling of neglect by their father, who was usually in Jakarta, and only saw them occasionally. These feelings seem to have been accentuated in the 1970s when — as will be recounted later — he married his fifth wife (one wife having died by then).

One curious feature of his private life was that none of his wives seemed to play any political role, that normally they kept away from Jakarta, and that they appeared to socialize rarely or never with his political associates there. This seemed to be a persistent pattern in later years too — one of the technocrats recounted that in the 1960s he had accompanied a delegation to Europe led by Hamengku Buwono; when he reached Jakarta airport to join the other delegation members, he became aware that one of the Sultan's wives was there to see her husband off. However, to his surprise and unease, she was not introduced to the delegation members.

SUMMARY

The two-year period under the Dutch was a useful apprenticeship for the new Sultan, and he was able to consolidate his personal authority and image in Yogyakarta and establish a modus vivendi with Dutch power. As the newest of the four Javanese rulers, however, he was less well known than the two Solo princes. In 1940, the Mangkunegoro was perhaps the most prominent — but not necessarily the most popular[199] — in the public mind, and certainly most prominent in the Dutch mind. The public perception of the new Sultan as his own man, and not excessively beholden to advisers in the court (as Pakubuwono XI was), would not yet have taken hold.

Whichever version of the contract negotiations we regard as more credible, their sheer length reinforces the case that Dorojatun tried to extract the best possible terms from the Dutch authorities. This first real evidence of his character would, however, have passed nearly unnoticed outside Yogyakarta. The sole contemporary commentary on the political contract notes that substantive issues must have been discussed in the negotiations, but indicates no awareness of serious disagreements.[200] Neither the Dutch Governor nor the new Sultan had any interest in publicizing the differences, whatever they were, which prolonged the negotiations. As 1942 arrived, and with it the threat of Japanese invasion, he was well placed to face the new challenges, but at this stage did not stand out from other traditional rulers.

Notes

1. The late Sudarpo Sastrosatomo said that Hamengku Buwono IX had recounted his father saying that he did not expect to live much longer, that colonialism was ending, and that Dorojatun must help to bring it down. Interview, 3 October 2003.
2. *Asiaweek* interview, 4 May 1986, p. 59.
3. He had suffered a heart attack on 31 August, complicated by diabetes — *Indische Gids*, vol. 2, 1939, p. 1057.
4. Westerkamp, pp. 13–16.
5. Purwokusumo, *Kasultanan Yogyakarta* [The Sultanate of Yogyakarta], p. 67.
6. *IPO* no. 43/1939, p. 769 — anonymous article in the monthly *Kawula*.
7. Some letters to Dorojatun from his father written in the 1930s are held by Princess Nindyokirono. Dorojatun must have written to his father in reply, but none of the family seemed to know whether any of these letters were still extant.

8. Larson, p. 7. Also Rotge, p. 11.
9. R. van Niel, "The Legacy of the Cultivation System", in *Indonesian Economic History*, edited by Booth et al., p. 76.
10. Boomgard and Gooszen (eds.), *Changing Economy in Indonesia*, vol. 11, *Population Trends 1795–1942*, p. 119.
11. Ibid., p. 120.
12. Suwarno, *Romusa*, p. 3. In 1749, when Pakubuwana II died, the combined population of the Solo and Yogyakarta principalities was estimated at 1.5 million: Kumar, p. 241.
13. Boomgard and Gooszen, p. 121.
14. *Ensiklopedi Nasional Indonesia*, vol. 17 (U–Zw), 1991, p. 387.
15. *Encyclopedie van Nederland Oost Indie*, vol. 1, p. 623.
16. *Djokja Solo*, op. cit., p. 41.
17. *Ensiklopedi Nasional Indonesia*, vol. 17, op. cit., p. 393.
18. *Djokja Solo*, p. 41.
19. Ibid., p. 42.
20. See previous chapter and Larson, op. cit., p. 470.
21. Mubyarto and Ace Partadireja, "An Economic Survey of the Special Region of Yogyakarta", *Bulletin of Indonesian Economic Studies*, no. 11 (October 1968): 29.
22. *Djokja Solo*, p. 53.
23. Verhoeff, op. cit., pp. 116–17.
24. Attachment to 1937 Yogyakarta *Memorie van Overgave*, Stok Report on Agriculture, p. 206.
25. *Mata Hari*, 1 February 1941, in *IPO* 6/41, p. 202.
26. Ricklefs, *A History of Modern Indonesia*, p. 93.
27. Moedjanto, *Konsep Kekuasaan*, p. 122.
28. Ricklefs, ibid., p. 94.
29. So described by Selosumarjan in "The Kraton in Javanese Social Structure", in *Dynamics of Indonesian History*, edited by Soebadio and du Marchie Sarvaas, p. 231.
30. This was the *Golek Menak Dewi Widyaningsih – Dewi Renggani*, still occasionally performed. See *Jakarta Post* of 6 September 2003.
31. See for example Anderson, Kumar, Ricklefs, Selosumarjan, Soemarsaid Moertono, and Moedjanto in the bibliography.
32. Moertono, *State and Statecraft in Old Java*, p. 56. Ricklefs (p. 18) renders *wahyu* as "supernatural radiance of legitimacy".
33. Ricklefs, *Seen and Unseen Worlds*, pp. 242–43.
34. Moertono, p. 40. Also Moedjanto, *Konsep Kekuasaan Jawa*, p. 121.
35. Ibid. (p. 122), summarizing a quotation from the *Suluk Garwa Kancana*. Also Ricklefs, p. 123.

36. Kumar, *Java and Modern Europe,* p. 403.
37. Kumar, ibid., pp. 394–95 and p. 404.
38. Kumar, *Java — A Self-Critical Examination of the Nation and its History*, p. 322.
39. Kumar, *Java and Modern Europe*, op. cit., pp. 382–83.
40. Ricklefs, *Seen and Unseen*, p. 122. See also Moertono, p. 137.
41. Ricklefs, ibid., p. xx. Both Ricklefs (p. 125 inter alia) and Kumar (p. 415) make the point that the notoriously syncretic Javanese see little or no contradiction between the Indic and the Islamic influences in their world view.
42. Reeve, p. 18, who points out the extensive use of this image by Ki Hajar Dewantoro.
43. *Sabda pandita ora kena wola-wali* — see Moedjanto, op. cit., p. 145.
44. Anderson.
45. Moertono, p. 138.
46. Kustiniati Mochtar in *TUR*, p. 63. *SO* — p. 47 — claims that the idea for the Serangan Umum came to the Sultan from *wisik*.
47. *TUR*, ibid.
48. Ricklefs, *Seen and Unseen Worlds*, op. cit., p. xix.
49. Mudjanto, p. 122.
50. Ricklefs, op. cit., p. xx.
51. Kumar, *Java and Modern Europe*, p. 392.
52. Kumar, ibid, p. 394.
53. He was just as fierce in his battles against fellow Javanese, but this is normally overlooked in nationalist accounts, Ricklefs op. cit., pp. 40–41.
54. Ibid., p. xxi.
55. Cf Kumar, op. cit., p. 395 on Sultan Agung and p. 397 on Airlangga.
56. *TUR*, p. 303, political contract, Clause 4. The Mangkunegoro house provides an exception of sorts. Succession through the female *line*, though not by *females*, has occurred on occasion, e.g., Mangkunegoro III was a son of the oldest daughter of Mangkunegoro II — Verhoeff, op. cit., p. 114.
57. See for an example, Southall, *Indonesia Face to Face*, p. 75, where this myth is repeated.
58. Van Klinken, *Migrant Moralities*, PhD Thesis, Griffith University, 1996, p. 77.
59. The English-language version was A.D.A. de Kat Angelino, *Colonial Policy*, abridged and translated by G.J. Renier, 2 vols (The Hague, Martinus Nijhoff, 1931).
60. Vandenbosch (op. cit., p. 71) mentions several Dutch thinkers, but the only Indonesian mentioned is the apostle of conservative "aristo-democracy", Noto Suroto.
61. Ibid., p. 71 n.
62. See, for example, Hatta's remarks in "Colonial Society and the Ideals of Social Democracy", in Feith and Castles, *Indonesian Political Thinking*, p. 33.

63. *Djawa* magazine 1940, p. 262. The museum was opened on 6 November 1935, and Dewantoro was a committee member alongside two princes from the kraton.
64. *Sinar Matahari*, 22 October 1942.
65. *Asia Raya* 1942–45 passim.
66. Reeve, *Golkar of Indonesia, an Alternative to the Party System*, pp. 9–20.
67. Dewantoro, *Karja II a*, p. 246, quoted by Reeve, ibid., p. 10.
68. Reeve, ibid., p. 12.
69. Ibid.
70. Goodwin, *Using Political Ideas*, pp. 316–17.
71. Shigeru Sato, op. cit., p. 16. For clarity, the term *ie* is a Japanese word, and is not the English abbreviation "i.e.".
72. Japanese unitary-state ideas were referred to by Professor Supomo in his speech to the Preparatory Committee (BPUPKI) in 1945 — see Feith and Castles (eds.), op. cit., p. 189.
73. Reeve, ibid., p. 19.
74. Ibid., pp. 28–29.
75. Amry Vandenbosch, *The Dutch East Indies*, p. 149.
76. The phrase "the right to self-rule does not extend to…" occurs repeatedly in the political contract, such as in articles nos. 21, 27, 33, 43 etc. *TUR*, pp. 334–70.
77. Ibid., p. 148.
78. See *Sedya Tama* of 16 November 1939, in *IPO* 46, p. 837. Even Dutch commentators drew attention to the trend — Mr H.G. Verhoeff, "De Herziening van de Politieke Verhouding tot de Vorstenlandsche Zelfbesturen" [Review of the Political Relationship with the Autonomous Princely States], *Koloniale Studien* (1940): 109.
79. Letter of 7 April 1939 to Governor General from Governor Bijleveld, MR 392 geh/39, p. 1.
80. Larson, *Prelude to Revolution*, p. 472 — "The political contract signed by the new Susuhunan led to a serious — perhaps fatal — loss of prestige for the kraton."
81. Purwokusumo, op. cit., p. 68.
82. Hamengku Buwono VIII actually spoke Dutch quite well, but after an incident where he overheard a senior Dutchman slur his proficiency, he afterwards refused to speak Dutch to Dutch officials. Westerkamp, p. 3.
83. Adam was born on 8 October 1890 in Situbondo, Java (NIOD 061950) and died in The Hague in 1978 (information from Mr Fred Adam, 18 September 2003).
84. S. Pompe, "A Short Review of Doctoral Theses on the Netherlands Indies Accepted at the Faculty of Law of Leiden University in the Period 1850–1940", *Indonesia* Magazine, no. 56 (October 1993): 82.

85. Lucien Adam, *De Autonomie van het Indonesische Dorp* [The Autonomy of the Indonesian Village], Melchior, Amersfoort, 1924.
86. In the mid-1920s as Controleur (i.e., Inspector) — *Darmo Kondo*, 2 July 1926 (IPO 30/26, p. 182).
87. *Stamboek* (Register of Colonial Officials), Folios 52 and 720, Nationaal Archief.
88. *Bijdragen tot de Taal- Land- en Volkenkunde*, no. 81, 1925, p. 424, article entitled *Zeden en Gewoonte en het daarmede Samenhangend Adatrecht van het Minahassische Volk* [Customs and Usages and the Associated Adat Law of the Minahasa People].
89. E.g., an article on Javanese mourning customs published in *Supplement op het Tri Windu Gedenkboek Mangkunegara VII* [Supplement to the Mangkunegoro VII Three-*Windu* Memorial Volume], Solo, 1940.
90. Vandenbosch, op. cit., p. 155n.
91. After release from internment in 1945, Adam wrote several friendly letters to van Mook during 1945–47. Van Mook archive NA 2.21.123, Inv no. 79 (Fiche 64).
92. The phrase is Anthony Reid's, in *Indonesian National Revolution*, p. 179.
93. Between the 49-year-old Adam and the 27-year-old Dorojatun, this might seem appropriate. In other cases, it was less so. The Governor General normally referred to the Sultan as his "grandson" — see the letter of 22 January 1921 from Governor General van Limburg Stirum to his 70-year-old "grandson" Hamengku Buwono VII on his abdication. *Indische Gids* 1, no. 43 (1921): 373.
94. For example, the photograph of the Sunan of Solo and the Dutch Governor on p. 6 in van Bruggen et al., *Djokja Solo Beeld van de Vorstenlanden* (hereafter *Djokja Solo*).
95. Photographs in for example *Djokja Solo*, op. cit., p. 57, and photographs in this book.
96. Obituary by L. Adam of 4 November 1939 in *Koloniaal Tijdschrift* no. 24/1940, pp. 1–3.
97. Governor's speech at the Sultan's enthronement, *De Locomotief*, 18 March 1940, recommending Van Vollenhoven's *Staatsrecht Overzee* [Overseas Constitutional Law].
98. *Moesson*, November 1989, *Een Jaar in een Paleis* [A Year in a Palace], article by Ingeborg van Epenhuysen – Tuckerman, p. 12.
99. MR 279/40, Governor's letter of 18 February 1940, p. 6.
100. *Moesson*, op. cit., p. 12.
101. MR 1283 geh/39, letter of 26 October 1939 from Bijleveld to Governor General, p. 1.
102. Ibid., p. 2.
103. Ibid.

104. Or even reactionary — see Sutherland, *Making of a Bureaucratic Elite*, p. 102.
105. Brown, *A Short History of Indonesia*, p. 123.
106. MR 1283 geh/39, letter of 26 October 1939 from Bijleveld to Governor General, op. cit., p. 2.
107. Letter of 26 October 1939 from Bijleveld to Governor General, ibid. It is strange that Bijleveld makes no mention of his forthcoming handover to Adam, which must have occurred in the following week. Bijleveld's reports never mention Adam and the latter's reports never mention Bijleveld.
108. MR 1350 geh/39, Raad van Indie decision of 8 November 1939.
109. Ibid., letter from Government Secretary F.C. Barbas of 23 November 1939.
110. See *Merdeka*, 12 February 1949, p. 8: "While there was no Sultan in Yogyakarta, the kraton was in uproar.... Eventually, victory went to Dorojatun's supporters."
111. *TUR*, p. 48. A similar process occurred when the present Sultan of Yogyakarta succeeded his father.
112. *Asiaweek* interview, loc. cit.
113. *TUR*, ibid.
114. *Kraton Jogja, The History and Cultural Heritage*, p. 122.
115. *Soerabaiasch Handelsblad*, 2 March 1940 (KPC).
116. Westerkamp, p. 12.
117. Vandenbosch, p. 151.
118. Purwokusumo, *Kasultanan Yogyakarta*, p. 67.
119. MR 279/40, Governor's letter of 18 February 1940, p. 4n and p 9.
120. Ibid., passim.
121. Ibid., p. 6.
122. Vandenbosch, ibid.
123. MR 279/40, Governor's letter of 18 February 1940, p. 15.
124. *Tempo*, no. 2, June 1980, pp. 6–7. Hamengku Buwono repeated the three points in his *Asiaweek* interview in 1986, with the slight difference that "they [the Dutch] wanted to make the 800 kraton guards soldiers in the Netherlands Indies Army. I said no." *Asiaweek* interview, loc. cit.
125. Sudarpo Sastrosatomo (interview, 3 October 2003) claimed that the Sultan wanted to form his own legion on the lines of the Mangkunegaran Legion. The Dutch official reports do not mention this.
126. Hamengku Buwono did not have a particularly reliable memory, according to George Kahin, who tried to elicit his recollections of the Madiun affair in the early 1960s — Feith papers, MON 78, 1991/09/012, item 198, Kahin/Feith letter of 20 December 1960, p. 1.
127. MR geh/40, Governor's letter of 29 November 1939, p. 7.
128. Political contract, Article 13, in *TUR*, p. 341.
129. Purwokusumo, *Daerah Istimewa Yogyakarta* [The Special Province of Yogyakarta],

p. 8, says that this stipulation was contained in the Patih's oath of office. The relevant clause of the 1940 political contract does not contain this.
130. *Sinar Matahari*, 20 July 1942 (KPC) reports a decision to change many names of official bodies from Dutch terms to Javanese (NB *not* Indonesian), including the change from *Raad van Advies* (Advisory Council) to *Amatyagana*.
131. Department of Social Affairs, *Riwayat Hidup Singkat Sri Sultan Hamengku Buwono IX* [Brief Biography of Sultan Hamengku Buwono IX], 1990, p. 11.
132. Selosumarjan, *Social Change*, op. cit., p. 50. He indicates that the Governor proposed an appointed Bale Agung, but this was rejected by Dorojatun as undemocratic. However, the Governor's reports never mention a Bale Agung.
133. *TUR*, op. cit., p. 308.
134. As noted above, a further confusing point is added in the 1986 *Asiaweek* interview, where Hamengku Buwono IX says that he rejected a Dutch proposal to make the 800 kraton guards officially soldiers in the Netherlands colonial army (KNIL). *Asiaweek* interview, loc. cit. Adam's reports make no reference to such a plan.
135. MR 13 geh/40, op. cit., Governor's letter to Governor General of 29 November 1939, p. 7.
136. Political contract, Article 32, in *TUR*, p. 351.
137. Adam is said to have told Dorojatun after one heated argument, "Your father would never have said that!", eliciting the reply, "That shows how little you knew my father." The exact topic of discussion remains unknown. Interview, Romo Noordi Pakuningrat, 20 August 2002. See the similar but not identical story on p. 41 of *TUR*.
138. The six children of Hamengku Buwono IX to whom I have spoken (in either formal or informal contexts) all said that their father had never spoken to them about the past, although two of them had begged him to do so. "It was enough that I did my duty", he is reported as saying.
139. MR 279/40, Governor's letter of 18 February 1940, p. 12.
140. A Dutch intelligence report of the Revolution period makes this claim — NEFIS files 1942–49, no. 06982 (held in Netherlands Foreign Ministry), CMI report no. 5676, of 20 March 1949.
141. Since 1933, Puruboyo had served as his father's private secretary and might well have felt better fitted for high office than his inexperienced younger brother. *Sinar Matahari*, 8 October 1943.
142. *Berita Buana* article, 5 October 1988, in *Sang Demokrat*, op. cit., p. 143.
143. Yogyakarta Resident Stok claimed in 1949 that the Sultan should observe the 1940 contract, *NIB*, vol. XVII, p. 671n.
144. Many years later, Hamengku Buwono referred to the possibility — *TUR*, p. 48.

145. Decree by Dutch Governor forbidding hoarding of Dutch currency, in *Mataram*, 10 March 1942 (KPC). Cribb, "Political Dimensions of the Currency Question 1945–47", *Indonesia*, no. 31 (April 1981): 114, notes that hoarding of the Netherlands Indies currency was quite common.
146. Djoeir Moehamad, *Memoar Seorang Sosialis* [Memoirs of a Socialist], pp. 307–8. Several witnesses (e.g., Mrs Rahmi Hatta in *TUR*, p. 213) testify to the Sultan's generosity with Dutch guilders after the Dutch occupation of Yogyakarta.
147. MR 279 geh/40, letter of 26 February 1940 from the Director of the Civil Service (Drossaers) to Governor General, where Drossaers agrees to the figures proposed by Adam.
148. Political Contract, Article 8, in *TUR*, p. 338.
149. *Indisch Verslag II* 1941 (p. 515) shows payments of fl 1,185,400 (Dutch guilders) in 1940 and fl 1,273,400 in 1941. The two amounts add up to fl 2,458,800, close enough to the scheduled two-year total of fl 2,460,000.
150. Purwokusumo, *Kasultanan Yogyakarta*, p. 64.
151. According to Larson, op. cit., p. 441 and p. 472.
152. Dutch commentators were more complacent — Verhoeff (op. cit., p. 118) wrote "it was to be expected that (the contract) would lead to disappointment and unease, but this was unimportant compared with the more general public interest".
153. Ibid., p. 112.
154. Ibid., p. 113.
155. Verbaal of 28 October 1939 (Letter P45, Subject — *Java Autonomous Regions*), p. 3.
156. Larson, p. 441.
157. Verbaal, op. cit., letter of 26 April 1939 from Governor General to Minister of Colonies, p. 2.
158. Ibid., second page (the first three pages of the Verbaal have no pagination).
159. MR 13/40, Governor's letter to Governor General of 18 February 1940, p. 1.
160. *Surabaiasch Handelsblad*, 2 March 1940 (KPC).
161. *De Locomotief*, 18 March 1940, p. 1, "Jogja's Jeugdige Sultan" [Jogja's Youthful Sultan].
162. *Djokja Solo*, p. 57.
163. *De Locomotief*, op. cit.
164. Ibid., *bintang pusaka* (lit "heirloom star").
165. Ibid.
166. Ibid. — *openhartigheid*, lit "openheartedness" or "honesty, straightforwardness".
167. E.g., *TUR*, p. 53. Sutrisno Kutoyo, *Sri Sultan*, op. cit., p. 28. *Djokja Solo*, op. cit., p. 5 (heading).
168. *Sri Sultan, Hari 2 Hamengku Buwono*, p. 28.

Dorojatun Becomes Sultan

169. Kutoyo, op. cit., p. 99, who adds that "The (Sultan's) statement certainly astonished the Dutch." They would hardly have been surprised that a Javanese Sultan described himself as Javanese.
170. Some Indonesian sources even add one word and quote this sentence as reading, "although I have had an extensive Western upbringing, I am and remain above all a Javanese (Indonesian)". For example, the Sultan's own brother Prince Prabuningrat, in *TUR*, p. 169.
171. *TUR*, p. 53.
172. Echols and Shadily, *Kamus Indonesia Inggeris*, 3rd ed., p. 395.
173. He later claimed that the "humiliating" conditions of the political contract were one cause of his nationalistic feelings. Van Kaam, "Een Vorstelijke rebel, Nederlands vergissing van 35 jaar geleden" [Princely Rebel, a Dutch Mistake of 35 Years Ago], *Vu* magazine, NIOD 081591, Natijd lists, p. 109.
174. *De Locomotief*, 18 March 1940, op. cit.
175. *Kraton Jogja*, op. cit., p. 103.
176. Westerkamp, p. 39, adding that he ensured that the coronation ceremonies were relatively modest.
177. See the renewed call for a Bale Agung in *Sedya Tama* of 18 November 1940, in *IPO* 47/4, p. 1107.
178. Article by "Andaja" in *Hidup*, 29 April 1949, MvD/CAD, NEFIS 1949, Bundle AA 21.
179. Ricklefs, op. cit., p. 163.
180. Department of Colonies report of 5 October 1939, quoted in Kwantes, *De Ontwikkeling van de Nationalistische Beweging in Nederlandsch Indie* [The Development of the Nationalist Movement in the Netherlands Indies], pp. 695–96.
181. Ibid.
182. C. Brown, *Short History of Indonesia*, p. 137.
183. Abeyasekere, *One Hand Clapping*, p. 54.
184. Sutherland, op. cit., p. 139.
185. Abeyasekere, p. 54.
186. Ibid., p. 55.
187. *IPO*, reported in inter alia *Tjaja Timoer* of 9 December 1940, p. 705.
188. Kahin, *Nationalism and Revolution*, p. 98.
189. *Djokja Solo*, p. 59.
190. Larson, p. 450.
191. *Djokja Solo*, p. 59.
192. Ibid., pp. 60–61.
193. Abeyasekere, op. cit., p. 67.
194. Sutherland, op. cit., p. 138.
195. *IPO* 17/41 of April 1941, p. 621.

196. *IPO* 17/41, ibid.
197. Ibid., p. 623, report in *Pewarta Umum* of 17 May 1941.
198. Abeyasekere, op. cit., ibid.
199. Larson concluded that the Mangkunegoro's prestige with his subjects was probably rather low at this time — Larson, p. 460.
200. Purwokusumo, *Kasultanan Yogyakarta*, op. cit., p. 68.

4

THE JAPANESE OCCUPATION

After a remarkably brief campaign during February to March 1942, the Japanese occupied virtually all of modern-day Indonesia. The biggest shock for the Allies had been the fall of the "impregnable fortress" of Singapore in mid-February 1942. From that point on, the Dutch knew that Java was gravely threatened and that they could lose their entire colony. Indeed, some already thought that their situation was hopeless.[1] They had already lost most of their naval forces in the Java Sea action.[2]

Hamengku Buwono, in what seems to have been his first ever radio address to his subjects,[3] admitted the seriousness of the situation "although it is in no sense hopeless". He advised the people of Yogyakarta to ignore stories that the enemy could not possibly reach Java, and called for a "realistic" attitude. The people should take appropriate security measures and follow the instructions of relevant official agencies, such as the Red Cross. He added that he had no wish to spread alarm, but needed to point out the gravity of the situation.

In their feverish preparations to defend Java, the Dutch colonial leaders quickly concluded that comprehensive defence of the island was impossible with the forces at their disposal.[4] The naval commander, Admiral Helfrich, contended that the main naval base, Surabaya, above all should be held, but the army commanders favoured West Java for the main troop concentration. Eventually the Governor General decided on 22 February to concentrate his forces in both East and West Java, and that "only Central Java should be largely denuded of forces, although that was also regarded as risky because of possible unrest in the princely states".[5] The relevant division Commander, Major General Cox, protested "because of the unfortunate effect on the Javanese princes and the people ... this means no less than a useless end to the so fruitful three hundred years of Netherlands Government".[6]

The Java princes were probably not informed of Dutch strategic planning, but the absence of Dutch defenders around Yogyakarta must have been evident to everyone.[7] Therefore, Hamengku Buwono was aware that the Dutch had abandoned Yogyakarta to the Japanese; and General Cox may well have been right in his assessment of the effect on the attitude of this particular Javanese prince.

The Dutch authorities offered the four rulers the opportunity to leave their principalities and seek safety under Dutch protection. According to Dutch records, the rulers were asked to join the Governor General in either Batavia or wherever else he might take refuge, probably Bandung. The Dutch believed rather naively that the Japanese would respect the Governor General's status, and that the princes would be safer with him. The Sunan of Solo was prepared to entertain the notion but Hamengku Buwono declined, saying that his place in times of crisis was with his people.[8] This was probably his first opportunity to exercise his own untrammelled political judgment, and to demonstrate his fitness to be Sultan.

Hamengku Buwono himself gives a different version. He says that the four princes were invited to flee to Australia (*not* Bandung) with Dutch officials, and that he and the others refused. He even adds that the Dutch had plans to abduct him and take him forcibly to Australia as a "hostage".[9] This testimony has to be taken seriously because it comes from the principal figure himself, and he repeated this claim in the 1986 *Asiaweek* interview, adding that the Dutch told him he should obey because he was an honorary general in the KNIL; he claimed further that an official called Westerhoff had been sent to "kidnap" him.[10] In his public statement reported in *Tempo* in the same year,[11] he repeated the kidnapping claim, adding that the plan miscarried because of the rapidity of the Japanese advance.

However, the kidnap claim raises many questions, e.g., why would the Dutch do this? Would they abduct only Hamengku Buwono? It is likely that the Dutch authorities were sincerely groping for ways of ensuring the local rulers' safety. It is also imaginable that they would see benefits in having tame local rulers ready to hand when and if they were able to reclaim their colony, but it is less credible that they would take them away by force. But whichever version of events one believes, the essential point was that Hamengku Buwono made a conscious decision to stay in Yogyakarta and face whatever risks emerged.

Public opinion in the Indies was confused. Leftish intellectuals, notably Hatta, Syahrir, and Amir Syarifuddin, regarded the new occupiers as fascists; but many were influenced by the popular Joyoboyo myths and thought that the Japanese were the "yellow men" who, the legend had it, would occupy Java for the time it would take for a maize plant to ripen, after which Java (or Indonesia) would gain its freedom.[12] On 5 March, as the Japanese attack was nearing its final stage, the Dutch Commander General ter Poorten admitted to two allied officers "that guerrilla warfare [against the Japanese] would be impossible because of the great hostility of the Indonesians towards the Dutch".[13]

In Yogyakarta, Indonesian nationalists were cordial towards the Japanese. In 1939, the Dutch Governor had reported that local leaders, such as "Mr Sumardi, Dr Sukiman, Wali Al Fatah and Ki Ajar [sic] Dewantoro, are positively disposed towards Japan, which they regard as the foremost Eastern nation."[14] He added that no Japanese had any contact with the Yogyakarta kraton.[15]

As the Japanese advanced, looting and anti-Chinese riots and robbery occurred in several locations on Java.[16] Yogyakarta suffered less than other cities, although the Dutch social club[17] in the Vereeniging building next to the Governor's palace, a bicycle shop, and several Europeans' houses were plundered, and some Europeans gathered in panic at the home of the Assistant Resident. Several thousand locals surrounded the house, but the Governor obtained the agreement of the incoming Japanese commander to employ armed police to disperse them.[18]

Early on 5 March, the Governor had received word that the scorched earth policy which had been applied elsewhere would not apply in Yogyakarta, and the city would not be defended.[19] When the first Japanese group arrived in Yogyakarta that evening,[20] the Governor asked them whether the Japanese would apply "international occupation law"; the answer was no, only Japanese military law would be in force.[21] The Japanese general[22] arrived later to the cheers of the many onlookers. Japanese troops were received by cheering crowds waving red and white flags when they entered Yogyakarta in some numbers the next day.[23] Initially they made few changes, leaving the Governor to run the principality.

OCCUPATION

The occupation of the Indies lasted from March 1942 until August 1945. Although the Japanese were often welcomed, their brutal and tactless behaviour and above all the privations to which they subjected the people as the war turned against them, led to widespread hatred by the end of the period.[24] Their attitude to the peoples of the occupied countries has been described as "at best paternal",[25] and as "arrogantly exhibiting a racial superiority".[26] Soon after their arrival, they scotched notions of immediate independence among the wilder nationalists.[27] Nevertheless, they released prominent nationalists from jail and sought their cooperation. From late 1942, Sukarno, Hatta and others were given positions of importance in various new organizations like the Hatta Kikan, the Putera, and so forth. Sukarno in particular took advantage of the new circumstances to establish himself as the most prominent indigenous leader, the man most likely to lead Indonesia to independence when it came.

The Japanese period made enormous differences to Indonesian life. Indonesians had seen haughty Dutch officials taken into captivity; they had seen Allied soldiers surrender virtually without a fight. They became used to hearing of the need to extirpate Western colonialism from Asia; to hearing the Allies described as the "enemy" and to "our troops" winning victories, and to the need to exert all efforts until "final victory" was won under Japanese leadership.[28] Strong condemnations of the Dutch era, Dutch governmental practices, and Dutch attitudes to Indonesians became the norm. Indonesian officials gained self-confidence as they moved into positions previously held by Dutchmen, and found that they could perform their duties competently.[29] In Yogyakarta, more citizens began to wear traditional Javanese dress as a means of proclaiming pride in their identity.[30] Above all, as Abeyasekere notes, "The Japanese had opened a Pandora's box by politicising new groups in society."[31] The Japanese increasingly tempted the Indonesians with the possibility of political independence, but this remained in the indefinite future until late 1944.

The new situation presented many challenges to a young Sultan. He had little choice other than to cooperate with the new conquerors, although by his own account he never trusted their promises.[32] It soon became evident that the Japanese would brook no opposition, and collaboration was the only practical approach.³³ Hamengku Buwono and the Sunan quickly issued statements offering their cooperation to the occupying forces and thanking Japan for freeing them from the Dutch.³⁴

In the first six weeks, the occupation authorities used Governor Adam to administer Yogyakarta. Adam called for calm, criticized the unruly behaviour of some locals, warned of firm action against any further disturbances, and banned street gatherings.³⁵ At the same time, the Patih announced that the Sultan had toured the city, that he was pleased that panic had not broken out when Japanese troops arrived, condemned the disturbances "at the Vereeniging building and elsewhere", and promised speedy punishment for malefactors.³⁶

A series of public notices appeared from the Governor while the Sultan was also active. As the principality was returning to calm if not normality, at the Governor's request,³⁷ Hamengku Buwono and the Patih visited Bantul on 11 March, Kulonprogo on 12 March, Gunung Kidul on 13 March, and Yogyakarta city on 14 March.³⁸ The Sultan familiarized himself with the security situation in the regencies, the reaction of the population to recent events, and the availability of foodstuffs and changes in economic circumstances.³⁹ He concluded that the public remained calm and undisturbed by the war. Some war damage was visible at Maguwo airport and the military barracks at Wonocatur.⁴⁰

Early evidence of Japanese ruthlessness emerged when three young Dutchmen, who had left their camps on an unauthorized family visit, were recaptured and immediately executed.⁴¹ All in Yogyakarta now knew that defiance of the Japanese was a perilous undertaking.

Relations with the Japanese

Both before and during the war, Japanese propaganda strongly emphasized pan-Asianism through such slogans as "Asia for the Asians", and succeeded in attracting a modicum of public sympathy in the Indies. The propaganda contained more than a little racial prejudice, but the prejudice was anti-Western and anti-European, so that it had some appeal to Indonesians, and the assumption that the Japanese had a right to dominate Asia was not quite so evident.⁴²

Japanese policy was initially ambiguous about the future of the principalities. In the first months the Japanese military government seriously considered abolishing them, although the four rulers received early assurances that the Japanese would protect their positions. In mid-March, senior members of the occupying forces (General Harada[43] and Colonel Nakayama)[44] visited Solo and presumably also Yogyakarta, to advise the princes that the system would continue more or less as under the Dutch administration.[45] Nakayama announced that the principalities would continue to be administered separately from Central Java province. The Badan Pengawas Kerajaan (BPK, or Bureau for Princely Territories) was established,[46] headed by a senior official (Kohri), with two deputies, S. Yoshigawa for Yogyakarta and H. Funabiki for Solo.[47] It appears that the latter two officials were based in the principalities, while Kohri may have been based in Jakarta.[48] They met the Sultan and Pakualam on 6 April, and the two Solo princes the next day.[49]

Despite the assurances made at the time, well-founded apprehension persisted in the principalities about Japanese intentions. Responding to this unease, the senior civilian official Miyoshi Shunkichiro visited Solo and Yogyakarta, met senior officials, and even studied the former Dutch political contracts.[50] Remarkably, he prepared two contradictory reports for Tokyo, one arguing for retention of the principalities and the other advocating abolition. Around this time, Col Nakayama returned from a meeting of the Southern Army command in Singapore, which strongly favoured retention of the principalities. After further correspondence between Jakarta, Singapore, and Tokyo, this was the ultimate decision.[51] Thus, like the Dutch the Japanese opted for "indirect" rule in Java and established correct relations with the Javanese princes.[52] On 1 August 1942, they formally recognized Hamengku Buwono as *Koo* (i.e., prince) of the Yogyakarta *kooti* (i.e., princely region).[53]

The other three princes were also confirmed as koos, causing surprise because the title of Koo seemed to confer equality on all four princes, whereas it had been generally recognized that the Sunan and the Sultan were the more senior.[54] But the installations occurred roughly in order of presumed seniority — the Sunan on 31 July, the Sultan on 1 August and the other two several weeks later.[55]

The Sunan, Pakubuwono XI, was recognized as *primus inter pares* among the four, although Mangkunegoro VII had held his position the longest. Pakubuwono had been in his position for slightly longer than Hamengku Buwono and was considerably older.[56] Pakualam VIII had become head of the Pakualaman house on 12 April 1937 following the death of his father,[57] three years before Hamengku Buwono became Sultan;

although the Pakualam was some years older, the two men established a harmonious and lifelong personal and political relationship.

The Sunan spoke for the four princes on the most important official event of all, the visit to Batavia by Prime Minister Tojo in July 1943. In the visit to the Commander-in-Chief in Batavia in December 1943, the Sunan spoke for himself and the Mangkunegoro, and the Sultan spoke for himself and the Pakualam.[58] In September 1944, the Sunan being ill, Hamengku Buwono spoke on behalf of the four princes at a further meeting with the Commander-in-Chief in Jakarta, expressing their appreciation of the promise of independence which had just been announced by Prime Minister Koiso.[59] During a further visit in April 1945, the role of spokesperson reverted to the Sunan.[60] After the death of Pakubuwono XI, the newly installed young Sunan (formerly Suryo Guritno) assumed his father's leading role in early August 1945, when the princes visited the Commander-in-Chief for the last time.[61]

The negotiation of the princes' new status was much less elaborate than in Dutch times. The official documents appointing the Koos appeared in the form of an order from the military government, supplemented by an amplifying instruction from the head of the military administration; and it is not clear whether any formal contract, as such, was ever signed by the Koos. The one-page order of 1 August by Commander in Chief Imamura records the appointment of Hamengku Buwono, specifies that the Kooti's territory is the same as that of the former Sultanate and that the Koo retains all his former powers, decrees that the Koo has the responsibility to administer the Kooti in the interests of its general prosperity, and establishes the Office of Sultanate Affairs (Kooti zimukyoku).[62]

A supplementary instruction records the Commander-in-Chief's power to appoint or dismiss the Koo and to appoint a *Somutyokan* (equivalent to the Dutch-era Patih),[63] stipulates that Military Government laws apply unless decreed otherwise, disbands the Sultanate army, permits the (re)formation of a palace guard but only with the agreement of the Office of Sultanate Affairs, and specifies that the latter (not the Sultan and not the *Somutyokan*) will control the police force.[64] The Kooti's draft budget had to be cleared with the Office of Sultanate Affairs before being made public.[65]

The documents appointing the Sunan are virtually identical to these,[66] although the budget clause specifies that the Sunan must "keep a reduced, sound budget by economising on expenditure as much as possible",[67] a much stronger formulation than the clause in the Sultan's document.

Evidently the Japanese had become aware of the Sunanate's reputation for lavish expenditure.

Not all of the decrees appointing the koos seem to be available, but they apparently took much the same form in each Kooti.[68] The supplementary instruction appointing the Mangkunegoro-Koo is almost identical to the Yogyakarta instruction, but with an important reference to the disbandment of the Mangkunegaran Legion,[69] a military body which had existed since the days of Governor Daendels in the early nineteenth century. The reference to the budget resembles the corresponding provision in the Sultan's document.[70] The princes knew that the Japanese, unlike the Dutch, would not have tolerated any protracted negotiations.

Relations between the four Javanese princes and the Japanese occupiers during the occupation are an obscure subject. Notwithstanding the probably self-serving anthropological theories heard occasionally in Japan in the 1930s to the effect that Japanese and other Asians were the "same race",[71] awkwardness in protocol terms could be expected in relations between prominent Indonesians and Japanese because of the Japanese assumption of racial superiority.[72] This was most clearly seen in the fact that apparently during the occupation, no Indonesian was ever placed in a position of seniority over any Japanese. A further implication of the Japanese approach was that no Indonesian could have higher social standing than any Japanese.[73] Even distinguished Indonesians were mistreated at times by relatively junior Japanese military officers.[74] How did this apply to relations between the Javanese princes and Japanese officials in the principalities? Some ambiguity was inevitable, because if Japanese were automatically superior to any indigene of the archipelago, then any Japanese outranked even the princes of Java. This implication was not explicitly stated by either side.

Throughout the occupation, the Japanese apparently complied with the Sultan's request that he be consulted whenever any demands were made on the Yogyakarta people.[75] He is also supposed to have ordered the Patih to take no important action without consultation with him,[76] and to have insisted that the Patih work from the kraton and not from his office in the Kepatihan building.[77] Hamengku Buwono also claimed that he was in constant conflict with Japanese authorities during the occupation.[78] In one interview, he said

> Joyoboyo made a prophesy that people from the north with short legs would come and stay as long as the age of maize. The grain ripens in

three months but the plant lives three years. I believed the prediction, so my dealings with the Japanese were businesslike [sic]. Many times they asked for more cooperation. They wanted rice and cattle and teak wood. I tried to lessen the people's burden. I only gave part of what they asked. They knew. They called me to Jakarta and told me to be more flexible, more helpful. I remained silent.[79]

Some secondary sources also indicate that he succeeded in keeping the Japanese at arm's length, supposedly unlike the two rulers in Solo.[80] A constant turnover of senior Japanese officials, especially the residents, supposedly arose from these tensions with the Sultan.[81] He was said to have rejected Japanese requests that his statements include the common punning slogan of the time — *Amerika kita strika dan Inggeris kita linggis*. ("We will iron out America and gouge out England.")[82]

A little independent evidence exists for some of these assertions: for example, former Governor Adam recorded that early in the occupation, one Japanese official from Semarang so offended the Sultan that he refused to receive him, a bold action at a time when reactions by Japanese to a loss of face were unknown and unpredictable.[83] None of Hamengku Buwono's statements indeed contain the well-known slogan mentioned above, which he may have felt was beneath his dignity. But it is unclear whether in fact senior Japanese officials constantly changed over as claimed. One key official, Resident Yamauchi, is recorded as occupying his position from August 1942 until August 1944, exactly two-thirds of the period that Hamengku Buwono was Yogyakarta-Koo.[84]

A potentially serious incident occurred early on, when local Japanese officials demanded a Javanese dance performance for a senior Japanese officer who was visiting very soon. Prabuningrat could not comply with this request because of lack of notice. He was interrogated about this refusal by Colonel Sato of the Kempeitai for four hours[85] before being released. Good relations were restored when — with more adequate notice — the visitor attended a traditional dance performance by the palace's best dancers.[86]

On the other hand, some coolness also existed between the Mangkunegoro and the Japanese. The Mangkunegoro retained a reputation for being pro-Dutch, and did what he could to help interned Dutch families.[87] Japanese officers were also said to have required the Mangkunegoro to bow first before they reciprocated.[88] The daughter of the former Dutch police chief in Solo was even arrested in November 1942 on suspicion of plotting with the Mangkunegoro against the Japanese.[89]

At first, the Japanese interned members of the Mangkunegaran Legion and the small Pakualaman Legion, but in due course they were released and both legions were abolished.[90] This accorded with the initial Japanese reluctance to allow any Indonesians to bear arms, a reluctance only partly overcome with the formation of the Peta in 1943.

One difference between Solo and Yogyakarta in the first weeks of occupation was the more active involvement in day-to-day administration of local officials, especially Governor Adam and the Patih Danurejo, who announced and implemented most of the military government's decrees. In Solo on the other hand, Japanese officials apparently announced their decrees themselves over Solo radio. Newspapers recommenced publication more quickly in Yogyakarta than in Solo.[91] These differences may indicate the emergence of a quick understanding between Hamengku Buwono and the Japanese authorities, although some credit may go to Governor Adam, who noted that the local military authorities were initially "not unpleasant" to deal with.[92] The atmosphere in Yogyakarta was better because of the comparatively peaceful commencement of the occupation there.

Apart from day-to-day contacts with Japanese officials in Yogyakarta, the princes occasionally called on the Commander-in-Chief in Batavia, and their representatives served on the Central Advisory Council (*Chuo Sangi-in*) which was established in 1943. One of Hamengku Buwono's representatives on that body was his brother Puruboyo,[93] and it was thus natural that Puruboyo would later serve on the body for the preparation of Indonesian independence (BPUPKI) in 1945.

The continued operations of Dutch officials under Japanese direction did not last long. In late March the governors of Solo and Yogyakarta were both downgraded from Governor to Resident without any official explanation.[94] This measure may have related to the Japanese decision to abolish the provinces and use the residencies as the main administrative unit.[95] Then on 21 April, most senior colonial officials across Java, including Governor Adam, were suddenly interned, amid accusations of abusing Japanese "goodwill".[96] Perhaps some plot had been discovered, but no further details about the reasons were given. Since the measure applied to most of Java, it cannot have arisen from events in Yogyakarta, although it is known that a senior Javanese official in the city had been given a large sum of money by the prominent colonial official Charles van de Plas for planned underground activities, which apparently led to nothing.[97]

The senior Dutch officials in Yogyakarta were paraded around town in the back of a truck, as a final humiliation before being interned in the Fort Vredenburg barracks.[98] From this time, the presence and influence of Dutch functionaries in Yogyakarta vanished from the principality after a colonial period of nearly two hundred years, only to emerge again briefly six years later during the Revolution.

Japanese Regulations

One of the assumptions of Japanese military rule was that the wartime economy could best be managed by constant regulation, especially of prices but also of trade. The proclivity to regulate everything was evident quite early, but became more marked as wartime shortages worsened. As early as mid-March 1942, rice rationing was introduced in the major cities, and a little later minimum purchase prices were set, to overcome the disruption caused by the war to normal credit arrangements and distribution patterns in the middle of the harvest season.[99] A further drastic measure was taken in Yogyakarta in July 1942, when the export of various commodities from the principality was banned.[100] Price controls were imposed on rents and major food commodities.[101] The intention of these measures was to check inflation and to ensure the availability of important commodities within the principality. Among unintended effects were the encouragement of the black market and cross-border smuggling, the distortion of market signals, and in particular the discouragement of local production of these commodities through the closing-off of available markets. If anything, the measures promoted inflation by creating local shortages.

The de facto autonomy given to the residencies resulted inter alia in the creation of a series of satrapies where individual residents issued their own economic regulations, ignoring the interests of neighbouring areas.[102] The distribution of important foodstuffs was more and more carefully controlled and rationed on a regional basis. In early August 1942, restrictions were placed on the import of rice into Yogyakarta.[103] By September 1943, announcements were appearing about the controlled distribution of rice to the thirteen subdistrict offices in Yogyakarta city.[104] This kind of effort was of course quite inadequate for the needs of the time.

Monetary policy during the occupation led to huge increases in money supply and contributed to runaway inflation, especially after the decision to permit the government bank to issue banknotes in April 1943.[105] Only in the 1960s were Indonesians again to experience inflation of this magnitude. For those, including Hamengku Buwono, who realized that the war was steadily going against Japan, the reasons for the already widespread[106] hoarding of Indies guilders would have been reinforced.

Even leading nationalists like Muhammad Hatta sympathized with the Japanese push for tight central controls, especially in the rice economy.[107] Few indigenous advisers had direct experience of local administration, almost all wished to eliminate the role of Chinese middlemen, but they had little grasp of the adverse effects in the villages of the regulatory straitjacket imposed by the Japanese and implemented by local Indonesian officials, many of them corrupt, high-handed and autocratic. By early 1945 signs of uneasiness were emerging about the rigid controls on commerce, for example in the recommendation by the Supreme Advisory Council that trade in strategic goods be liberalized between residencies.[108]

The drought of 1944 and government demands for one-third of the rice crop severely affected the poorer areas across Java. Around Solo, deaths from malnutrition were reported from the impoverished districts of Wonogiri, Karanganyar, and Boyolali. Many villagers sold all available property such as cattle, land and jewellery to obtain food.[109] The burdens on the peasantry and especially the landless peasantry became more and more unbearable; and by late 1944 there were reports of farmers in Java tilling the fields naked because of lack of clothing, and people dying of hunger by the roadside. In the latter stages of the occupation, "never before was there so much tension, so much want of everything, so much fear".[110]

The scanty available evidence does not permit firm conclusions about Yogyakarta's experience compared with other regions. Some informants reported extensive hardships, "having to eat banana [tree] trunks, to wear rags or rice sacks instead of cotton clothes, and having to make sandals out of old tyres".[111] Selosumarjan, as a local government official in Kulon Progo to the west of Yogyakarta city, recounts that almost all inhabitants of the region, including senior officials, had meagre supplies of clothing, but that he saw no signs of the gross suffering reported elsewhere, and that despite the widespread scarcities, no one actually died of hunger.[112] A Eurasian who lived outside Yogyakarta reports seeing no signs of starvation among the people.[113] On the other hand, a witness in Yogyakarta city saw increasing numbers of beggars near the end of the occupation, and even the circulation each evening of a cart which picked up the corpses of the dead.[114]

SULTAN'S ROLE

Public Works — The Mataram Canal

An important public works project was completed during the Japanese period, the Mataram Canal[115] linking the Kulon Progo and Garo rivers in the mountains and proceeding thirty kilometres to Yogyakarta city. This was to provide irrigation for up to 10,000 hectares of farming land and fresh water to the city, and was also intended to assist with flood alleviation. Hamengku Buwono and the Pakualam visited Kulon Progo in July 1944, inspecting existing irrigation works and the region through which the new canal would run, from the mountains to the Kulon Progo estuary. The region included the Godean area and Kemusuh village, the place of origin of a young Peta recruit, Suharto, who at the time was in Bogor on a training course.[116] The next week, the two princes attended the formal inauguration of the project, at which Hamengku Buwono thanked the Japanese administration for providing a million guilders for the enterprise.[117]

The propaganda for the canal, described as "the largest water supply project in Java",[118] claimed that although in the Dutch period irrigation and waterworks were aimed at providing water for Dutch-owned industry, the Mataram canal would supply water for the ordinary people.[119] This was partly true in that many irrigation works in the Dutch period had benefited large Dutch-owned enterprises; but it was also a rationalization of the collapse of the sugar industry during the period.[120] Any decline in the sugar industry meant a slump in the Sultan's private income, because he gained much more rental from sugar companies than from rice farmers.[121] He inspected the new canal on its completion in July 1945, and received briefings from the chief engineers.[122] His role in promoting the project later drew rare specific praise from the Japanese Resident.[123]

The Romusha Question

Under the Japanese *romusha* programme that commenced in October 1943, hundreds of thousands of labourers were recruited and sent away from their home areas, many out of Indonesia, to work under miserable conditions on Japanese construction projects, including the Burma–Siam railway. The pay was poor, the treatment was harsh, and many labourers died.[124] Sato's estimate is that perhaps as many as ten million men were recruited for at least temporary romusha work within the Indies (much higher than some previous estimates).[125] Of these, about 160,000 romusha were sent out of Indonesia and about 135,000 returned, an attrition rate of about 15 per cent (much lower than some previous estimates, but still a grim statistic).[126]

Many accounts of Hamengku Buwono's life[127] assert that he succeeded in limiting the numbers of romusha sent out of Yogyakarta, by arguing that he needed the maximum amount of labour for his own ambitious programme of public works, especially the Mataram canal. His interest in public works and irrigation projects is attested,[128] but unfortunately the evidence provides little support for the claimed connection with the romusha programme. Romusha labour was indeed employed on the Mataram canal and other public works programmes, and romusha working on the project were not, perforce, employed elsewhere.[129] But it is questionable whether appreciably fewer romusha were sent from Yogyakarta compared with other regions. Available figures are conflicting and probably unreliable, but one official document appears to indicate that more romushas were actually recruited and sent away from Yogyakarta in 1944 than were requested. This boasts that 17,000 men were sought in that year but that the local authorities were able to round up 18,567.[130]

This was a small number compared with the total numbers of romushas recruited across Java. But it seems unnecessary to make any link between the Mataram canal and the romusha programme; the canal was an important and enduring achievement, and to the extent that Hamengku Buwono deserves credit for it, he should receive the credit, without excessive additional claims being made. The argument that numbers sent away from Yogyakarta were much lower than they would have been might be bolstered if unusually large numbers were used on the Mataram project, but the available sources do not provide any workforce figures. If there was such an effect, it seems to have been at best a minor one.

The romusha question remains a contentious issue in assessing the reputation of all Indonesian leaders of the period. Debates have usually centred on the role of Sukarno, in publicly encouraging thousands of youths to join the programme, which promised regular work and pay to many who otherwise had little prospect of either, but which proved a cruel deception. Challenged later about this, Sukarno argued that he helped (in some undefined way) to alleviate the worst effects of the programme, and that another leader would have been less attuned to the needs of the people involved.[131] Critics of Sukarno regularly drew attention to this emotive subject in later years.[132]

Hamengku Buwono seems to have had no direct public role in encouraging romusha recruitment. His visit to Yogyakarta romushas in West Java, described below, demonstrates some concern for their welfare. But the argument that he moderated the effects of the programme by keeping romusha workers in Yogyakarta rather than allowing them to be sent outside might be seen as a rationalization, albeit a stronger one, along the lines of Sukarno's argument. That such arguments were necessary reveals the sensitivity of the issue, although the obvious counterargument is that Indonesian leaders could do little in the face of ruthless Japanese determination to recruit the maximum workforce possible.

In some localities, officials actively undermined Japanese recruitment efforts, apparently independently rather than by instruction from Hamengku Buwono. Selosumarjan[133] recounts the acuteness of the dilemma faced by local officials at the time. Sub-district chiefs (*panewu*s) like himself were responsible for recruiting romusha, and he was aware from widespread rumours that those who failed to do so could be severely punished by the Kempeitai.[134] On the other hand, the rumours had it that sending young men to the programme would condemn them to mistreatment, low pay and possibly even death. He outlined the dilemma frankly to the local youth, and advised them to enlist with the romusha office in Yogyakarta, but then to vanish and if possible stay quietly with relatives outside their home area.[135] He records that, despite his fears, no Japanese troops ever visited his sub-district to seek out the missing romusha. After the war, several young men told him that they had successfully followed his advice.[136] A strategy of this kind, in what must have been a no-right-answers environment, was probably of limited practical utility, because the presence of youths in any numbers outside their home areas would have been nearly impossible to conceal.

A perhaps more plausible contention than the claim about the romusha programme is that Hamengku Buwono deceived the Japanese by presenting misleading economic statistics which (over)emphasized Yogyakarta's poverty, thereby helping to limit their demands for supplies and labour.[137] The method apparently involved minimizing statistics of rice production, arguing that Yogyakarta ran constant food deficits, and that the quantity of arable land was very small. He therefore sought funds for irrigation projects, which he succeeded in obtaining, as we have seen. Selosumarjan too claimed to have successfully minimized food production figures for his remote sub-district in his reports to the Japanese authorities.[138]

Nevertheless, doubts must also arise about some of these claims. It would have taken only one disgruntled local official to report the deception to the Japanese for the young Sultan to be in serious trouble. Japanese officials were notoriously sensitive about being made fools of, and the risk was a real one. The rank of Sultan did not always convey immunity, as the example of the Mangkunegoro perhaps showed, not to mention the arrest of twelve sultans in West Kalimantan during September 1943 to early 1944, charged with anti-Japanese plotting.[139] It is rather more believable that Hamengku Buwono and his officials constantly used available factual and unfalsified information about Yogyakarta's very real poverty as an argument against excessive demands being made on Yogyakarta's resources. The actual statistics for food production were presumably depressing enough (and vague and uncertain enough) without the need to falsify them.

Moreover, one of the few available factual indicators, the figure for rice delivery to the military government, does not support the notion that the Yogyakarta region performed markedly worse than other regions. In 1944, a year of desperate drought across Java, Yogyakarta delivered 90 per cent of its government-determined quota of rice; Solo actually delivered 104 per cent,[140] though once again we must guard against excessive faith in the reliability of the figures.

Perhaps surprisingly if we bear in mind his later involvement in defence matters, Hamengku Buwono seems to have had few direct links with the military organizations formed by the Japanese. Although several high-ranking princes from Solo (notably Jatikusumo) joined the Peta when it was formed in 1943, no senior member of the Yogyakarta kraton appears to have done so. Hamengku Buwono made little comment initially about the Peta, but he fulsomely praised the morale and resolution of local Peta and Seinendan (army youth auxiliary) recruits during his tour of East Java in January 1944.[141] In March 1944 he noted approvingly the creation and activities of the Peta, the Keibodan (auxiliary police), and the Seinendan.[142] In September 1944, commemorating the Peta's first anniversary, he remarked that "history has repeatedly shown that a nation which lacks strong defence forces will certainly not be able to preserve its independence",[143] with the implication that the "nation's" defence forces could or should be used to restore its independence, leaving open against whom the effort might be made.

The Pakualam

It is from the occupation that Hamengku Buwono's close relationship with Pakualam VIII can be dated. The two princes formed Yogyakarta-wide branches of major organizations such as the Putera and the Jawa Hokokai (Java Service Association) rather than forming separate branches in each of the two principalities,[144] and measures were taken to foster closer relations between the Yogyakarta bureaucracy and the Pakualaman.[145] The two Koos inspected public works projects such as the Mataram Canal as well as light industry and animal husbandry facilities in the Yogyakarta area.[146] They also travelled together around Java late in the occupation.

Suryodilogo, described as "very ambitious" in a Dutch official report,[147] succeeded his father Pakualam VII in 1937, supported Hamengku Buwono and the Republic during the Revolution, stood in for the Sultan for many years as Deputy Governor of the Yogyakarta Special Region, became Governor (or Acting Governor) himself after Hamengku Buwono's death, and survived long enough to join Hamengku Buwono X in calling for Suharto to step down in 1998. He has received minimal coverage in the history books, and is usually regarded as no more than Hamengku Buwono's cipher, with no ideas or programmes of his own.[148] He bears much responsibility for allowing the Yogyakarta administration to decline from its status in the Revolution as the centre of local government reform to a static backwater in the 1970s.[149] But he had sufficient political acumen to follow and support Hamengku Buwono all along the line.[150] He deserves at least some credit for resisting Dutch blandishments in 1949. Pakualam VIII is a remarkable example of political survival, and it is hard to believe that the result was a matter of pure luck. Nevertheless, his reputation, both political and personal, has always been dim, and unlike Hamengku Buwono, he never had a national political role.

Tours

As the occupation advanced, Hamengku Buwono gave more and more indications of wanting to be an activist Sultan. In early 1944 he toured his entire principality, an unprecedented operation for a Javanese prince. Over a period of several weeks, he and a selected group of officials visited village after village, sometimes on horseback, sometimes even on foot.[151] He made more visits to villages in May and July 1944 after *pamong praja* meetings,[152] and a further extensive tour in June 1945.[153] Around this time Hamengku Buwono first met and recruited to his personal staff an intelligent and capable young *panewu* called Selosumarjan, who became one of his closest associates and advisers for the next thirty years.[154]

In January 1944, the Sultan toured East Java, including Surabaya, Mojokerto, Mojopahit (the centre of the ancient Javanese kingdom), and Gresik, and visited famous grave sites such as the tombs of Sunan Giri and Syech Maulana Malik Ibrahim.[155] With the Pakualam he visited West Java in May, visiting ports and mines, meeting officials, and meeting Yogyakarta romusha who had been transferred there.[156] He again visited East Java, primarily Madiun and Kediri, in August, when with the Mataram Canal in mind, he inspected a major water supply and flood alleviation project.[157]

RELATIONS WITH THE NATIONALISTS

It is unclear when Hamengku Buwono first met Sukarno.[158] It appears to have been some time during 1943 when Sukarno was making one of his tours of Java in his role as head of Putera. The Sultan's uncle Suryodiningrat was the head of the local Putera branch.[159] The first contact was a very brief meeting in which introductions were effected but no substantive discussion took place.[160] In such modest fashion began a key relationship in Hamengku Buwono's political life. Although the two men were both Javanese, they had sharply differing backgrounds, family circumstances, political attitudes and personalities, as well as being of different generations. The Sultan was a "pure Javanese" from one of the oldest princely houses in Java. By contrast Sukarno was an outskirter, and although of the *priyayi* class, he was a half-Balinese from the comparative periphery of East Java.[161] Sukarno belonged to the first generation of Indonesian nationalists which had come of age, struggled, and suffered in the moderately hopeful 1920s and the grim 1930s, whereas Hamengku Buwono had been at school. In December 1930, when Sukarno was sentenced to four years jail, the Sultan was already safely in the Netherlands. Sukarno's attitudes and political beliefs were already widely advertised and celebrated, whereas the Sultan's few public statements had been bland, orthodox and probably little noticed outside Central Java.

Sukarno was a magnetic and confident public speaker, at home on the hustings,[162] as well as a writer of copious political tracts.[163] Up to this stage, Hamengku Buwono had received no opportunity to express his political views with any freedom, and although he was to prove a competent (if dull) public speaker, he could not — and made no attempt to — create the excitement which Sukarno could inspire. Sukarno was a famous rebel against the Dutch colonial system, whereas the Sultan had collaborated with the Dutch for two years before the Japanese arrived. They were very different in their attitudes to the enjoyment of pomp and luxury, towards women,[164] and even towards the education of their children.[165] The relationship was not a meeting of minds, but the two men were able to cooperate well, although normally at a distance, throughout the Revolution.

Sukarno is not on record with his opinion of the Sultan, but he probably felt some initial suspicion. The nationalist credentials of the Yogyakarta royal house were scanty, and references to the glorious Prince Diponegoro were only a reminder of the quiescence of the sultans since that time.[166] Sukarno would have reflected on the privileges enjoyed by Javanese princes and the luxury in which they lived, compared with the life of the ordinary Marhaens whose interests he represented. The Sultan was a newcomer to the nationalist movement, and the nationalists would have been uncertain whether his attitude was feigned, or forced on him by popular sentiment. Such suspicion would have been gradually dispelled, especially after the Republican government's move to Yogyakarta in January 1946.

Hamengku Buwono would have greatly respected Sukarno as the foremost nationalist leader, and must have recognized his charismatic hold on the masses. But the differences in their personal styles may have led him to doubt Sukarno's grasp of administrative realities. Might the Javanese prince have distrusted the flashy oratory of this popular demagogue, and wondered whether he had the sober persistence to run a modern state? These differences reflected some elements of the distinction between the "solidarity maker" and the "administrator" described by Feith.[167] But this possible source of conflict remained well in the background during the Revolution and only became starkly evident years later, in the 17 October 1952 affair.

Hamengku Buwono was probably more compatible with Mohammad Hatta, as both had received a European education and both were cautious and pragmatic by nature. But they were also separated by a social and ethnic gulf, as Hatta was Sumatran and the Sultan Javanese, and Hatta was wary of feudalism. The time of their first meeting is even less clear than that between the Sultan and Sukarno. Hatta chose Hamengku Buwono as his Minister of Defence in two successive cabinets of the period August 1949 to September 1950, and he would not have done this without a favourable assessment of the Sultan's capacities. Both men shared many of the features of the administrator type, in Feith's terms. Nevertheless, the Sultan's political stance must have been unclear to the nationalists during the Japanese period.

Although we have to exercise care in approaching this kind of evidence, one pointer to his attitude is his public statements during the Japanese occupation. Unlike the practice during the Dutch period, the Javanese princes were required to make frequent statements.[168] The statements always followed standard patterns, but the differences between them indicate that some measure of latitude existed.

Up until 1944, it was rare to find the word "Indonesia" in Hamengku Buwono's brief and orthodox speeches or published statements.[169] Rather more common was the term "Jawa" or "Jawa Baru" (New Java), a term favoured by the Japanese.[170] Until very late in the occupation, the Japanese were vague about both independence and what kind of entity might become independent. The term "Jawa Baru" left the suspicion that Java might become independent by itself if independence was to occur at all.[171] As we have seen in the early years of the nationalist movement, the idea of an independent Java had been quite current, although it was later overtaken.[172] During Prime Minister Tojo's visit in 1943, the Javanese princes did not mention "Indonesia" once in their welcoming speeches, while Sukarno did so ten times. Sukarno was prepared at times to run well ahead of Japanese policy,[173] but the Javanese princes were far more circumspect.

The terminology may have arisen among the Japanese merely as a matter of convenience because of the three-way administrative division of the Indies under the Japanese occupation. Quite different policies towards Indonesian nationalism were adopted in each part, and levels of political sophistication differed considerably from region to region.[174] The Japanese administrative divisions, whether deliberately or not, effectively cut off some groups of politically minded Indonesians from each other, even more than the Dutch had done.

Whatever the reasons, the relative absence of the word "Indonesia" in most of Hamengku Buwono's statements up to 1944 is curious, and does not provide evidence on his part of strong nationalist feeling, or at least strong Indonesia-oriented nationalist feeling. Had he been prepared to demonstrate his nationalism a la Sukarno, he could surely have used the word "Indonesia" more frequently without exciting Japanese reaction.[175] In his statements during this period, he was, like the other princes, concerned to be as inoffensive to the occupiers as possible, a politically prudent approach in the circumstances.

For the most part, his statements repeated all the orthodoxies of the Japanese period. He normally expressed thanks to the Military Government for whatever action it had recently taken, called for the people to demonstrate unity, and praised the resolution, bravery and skill of the Japanese armed forces. As the war turned against Japan, appeals for the people to make all sacrifices to defend Java to achieve "final victory" came to predominate.[176]

Hamengku Buwono sounded at times like a strong advocate of pan-Asian solidarity: "As long as the enemy's military forces are present in the region, the peoples of Asia will not know peace and security. Because the enemy's objective is solely to divide and rule the peoples of Asia, to weaken and arbitrarily oppress them, as shown by their wicked behaviour in ordering soldiers from Chungking, Africa and India to fight in the front lines as cannon fodder, so that they [the enemy] can flee and save themselves."[177] He described the Allies as "capitalists and imperialists" in the 1944 New Year speech.[178]

The forcefulness of these anti-colonial sentiments may reveal genuine feeling despite the requirement to say what the Japanese wanted. Although the evidence is thin, it is easy to believe that Hamengku Buwono held definite and perhaps even strong anti-colonial opinions by this time, both anti-Dutch and anti-Japanese. His consistent support for the Republic during the Revolution was not something which could have sprung fully armed from his head; it must have emerged from earlier experiences, awaiting only the appropriate time and circumstances to give it expression.

PREPARATIONS FOR INDEPENDENCE

In September 1944 Prime Minister Koiso publicly confirmed Japan's intention to grant independence to Indonesia, an undertaking met with delight by the nationalists. Although Japanese motives were transparently much more focussed on marshalling the maximum support for the war effort and much less on Indonesian political aspirations, previous undertakings had been given concrete form, and public display of nationalist symbols like the Indonesian flag and anthem was at last permitted.

A public meeting in the town square, attended by Hamengku Buwono, the Japanese Resident, the Pakualam and other dignitaries witnessed probably the first ever public raising of the Indonesian flag in Yogyakarta.[179] A crowd estimated at over 100,000, reportedly the largest public meeting ever seen in the city to that time, saw an aircraft scattering leaflets containing a message from "our Great Leader[180] Ir Sukarno" and heard speeches from a local Hokokai leader, from senior Kraton official KRT Notonegoro "representing the Indonesian community", and from leaders of the Chinese, Eurasian, Indian and Arab communities.

Nevertheless, the military government was very slow in fulfilling its promise, and the nationalists were extremely impatient by the time the membership of the Badan Penyelidik Usaha2 Persiapan Kemerdekaan Indonesia (BPUPKI, or Committee to Investigate Preparations for Indonesian Independence) was announced in April 1945.[181] It held its first meeting in Jakarta on 28 May 1945.[182] Prominent Yogyakarta personalities like Dr Sukiman Wiryosanjoyo, Ki Hajar Dewantoro, Sayuti Melik, Abdul Kahar Muzakkar and Ki Bagus Hadikusumo were members, as were two of the Sultan's brothers, Puruboyo and Bintoro. But the Yogyakarta representatives did not constitute a united bloc, still less a royalist bloc. Sukiman and Hadikusumo were Muslim politicians, whereas Sayuti Melik was a radical youth representative.[183] Another representative was Suryoamijoyo, the well-known Surakarta prince.[184]

The Javanese princely houses could not complain of a lack of opportunity to participate in the debates. Bintoro and his fellow Yogyakartan Ki Bagus Hadikusumo shared a desk immediately behind Sukarno and Mohammad Yamin and just in front of Mohammad Hatta, whereas Puruboyo's place was immediately in front of Haji Agus Salim.[185] But the princes played virtually no active role.[186]

The meeting was chaired by the respected but reactionary[187] Dr Raden Rajiman Wediodiningrat, who had been a court doctor at the Surakarta palace and also a prominent figure in Budi Utomo.[188] Reading the debates sixty years later, one is struck by the air of excitement and innovation, a feeling that anything was possible in the new circumstances, and that speakers were free to be politically creative about the boundaries and nature of the country. Mohammed Yamin for one dreamed of a single unified pan-Malay nation,[189] ignoring colonial boundaries.[190]

Of interest to the kratons was the first subject of debate, whether Indonesia would be a monarchy or a republic. The Japanese had apparently envisaged a Javanese or perhaps Indonesian monarchy, a concept fully in accordance with their own constitutional system, and had canvassed the possibility of placing the Sultan of Yogyakarta in that capacity.[191]

By mid-1945, although Hamengku Buwono was still quite young (only 33), he would have stood out among the four princes because succession in the two Solo houses had just occurred or was about to occur — the previous Mangkunegoro had died in 1944,[192] and around the time of the BPUPKI debates, the Sunan too had fallen ill, eventually dying in June 1945. Thus, in mid-1945, both Solo rulers were inexperienced young men in their twenties.[193] The other ruler, the Pakualam, headed much the smallest of the four principalities and could be ruled out on that basis. Hamengku Buwono was also the best qualified educationally. It was assumed that — given the demographic realities of the archipelago — any king of Indonesia would have to be Javanese.

A group of monarchists met in Magelang and agreed to propose the Sultan as the head of the new state,[194] and the idea was welcome to the Japanese and to a large segment of the local civil service.[195] Many local public servants, the conservative pamong praja who had spent the first part of their careers under the Dutch, might well have seen a new monarchy as a return to the reassuring predictability of the past. Curiously enough, Hamengku Buwono himself later denied ever having received approaches from the Japanese along these lines.[196]

But the monarchy option was quickly discarded. Kanahele notes that the multiplicity of royal houses in Indonesia had a dampening effect on the proposal, because no single ruler had wide recognition or acceptance.[197] Moreover, the princes from Yogyakarta and Solo did not speak up for monarchy in the BPUPKI. The task was left to the Eurasian representative P.F. Dahler from Semarang. Dahler had been born in Semarang in 1883 and was a prominent but maverick leader of the Eurasian community, having been a member of the Volksraad during 1929–30.[198] Dahler reminded his hearers that he had held and expressed his views for many years. Although he had previously been "100 per cent republican", he now believed that monarchy represented the "best pattern of human and religious progress in the world, because a king always represents God on earth".[199] Nevertheless, if the majority favoured a republic, he would not stand in the way.

Other delegates did not find this persuasive. Susanto believed that none of the current princely rulers could be sure of universal support.[200] Mohammed Yamin too pointed out the presence of "over 300" principalities in Indonesia and asserted that the forty-year-old nationalist movement had been based on republican principles.[201] The Yogyakartan Sukiman contended that a republic was more consistent with an Islamic state, which he favoured.[202] His fellow Yogyakarta Muslim leader Hadikusumo advocated a non-hereditary head of state chosen by the people through a basis of consensus.[203] The Yogyakarta delegates clearly had no intention of nominating their Sultan as a future king of Indonesia, and in fact no individual candidate was mentioned in the BPUPKI debates.

The vote decisively favoured a republic — fifty-five against six. Although the records do not reveal the identities of the six monarchists, we could assume that Dahler was one of them; the two Yogyakarta princes and the prince from Solo may have been three of the other five, but no firm evidence exists for this.

Indonesia would be a republic, but the status of the four Kootis was still unclear. In the princes' only contribution to the constitutional debates, Puruboyo argued for retention of the principalities, to avoid unsettling the population. Sukarno was doubtful, seeming to believe that the vote against monarchy had settled the matter, but after intervention by Hatta, it was decided to leave the principalities as they were.[204] Thus, the political future of the principalities and of Hamengku Buwono himself had passed a further test, and this vague decision opened the possibility that the future Indonesian Republic could encompass some kind of feudal entity.

DEVELOPMENTS IN YOGYAKARTA

Hamengku Buwono's power, at least in the early stages of the occupation, appears to have been nearly as circumscribed as under the Dutch. Executive power remained with Japanese colonial officials, assisted by the Patih and the Javanese bureaucracy. The Japanese functionaries of the time were, however, much less experienced than Dutch colonial officials, and they may therefore have been more reliant on local expertise.

One early decision taken by Hamengku Buwono in late July 1942 was to change the names of many local government instrumentalities from Dutch terms to Javanese (and *not* to Indonesian terms).[205] Another story, which is unconfirmed, is that the Sultan quickly changed most street names in Yogyakarta soon after the Japanese entry to the town, eliminating all Dutch-language names and forestalling any similar effort by the Japanese.[206]

Later in the occupation, Hamengku Buwono gained some measure of increased day-to-day authority and was able to institute some substantive reforms. This was perhaps one result of the vague promise of greater Indonesian participation in government by Prime Minister Tojo in mid-1943, which was given some veneer of reality by the creation of the Central Advisory Council (*Chuo Sangi-in*), regional advisory councils and the appointment of Indonesian advisers (*sanyos*) to major government departments.[207] There followed an announcement in November of the handover of "a majority" of administrative powers to the Kootis, including financial functions.[208]

By 1944 Hamengku Buwono had opened entry to the public service to all classes and groups in society, whereas previously few civil servants of non-noble birth had been admitted.[209] He also experimented with changes in local administrative arrangements, such as the creation in 1944 of committees of local worthies to assist the *panewus*.[210] In late 1944, he issued instructions for more intensive training of junior civil servants.[211] He abolished the district as a separate entity,[212] laying emphasis on the sub-district as the basic administrative unit. He also abolished special courts for citizens of noble birth.[213] Not all of these experiments were successful, as Selosumarjan reveals.[214]

As the health of the Patih, Prince Danurejo, was occasionally delicate from the end of 1944, Hamengku Buwono took up an increasingly large role in government.[215] On 17 July 1945 Danurejo resigned after twelve years' service in the position.[216] The reason given publicly was his age (seventy-two) and length of service, and the Sultan awarded him a higher title and a pension.[217] The Sultan announced his intention to fill the position himself, and from 1 August 1945, he worked regularly in the Kepatihan building. From this time on, he insisted on receiving Japanese visitors in the Patih's office and not in the kraton.[218] Therefore, he attained the objective he claimed to have sought in the negotiations with the Dutch Governor, that of abolishing the position of Patih. Thus ended a post which had existed for nearly 200 years, from the days of Hamengku Buwono I.[219] Perhaps surprisingly, given that the decree establishing the Yogyakarta Kooti specifies that the Military Government appoints the Somutyokan, the local Japanese authorities seem not to have reacted to Hamengku Buwono's initiative.[220]

Hamengku Buwono's decision to become an executive Sultan raised constitutional questions which were still not settled in Yogyakarta into the twenty-first century.[221] The previous system, with all its imperfections, might conceivably have developed into a constitutional monarchical system, with the Patih (or equivalent) playing the role of an executive prime minister or premier, while the Sultan remained above politics as an invulnerable head of state or head of region. But for an educated Sultan trained in the arts of government, such a passive role was unthinkable, and few in Java knew or understood the concept of a constitutional monarch, despite the Dutch example.

Nevertheless, an executive monarch could risk his whole dynasty through an unwise political choice; he could lose control of political events as the Sunan and Mangkunegoro later did in Solo. By having to deal day-to-day with the occupying power, other political actors, officials and supplicants, he risked loss of face or direct political blame if his decisions went wrong; the Patih in previous days had acted as a useful buffer or screen, whose decisions could be qualified, amplified, or if necessary disowned.[222] The decision meant losing some of the aura of mystery which surrounded the person of a Javanese monarch. Selosumarjan notes the unease in some court circles at the time because of the risks.[223]

Hamengku Buwono formed a new superstructure of government, with himself as head and Puruboyo and Bintoro as his deputies.[224] He had already shown signs of activism, including his tours of the Yogyakarta principality, chairing the pamong praja meetings from early 1944,[225] and his tours of other parts of Java. As it turned out, in one respect his timing was impeccable, because the risk involved in engaging in discussion, negotiation and possibly direct dispute with the occupying authorities soon vanished as the Japanese regime had only weeks to run.

But the inexorable decline in the war economy was a phenomenon no ruler could ward off. Quite apart from the doubt about the claim that Hamengku Buwono managed to check Japanese ambitions in the romusha programme, it is problematic whether the people of Yogyakarta were relatively better off than any other group in Java. This is of course no discredit to Hamengku Buwono. The one large advantage they enjoyed, of incalculable value as it turned out, was the presence of a well-established, popular and determined local leadership.

SUMMARY

As the twentieth century advanced, the Javanese kratons had come increasingly under threat. One challenge came from the colonial authorities, who progressively whittled down the power of the princes. A more subtle and generalized challenge emerged from the way of life and approaches to government represented by the colonial enterprise in general, and some reforms promoted by the Dutch — such as certain public health measures, the proposed creation of advisory bodies like the Bale Agung, and a much greater discipline over royal finances and government finances in general — were disliked and at times subverted by local rulers. Although the Mangkunegoro cultivated an appreciation of Dutch culture and his kraton tried to combat the power of the Sunanate, the Sunan adopted a cooler attitude to the Dutch and some of his relatives openly sympathized with the nationalist movement. In Yogyakarta, Hamengku Buwono VIII preserved his power in the kraton but made little attempt to challenge the Dutch outside it. By the end of Dutch rule, his son had made some changes in the kraton, but no change to the essential power structure had occurred before the Japanese occupation, apart from the semi-political role of the PKN led by Suryodiningrat.

Another potential threat was the rising nationalist movement; and as we saw in the previous chapter, the kratons — or at least the rulers — generally kept their distance, with the possible exception of the Sunanate. The nationalists — divided, demoralized, their leaders mostly in exile — would not have seemed immediately menacing to the kratons in 1942. In Yogyakarta, the popularity of the PKN in the 1930s may well have led some of the nobility to believe that the nationalists had been, or could be, outflanked.

The Japanese posed a new series of challenges. Their decision to maintain the rulers in position would have seemed encouraging at first, and the rulers were aware of the compatibility between their own feudal status and the semi-divine position of the Japanese Emperor. But the open ruthlessness of Japanese rule would have made them at best fearsome and unpredictable allies, and the growing privations inflicted on the ordinary populace led to an uneasy awareness that the inevitable unrest could be directed not only against the Japanese but also at the Javanese elite. The rulers' consciousness of their own lack of power must have become even sharper under the Japanese than under the Dutch.

Hamengku Buwono seems to have walked a fine line between regular protests and representations to the Japanese about their demands on local resources and their behaviour towards the local population, and the risk of offending the Japanese beyond their willingness to preserve him in his position. Given the vagueness of available Indonesian versions of events and in the absence of relevant Japanese sources and accounts, the details of these conflicts are now shrouded in obscurity. The Japanese occupation is a particularly impenetrable period of Indonesian history, and available sources are sparse and not always reliable. Any conclusions about the period must thus be drawn with some care and with appropriate caveats.

But the widespread belief among a number of observers — while not wholly supported by corroborative evidence — that he kept the Japanese at arms' length, the limited corroboration from Governor Adam, and his own testimony to this effect lend credence to the conclusion that Hamengku Buwono did his best to protect his people, with varying success, from the worst features of the Japanese administration, and succeeded in maintaining at least the appearance of coolness towards the ruling power, rather as he had done in his dealings with the Dutch. A reputation for distant relations with the occupying power did him no harm with anti-Japanese nationalists, notably Syahrir and the left wing, who came to power in late 1945 after the proclamation of independence.

Hamengku Buwono was fortunate in the timing of events. By the end of the Japanese occupation, he was thirty-three years old, he had been Sultan for over five years, was now thoroughly familiar with his own principality, and had some current knowledge of and exposure in the rest of Java. He had established a degree of recognition and popularity among his own subjects, and had met many of the personalities who would be important during the Revolution. His relatives had dealt regularly with leading nationalists in such bodies as the Putera, the Chuo Sangi-in, and the BPUPKI. Even though the move to make him king of Java (or Indonesia) had failed — to the extent that it was a concerted move and to the doubtful extent that he encouraged it or had anything to do with it — the mere emergence of such a suggestion demonstrated the regard in which he was already held.

Notes

1. L. de Jong, *Het koninkrijk der Nederlanden in de Tweede Wereldoorlog* [The Kingdom of the Netherlands in the Second World War] (14 vols., The Hague/Leiden 1969–91), vol. 11, part a, p. 992.

2. Ibid., pp. 930–38.
3. *IPO* reports 1942, February 1942, p. 243, quoting an account in *Sedya Tama*, 14 February 1942.
4. De Jong, op. cit., pp. 993–94. The KNIL forces numbered about 18,000 reasonably well-armed infantry, but with severe shortages of tanks, artillery, and air defence weaponry; their morale was very doubtful. To these were added 2,200 very recently arrived Australians, a United States artillery unit of 5,000 men, and some 5,000 scattered British RAF personnel from Singapore with virtually no arms. The Japanese were estimated at 150,000–200,000 men.
5. Ibid., pp. 994–95.
6. Ibid., p. 995.
7. It was certainly evident to the local Dutch community — on 28 April 1942, the indomitable Dutch diarist Adriana Modoo noted that on 1 March the airport was cleared of all military supplies. She concluded: "Then we understood that our region would not be defended" (NIOD Diary no. 198, p. 4).
8. Letter from P. Idenburg to A.G. Vromans of the (then) Royal Institute for War Documentation (RIOD, now NIOD), 22 June 1961 (NIOD 060034).
9. *TUR*, p. 58. See also the account in *TUR*, p. 56, recounting a meeting between the Governor General, Governor Adam and Charles van der Plas, where the plan to have the rulers flee to Australia was supposedly decided.
10. *Asiaweek* interview, 4 May 1986 (vol. 12, no. 18), p. 59. Also Badan Musyawarah Musea Daerah Istimewa Yogyakarta, *Sejarah Perjuangan Benteng Proklamasi*, p. 21.
11. *Tempo*, vol. 16, no. 26, 23 August 1986, p. 15.
12. Kanahele, *The Japanese Occupation of Indonesia*, p. 17.
13. De Jong, ibid., p. 1079.
14. MR 409/40, Fiche 1784, *Bewaking Japansche Expansie, 2de Helft 1939* (Monitoring Japanese Expansion, 2nd Half of 1939 — Yogyakarta), report by Governor, p. 7.
15. Ibid., p. 9.
16. De Jong, pp. 1079–82.
17. NIOD 037965. Letter by L Adam to Vromans, of the (then) RIOD, 2 April 1957, p. 3.
18. De Jong, op. cit., p. 1082. The Adam letter mentioned above (NIOD 037965) does not record this.
19. NIOD 037965, Adam letter, 2 April 1957.
20. This detachment seems to have belonged to the Kaneuchi Unit (headed by Major Kaneuchi), of the 2nd Battalion of the 124th Infantry — see "The Conquest of Java Island, March 1942", from <http://www.geocities.com/dutcheastindies/java.html>. Later the Sakaguchi Detachment, headed by Maj Gen Shizuo Sakaguchi, briefly established its headquarters in Yogyakarta. It was later deployed to Burma — ibid.

21. Ibid., p. 3. Although in fact the Japanese left Dutch colonial law largely in place. Ricklefs, *History*, p. 189.
22. Presumably Maj Gen Sakaguchi mentioned above, though I have no confirmation of this.
23. *East*, op. cit., p. 80, Moltzer interview, code no 1121.1; also Adam, NIOD 037964.
24. Ricklefs, *History*, p. 190. See Hatta, "Political Manifesto of November 1945": "The Japanese looked upon Indonesians as mere cattle". Feith and Castles, *Indonesian Political Thinking*, p. 51.
25. Tarling, *A Sudden Rampage*, p. 175.
26. Benda, *The Crescent and the Rising Sun*, p. 122. "(The Indonesians) have been lazy coolies for the Dutch." — Sekidoho (Japanese Army daily newspaper), quoted in Shigeru Sato, *War, Nationalism and Peasants*, p. 13.
27. I.J. Brugmans, *Nederlandsch — Indie onder Japanse Bezetting* [Netherlands Indies under Japanese Occupation], p. 477.
28. *Asia Raya* 1942–45 passim.
29. Kahin, *Nationalism and Revolution*, pp. 132–33.
30. H. Wallace, "Social and Cultural Interaction between the Japanese and the Indonesians in Java 1942–1945" (PhD thesis, Monash University 2002), p. 131. Wallace here is quoting Friend (*The Blue-Eyed Enemy*, p. 146).
31. Abeyasekere, *One Hand Clapping*, p. 94.
32. *TUR*, p. 62.
33. "The issue of 'collaboration' was, by and large, decided by the mere presence of naked military power." Benda, op. cit., p. 107.
34. *Berita Umum*, 20 March 1942.
35. *Mataram*, 7 March 1942 (KPC).
36. Ibid.
37. NIOD 037965, letter of former Governor Adam.
38. *Mataram*, 13 and 16 March 1942 (KPC).
39. Ibid.
40. *Mataram*, 16 March 1942 (KPC).
41. Tokyo Exhibits series in NIOD, prosecution document no. 5681 (NIOD exhibit no. 1703), p. 5, and *East*, p. 143 (Doppert interview, Code no. 1194.2).
42. Wallace, op. cit., p. 24.
43. Deputy Chief of Staff of the 16th Army. He became Commander-in-Chief in 1943.
44. Colonel Nakayama Yoshito is noted as Head of the General Affairs Office of the 16th Army, a key position in the military government, during 1942–1943, in Sato, op. cit., p. 24, p. 42, etc. Nakayama had joined the economic negotiations between Japan and the Dutch East Indies in 1940–1941 (Sato, p. 240, n 31), had helped plan the attack on the Indies in 1942 and was later involved in

the negotiations with Sukarno and Hatta which led to the formation of the Putera (ibid., p. 51).
45. Soejatno Kartodirdjo, *Revolution in Surakarta 1945–50*, p. 27. The visit is referred to by the Solo delegate Prince Suryoamijoyo in the BPUPKI debates (*Risalah Sidang Badan Penyelidik Usaha2 Persiapan Kemerdekaan Indonesia [BPUPKI]*, p. 354. Henceforth cited as *Risalah*).
46. The Japanese term was *Kooti Jimukyoku*. Reid and Okira, op. cit., glossary, p. xi.
47. Soejatno, ibid.
48. Soejatno, ibid., mentions Funabiki's activities in Solo, but does not refer further to Yoshigawa, and I have found no reference to the latter in the Yogyakarta press.
49. Ibid.
50. Miyoshi Shunkichiro "The Japanese Policy towards the Sultans' Autonomous Regions", in Reid and Okira, op. cit., pp. 116–18.
51. Ibid., p. 118.
52. Benda, op. cit., p. 149.
53. *Asia Raya*, 1942–45, passim, e.g., 17 August 1942, 7 July 1943 etc.
54. The Sunan and Sultan were apparently displeased by this — Reid and Okira, op. cit., p. 120.
55. Reid and Okira, op. cit., p. 118.
56. He was 59 years old in 1942, about 30 years older than Hamengku Buwono.
57. *Indisch Verslag* 1937 (Indies Report), p. 437.
58. *AR*, 2 December 1943.
59. *SM*, 11 September 1944.
60. *SA*, 26 April 1945. The Sunan died less than two months later.
61. *SM*, 8 August 1945.
62. Purwokusumo, *Daerah Istimewa Yogyakarta* [Special Region of Yogyakarta], p. 5. This is slightly confusing, because — as noted above — Soejatno indicates that the Koti zimukyoku had been established earlier. Imamura's decree was perhaps a formalization of the office's status.
63. The former Patih Danurejo became Somutyokan of Yogyakarta on 11 September 1942. Suwarno, "Hamengku Buwono IX dan Sistem Birokrasi Pemerintahan Yogyakarta 1942–74, Sebuah Tinjauan Historis" [Hamengku Buwono IX and the Bureaucratic System of the Yogyakarta Government 1942–74, Historical Review], p. 443.
64. Purwokusumo, *Daerah*, op. cit., p. 6.
65. Ibid.
66. Soejatno, ibid., p. 30.
67. Reid and Okira, p. 119.

68. Miyoshi's account confirms this — Reid and Okira, p. 118.
69. Copy of supplementary document appointing Mangkunegoro VII of 14 August 1942, received from Mrs Madelon Djajadiningrat-Nieuwenhuis, August 2003; originally from the Mangkunegaran archives.
70. Ibid.
71. Sato, op. cit., p. 16. Also Wallace, op. cit., p. 40.
72. Wallace, pp. 4–43.
73. Benda, op. cit., p. 122.
74. The best-known example was the slapping of Sukarno's face by a Japanese air raid warden, to the great annoyance of Commander in Chief Imamura — see Imamura, "Memoirs", in Reid and Okira, op. cit., p. 61.
75. Interview, Professor Selosumarjan, 31 July 2002.
76. *TUR*, p. 59.
77. Sudarisman Purwokusumo, "Sebuah Tinjauan tentang Pepatih-Dalem" [A Note on the Patih], p. 58.
78. TUR, ibid., p. 62.
79. *Asiaweek* interview, 4 May 1986 (vol. 12, no. 18), p. 59.
80. For example, *Djokja Solo*, p. 70.
81. *TUR*, p. 60, caption to photograph 39.
82. Prabuningrat in *TUR*, p. 169.
83. NIOD 037967, Adam letter, p. 5.
84. *Djokja Solo*, op. cit., p. 68, records Yamauchi's arrival in August 1942 and his replacement in August 1944 by Imahi (alternative spelling "Imai"). Imahi was replaced by a certain Ishikawa some time in 1945 — *SM*, 2 August 1945.
85. Kutoyo, "Sri Sultan Hamengku Buwono IX, Riwayat Hidup dan Perjuangan" [Sri Sultan Hamengku Buwono IX, His Life and Struggle], pp. 113–14, based on an interview with Prabuningrat.
86. Ibid.
87. NIOD 025508, interview with S.U. Zuidema, p. 1. See also *Djokja-Solo*, p. 68 and p. 70.
88. NIOD 025508, ibid.
89. NIOD 019431, interview with former police chief of Solo, Gerhardus de Lang, 1 May 1946, p. 1. Also *Djokja Solo*, p. 70.
90. *Pemandangan*, 6 April 1942, "Keadaan di Vorstenlanden dan sekitarnya" [Situation in the Principalities and Environs].
91. Ibid.
92. NIOD 037967, Adam letter, op. cit., p. 5.
93. "Almanak Asia Raya 1944" [Asia Raya Almanac 1944, the annual almanac of the Jakarta daily], list of Advisory Council members, p. 95.
94. *Soerabaiasch Handelsblad*, 27 March 1942 (KPC). This report foreshadowed the change which was officially announced a little later — see *Pemandangan*, 6 April 1942 and *Kan Po*, 5 April 1942.

95. Sato, op. cit., p. 128.
96. *Soerabaiasch Handelsblad*, 22 April 1942 (KPC).
97. Adam letter of 2 April 1957, attachment headed *Rectificatie van Chronologie betr. Yogyakarta* [Correction of the Yogyakarta Chronology], p. 1; NIOD 037965.
98. Interview with Fred Adam, 18 September 2003.
99. Sato, op. cit., p. 115.
100. *SA*, 11 July 1942, announcing a ban on the export of, inter alia, coconuts, coconut oil, soap, peanut oil, matches, and materials for making cloth.
101. Ibid. The commodities were the same as those listed above (except for items connected with the making of cloth).
102. Sato, op. cit., p. 129.
103. Sato, ibid., table 6.9.
104. *SA*, 10 September 1943.
105. Shibata Yishimasa, "The Monetary Policy under Japanese Administration", *Japan, Indonesia and the War*, p. 191.
106. Cribb, "Political Dimensions of the Currency Question 1945–47", *Indonesia*, no. 31 (April 1981): 114.
107. Sato, pp. 141–43.
108. Anderson, *Some Aspects of Indonesian Politics under Japanese Occupation 1944–1945*, p. 13.
109. Soejatno, op. cit., p. 43.
110. Abu Hanifah, *Tales of a Revolution*, p. 141.
111. Ben White, "Towards a Social History of Economic Crises: Yogyakarta in the 1930s, 1960s and 1990s", Chapter 11, in *Indonesia in Transition: Rethinking 'Civil Society', 'Region' and 'Crisis'*, edited by H. Samuel and H. Schulte Nordholt, p. 198.
112. Abrar Yusra, op. cit., p. 118.
113. *East* CD-ROM, S.A. Martherus, code no. 1325.2 (01).
114. *East* CD-ROM, H.L. Doppert 1194.1 (10).
115. Called *Gunsei Hasuiro* or *Gunsei Yosuiro* by the Japanese — *TUR*, p. 61. The term "Mataram Canal" (Selokan Mataram) occurs in at least one contemporary press report — *Sinar Matahari*, 17 July 1944.
116. *SM*, 17 July 1944. On Suharto at this time, see Elson, *Suharto*, p. 33.
117. Ibid., 21 July 1944.
118. *AR*, 28 July 1944.
119. *SM*, 7 July 1945.
120. A report gives sugar production in Java as 1,325 million tons in 1942, declining to only 84 million tons in 1945; 85 mills were operating in 1942, compared with 13 in 1945. NIOD 012569–012582, report in English headed *XII-C. Summary of the Sugar Industry* (nd – late 1945?).
121. Sato, op. cit., p. 97.

122. *SA*, 6 July 1945. The two leading engineers on the project were named as "Ir Hiromatu" (sic – probably Hiromatsu) and Ir K.R.T. Martonegoro.
123. *SM*, 2 August 1945. Remarks by Resident Ishikawa at commemoration of third anniversary of Hamengku Buwono's appointment as Yogyakarta-Koo.
124. See Tokyo Exhibits series in NIOD, de Weerd report, prosecution document no. 5681, NIOD exhibit no. 1703, p. 12.
125. Sato, p. 158.
126. Ibid., p. 160. Sato radically revises earlier estimates, which were based on a report by the Dutch officer de Weerd in 1946 (Tokyo Exhibits series in NIOD, prosecution document no. 5681, NIOD exhibit no. 1703, loc. cit).
127. For example, *TUR*, p. 61.
128. For example, in a speech commemorating the anniversary of his elevation as Yogyakarta-ko, he mentioned water supply and the building of dams as the first item in a list of desirable government activities. *SM*, 3 July 1943.
129. *SA*, 6 July 1945. This confirms the use of romusha labour.
130. NIOD 1727a, Tokyo Exhibits document no. 5710, entitled *AFA Translation no. 8, 12 August 1945, NADA Djokjakarta Labour Order no. 1*.
131. Brown, *Short History of Indonesia*, p. 147.
132. When the Madiun revolt commenced, PKI leader Muso said, "Has Sukarno forgotten that he produced two million romushas for the Japanese and hundreds of thousands of them died?" *De Locomotief*, 20 September 1948.
133. Quoted in Abrar Yusra, op. cit., p. 113.
134. Ibid., p. 114.
135. Ibid., p. 115.
136. Ibid., p. 116.
137. *TUR*, op. cit., ibid. See also Kutoyo, op. cit., p. 116.
138. Abrar Yusra, op. cit., p. 110.
139. Ricklefs, *History*, op. cit., p. 191.
140. Sato, op. cit., p. 122, Table 6.4.
141. *SM*, 30 January 1944.
142. *SM*, 1 March 1944.
143. *SM*, 3 October 1944.
144. Sultan's statement on the creation of the Java Hokokai, *SA*, 5 March 1944.
145. *SA*, 5 September 1943.
146. *SM*, 7 July 1944.
147. Handover report (*Memorie van Overgave*) of 1937 by Governor Bijleveld, NA 2.10.39 (fiches 1–4), p. 47.
148. Beginning with the "Tull report" of 1945 (NIOD 007428, Tull report Part 2, p. 5), "the other prince seemed less whole-hearted [than the Sultan], but was not allowed to open his mouth".
149. "Yogyakarta mati, dibunuh oleh Pakualam" [Yogyakarta is dead, killed by

the Pakualam]. Anonymous source quoted in *Tempo* magazine article on Yogyakarta, 11 December 1971, p. 13.
150. The Pakualam's attitude was influenced by the strong advice of his mother to associate himself with Hamengku Buwono, according to Purwokusumo, *Peranan Beberapa Tokoh Wanita di Puro Pakualaman* [The Role of Several Leading Women in the Pakualaman Palace], p. 29.
151. Abrar Yusra, op. cit., p. 126.
152. *SM*, 2 June 1944 and 6 July 1944.
153. *SM*, series of articles on 15, 18, 19, 21, 23 25, 26, 27, 28, 29 June, and 2 July 1945.
154. Selosumarjan, born near Yogyakarta in 1915, was educated in the Dutch school system, became a Yogyakarta civil servant in the 1930s, was Panewu in Lendah and then *wedana* (assistant regent) in the Yogyakarta sultanate from 1944 to 1946. In the Revolution, he was a staff member in Hamengku Buwono's office, and in 1949, a trusted emissary between the Sultan and the local bupatis. From the 1950s to the 1970s, he seems to have been in effect principal private secretary to Hamengku Buwono in whatever position the latter occupied; although he took three years off from 1956 to 1959 to write his PhD thesis at Cornell, published as *Social Change in Jogjakarta*.
155. *SM*, 30 January 1944.
156. *SM*, 25 May 1944.
157. *SM*, 4 August 1944. This was the Neyama tunnel constructed near Kediri in 1944–45 with romusha labour, described critically but in detail by Sato, op. cit., pp. 190–98.
158. In a 1986 interview, Hamengku Buwono said, "During the Japanese occupation, Sukarno and Hatta visited me. My first contact had been during the Dutch time." *Asiaweek* interview, 4 May 1986 (vol. 12, no. 18), p. 60. A meeting in the Dutch period in fact appears improbable, as both leaders were then in exile far from Yogyakarta.
159. *SM*, 20 November 1943.
160. *TUR*, p. 63. Both attended a meeting of the Yogyakarta Hokokai on 22 March 1944, where Sukarno made a speech, but this was probably not their first meeting — *SA*, 25 March 1944.
161. Legge, *Sukarno*, op. cit., p. 16.
162. Legge, ibid., pp. 91–92 and passim.
163. For example, *Indonesia Menggugat* and *Dibawah Bendera Revolusi*, written during the Dutch period.
164. I have only lightly explored Hamengku Buwono's private life. It is sufficient to note here that he was not accused of the sort of sexual misbehaviour for which Sukarno became notorious. Hamengku Buwono married five times in all, four times to Javanese women associated with the kraton; when one of his

original four wives died, he married a Sumatran (Norma Musa), who became Princess Nindyokirono. He was not known to take concubines (*priyantun-dalem* and *lelangen-dalem* in Javanese — Taylor, op. cit., p. 162), although an affair with a princess from Solo is rumoured.
165. M.H. Bro, *Indonesia: Land of Challenge* (New York: Harper, 1954), pp. 91–94. She quotes (p. 94) the "often-heard comment": "If the Sultan's children could go to a public school, why not the President's?"
166. "Batavia parked on Central Java's minithrones a succession of utterly pliable, mediocre, fainéant princelings": Anderson, "Professional Dreams", in his *Language and Power*, p. 289.
167. Feith, *Decline of Constitutional Democracy*, pp. 33–34.
168. These included "most Japanese calendar festivities, such as the Emperor's birthday, the anniversary of Pearl Harbour, the anniversary of the Japanese arrival in each area, the 'acceptance' of each Japanese concession towards independence". Anthony Reid, "From Briefcase to Samurai Sword", in *Southeast Asia under Japanese Occupation*, edited by McCoy, p. 22.
169. A count of the terms used in his speeches show "Jawa Baru" or "Jawa" predominating until mid-September 1944, after which, the term "Indonesia" becomes the norm.
170. Dahm, *Sukarno and the Struggle for Indonesian Independence*, p. 242, indicates that the Japanese seemed to recognize Sukarno only as a leader of the "New Java".
171. Ricklefs (*History*, op. cit., p. 197) indicates that in July 1945, "the Japanese army and navy ... decided that Java should be given independence by early September and the other areas soon after".
172. See van Klinken, *Migrant Moralities*, for an account of this thinking in the 1920s, p. 103.
173. Dahm, *Sukarno and the Struggle for Indonesian Independence*, p. 242.
174. Kanahele, op. cit., p. 37 and p. 138.
175. Once the word "Indonesia" had become more acceptable after September 1944, he and the Pakualam used it more frequently than the two princes of Solo.
176. E.g., address to the Yogyakarta Hokokai branch, in *SM*, 2 May 1944, and statement on first anniversary of founding of the Peta, in *SM*, 3 October 1944.
177. Speech by Yogyakarta-Koo on his inauguration as head of local Hokokai branch, *SM*, 13 March 1944.
178. *SM*, 1 January 1944.
179. *SM*, 14 September 1944.
180. Ibid. *Pemimpin Besar* in Indonesian, perhaps the first time Sukarno received the appellation.
181. Some Japanese felt that the delays were a "betrayal" of Japanese promises — see Nishijima Shigetada, "Testimony — Indonesian Independence and Revolution", edited by Reid and Okira, op. cit., pp. 262–63.

182. Anderson, op. cit., pp. 16–18.
183. Sukiman was a Masyumi leader at this time and was later Prime Minister from 1951 to 1952. Hadikusumo was General Chairman of Muhammadiyah during the Japanese period.
184. *Risalah*, p. lviii.
185. *Risalah*, p. lcx.
186. Some proposals about the nature of the Indonesian state were apparently put to the BPUPKI by a Yogyakarta kraton functionary. See Suwarno, op. cit., pp. 161–64.
187. Speech to Budi Utomo meeting in which he opposed the introduction of Western science to Java, in Larson, *Prelude to Revolution*, p. 135.
188. Reid, "The Nationalist Quest for an Indonesian Past", p. 282, in *Perceptions of the Past in Southeast Asia*, edited by Reid and Marr (Singapore: Heinemann, 1979).
189. *Risalah*, p. 29.
190. Ibid. The head of the PETA-equivalent in Malaya (also called PETA), Ibrahim Yaacob, who wanted Malaya to join Indonesia, visited Jakarta in August 1945, but was told that the Indonesian nationalists were not ready to fight the British as well as the Dutch — Kratoska, op. cit., p. 303.
191. Theodore Friend, *The Blue-Eyed Enemy*, p. 111.
192. Mangkunegoro VII, originally R.M. Suryosuparto, was a son of Mangkunegoro V, had become Mangkunegoro on 3 March 1916, had worked in the bureaucracy, chaired Budi Utomo from 1915 to 1916, and been a member of the Volksraad from 1918 to 1921. Soejatno, op. cit., p. 36.
193. The new Sunan, Pakubuwono XII, had been born as Raden Mas Suryo Guritno in 1925, had become crown prince as KGPH Puruboyo in 1943, and thus became Sunan (and Solo Koo) at the age of twenty. The new Mangkunegoro VIII, originally BRM Saroso and born in 1920, had a Dutch-style education in Java, had attended military training in Bandung for the Reserve Officer Corps, and had received Peta training in 1943. Soejatno, ibid.
194. Kanahele, ibid., p. 210.
195. Despite the remarks by Yogyakarta representatives like Hadikusumo, the Japanese eyewitness Ichibangase, op. cit., p. 2 (*Report on the Preparative* [sic] *Committee for Indonesian Independence*) says that "those from Surakarta and Yogyakarta provinces and one half of the bureaucracy" favoured monarchy.
196. *TUR*, p. 63.
197. Kanahele, p. 319.
198. NIOD — 081578, *Notities betreffende de 'Dahler-kwestie'* [Notes on the "Dahler question"], by C.M. van Diemen, no date but around 1949.
199. *Risalah*, p. 130.
200. Ibid., p. 129.
201. Ibid., pp. 133–34.

202. Ibid., p. 142.
203. Ibid., p. 128.
204. *Risalah*, p. 348. Sukarno had strongly criticized feudalism in the past — see Feith and Castles, *Indonesian Political Thinking*, p. 31.
205. *SM*, 28 July 1942 (KPC).
206. The Japanese certainly had a general policy of changing all street names from Dutch to Japanese or Malay names, as a further means of expunging all reminders of Dutch rule. NIOD Tokyo Process exhibit no. 1351, "De Weerd report", *The Japanese Occupation of the Netherlands Indies*, doc no. 2750, p. 5.
207. Benda, op. cit., p. 137.
208. *Kan Po* no. 31/1943, Military Government decree of 15 November 1943. Despite the claim about the devolution of financial powers, the list quoted in the decree did not include them.
209. Selosumarjan, *Social Change*, p. 56, gives the date of this change as 1943, but Purwokusumo (*Tanggapan*, op. cit., 27) says 1944. The later timing is more credible, if we assume that more powers had been passed over later in the occupation.
210. Ibid.
211. CAD, NIGIS reports, Bundle AA7, p. 3/132A, monitoring Yogyakarta radio broadcast of 23 December 1944.
212. Ibid. Purwokusumo places this change in April 1945 — Purwokusumo, *Tanggapan*, op. cit., p. 2.
213. *TUR*, p. 64. This occurred in 1947 according to Selosumarjan, op. cit., p. 122.
214. Selosumarjan, op. cit., p. 57.
215. Purwokusumo, *Tinjauan*, op. cit., p. 59.
216. *AR*, 17 July 1945.
217. Ibid., some sources, e.g., *Djokja-Solo*, op. cit., p. 70, claim that Danurejo died in August 1945; but this seems incorrect. Purwokusumo (*Tanggapan*, op. cit., p. 24) says that Danurejo died in 1946.
218. *Djokja-Solo*, ibid.
219. The Pakualam also abolished the position of his Patih during this period — Ricklefs, *History*, op. cit., p. 269, and Selosumarjan, op. cit., p. 53.
220. Purwokusumo, *Tinjauan*, op. cit., p. 63.
221. After some years of heated debate about a new draft law on "Specialness" (*keistimewaan*), the issue finally reached the national parliament and was temporarily settled in 2012 with a new law on Yogyakarta's Specialness, Law 13/2012, confirming the special status of the Yogyakarta princes.
222. Selosumarjan, p. 52.
223. Ibid.
224. *SM*, 2 August 1945.
225. *SM*, 5 June 1945.

5

REVOLUTION — FIRST PHASE

The proclamation of Indonesian Independence by Sukarno and Hatta on 17 August 1945 had immediate effects in Yogyakarta. That afternoon Ki Hajar Dewantoro led a small Taman Siswa group through the streets welcoming the proclamation.[1] The next day Hamengku Buwono sent congratulatory telegrams to the two proclamators and to Dr Rajiman. The first two cables read "I as Jogjakarta-koo extend my congratulations on the proclamation of the Republic of Indonesia and the appointment of Your Excellencies as President/Vice President."[2] These were followed up with further joint telegrams with the Pakualam, in virtually identical terms.[3] The need for the joint cables suggests some initial lack of coordination.

In early August, with Japanese concurrence, the nationalists had formed a new committee to prepare for the transfer of government powers, called the Committee for the Preparation of Indonesian Independence (Panitya Persiapan Kemerdekaan Indonesia [PPKI]), with membership based on — but smaller than — the BPUPKI.[4] After the proclamation, the committee quickly approved the draft constitution and appointed Sukarno and Hatta as President and Vice President.

The two Yogyakarta leaders sent a congratulatory cable to the Committee,[5] of which Hamengku Buwono's brother Puruboyo was a member. It may seem incongruous now that they also dispatched messages of thanks to Japanese authorities in Jakarta,[6] but at the time this must have seemed a prudent course of action. Hamengku Buwono's statement welcoming the Proclamation contained — for the last time — the ritual thanks to the Japanese which his messages of the past three years had contained.[7] Headed "Let us appropriately repay Dai Nippon's kindness", the statement pointed out that a strong desire for independence was insufficient in itself and that Indonesia needed to build up the capability to *retain* independence, bearing in mind that this was "an age of crisis". Community groups should submerge their narrow interests to create "a comprehensive and strong unity."[8] Appeals for unity at this early stage only illustrated the fears of disunity which already existed and foreshadowed the difficulty of the task which lay ahead.

The Preparatory Committee confirmed that Java would remain divided into three provinces, but that the *kooti*s would be separate. The new Department of Home Affairs would manage the public service, the police, land and the principalities. By implication, this placed the principalities under the first Minister of Home Affairs.

Hamengku Buwono held a meeting of the Yogyakarta Hokokai, which resolved that the region support the national leadership "with all their might", and a further cable to that effect was sent to Sukarno on 21 August.[9] From meetings of this kind and from other soundings of popular opinion, it became evident that the public strongly favoured the actions Hamengku Buwono had already taken. Yogyakartan enthusiasm for Indonesian independence had already been shown after the promise of independence made by Prime Minister Koiso, in the large meeting of September 1944 described in the previous chapter.

Nevertheless, it is pertinent to explore his reasons for joining the Republic. It is arguable that one of his prime but unstated ambitions throughout his career was to preserve his dynasty in some form and pass it on to his successor. Joining the Republic may well have seemed, somewhat paradoxically, the best option to preserve the succession by allying himself with the strong nationalistic emotions which were now being unleashed.

But first let us examine his options in this new, hopeful but also quite dangerous period of his life. In ascending order of likelihood, at least from the nationalist viewpoint, these would have been:

- to reject the Republic and declare allegiance to the Dutch, perhaps with reference to the 1940 contract which had cost him so much time and effort;

- to declare Yogyakarta an independent state;
- to wait and see;
- to declare support for the Republic, abdicate as Sultan and declare that he regarded himself as an ordinary citizen of the new state;
- what he actually did, namely to join the Republic while preserving the Sultanate.

Accounts of the period take for granted that the last option was his only choice, but other options were at least thinkable and one or two had elements of attraction. The option of declaring for the Dutch may look preposterous now and must have looked unlikely even then. He felt entitled to believe, with many Republicans,[10] that the Dutch had forfeited their claim to Indonesia by their failure to defend it from the Japanese. The Dutch had invited him to flee Yogyakarta when the Japanese invaded,[11] and by his decision to stay with his people, he had secured the people's trust while the Dutch had lost it. The Dutch defeat in 1942 had arguably voided the 1940 contract; among the long list of powers excluded from the Sultan's ambit of self-rule in Article 21 was the defence of the principality.[12]

Dutch and Allied forces were still far away from Java in August 1945, and their absence reinforced the feeling that independence for Indonesia would come now or never. Nevertheless, an element of risk existed in joining the Republic quickly. The Dutch might come back. They were part of the victorious coalition which had dropped the atomic bomb on Japan, and if they gained the support of their allies, especially the United States, they would be formidable adversaries for the new Republic. The Japanese retained strong forces in Indonesia and might turn on the Republic with unpredictable results.

The notion of declaring his own independence can be quickly dismissed.[13] Although no democratic assessment of public opinion was ever held, it appeared that the people favoured the Republic, and the idea of a separate Yogyakarta never entered their thoughts. The Yogyakarta sultans traced their descent from Sultan Agung's state of Mataram, but the Yogyakarta principality had been created a century later by splitting the kingdom; and Yogyakarta had never been an independent state.[14] The Sultan could not expect his small realm, with a weak and untried army, to survive if it antagonized the Republic, the Dutch and their allies and possibly the Japanese as well.

The option of doing nothing for the time being had its attractions. The Republic was a largely unknown quantity, Hamengku Buwono barely knew Sukarno and Hatta, and he only knew of the constitutional committee debates at second hand. The kootis were to be preserved under the new constitution, but the arrangement might not last. Although extreme left-wing opinion had had little opportunity to express itself as yet, he must have known that republican radicals had little time for traditional privilege. The still well-armed Japanese might react savagely against Republican claims, but would be unlikely to do anything drastic against one of their own *Koo*s who was not provoking them. The same might apply to the attitude of the Allies. Hamengku Buwono might be better off waiting to see which way the wind was blowing and joining the winning side when the situation was clearer.

The fact that he did not do so but immediately declared his adherence to the Republic could be seen as a principled declaration of his political attitude. It could be seen as an astute summing-up of the political potentialities of the situation, and especially the temper of his own people. It might also be seen as the best way of preserving his dynasty.

In Sumatra, similar dilemmas confronted the traditional rulers in a much sharper and even tragic form. None could cope with the passions unleashed after the Japanese surrender, and many were deposed or even murdered. Even the most progressive leader, Sultan Syarif Kasim of Siak, who recognized the principle of *kedaulatan rakyat* (people's sovereignty) and tried to establish constructive relations with the Republicans, was eventually constrained to abdicate.[15] Thus, the traditional rulers in Java and Sumatra, apart from Hamengku Buwono, never survived as a class to find meaningful new roles in an independent country, unlike their counterparts in Malaya.[16]

Hamengku Buwono's most radical option, that of joining the Republic by abolishing the Yogyakarta principality, has its theoretical logic. In most republics, a basic assumption is that citizens are equal before the state and before the law, and ascribed status has a lesser role than in a monarchy or tyranny. Although republicanism did not necessarily mean democracy, and the Greek, Roman, and even American republics retained all kinds of privileges and discrimination against underclasses (slaves, women, non-property-owners), one of their number would only achieve primacy with their consent. All disliked, at least in theory, the preservation of privilege based on noble birth, and one of the aims of the American Republic in 1876 was to abolish the privileges of the English aristocracy, while preserving the status of the propertied gentlemen who created the American Republic.[17]

Although in constitutional terms it seemed contradictory to join a republic while remaining a Sultan, such abstract considerations carried little weight in 1945. In Hamengku Buwono's thinking, abolition of his own status and authority could well lead to chaos, and such a result would not promote Indonesian independence. It was not clear to whom he could pass over his power if he did step down, and there was certainly no one to whom he could bequeath his status and prestige. The BPUPKI had preserved the status of the kootis, so that, on one possible interpretation, he would contradict the new dispensation if he did abdicate. Hamengku Buwono knew that the standing of the Republican leaders, notably of Sukarno and Hatta, was high, and in particular Sukarno's profile and popularity seemed a good sign that the Republic could survive.

The decision had long-term consequences for the survival of the sultanate, but it also had implications for the kind of state which Indonesia would become, and for the complex of ideas surrounding what it meant to be "an Indonesian". Now that independence was proclaimed, what was "Indonesia" and what was "an Indonesian"? The decision by the BPUPKI to preserve the principalities implied the validity of some form of feudal identity within the country. As would be seen by the ultimate fate of Solo, the exact status of the principalities would not be worked out for some time; but it was at least left open that the country could include non-republican (and perhaps also non-democratic) entities. The decision implied a tacit acceptance that ascribed status could have continuing authenticity in the Indonesian Republic. A good Indonesian Republican could be a prince and could retain that status. He had the chance to prove that this was possible.

In late August Hamengku Buwono contacted the two princes in Solo and discussed ways of formalizing their adherence to the Republic.[18] Some of the euphoria of the independence proclamation had worn off, and he had issued a statement calling again for unity "at this difficult and unpredictable time".[19] He called again for "a disciplined and sturdy unity, involving mutual respect and avoiding discrimination between groups and races".[20]

On 4 September the two Solo princes got in first with their formal statements joining the new state, including the assertions that the Sunanate and Mangkunegaran, which both had "the status of a kingdom", were each a "special region" within the Republic; and that they both held "all power" within their realms. Both statements added that the relationship between the principalities and the Republic was a direct one.[21] The notion of a "special region" seemed to be a legitimate interpretation of the vague conclusion about the principalities reached by the Constitutional Committee.

The Sultan and Pakualam followed four days later[22] with nearly identical declarations. But they each claimed a direct relationship with the *President* (and not just the Republic), a subtle strengthening of the similar clause in the Solo statements. This might also indicate a rejection of the idea, implied in the government announcement on the functions of the Department of Home Affairs, that the princes would be subject to the Home Affairs Minister. Nevertheless, in his study of the period, Selosumarjan confirms that both the Yogyakarta rulers were responsible to that Minister.[23]

The two princes announced the merger of their two realms, in which the Sultan became head of the Special Region of Yogyakarta and the Pakualam his deputy, an arrangement which was to continue for the next thirty-three years.[24] In early September, two representatives of the Jakarta Government arrived in Yogyakarta with a formal recognition of the Special Region signed by Sukarno and backdated to 19 August.

The Yogyakarta region formed its own Regional Indonesian National Committee (Komite Nasional Indonesia Daerah [KNID]). The committee comprised eighty-four members, with a majority of supporters of Hamengku Buwono. Even the more left-wing members were prepared to accept his role.[25] Politically aware members of the local Hokokai branch apparently formed the KNID without the Sultan's involvement, and only sought his imprimatur later.[26] Initial differences between groups who had collaborated with the Japanese and those who had not were resolved in agreement to follow the Sultan's lead.[27]

KOTA BARU EVENTS

Tensions rose in Yogyakarta and indeed across Java as many nationalists, especially the radical *pemuda*,[28] strove to seize arms from the Japanese and to take action against all Dutch interests. Unfortunately, this meant in some cases indiscriminate killings and assault against any Europeans, Eurasians and Chinese they could find, as well as the Japanese.[29] Yogyakarta seems to have been free of such incidents, but hatred of the Japanese, and especially of the Kempeitai, was as bitter here as elsewhere, and by early October matters were reaching a head.

During September more and more incidents occurred. Hamengku Buwono persuaded the Japanese to concede after a confrontation between Japanese guards and pemuda groups who wished to raise the Indonesian flag at the Resident's palace.[30] On 26 September, most government offices, companies, and factories were taken over by Indonesian officials led by police chief R. Sudarsono,[31] and the *Sinar Matahari* newspaper offices were occupied and its equipment used to produce the first edition of *Kedaulatan Rakyat* (People's Sovereignty),[32] the daily which was still appearing sixty years later. The Kido battalion barracks at Kota Baru, housing Kempeitai elements, remained untouched for the moment.

The first officials of the office for the Recovery of Allied Prisoners of War and Internees (RAPWI) had arrived in Semarang by this time. One of them visited Yogyakarta and was received with much pomp, obviously aimed at impressing him. He concluded that the Sultan had thrown in his lot with the nationalists, and was more or less in control.[33] The visitor was probably the first European to meet Hamengku Buwono in over three years. Hamengku Buwono complained of food shortages in his region, and thus was reluctant to accept the transfer into Yogyakarta of any internees.[34] The visitor noted the popularity of the independence movement: "On the Indonesian side evidence of the strength and purpose of the Nationalist movement existed everywhere. Not a house, nor a public building lacked its Indonesian flag."[35]

Immediately thereafter, all communications between Yogyakarta and the outside world were temporarily cut off by the Indonesians.[36] On 6 October pemuda groups attacked the Kido barracks,[37] and after some bloodshed succeeded in capturing most of the weapons there.[38] A Japanese surrender was arranged after talks between the Japanese resident and the Sultan.[39] In other incidents in Central Java, the Japanese surrendered their arms with only a token struggle after phone calls from senior officers in Jakarta.[40] The Japanese commander in Central Java, General Nakamura, said that to avoid a serious situation he had agreed to surrender all weapons in Yogyakarta to the Sultan.[41] These events were paralleled in Solo, where the Japanese forces had agreed to yield to the local KNI. This occurred relatively peacefully on 5 October. Only the Kempeitai resisted, but even they eventually surrendered on 11 October after some bloodshed.[42]

In his most internationally oriented address to date, marking two months of Indonesian independence, Hamengku Buwono said that Indonesia had already striven for two months to convince the outside world that it had a well-organized government, strongly supported by the Indonesian people, unlike NICA[43] "which was solely based on the Dutch desire to colonise the Indonesian people again".[44] The world did not realize how the Indonesian people had changed in the past three years. "Whatever the attempts by NICA to deceive the outside world, the Indonesia people will always stand behind the government's policy of firm resistance combined with diplomacy."[45] He added that the sacrifices already made by "heroes" demanded that Indonesia should continue the struggle. The right of subject peoples to decide their own fate had been acknowledged by the Allies in the Atlantic Charter.[46]

The references to international circumstances may reflect his greater awareness of developments in Jakarta, including Syahrir's rise to power and his analysis of Indonesia's need to convince Western countries of the justice of the Republican cause, which was shortly to appear in his influential booklet *Perjuangan Kita* (Our Struggle).[47] Nevertheless, the ambiguity of Hamengku Buwono's reference to struggle *and* diplomacy reflected the tension between the revolutionary spirit of the many radical pemuda groups and the greater caution of the older, Western-educated leaders.

INTERNEES AND MINORITIES

During this time, many Dutch citizens and Eurasians in the region exchanged imprisonment by the Japanese for imprisonment by the Indonesians.[48] Some reports refer to low-level mistreatment of the Dutch community in Yogyakarta, especially relating to internment without warning, separation of families, and at times poor rations, although there are no reports of physical abuse. Conditions in the camps seem however to have been reasonably good, and Red Cross visits and parcels were received.[49] Inmates reported receiving food from the Sultan,[50] although at the time he publicly denied press reports that he had done so. Responding to an Antara report on the matter, Hamengku Buwono stated indignantly that he had had no contact with the internees; he regarded as a personal attack any statements which falsely used his name in this way. It might seem peculiar that he would have to deny behaving in a humanitarian manner, but his vehemence may indicate the political dangers of seeming too sympathetic to the Dutch or Eurasians.[51]

From the Japanese period on, private charities had continued efforts to support needy minority groups in the region. The local Red Cross somehow carried on during the Japanese occupation and into the period of the Revolution,[52] supplying small amounts of cash and food to destitute families, including Ambonese, Eurasians, and Menadonese. Immediately after the Japanese capitulation, the organization requested the senior palace official, Honggowongso, for permission to take over direct management of this charity work. After consulting the Sultan, Honggowongso rejected the request "with an eye to the volatile political situation".[53] Even at this early stage, Hamengku Buwono had to insist on Republican bureaucratic cover for humanitarian work. He was only too conscious of the political sensitivity of helping distrusted minorities like the Eurasians and Ambonese.

The senior official Notonegoro chaired a new committee handling the affairs of the internees and charity organizations.[54] Policy was complicated by wider political considerations, not least the fear that once all the internees reached safety, the Dutch forces would be freer to act against the Republic, and the likelihood that the younger males might return as Dutch soldiers.[55] In these talks the Indonesian government also demanded reciprocal releases of Indonesian political prisoners.[56] By early 1946 Hamengku Buwono was sending representatives to meetings at the Allied Headquarters in Jakarta.[57] One of his brothers organized the evacuation of Dutch and Eurasian internees from Yogyakarta, and eventually all reached Surabaya, Semarang or Jakarta,[58] although the process was excruciatingly slow, lasting into 1947.[59] The Sultan told a meeting in the town square when a group of Dutch internees were being sent to Jakarta that the true meaning of *merdeka* was independence for all, not only for Indonesians.[60] This sentiment was not often heard in Republican circles.

HAMENGKU BUWONO, THE MILITIA AND THE ARMY

Large numbers of pemuda roaming the countryside with weapons seized from the Japanese were a potential threat to *any* centres of authority. In August Hamengku Buwono had announced that pemuda wanting to help the Republic should report to his office,[61] and he had met local youth leaders and obtained their agreement to this.[62] Around mid-October, Selosumarjan visited Magelang for a conference of armed youth groups which turned out to be dominated by the re-emerging communist party.[63] Hamengku Buwono was alarmed at rising left-wing influence and resolved to forestall a similar situation in Yogyakarta. After a meeting with about fifty leading youth figures,[64] he presided over a parade in the town square inducting large numbers of youths into the Laskar Rakyat Mataram (Mataram

People's Militia),[65] later known as the Tentara Rakyat Mataram (Mataram People's Army).[66] He formalized the creation of the force by a decree of 26 October[67] and was named as its first Commander with Selosumarjan as Chief of Staff.[68] These actions preceded by four days an announcement by the Army leadership mandating the creation of a Laskar Rakyat across the entire country.[69]

It is from this period that the army came to accept Hamengku Buwono as a kind of honorary senior officer. The process whereby he gained the status is shadowy, although the prescient formation of the Laskar Rakyat had something to do with it. Along with the other three Java princes he was also named to the army's Supreme Council,[70] and he was awarded an honorary General's rank as early as November 1945.[71] Anderson notes that he was "treated as a general officer" by senior army commanders.[72]

But the extent of his military expertise was slight. His only military training was in the Leidsche Corps at Leiden University years before, and he never commanded troops in the field at any time. Nevertheless, the unorthodox way in which the Indonesian armed forces originated meant that many Indonesians of little military background could command armed units, and Hamengku Buwono's claim to authority was as strong as many of them. This was also a period (unlike the Dutch era)[73] when he was fond of wearing military uniform, and several photographs testify to this.[74]

On two known occasions he sought to experience the reality of war. In November 1945, about ten days after the appalling bloodshed of the battle of Surabaya and while sporadic clashes were still occurring, Hamengku Buwono drove "incognito"[75] to Mojokerto, accompanied by Bintoro and Mohammad Saleh, the head of the Yogyakarta KNID. There they met East Java Governor Suryo and reached the outskirts of Surabaya. The next day, with the Governor and local Resident, he visited Gresik.[76] Hamengku Buwono told the press "The battle of Surabaya demonstrated the cruelty of the British, and showed us that the policy of diplomacy (*diplomasi*) is inappropriate." While praising the courage of the youth, he called for stronger coordination of army units.[77] His criticism of diplomasi might be taken as condemnation of official policy, but since the Syahrir cabinet had been formed only a week before, the government was not necessarily the direct target of his remarks. Emotional reactions could be expected from any Indonesian leader viewing the carnage around Surabaya.

The visit gave rise to a modicum of unconfirmable legend. Somewhere to the east of Madiun, Hamengku Buwono's jeep was stopped by an unidentified armed group, who enquired where "Dorojatun" was. He calmly answered "I am Suyono" and was allowed to proceed.[78] Later Hamengku Buwono heard that the intercepting group were agents of the dreaded colonial official van der Plas, who had become aware of his presence in the area and wished to abduct and even assassinate him.[79] Such was van der Plas's reputation[80] that any anti-Republican groups were regarded as his creatures.[81]

To boost the morale of the Yogyakarta fighters, he also visited the Ambarawa front with the prince from Solo, Jatikusumo, who was already a senior officer in the newly formed Tentara Keamanan Rakyat (TKR)[82] (People's Security Army, later Tentara Rakyat Indonesia (TRI) — Indonesian People's Army, and then Tentara Nasional Indonesia (TNI) — Indonesian National Army). The news of a ceasefire ordered by the central government came soon after he arrived at the front, so that his opportunity to support the troops was brief. These episodes revealed a strain of youthful adventurism which was rarely to reappear. They also showed his determination to identify himself with the revolutionary pemuda, a no doubt sincere but also politically shrewd stance to take.

His identification with the TKR was reinforced at the historic inaugural meeting of senior officers in Yogyakarta in mid-November, which was an attempt to unify the disparate Republican forces which had sprung up like dragon's teeth across the archipelago. The meeting elected Colonel Sudirman,[83] the Banyumas leader, as its first Commander-in-Chief and chose Hamengku Buwono as the first Minister of Defence, but very soon the news arrived that the Jakarta-based Prime Minister Syahrir had named Amir Syarifuddin as Defence Minister. This almost certainly arose from a lack of coordination rather than from deliberate provocation on either side, but it was one of the first manifestations of uneasy civil–military relations which would colour Indonesian politics for years to come.

Syahrir, who at this stage may not even have met Hamengku Buwono, needed as Prime Minister to control such an important ministry as Defence and had wanted a close colleague like Syarifuddin in the post. He was however constrained, after some weeks, to endorse Sudirman as Armed Forces Commander in Chief (*Panglima*); but it soon became clear that Sudirman, like many in the TKR, strongly opposed Syahrir's policy of negotiating with the English and the Dutch.[84]

During October and November, inflammatory broadcasts by the Republican radio in Yogyakarta had sufficiently irritated the British that they launched a series of air raids against it.[85] Hamengku Buwono protested at the attacks which endangered his people,[86] and he and the Pakualam visited the affected areas and the victims in hospital.[87]

Negotiations about the Republic's status, first with the British and then with the Dutch with growing UN involvement, were an increasing source of public attention and much dissension on all sides. The main milestones in the negotiations were the Linggajati Agreement of March 1947 and the Renville agreement of January 1948. Both sides struggled for advantage and for international recognition and support, and military clashes continued sporadically, amounting to all-out war during the two major Dutch attacks in mid-1947 and December 1948. To the irritation of the Republicans, the Dutch authorities also made strenuous efforts to create separate autonomous states, especially outside Java, with the help of compliant local leaders[88] who formed the Bijeenkomst voor Federale Overleg (BFO — Federal Consultative Assembly). The latter were regarded as puppets by the Republicans, and indeed few Federalists survived to play any political role after the transfer of sovereignty. Prominent federalists included Hamengku Buwono's former classmate Sultan Hamid II of Pontianak (Borneo), and Sukawati and Anak Agung (East Indonesia).

Lieutenant Governor van Mook's ambitions reached a climax in the Malino conference in Sulawesi in July 1946.[89] The Republic refused an invitation to attend. The transparent aim of the Dutch in establishing the federal states was to create a United States of Indonesia in which the Republic, if it participated, would be only one constituent among many others and could be outvoted.

MOVE OF GOVERNMENT TO YOGYAKARTA

In January 1946 the Republican Government moved from Jakarta to Yogyakarta. The Yogyakarta KNID, headed by Mohammad Saleh,[90] had urged the Central Government in early December to relocate to Central Java because of lack of security in Jakarta. The KNID also requested the Steering Committee of the Central KNI (the de facto national parliament) to do the same.[91] The KNID had been alarmed at an attack on Prime Minister Syahrir in Jakarta by a KNIL (Dutch colonial army) group in late 1945 and believed that for their safety, the central government should move.[92] Sukarno himself apparently chose Yogyakarta as his new domicile.[93] Another account gives as the government's reasons for the choice of Yogyakarta: its relative remoteness from Allied forces, its good communications with other important centres, the location there of the TKR headquarters, and the fervent local support for the Republic.[94]

Although the KNID leadership made the initial approach, they would certainly have consulted Hamengku Buwono at an early stage. He may have discussed the move with Sukarno, Hatta, and Syahrir during their visit to Yogyakarta on 18 December.[95] Syahrir, as the main negotiator with the Dutch, had to stay in Jakarta, but the President, Vice President, and many public servants moved to Yogyakarta. These included Sukarno's and Hatta's staff, the Minister and the nascent Ministry of Defence, and several sections of the Information Ministry.[96] Other ministries followed later, although several were relocated to other towns in Central Java, like Purwokerto, Klaten, and Magelang.[97]

On the evening of 2/3 January 1946, a special train surreptitiously conveyed Sukarno, Hatta, and their households from Jakarta to Yogyakarta,[98] where Hamengku Buwono had prepared accommodation and office facilities for them. He greeted them on arrival at Tugu railway station, and Sukarno was accommodated in the former palace of the Dutch Governor. This development was an important step in the association of the Yogyakarta principality with the Republic. Hamengku Buwono was binding himself even closer to the Sukarno and Hatta leadership; and Yogyakarta was to become the legendary "capital of the Revolution". At the same time, his own authority was strengthened by the presence of the central government in his city.[99] By contrast, Solo became a convenient centre for opposition politics, being close enough to affect the Republican government in Yogyakarta, but far enough away for dissidents to organize and to express their views with freedom.[100] Solo became a centre for the Persatuan Perjuangan (United Struggle), which favoured Tan Malaka and his rejection of Syahrir's policy of negotiation.

Shortly after the move, the Consul General of China visited Yogyakarta, as the first official visitor to the Republican Government in its new location, and paid formal calls on the President, the Vice President, and the Sultan as head of the Special Region.[101] Later visits by diplomatic representatives, the consular commission, the future UN Good Offices Commission and even Dutch official visitors (as occurred in 1946 and mid-1947) generally followed this pattern, and thus, Hamengku Buwono gradually became better known in the outside world. He also received various callers from elsewhere in the archipelago.[102]

Not long after decreeing the takeover by the government of all local Japanese firms,[103] Hamengku Buwono visited light industrial concerns across the region.[104] A statement during the visits contained some interesting and rare (for him) ideological points. He declared that Indonesian workers were demonstrating their ability to keep industries operating without foreign management, further confirming Indonesia's readiness for independence. Workers appreciated that they were working not only for themselves but also for the people and the nation. The people of Indonesia were not attracted to "syndicalism and capitalism"; Indonesian democracy was and should be based on cooperation (*gotong royong*). Workers could not base their struggle on individualism which would separate them from other groups. Rather, they had to base themselves on *gotong royong* "so that workers, farmers and similar groups will strive together for the interests of the whole Indonesian people and nation". His statement went on to make suggestions on opportunities for possible future industrial development in the region, noting his efforts to provide more autonomy to Yogyakarta's villages and to promote cooperatives.[105]

We cannot make too much of these brief remarks, but some comments are possible. Hamengku Buwono would probably have denied it, but his efforts to transform villages into more self-reliant units might owe something to the former Dutch Governor, only just released from an internment camp, who many years before had written a thesis on *The Autonomy of the Indonesian Village*. The reference to cooperatives may reflect the influence of Hatta, a known enthusiast for cooperatives, whom he would have met several times by this stage and to whom he was to grow increasingly close in the next few years.

His remarks on the necessity to base democracy on *gotong royong* and for the need for all groups to subordinate their interests to the greater good are hardly the standpoint of a committed supporter of Western-style, individualist, "fifty per cent plus one" democracy. Many Indonesian leaders disliked significant elements of European- or American-style democracy and canvassed the necessity of adapting foreign models to Indonesia's different political and social needs. The need for orientation towards and responsibility to the wider social group was commonly expressed in dominant ideologies in later times. Such sentiments were expressed by Sukarno in justifying Guided Democracy and Suharto in asserting the ideology of the New Order. The importance of unity among and between different groups in society, and the need to avoid disruptive factionalism while ensuring representation of all groups, was emphasized in different ways by both men.[106] Sukarno detested the social disunity created by partisan politics in the democracy of the 1950s. In his speeches leading up to the inception of Guided Democracy, he too emphasized the importance of *gotong royong*.[107] From a very different standpoint, Suharto too was later to criticize social disunity, but his target was the disunity created by the PKI and other groups,[108] and it was Suharto who much later gave the doctrine of representation of "functional groups" a new and powerful meaning.

As the national government settled into its new location and negotiations in Jakarta wore on, Yogyakarta developed a new atmosphere. Conferences of major organizations were held, visitors came and went, the government tried to consolidate itself, and refugees arrived.[109] "Yogyakarta was full of strange, fanatical young men coming and going between the so-called fighting fronts, and of frenzied refugees from areas occupied by the allies."[110] Leaders in Yogyakarta could easily become impatient with the tortuous negotiations in Jakarta. "In the old royal city of Yogyakarta, where not a single allied soldier could be found, and where the exhilaration of merdeka could be freely experienced, all the variegated forces of the independence movement were gathered."[111] The Yogyakarta KNI, headed by Mohammad Saleh who was known to favour "struggle" (*perjuangan*) rather than diplomasi, cabled Prime Minister Syahrir with the demand that it would only accept "100 percent independence" (*Merdeka 100%*, the slogan of the Tan Malaka opposition).[112]

If the town differed in tone from Jakarta which was becoming increasingly dominated by the Allies, it also differed from Solo. By early 1946 the febrile situation there was going from bad to worse. Both royal palaces had struggled to preserve their separate identities and had blocked Republican attempts to unify the administration of the Special Region. Pemuda groups became more and more impatient with both palaces. The news of the Sunan's affair with a Eurasian woman, at a time when Eurasians were commonly regarded as Dutch spies, sharpened public feeling.[113] In January 1946 hundreds of pemudas from the Barisan Banteng (BB) surrounded the kraton and kidnapped the Sunan, his mother-in-law, and his adviser Prince Suryoamijoyo.[114] They were held for three days, and the Sunan never really overcame the attendant loss of prestige. By May, he was announcing that the Special Region could be abolished "if the people wished it".[115] By this time, many civil servants were following the instructions of the local KNI and ignoring the kepatihan.

After attempts at mediation by the government amid growing oppositionist fervour, all four local kabupatens separated themselves from the Sunanate, and senior army officers publicly supported the opposition. The government vainly tried to bring in the popular governor of East Java (Suryo) to control the situation, and then ordered the arrest of senior Barisan Banteng (BB) leaders.[116] But after angry public reactions, Sudirman himself released the BB leaders. An emergency cabinet meeting resulted in the formation of a new government in the region, abolishing the Sunanate and Mangkunegaran,[117] followed by the declaration of a state of emergency several days later. Soejatno concluded that this episode amounted to a genuine social revolution where the feudal and bureaucratic power of the nobles and *pamong praja* was replaced by new forces.[118]

Soon after, Syahrir's kidnapping in Solo in the June 1946 affair illustrated both the weakening of his influence and the profound divisions within the Republic. Syahrir was quickly released after an appeal by Sukarno,[119] and the government rounded up the leaders of the kidnap plot, including the head of the Yogyakarta KNID, Mohammad Saleh.[120] In a further dramatic development, Mohamad Yamin, Sudarsono (now a Major General), and others confronted Sukarno with a series of demands which would have amounted to abandonment of diplomasi. Sudarsono and his associates were quickly arrested, and the leaders of the affair subsequently stood trial, which revealed much detail about the events of the time but left obscure Sudirman's ambiguous role.[121] As a result, the Tan Malaka group was severely weakened.

Hamengku Buwono seems to have played no part in the affair, but because of the involvement of such Yogyakarta personalities as Sudarsono and Mohammed Saleh, he and the Yogyakarta region could not have been indifferent. He never made a public comment on the affair, but he would almost certainly have supported the central government. Public opinion in Yogyakarta would have been ambivalent at first, because the local legislature was impatient of diplomasi and the local newspaper *Kedaulatan Rakjat* was sympathetic to Tan Malaka and very critical of Amir Syarifuddin.[122] But after six months' experience as the capital city of the Republic, the populace would have been suspicious of opposition action, centred in the rival city of Solo, which was presented publicly as an attempt to overthrow the central government.

An account by a visiting Dutch journalist/politician describes attitudes in the Yogyakarta palace around August 1946.[123] A brother of the Sultan tells the visitor of the close relationship between the palace and the Republic. Asked about the possibility of violent social revolution in Java as in Sumatra, the prince replies that such behaviour in Yogyakarta is out of the question. But if by "social revolution" is meant the creation of a modern state, the elimination of illiteracy and the improvement of social welfare, these are Republican goals which the Sultan fully supports. The visitor recounts the colonial attitudes he has just encountered in Batavia and the belief there that the population really supports the Dutch queen against the "fascist Republic" and that the nobility and the former colonial officials are hoping to be liberated from its clutches.[124] The prince replies: "What a false idea of relationships within the Republic! If it must come to fighting, the Sultan will do his utmost to resist the restoration of Dutch authority.… We are nationalists too."[125] This was all too sadly prophetic of events two years later.

In a broadcast to mark the anniversary of the proclamation, Hamengku Buwono praised the revolutionary spirit of the youth who confronted the Japanese the previous year.[126] The whole Indonesian people desired independence, and this was evident even among the federalists at the recent Malino conference. Although the Dutch based their claims on past history, the Republicans based theirs on their current identity as a free people, who wished to cooperate closely with other peoples in building a new world based on law, security and welfare. "If the Dutch, influenced by a small group of colonialists and capitalists, want to assert their colonial intentions, they will not have their way against the gentle[127] Indonesian people, who are … determined to show the world that they are now mature, and capable of managing and defending their own country."[128] Hamengku Buwono referred again to the Atlantic Charter.[129]

A report by a Dutch delegation[130] which visited Yogyakarta and East Java in September 1946 reported that food supplies in these areas appeared adequate and at normal levels for the time of year, and the state of public health seemed satisfactory. The main problem was scarcity of suitable transport, severely hampering efforts to deliver foodstuffs to deficit areas. The availability of clothing in the region was "moderate to good" as textile supplies had become available from stocks in Japanese warehouses. Western clothing was more commonly worn than before, perhaps because it demanded less cloth.[131] The rice fields revealed normal planting patterns, but fertilizer was almost non-existent. The forests had been badly damaged by uncontrolled cutting for fuel. The overall impression in the towns was of reasonable order and tidiness.[132]

The delegation noted greater self-confidence among the Indonesians "accompanied by the disappearance of docility and submissive attitudes", and a strong desire for "merdeka ideals". Nationalistic feelings were commonly mixed with the desire for social change, with little attempt to distinguish between the two. No raw anti-Dutch hatred was encountered,[133] but the prevalence of uniforms and the Japanese-style drilling of many groups of young men was an uncomfortable reminder of the Japanese period. The key role of Sukarno was emphasized.[134]

Hamengku Buwono told the delegation that land availability was a very sensitive question in his region; restoration of the sugar industry would be difficult and it could not be returned to its pre-war condition; local farmers would accept the presence of sugar mills only if they shared the benefits.[135] Sugar had always been a sensitive issue because of resentment of the takeover of rice land for the use of Dutch-owned sugar mills. We have seen in Chapter 4 that the issue was exploited by the PKN in the 1930s, and the alleged indifference of the Dutch sugar industry to local farmers' interests was mentioned in the propaganda for the Mataram canal during the Japanese period. In April 1946 discontent among peasants in Yogyakarta had led to the blocking of irrigation channels and destruction of some crops.[136]

HAMENGKU BUWONO IN THE NATIONAL GOVERNMENT

Hamengku Buwono gained a new role when Syahrir named him as Minister of State for Special Region Affairs in his third cabinet.[137] Syahrir probably appointed Hamengku Buwono because of his growing reputation as a moderate reformer. The emergence of Yogyakarta as a pilot area for a variety of democratic reforms made it a model for other regions.[138] The Dutch Colonies Ministry noted the juxtaposition in the ministry of several figures (like Syahrir himself and Amir Syarifuddin) who had been jailed under the Dutch regime, together with "the Sultan of Yogyakarta who had previously been very closely connected to us".[139]

Hamengku Buwono now for the first time performed official functions which stretched outside his own domain. He joined a Republican delegation which visited Jakarta for talks with the Dutch,[140] probably his first visit to

Jakarta since the proclamation. He seems also to have joined the negotiating committee examining the conditions of Indonesian prisoners held by the Dutch.[141]

After the abortive attempt to name him as Minister of Defence eleven months before, he had thus finally entered the national political arena, and his first attendance of cabinet meetings in 1946 was the beginning of a long involvement in national politics, ending with attendance of his last cabinet meeting in 1978. Although the majority of his cabinet colleagues were party political figures, he was always described as "non-party", an appellation he abandoned only when he joined Golkar twenty-five years later. The non-party identification gave him an air of being above everyday partisan politics and a lasting impression of detachment commensurate with his princely status.

He remained one of several ministers of state in successive cabinets over the next three years, rising to Coordinator of Internal Security and Minister of Defence in the dramatic years of 1948 and 1949. His role as Minister of State apparently included providing advice to other regions on the reforms he was conducting in Yogyakarta; he later described himself as a "troubleshooter".[142] October 1946 found him in Solo advising the local authorities, and travels further afield were foreshadowed "because of the large number of special regions in Indonesia (over 300)".[143] It was not an easy task even to visit such regions, many of which existed only in theory in any case. He had already visited Sumatra's east coast in March 1946,[144] apparently to investigate the position of the traditional rulers and their families who had been interned by local Republicans. He later described his role as an attempt to "solve the problem of the social revolution" in Sumatra,[145] a near-impossible enterprise.

In April 1947, he toured Sumatra again, visiting Pematang Siantar, Bukittinggi and Medan. He warned the people of Bukittinggi[146] that the recently signed Linggajati agreement did not guarantee independence, drawing attention to Dutch activities which were prejudicial to the Republic.[147] To TNI officers in Pematang Siantar, he again emphasized the need for unity between the army, government and people.[148] He also held talks with the Republican mayor of Medan.[149] Later, in 1948, plans were made by Sukarno and the Sulawesi Republican leader Dr Sam Ratulangie to have the Sultan head a Republican mission to Sulawesi to promote the role and influence of the Republic there, but this proved impossible for practical reasons.[150]

LOCAL REFORMS

Hamengku Buwono instigated a series of reforms in Yogyakarta during 1945–48. He decreed that henceforth all official business should be carried out in Indonesian rather than Javanese,[151] in May 1946 he created a Yogyakarta City Council,[152] commenced a range of economic projects, and later formed representative political institutions in the entire province down to the village level.[153] The village elections involved a franchise of all inhabitants over the age of eighteen, the separation of village executive and legislative organs, and the mergers of villages into larger and more viable entities.[154] He assigned various palace buildings and later provided land to the new national university which was to become one of Indonesia's best known educational institutions, Gadjah Mada University. In December 1945, the Steering Committee of the Yogyakarta KNI debated a new draft constitution for the special region.[155] It was from these measures, coupled with the invitation to the Republican government to move to Yogyakarta, that his reputation as a reforming leader really began. Among these developments, in July 1947 Hamengku Buwono nominated Sudarisman Purwokusumo as mayor of Yogyakarta city, a post which he held for the next twenty years. During the Revolution, he was a useful ally for Hamengku Buwono.[156]

After Hamengku Buwono's appointment to the ministry, his reputation was growing: "The Sultan has essentially anticipated the revolution. He has created a state structure in his region which accords fully with people's sovereignty. Moreover, his leadership of the public service and of the people which he conducted personally by descending from his throne has made him loved."[157] Such reactions allayed fears in kraton circles that he was sacrificing his standing by becoming more accessible to the common people.

In November 1946, the British had handed over responsibility to the Dutch and had withdrawn from the Indies. Some months later, the last of the Dutch and associated internees were evacuated from Republican camps, and the Dutch were freer to take military action.[158] Nevertheless, a brief period of hope emerged that same month when Prime Minister Syahrir and the Dutch signed an agreement at Linggajati in West Java in which the Republic was recognized as the de facto power in Java and Sumatra. The agreement came under immediate attack from radicals in Indonesia and conservatives in the Netherlands; Indonesian radicals led by Tan Malaka excoriated the agreement as a feeble backdown by a government under pressure from the Dutch and the United States.

After a visit to Yogyakarta with an official delegation,[159] the colonial official P.J.A. Idenburg, who had known Hamengku Buwono in earlier times, described him as a Javanese prince of "high calibre" who had managed to maintain his standing even in the difficult Japanese period and had shown a keen appreciation of the new circumstances. Hamengku Buwono told Idenburg of his current threefold role, as ruler of the Sultanate, Governor of the "wider Yogyakarta territory" (whatever that meant), and also Minister of State. But as in the conversation with the Dutch delegation the year before, he confined himself to local matters, even disclaiming knowledge of national political affairs and discouraging Idenburg from attempting to discuss them.

Idenburg nevertheless concluded:

> He is an impressive Javanese personality and my personal impression is that his thoughts and vision about Java's future go in a quite different direction from those of the present men in power. But he has endless patience and is not a figure who would act in a spontaneous and unprepared manner when the aims of the action are not assured, and I believe that an essential element of these aims would be the greatest possible autonomy for Java, under the direction of the Sultan.[160]

This judgement nourished ideas that Hamengku Buwono was cannily biding his time and awaiting the moment when he could split off from the Republicans. In this the Dutch underestimated his nationalism and overestimated his ambition. An intriguing feature of Idenburg's comment is the reference to "Java" and not Indonesia, as if the Sultan was only concerned with the one island.

THE FIRST DUTCH ATTACK

By mid-1947 the Linggajati process was reaching a dead end. In further negotiations, Syahrir was forced to make damaging concessions, among others accepting that the Dutch crown could in effect control Indonesian foreign policy, a concession unacceptable to many of his supporters. The Syahrir government fell in June when other members of the left wing withdrew support.[161]

Divisions within the Republic and increasing Dutch impatience and assurance of their military superiority led to greatly heightened tension. In July 1947 the Dutch launched their first major offensive against the Republic, occupying large areas of Java and Sumatra, especially major towns, oil fields and coal mines. Van Mook and army commander General Spoor wanted to finish the job by occupying Yogyakarta,[162] but after strenuous international efforts to restrain the Dutch as well as their recognition of the need to absorb their gains, they stopped short of attempting to occupy all Republican territory. During the attack, many important Republican leaders (not including Hamengku Buwono) were evacuated to areas outside Yogyakarta, but after the subsequent ceasefire on 4 August, they returned.[163]

Hamengku Buwono told the Council of Youth Leaders that now was the time to do more and talk less. He called for measures to avoid public panic "such as had occurred following the recent bombing of the Maguwo airport"; he sought to preserve normal trading and commerce as much as possible and to avoid sharp increases in prices. He asked the Chinese community to cooperate with these efforts.[164] Some weeks later, he was threatening the fiercest possible defence of Yogyakarta if the Dutch were to attack it.[165] Behind the scenes he was encouraging firm resistance to the Dutch, even supporting a small Muslim group's determination to launch a holy war (*perang sabil*) against the foreign invaders.[166]

He made a considered public response to the Dutch attack in early August in a radio broadcast, where he asserted that despite the Republic's efforts for peace, the Dutch had launched a colonial war:

> This evening I direct my remarks to the people of the Special Region of Yogyakarta. The Dutch have left the path of peace and have taken up arms. Our government had shown its goodwill in efforts to reach a peaceful solution, but sadly this was of no avail and the Dutch have begun a colonial war. The Dutch want to rule over us again, an aim which we cannot tolerate. I call on every Indonesian youth who wishes to defend his homeland to report to one of the [military] headquarters in the city. The blood of Mataram flows in each citizen of the Special Region, a people who earlier were well-known for refusing to be dominated by anyone. The struggle which is being conducted now will decide the fate of our country. No one knows what the future will bring. To uphold the honour of our land and people I call on all inhabitants to play a real part in the defence of this region. A country which takes up arms against tyranny will be respected by all the great powers. Now is the time to shun emotion and divisive factionalism. As you all know Maj Gen Urip Suharjo [*sic*] has

been named as the Military Governor of this region. I call on the Chinese community to support us in this difficult time through financial support to the military headquarters and through helping to maintain law and order. This is also in your own interest. Take care that you do not help the enemy in his effort to tyrannise over us again. Keep your shops open and do not hoard supplies. I call on each citizen to defend this province so that our people will be respected by all nations. Merdeka![167]

Here, clearly and simply, was a statement of his anti-colonial beliefs, his support for the Republic, his rejection of the reimposition of Dutch rule, and his acceptance of the need for forcible resistance if armed conflict could not be avoided. Doubtless because he was addressing a Yogyakarta audience, Hamengku Buwono's call to Mataram's patriotism had a Javanese element to it. One wonders whether locally resident non-Javanese felt excluded by this call to arms; and the reference to the Chinese, while understandable in the style of the time, could only reinforce stereotypes about this vulnerable community. Nevertheless, his relations with the Chinese community were generally cordial and trusting.[168] His suspicion of the Dutch was shown when he advised a delegation from West Java not to trust Dutch promises, because their sole aim was to oppress the Indonesian people once again.[169]

A NEFIS intelligence analyst commented: "The Sultan is fully convinced that the foundation of an independent Republic is the best outcome for his people.... He does not hate the Dutch but sees no benefit in Dutch policy based on pre-war assumptions.... His radio broadcast must be seen as a true reflection of his innermost convictions.... [But] clearly he is not aware of the true intentions of the Dutch Government.... The Sultan's stance must be seen as similar to that of other Javanese intellectuals ... who see the return of the Dutch as meaning the restoration of the pre-war social order", where the Dutch were seen to be first and the Javanese last.[170] This pertinent intelligence assessment evidently went unnoticed in Dutch official circles, and many continued to believe, like Idenburg, that the Sultan's secret objectives diverged from those of the Republic. The "let-out" in the assessment was the claim that he had misunderstood the true benevolence of Dutch policy, so that officials might believe that Hamengku Buwono could be talked round if the Dutch obtained access to him.[171]

In September 1947 Hamengku Buwono became Military Governor of the Yogyakarta Special Region, replacing Urip Sumoharjo. He thus for the first time combined the functions of the civilian and military powers in his own region;[172] this might be regarded as the pinnacle of his career in terms of day-to-day power in the principality. The new post was no sinecure, and as more refugees, as well as evacuated soldiers, streamed into Yogyakarta, levels of tension among disparate groups led to a number of clashes. This was perhaps inevitable when many armed units, some of them speaking different languages, were quartered around the town and environs. Nasution reports an actual exchange of fire between Siliwangi and naval units near the well-known restaurant Toko Oen in the main street, and further incidents among military units guarding various strategic locations in the city. Hamengku Buwono managed "with great difficulty to restore a tranquil atmosphere with Army and Police help".[173] These incidents must have been very alarming, raising as they did the fear of anarchy which had become familiar in Solo and some other towns in Java.

NATIONAL DEVELOPMENTS

After further negotiations, Prime Minister Amir Syarifuddin found himself in a similar position to his predecessor Syahrir, having to make further concessions in an effort to avoid major conflict, in the hope that international pressure would restrain Dutch ambition. The Renville agreement was signed in January 1948, and involved several contentious concessions to the Dutch position. These were made under heavy American pressure, but the American representative on the UN Good Offices Commission made several assurances to the Republicans, especially about future planned plebiscites in Dutch-occupied areas which the Republicans were confident of winning.[174] A strong implication of the American assurances was that the United States would continue to support the Renville agreement.

Many Republicans regarded the agreement as a humiliation, especially as it involved the withdrawal of Republican forces from areas which they held, notably the withdrawal of the entire Siliwangi division from West Java.[175] Amir quickly lost support and resigned after only two weeks. Negotiations nevertheless continued under a new "presidential" cabinet headed by Vice President Hatta, in which Hamengku Buwono retained his post as Minister of State, and Hatta dedicated himself to implementing the Renville agreement. He also began reorganizing the armed forces, dismantling the political apparatus established by Amir and weakening the influence of the left within the army.[176]

The cabinet had several anxious discussions about their approach to the troubled Solo region, especially the appointment of a new military governor to restore order. Hamengku Buwono gave a counsel of perfection, arguing that the new military governor should be a man whom the troops would obey, that clear instructions should be given, and a clear policy plan prepared.[177] The appointment was so contentious that it was not until September, on the eve of the Madiun affair, that the cabinet appointed Gatot Subroto as Military Governor of the Solo area.

During 1948, conditions in Yogyakarta and central Java steadily worsened as more refugees arrived, and as the Dutch blockade tightened its grip. George Kahin visited the city at this time and noted, "Driving on we passed only one automobile, but as we became closer to the city soon began to encounter an increasing number of carts and bicycles, that constituted its almost exclusive means of transport.... Most of the people looked thin and undernourished."[178]

The Chinese community also came under pressure and, in some cases, actual attack, and Hamengku Buwono was forced to assure the Chinese consul that "We will do our best to prevent such incidents and we will take preventive measures."[179] It is in scattered evidence like this that we can catch the tone of the experienced administrator.

Hatta appointed Hamengku Buwono as Coordinator of Internal Security around this time, although little is known about the background to the appointment. Hatta laconically mentions that he had to take the Defence portfolio himself because the Sultan had refused it, but he gives no further details.[180] Hamengku Buwono's reluctance is hard to explain, but perhaps he was still smarting over his experience in 1945.

The next major crisis in a year of crises was the Madiun affair.[181] The disillusion of the left wing with the policy of negotiation, coupled with the unheralded arrival from Russia of the veteran communist leader Muso, led to increasing radicalism on the left, including Amir's startling announcement that he had long been a secret PKI member. Muso's new leadership — bolstered by his recent arrival from the centre of world communism — was quickly accepted by the PKI and associated organizations, including important figures like Amir, Alimin, Setiajit and Tan Ling Jie. Muso, as a Moscow-line communist, was however unacceptable to the Tan Malaka left, which prided itself on its independence from foreign influence.

A multi-sided conflict in Solo between leftist forces and various elements of the official army, including Siliwangi units, led to a government crackdown. After heavy fighting, the pro-government Siliwangi and its allies eventually expelled leftist units from the city.[182] Apparently fearing further assaults from the government, PKI forces in Madiun launched a local coup on 21 September, which was subsequently endorsed by Muso and Amir, who were touring outside Madiun at the time. In such an uncoordinated and unprepared manner did the communist challenge come to a head.

The next day Hamengku Buwono[183] as Security Coordinator met Sukarno to discuss the matter, and they sent for Colonel Nasution. Sukarno asked Nasution to prepare a plan to quell the revolt, for discussion and approval in cabinet. Nasution argued that no time should be lost because the Madiun uprising should be squashed before it spread.[184] He feared that other disaffected commanders in East and Central Java might join the revolt.[185] Sukarno said that Nasution was free to make immediate preparations. The subsequent cabinet meeting empowered Sudirman "to take necessary action to safeguard the nation".[186] In the meantime, Nasution had convened a meeting of commanders and issued the necessary orders. The next morning, Sudirman placed Nasution in strategic command of the operation.[187]

Republican leaders, including Sukarno, Hamengku Buwono, Sudirman, and the Masyumi leader Sukiman, made broadcasts[188] rejecting the coup and calling on the people to support the legitimate government. Hamengku Buwono called on the people to stand by the Hatta government, asserting that it stood for the development of the country while Muso and the communists only desired destruction.[189] Siliwangi units and other government forces advanced on Madiun and quickly defeated the communists; both Muso and Amir were killed. During the period the atmosphere in Yogyakarta was tense at times, especially when a PKI death list was reportedly found. Some notables moved to the Yogyakarta Police Headquarters to avoid possible communist death squads.[190]

In his 1986 *Asiaweek* interview, Hamengku Buwono hinted intriguingly at a further background role for himself in the Madiun affair (words in square brackets in the original):

> In Madiun I proposed strengthening the military, but Muso [a communist leader] had arrived already. I was told East Java commander Sungkono wanted to join him. I went in my own car and the Governor of East Java, Pak Suryo, and the head of the provincial police were behind me in their own car as far as Solo. They must have gone to a restaurant. At Walikukun I saw these black people, the warok [tough mystics, used

by the communists] sitting by the roadside smoking. Two hours later a courier reported that Suryo and the police chief had been murdered at Walikukun half an hour after I went through.[191]

Suryo — who had moved by then from East Java to Yogyakarta to chair the Supreme Advisory Council (DPA) — was indeed killed at Walikukun, which lies between Solo and Madiun. Nasution[192] notes that on 9 November 1948, as the Madiun affair was entering its final stages, Suryo and two others were killed by pro-PKI forces at Walikukun; he does not mention Hamengku Buwono. A discrepancy is Nasution's claim that the murders of Suryo and the police chief only became known after two days when the bodies were discovered, while Hamengku Buwono claims to have found out two hours later from a courier. Since Hamengku Buwono knew Suryo and had visited him in East Java just after the November 1945 Surabaya fighting (see previous chapter), it is highly credible that two such prestigious figures might be called on to perform some role in resolving the Madiun affair, but nothing more is known about the episode.

For the purposes of our story, Hamengku Buwono had again given his support to the official Republican government against a challenge to it. This was predictable enough, because he had already identified himself firmly with the Sukarno-Hatta leadership, and had established the Laskar Rakyat Mataram partly to block communist influence on local youth. He knew that a PKI government would have little use for feudal leaders, no matter how progressive.[193] If a Dutch intelligence report is to be believed, Hamengku Buwono had already had severe differences with Amir Syarifuddin when the latter was Prime Minister.[194]

In Hamengku Buwono's new capacity as security coordinator, he made a further proposal for the governance of the Solo area, which he frankly likened to "the Wild West".[195] Reporting to Hatta that the best approach was to use those administrative organs which were still in reasonable shape (as well as incorporating the princes so that they would not "become an anti-revolutionary force"), he proposed a Solo Special Region with its own identity but guided by legislation already in force in Central Java.[196] The structure would be headed by a Governor, assisted by a seven-person Governing Council;[197] five of these would be nominated by the local legislature, and one member (each) nominated by the Sunan and Mangkunegoro. The Governor would be appointed by the President, and assisted by an Advisory Council "consisting of the Sunan and the Mangkunegoro".[198]

Hamengku Buwono's acceptance of the political unreliability of the Sunan and Mangkunegoro is revealing, but he was not prepared to discount their potential popular attraction, and he could no doubt tell the Solo princes that with this proposal he had done the best he could for them. To anti-feudal Republicans, he could point to the relatively small influence which the Solo nobles would have in the government, given their minor representation in the proposed new structure. The proposal was also calculated to appeal to local sentiment in Solo, where the incorporation into Central Java had never been popular. But it did not explain how to overcome the extreme factionalism in the city, including the rivalry between the two kratons which had negated previous attempts to unify the city government. Admittedly, having expelled the leftists from the city, the central government now had its best chance in years to bring some order to the area. But the timing of the proposal was unlucky — six weeks after it was made, the Dutch launched their second major attack.

Even more important than efforts to pacify Solo was the need to prepare against such an attack. During the Madiun affair, the Republic had to keep many troops on the demarcation lines, because of the fear that the Dutch might take advantage of the internal conflict to launch a decisive strike.[199] During 1948, the Republican leaders discussed contingency plans against a further Dutch attack. The intention was that the leadership would join the guerrilla struggle, and all ministers apparently agreed to this, although Hamengku Buwono said he would stay in the palace.[200] The contingency plans had a military and a political dimension, but while some military plans were in place, they were not fully implemented in the confusion of the actual Dutch attack. Nasution recounts frankly that although the army headquarters was able to withdraw more or less as planned to a station five kilometres north of Prambanan, many important documents had been left behind and civil defence preparations were non-existent.[201] The national government was caught by surprise, but at the regional level, plans for an underground civilian government had been prepared. We will describe further these plans and how they worked out in practice in the following chapter.

SUMMARY

Hamengku Buwono cemented his reputation as a progressive reformer in this period. Although a reasonable amount is known about the series of measures and reforms introduced in the first phases of the Revolution, very little has emerged about the process by which these reforms were conceptualized and formulated. Hamengku Buwono had in the kraton some senior and experienced administrators such as Honggowongso and Notonegoro, as well as his experienced brother Puruboyo, and his other brothers Prabuningrat and Bintoro, and able young officials like Selosumarjan, although their exact roles in relation to the reform programme are almost totally unknown. But the existence of experienced and capable officials alongside promising new ones illustrates one aspect of Hamengku Buwono's career, namely his ability to find suitably talented associates, who repaid his confidence in them and to whom he could delegate substantial responsibility.

In this period, Hamengku Buwono finally emerged as the anti-colonial nationalist he had perhaps already been for many years, and his commitment to more democratic forms and representative institutions also became evident. In a dangerously volatile polity, he succeeded in capturing and keeping a great deal of popular support and even affection, an affection he retained for the remainder of his long career.

How did he do this? Several factors came into play. The first was his exploitation of his status as Sultan which still had powerful appeal among some sections of the Yogyakarta community, notably the older generation, the nobility, many sections of the bureaucracy, and the rural areas. This by itself was insufficient to ensure survival, as demonstrated by the circumstances of Solo and especially Sumatra. But to this Hamengku Buwono added several crucially well-judged decisions, especially the swift adherence to the Republic, the creation of the Laskar Rakyat, and the move of the central government to Yogyakarta. The presence of the government in his city was probably enough by itself to strengthen his hold on his people, but he had already established a wide degree of personal popularity and acceptance.

For Dutch officials, memories of his relatively smooth cooperation with them before the Japanese occupation, and Hamengku Buwono's reticence about national politics in their sporadic contacts with him after the Proclamation provided enough grounds to believe that given the right circumstances he might collaborate with them again. They were aware of his consistently anti-colonial statements between 1945 and 1948, but were somehow reluctant to take them at face value. The extent to which they deceived themselves about him was to appear in 1949.

For the Republicans of virtually every stamp, Hamengku Buwono had proved himself in the past three years, especially in contrast to the more erratic and inflexible performance of his counterparts in Solo. His reform measures, the creation of the Laskar Rakyat Mataram, his strong pro-independence stance, and his close association with the Republican leadership left little room for doubt about his loyalty. Most would have been startled to hear the Dutch doubts on the point. For all but the most radical nationalists, a part of Hamengku Buwono's popularity would have been the unstated cachet of having a real Sultan in their ranks; the cause was so compelling and so justified that a scion of the traditional Javanese nobility had become a dedicated Republican.

For leaders like Sukarno and Hatta, Hamengku Buwono became an increasingly trusted colleague, especially after the move to Yogyakarta, and even more so after Hatta's assumption of the Prime Ministership in early 1948. Yogyakarta was the Republic's base area, and Hamengku Buwono's local popularity reinforced the wider popularity and exposure of Sukarno and other leaders. The assurance of fervent public support and competent and innovative government in a stable Yogyakarta added credibility to the Republic, both in other regions of Indonesia and internationally.

Notes

1. Abrar Yusra, *Komat-Kamit Selosoemardjan* [The Murmurings of Selosumarjan], p. 144.
2. *SM*, 18 August 1945.
3. Ibid., 20 August 1945.
4. Kahin, *Nationalism and Revolution*, p. 127.
5. Abrar Yusra, op. cit., ibid.
6. *SM*, ibid., five cables to senior Japanese officials including the Commander-in-Chief.
7. It is not entirely clear whether even at this stage leaders in Yogyakarta were aware of the Japanese surrender.
8. *SM*, op. cit.
9. *SA*, 22 August 1945.
10. E.g., the remarks of Haji Agus Salim quoted in Hatta, *Mohammad Hatta, Indonesian Patriot, Memoirs*, p. 247, and *Wilopo 70 Tahun* [Wilopo at 70], p. 43.
11. See previous chapter and *TUR*, p. 58.
12. *TUR*, Annex to contract, item (1), p. 327.
13. Some Indian rulers, whose realms had been independent in the past, believed in the late 1940s that independence for India could mean independence for

them too. They were quickly disabused, although six were allowed some privileges until all were abolished in the 1970s. Collins and Lapierre, op. cit., p. 209 and p. 245.
14. Surprisingly, the idea of an independent Yogyakarta was raised in recent years in the heated debates about the Special Region's *keistimewaan* (specialness), leading up to the new Law on Specialness passed by the national Parliament in 2012. See, for example, Heru Wahyukismoyo, ed., *Keistimewaan Jogja vs Demokratisasi* [Yogyakarta's Specialness versus Democratization], Bigraf Yogyakarta, 2004.
15. *KR*, 9 April 1947. Also Ariffin Omar, *Bangsa Melayu* [The Malay People], p. 68 and p. 85.
16. Khoo Boo Teik, *Paradoxes of Mahathirism*, p. 207, notes that the sultans eventually became "symbols of the special position of Malays in Malaysia".
17. See, for example, Appleby, *Liberalism and Republicanism in the Historical Imagination*, p. 217.
18. Informant no. 2, interview, 3 October 2003, who, on the basis of conversations with Hamengku Buwono in the 1960s and 1970s, is certain that he took the initiative here. The similarity between the statements by the four princes argues for fairly close coordination of some kind.
19. *SM*, 30 August 1945. "Pada waktu yang sulit dan muskil ini." The reasons for the gloomier tone of this statement are unclear; perhaps Dutch rejection of the proclamation had already become known.
20. Ibid.
21. *Sinar Matahari*, 4 September 1945. Both statements are dated 1 September 1945.
22. *Sinar Matahari*, 6 September 1945. Both statements are dated 5 September.
23. Selosumarjan, *Social Change in Jogjakarta*, organizational diagrams, pp. 418–19.
24. Ibid., p. 63. Selosumarjan dates the merger from September 1945, but indicates that it was only formalized by a decree in 1952.
25. Suwarno, *Hamengku Buwono IX dan Sistem Birokrasi Pemerintahan Yogyakarta 1942–74, Sebuah Tinjauan Historis* [Hamengku Buwono IX and the Bureaucratic System of the Yogyakarta Government 1942–74, a Historical Review], p. 168. Suwarno says the KNID was formed during September.
26. Selosumarjan, op. cit., p. 62.
27. Suwarno, op. cit., p. 168. Suwarno divides the KNID into ten groups, including former Hokokai members, former Dutch-era party figures, PKN representatives, Taman Siswa, police and journalists.
28. *Pemuda* — Indonesian term meaning "youth", commonly used in the Revolution for groups (or gangs) of young men.
29. Many accounts tell of the terror and insecurity felt by Dutch and Eurasians, especially women, during the so-called *siap* period. See Willems and de Moor,

eds., *Het Einde van Indie, Indische Nederlanders tijdens de japanse bezetting en de dekolonisatie* [The End of the Indies, Eurasians during the Japanese Occupation and the Decolonisation Period], p. 11, p. 129 and pp. 188–98.
30. *KR*, 14 September 1995, commemorative article by P.J. Suwarno. Incidents involving the Indonesian flag were occurring all over Java — Kahin, op. cit., p. 137.
31. *KR*, 10 October 1994, commemorative article by P.J. Suwarno.
32. *KR*, ibid., 14 September 1995.
33. NIOD 007142 — Sitrep no. 14 of 5 October 1945, signed by Flt Lt Ball "on behalf of CO 5 RAPWI Contact team", apparently written by Wg Cmdr Tull.
34. Ibid. Strangely, this report fails to mention the internees already in the Yogyakarta area.
35. NIOD 007149, Tull report ("Extracts from the report of Wg Cmdr Tull"), p. 3.
36. NIOD 007112, report of Maj Gen Nakamura, attached to letter of 31 October 1945 from Lt Gen Nagano to Maj Gen Hawthorn, Commander Allied Land Forces.
37. The Japanese were led by Major Ohtsuka, a Kempeitai officer later sentenced to death for war crimes — NIOD 008755, p. 4, Roodnummer 336, Temporary War Tribunal records, Batavia.
38. *Sejarah, Perjuangan Yogya Benteng Proklamasi* [The History of Yogyakarta as a Bastion of the Proclamation — cited below as *Sejarah*], p. 56, says 21 Indonesians were killed and 32 wounded, without giving Japanese casualty figures. See also NIOD 007139.
39. *KR*, ibid., and *TUR*, account by Prabuningrat, p. 170.
40. Anderson, op. cit., p. 145n.
41. NIOD 7143, Report by Tull to RAPWI Control Staff in Batavia, 7 October 1945.
42. Soejatno, *Revolution in Surakarta 1945–50*, PhD thesis, ANU, 1982, pp. 68–70.
43. Netherlands Indies Civil Administration.
44. *KR*, 18 October 1945.
45. Ibid., "firm resistance combined with diplomacy" is a free translation of *perjuangan-diplomasi* (literally "struggle-diplomacy"), an intriguing combination of two terms which were becoming very common, but which were usually taken as antithetical or even contradictory.
46. Ibid. References to the ideals of the Atlantic Charter were common in Republican statements.
47. Kahin, op. cit., p. 152, and (on *Perjuangan Kita*), pp. 164–65.
48. See M. van Delden, *Orde in de Chaos? De internering in en evacuatie uit de Republikeinse kampen* [Order in Chaos? The Internment in and Evacuation

from the Republican Camps], edited by Willems and de Moor, op. cit., pp. 188–207.
49. *East* CD-ROM — interview with S.A. Martherus, 1325.2. One Red Cross visit to Yogyakarta occurred in January 1946, not long after the central government moved there (see *Kronik Revolusi Indonesia* — henceforth cited as *KRI* with year number — *KRI 1946*, p. 13).
50. *East* — interview with L.R. Lux, no. 1217.1, p. 165.
51. *KR*, 26 January 1946.
52. "Szabo report" dated 25 April 1947, NIOD, Attachment to Diary no. 195, envelope no. 2.
53. Szabo report, op. cit., p. 7.
54. NA 2.21.036.02, part 125, Collectie Buurman van Vreeden, *Chronology of 1945*, p. 7. This gives the date of formation of the committee as 31 August.
55. NEFIS/CMI report held in Dutch Foreign Ministry, Inv no. 00922, letter by General Spoor of 27 April 1946 to C in C AFNEI, reporting on Republican meetings on these matters in Yogyakarta and Solo, chaired by Sukarno, some of which were attended by Hamengku Buwono.
56. Van Delden, in *Het Einde van Indie*, op. cit., p. 194.
57. *NIB*, vol. 3, p. 243, record of meeting of 17 January 1946, chaired by Brigadier Wingrove. The Sultan's representative was Dr Mangudoyo.
58. NIOD 081 487, copy of an account by L. and J. Doppert in *De Paal* magazine (date not given, no. pagination), *Een Portie Nasi Rames* [A Helping of Rice].
59. For example, in October 1946, large numbers were still being transported from Central Java — see report in *KRI*, 1946, p. 419. By November 1946, across all of Java, there still remained 25,000 internees, according to Dutch estimates, while the Indonesian estimate was 9,000 (Van der Post, Laurens, *The Admiral's Baby*, p. 247).
60. Article in *Moesson*, vol. 32, no. 16, 1 April 1988, by Mrs van Lith-van Schreven, p. 5.
61. *SM*, 20 August 1945.
62. *SM*, 23 August 1945.
63. Yusra, op. cit., p. 147.
64. Suwarno, *Hamengku Buwono IX*, op. cit., p. 185.
65. *Sejarah*, op. cit., p. 59.
66. *SM*, ibid. The first field commander was Sutarjo, known as Bung Tarjo — ibid.
67. NIOD 061314, text of Maklumat no. 5, in NEFIS Publication 15, 22 July 1946: *Laskar Rakjat van Java en Madura* [The People's Militia of Java and Madura], p. 3.
68. *TUR*, p. 69.
69. Ibid.
70. *KRI*, 1945, p. 112.

71. NA 2.10.17, Procureur Generaal Archive Part 367 (henceforth Proc Gen), NEFIS documents, report of monitoring of Radio Pemberontakan Jogja (Rebel Radio Jogja), 25 November 1945.
72. Anderson, op. cit., p. 247n.
73. Former Governor Adam testifies that the Sultan rarely wore uniform during the time when Adam knew him — Adam letter of 2 April 1957 to the RIOD, attachment headed *Rectificatie van Chronologie betr. Jogjakarta* [Correction of the Yogyakarta Chronology], p. 3; NIOD 037965.
74. E.g., *TUR*, p. 68, p. 94, and p. 146. Anderson (op. cit., ibid.) records his attendance at military meetings in uniform.
75. His puckish enjoyment of incognito appearances and his dislike of excessive deference is attested in several accounts over the years. The standard story in Indonesian accounts (e.g., *TUR*, p. 99) is his giving a lift to a woman trader who was proceeding to market with her goods, some time in 1946. On arrival, she asked how much the fare would be and was irritated when he refused the money proffered, thinking he was holding out for more. After he drove off, she supposedly fainted when advised of the driver's identity. He was also supposed to have made several incognito visits to villages and markets shortly after becoming Sultan — article by "Andaja", in *Hidup*, 29 April 1949, from MvD/CAD, NEFIS 1949, Bundle AA 21.
76. *KR*, 22 November 1945. This gives 20 November as the date of arrival in Mojokerto.
77. Ibid.
78. *TUR*, p. 95.
79. *TUR*, ibid.
80. "Dr van der Plas became a semi-legendary figure in Indonesia with nearly as much fantasy as fact attaching to his name". Kahin, op. cit., p. 379n.
81. Nayono, "Meneladani Sikap dan Tindakan Sri Sultan Hamengku Buwono IX dalam Perjuangan Nasional Bangsa Indonesia" [Emulating the Attitude and Actions of Sri Sultan Hamengku Buwono IX in the National Struggle of the Indonesian People], in Sulistya et al., eds., *Reformasi dan Pembangunan Bangsa* [Reform and National Development], Yogyakarta: Museum Benteng Yogyakarta, 1999, p. 2, adds that the Sultan's journey became known to East Java Governor Suryo, who was horrified at the risk to the Sultan and ordered that he be prevented from proceeding, so that he was stopped near Gresik and escorted back to Central Java, the venture ending in anticlimax.
82. Ibid.
83. *KRI*, 1945, p. 140.
84. Kahin, p. 176.
85. *Kota Yogyakarta 200 Tahun* [Yogyakarta City 200 Years], p. 31. Also *KRI 1945*, ibid., p. 186 (25 November) and p. 195 (27 November).

86. *KR*, 29 November 1945. Also, IMG, file 010A/46, NEFIS Semarang radio monitoring Report no. 30, 30 November 1945.
87. *KR*, 26 November 1945.
88. The first such state, East Indonesia, was created as early as December 1946. Kahin, p. 355.
89. Reid, *Indonesian National Revolution*, pp. 108–9.
90. Muhammad Saleh Werdisastro was a Madurese born in Sumenep in 1908. He studied at various teachers' training schools and pesantrens in Java, headed a private school in Sumenep, and then taught at a Muhammadiyah MULO (middle school) in Yogyakarta before joining the PETA. He was head of the Pemuda Muhammadiyah in Madura from 1933 to 1941 and became a Peta *daidancho* (battalion commander) in Yogyakarta under the Japanese. He became the first head of the Yogyakarta KNI when it was formed and was very influential among local pemuda groups. He suffered an eclipse when he became involved with the 3 July 1946 Affair — Anderson, op. cit., p. 21, p. 371, and p. 435, also p. 396 on Saleh's relations with the pemudas.
91. *Merdeka*, 8 December 1945.
92. Sudarisman Purwokusumo, *Tanggapan atas Disertasi berjudul "Perubahan Sosial di Yogyakarta"* [Reaction to Dissertation entitled "Social Change in Yogyakarta"], p. 37.
93. Purwokusumo, ibid. Hamengku Buwono in the 1986 *Asiaweek* interview, says that Sukarno sent his staff member Sartono to enquire whether the move would be acceptable — 4 May 1986 (vol. 12, no. 18), p. 59.
94. Moedjanto, *Kasultanan Yogyakarta dan Kadipaten Pakualaman* [The Yogyakarta Sultanate and the Pakualam Principality], p. 92.
95. *KRI*, 1945, op. cit., p. 255.
96. *Merdeka*, 8 January 1946.
97. Subadio Sastrosatomo, *Perjuangan Revolusi* [The Revolutionary Struggle], p. 203.
98. *KRI*, 1946, p. 5.
99. "Since the government could not permit unrest and disturbance in its own seat of power, its presence reinforced the authority of the Sultanate." Anderson, op. cit., p. 356.
100. Ibid., p. 357.
101. *KRI*, 1946, p. 46.
102. Three Sumatran journalists briefed him in March 1946 on the Sumatran social revolution, concluding that the situation in Java was very different — *Merdeka* 25 March 1946. As already noted, a Red Cross delegation met him in early 1946 — *KRI 1946*, p. 13. The Dutch delegation led by van Mook's chief of cabinet P.J. Koets met him during a visit in September 1946 — *NIB* vol. 5, p. 489.

103. *Merdeka*, 25 March 1946. This no doubt formalized a de facto situation dating from the previous October.
104. *KR*, 22 April 1946.
105. *KR*, ibid.
106. See Sukarno's *konsepsi* speech of 21 February 1957, in Feith and Castles, *Indonesian Political Thinking*, p. 85, on the disruptive effects of democratic opposition.
107. Ibid.
108. Suharto, "Ending Three Deviations", ibid., p. 146.
109. One early estimate was that Yogyakarta's population had swelled to 1.5 million by late 1947 — *Suluh Rakjat*, 25 April 1949.
110. Van der Post, op. cit., p. 260.
111. Anderson, op. cit., p. 300.
112. *KRI*, 1946, pp. 75–76, cable of 13 February 1946.
113. Anderson, op. cit., p. 355.
114. Soejatno, op. cit., pp. 105–6.
115. Ibid., p. 108.
116. Anderson, op. cit., p. 363.
117. Ibid., pp. 364–65.
118. Soejatno, op. cit., p. 118.
119. Anderson, ibid., p. 390.
120. Soejatno, op. cit., p. 95.
121. Anderson, ibid.
122. Ibid., p. 328, reporting *Kedaulatan Rakjat*'s strong criticism of the arrest of Tan Malaka in March 1946.
123. "Pieter 't Hoen" (F.J. Goedhart), *Terug uit Jogja* [Back from Jogja], pp. 36–38. Unusually for a Dutchman in this early period, the writer was sympathetic to the Republic's aspirations, and recognized Sukarno as a genuinely popular and charismatic leader. "Pieter 't Hoen" was the pen-name of the left-wing Labour Party member, F.J. Goedhart.
124. Ibid., p. 9.
125. Ibid., p. 38.
126. Van Helsdingen, ed., *Op Weg naar Nederlandsche-Indonesische Unie* [On the Way to a Netherlands — Indonesian Union], p. 197. This is a Dutch translation of the talk dated 15 August 1946, which would have been delivered in Indonesian.
127. This word was presumably meant ironically.
128. Ibid.
129. *Patriot*, 14 September 1946.
130. *NIB*, vol. 5, pp. 207–13.
131. Ibid., p. 209.
132. Ibid., p. 210.

133. Ibid., pp. 211–12.
134. Ibid., p. 212.
135. *NIB*, vol. 5, p. 489, meeting of Commission-General chaired by Professor Schermerhorn, The Hague, 4 October 1946, briefing by Koets on his visit.
136. Reid, op. cit., pp. 128–29.
137. Kahin, p. 194. Also *KRI 1946*, p. 420.
138. Kahin, ibid., p. 194n.
139. *NIB*, vol. 6, p. 490, report of meeting between Colonies Minister Jonkman and his division chiefs, 29 October 1946.
140. *Merdeka*, 29 October 1946.
141. Proc Gen, op. cit., sheet entitled "Hamengku Buwono IX", quoting report in *Het Dagblad*, 29 October 1946.
142. *Asiaweek* interview, op. cit., p. 60.
143. *Merdeka*, 25 October 1946.
144. *NIB*, vol. 8, p. 462, political report for March–April 1946 by Adviser for Sumatran Political Affairs van der Velde.
145. *Asiaweek* interview, 4 May 1986 (vol. 12, no. 18), p. 60.
146. Proc Gen, op. cit., sheet headed *Overgenomen uit B K E 243* [Taken from BKE 243 — meaning unknown], dated 19 April 1947.
147. NA 2.10.17, NEFIS radio monitoring reports, radio report from Bukittinggi, 18 April 1947.
148. Ibid., NEFIS monitoring reports, recording a meeting of 22 April 1947 at the TNI officers' mess in Pematang Siantar.
149. Proc Gen, op. cit., page headed *Overgenomen uit B K E 238* [Taken from BKE 238].
150. Proc Gen, op. cit., NEFIS document headed *Pakoebowono* [sic], *Sultan van Djocja*, March 1948. The plan for a "goodwill mission" is also reported in *Min Pau*, 27 March 1948.
151. *Sang Demokrat*, p. 213 (reprinting report in *Tempo*, 8 October 1988).
152. MvD/CAD, Bundle AA 22, NEFIS 1947–49, NEFIS Semarang files, report of 15 January 1948, *Installation of Yogyakarta City Council*.
153. This had been already foreshadowed as early as December 1945 — *KRI 1945*, p. 213.
154. Kahin, in *TUR*, p. 176. Unfortunately very little detail about these local elections appears in the public record.
155. *Merdeka*, 10 December 1945. By January 1946 a draft was ready for the plenary to consider — *KR* 19 January 1946.
156. Selosumarjan, *Social Change in Yogyakarta*, p. 80. Purwokusumo was born in Yogyakarta in 1913, educated in the Dutch school system, joined various youth movements in the 1930s, and worked for *Sedya Tama* daily's office in Jakarta. In the Japanese period, he worked in the Information and then Finance departments in Jakarta. He joined the Sultanate service in 1944, and during

the Revolution headed the regional information bureau, then became secretary of the Regional Defence Committee, before becoming Mayor of Yogyakarta in July 1947. As a PNI leader, he had by the mid-1960s come to be identified with the Old Order, became a target for anti-Sukarno forces in 1966, and was forced to resign as Mayor at the end of that year. Biographical information mainly from Suwarno, *Hamengku Buwono IX*, op. cit., pp. 446–47.

157. *Merdeka*, 3 October 1946. The word "loved" was *dicinta* in the original. The article is unsigned.
158. Van Delden, in *Het Einde van Indie*, op. cit., p. 205.
159. NA 2.10.14, Inv no. 2831, Idenburg report, *Indrukken omtrent Djocja* [Impressions of Jogja], May 1947.
160. Ibid., p. 3.
161. Soejatno, op. cit., pp. 129–30.
162. Heijboer, *De Politionele Acties* [The Police Actions], p. 45.
163. Abu Hanifah, op. cit., p. 269.
164. Proc Gen, op. cit., single sheet headed "Overgenomen uit RVD dd 24 Juli '47 DN 1164; boodschap van Z V H de Sultan van Djocja" (this [probably] means "monitored from Radio Free [?] Democracy [?], of 24 July 1947 DN 1164; Message of H H the Sultan of Jogja").
165. *Sin Min*, 9 September 1947.
166. Netherlands Foreign Ministry NEFIS files, Inv no. 6910, letter of 31 July 1947 from Markas Angkatan Perang Sabil Jogja-Kedu, signed by Moh Syarbini, on which Hamengku Buwono noted "no objection".
167. Proc Gen, single sheet headed *Overgenomen uit Sub. Div. Mon RRI S'baja 106* [sic] (probably = "taken from sub division monitoring Indonesian Republic Radio Surabaya 106"), dated 9 August 1947.
168. "From the period of the Japanese occupation, Hamengku Buwono IX always consulted the Chinese community about all important issues. Also thanks to the Sultan, Chinese in Jogja were spared any physical abuse or violence". Didi Kwartanada (a Chinese-Indonesian born in Yogyakarta), quoted in *Kompas*, 14 May 2005.
169. Proc Gen, op. cit., running sheet entitled "HAMENGKOE BOEWONO IX", with entries from October 1946 to early 1948.
170. Ibid., one-page report entitled "Sultan of Yogyakarta anti-Netherlands?" of 6 October 1947. The report was prepared by an anonymous NEFIS analyst basing his comments on the reactions of an anonymous Javanese informant.
171. In at least one known case, Hamengku Buwono's public statements convinced a possible Dutch combatant not to join the struggle. A former classmate at Leiden many years later told Hamengku Buwono that he had decided not to rejoin the Dutch military after reading a newspaper report of the Sultan

telling the Dutch not to return to the Indies — *East* CD-ROM, code no. 1020.1 (11), interview with S. Kamminga.
172. Proc Gen, op. cit., running sheet headed "HAMENGKOE BOEWONO IX". This gives the date of appointment as 6 September 1947.
173. Nasution, op. cit., vol. 7, p. 213.
174. Kahin, op. cit., pp. 226–29.
175. A near-final figure of 28,735 Siliwangi troops was given by the military observers of the Good Offices Committee on 21 February 1948 — *NIB*, vol. 13, p. 10, doc 5.
176. Hatta, op. cit., p. 281. Also Soejatno, p. 161.
177. *NIB*, vol. 16, p. 720, attachments, doc no. 18, record of Indonesian cabinet meeting of 9 March 1948. This was a series of records of cabinet meetings in 1948 captured after the Dutch surprise attack of 19 December 1948.
178. Kahin, *Southeast Asia, a Testament*, p. 38.
179. NEFIS/CMI files in Netherlands Foreign Ministry, Inv no. 6909, letter of 13 July 1948 from Chinese Vice Consul New Shu Chun, on which Hamengku Buwono noted in English and Dutch, "Already received from CHTH [Chung Hwa Tchung Hui — a prominent Chinese-Indonesian association]. We will do our best to prevent such incidents and we will take preventive measures. Ik zal zelf tekenen." (= I will sign myself). Sporadic anti-Chinese violence however continued during 1948, including the murder of a Chinese shopkeeper in Yogyakarta in October — Nasution, vol. 8, p. 436.
180. Hatta, *Hatta Indonesian Patriot, Memoirs*, p. 280. The exact timing of the appointment as Coordinator of Internal Security is hard to pin down. Official accounts listing Hamengku Buwono's appointments (e.g., *Riwayat Singkat dan Perjuangan Sri Sultan Hamengku Buwono IX*, p. 6; and *TUR*, p. 375) date the appointment from August 1949, but other accounts describe him as Coordinator of Internal Security at least from the Madiun affair in September 1948, e.g., Nasution, vol. 8, p. 74 and p. 239.
181. See the extensive list of works on the Madiun affair in Said, *Militer Indonesia dan Politik: Dulu, Kini dan Kelak* [The Indonesian Military and Politics: In the Past, the Present and the Future], p. 44n. Kahin has a detailed account (pp. 290–300).
182. Kahin, *Nationalism and Revolution*, op. cit., pp. 288–90.
183. Nasution confirms being brought by Ali Sastroamijoyo to the palace to see Sukarno and Hamengku Buwono that morning — *TUR*, p. 180.
184. Nasution, op. cit., vol. 8, pp. 239–41.
185. Hamengku Buwono understood that the Madiun commander Sumarsono hoped for support from East Java commander Sungkono. Kahin letter to Feith, Feith papers, MON 78, 1991/09/012, item 198, 20 December 1960.
186. Nasution, vol. 8, op. cit., p. 241.

187. Elson, *Suharto*, p. 26.
188. *De Locomotief*, 20 September 1948.
189. Proc Gen, op. cit., sheet entitled *HAMANGKU* (sic) *BUWONO IX* (undated, but around December 1948).
190. Abu Hanifah, p. 287.
191. *Asiaweek* interview, op. cit., 4 May 1986, vol. 12/18, p. 60. Words in square brackets in the original.
192. Nasution, op. cit., vol. 8, p. 364.
193. "All vestiges of feudalism must be liquidated" — Muso in August 1948, as reported by Kahin in *Southeast Asia, a Testament*, p. 52.
194. This document (uncorroborated by any other source) claims "the extreme leftist Amir Syarifuddin regarded any remnant of feudalism as a thorn in the side, and the Sultan led an extensive underground campaign against him, with some success". Paper prepared for the Dutch cabinet meeting of 21 March 1949, headed "The Standpoint of the Sultan of Yogyakarta." The unsigned paper was apparently written in the Overseas Territories Ministry.
195. NEFIS/CMI files held in Foreign Ministry, attachment to CMI document 5235, NEFIS files 1942–49, no. 06545. Letter from Hamengku Buwono of 2 (?) November 1948, headed, *Usul tentang pembentukan dan susunan Pemerintah Daerah Surakarta* [Proposal on the formation and structure of the Surakarta (i.e., Solo) Regional Government] (cited below as *Usul*).
196. *Usul*, in NEFIS/CMI files, op. cit., p. 1.
197. Ibid., *Dewan Pemerintah* in original.
198. Ibid., p. 2.
199. Kahin, *Nationalism*, op. cit., p. 295.
200. *Asiaweek* interview, 4 May 1986 (vol. 12, no. 18), p. 59.
201. Nasution, vol. 10, op. cit., p. 4.

6

REVOLUTION — THE DUTCH ATTACK AND AFTERMATH

On 19 December 1948, Dutch troops attacked and occupied Yogyakarta, capturing virtually the entire Republican leadership, including Sukarno, Hatta, Syahrir, and many others. The captives were quickly exiled to various locations, and the three mentioned above ended up on Bangka island. After the attack, Syafruddin Prawiranegara led a defiant Emergency Government from his base in Sumatra. For the time being, Sultan Hamengku Buwono and the Pakualam were left alone in their palaces.

As soon as the attack became known, an urgent cabinet meeting considered the options. Because many ministers were out of Yogyakarta, the numbers attending were small.[1] Prime Minister Hatta was in Kaliurang, where, although recovering from a minor illness, he had been conducting talks with the UN Committee of Good Offices representatives, especially the Australian representative Critchley, and Hamengku Buwono, who was also slightly ill,[2] volunteered to fetch him. At this stage Sukarno was still assuming that he and Hatta should take to the hills and try to evade capture.[3]

Accompanied by Sutan Syahrir, Hamengku Buwono stopped at the Kepatihan building to tell Honggowongso to prepare a refuge for the Central Government in the Gunung Kidul area, as previously planned.[4]

They drove towards Kaliurang but encountered Hatta in Pakem Street (now Jalan Kaliurang) in the city, which was already under heavy Dutch bombardment, after which they returned to the presidential palace at about 11 a.m. By the time they had returned, the cabinet meeting had apparently already concluded.

Col Simatupang had counselled the leadership to retreat to Wonosari,[5] but Sukarno changed his mind and decided to allow himself to be captured by the Dutch. One reason for this was that the leaders would need to be guarded by at least one battalion of soldiers, and the TNI could not spare so many. If the leaders stayed in Yogyakarta, they could also remain in contact with the GOC representatives as long as possible.[6] Another rationale was that it would be much easier for the Dutch to assassinate the Republican leaders in some remote region, than if they were captured in the centre of the capital before many witnesses. Nevertheless, many in the army regarded the decision as cowardly, especially after Sukarno's previous boasts about leading the guerrilla war himself if the Dutch were to attack again,[7] and this episode was a reason for the subsequent widespread military distrust of civilian politicians.[8]

Sukarno's and Hatta's intention to go underground had earlier seemed genuine, and Hatta had even inspected a proposed emergency airfield south of Yogyakarta from which the leaders could, under one possible option, be flown to Sumatra if the Dutch attacked.[9] In November a high-level committee including Hamengku Buwono, Moh Natsir, and military leaders had approved these emergency plans, accompanied by plans for scorched-earth tactics, preparation of bases, and administrative arrangements.[10] But the military leadership had apparently had insufficient time to elaborate the plans and communicate them to the lower levels before the Dutch offensive.

Many military units were unprepared for the Dutch attack, but were nevertheless on alert because a series of military exercises had been planned at this time.[11] Thus, in an uncoordinated and untidy way, local forces were able to retreat outside the city and regroup. Civilian organs of the central government were often caught quite unawares, and many senior officials and their records were captured.[12] The Yogyakarta regional government was not quite so unready, as will appear below.

The Dutch had calculated on presenting the world with a fait accompli, but much of world opinion was outraged because the assault breached undertakings in the Renville Agreement, which included recognition of the Republic's de facto authority in Java, Sumatra and Madura. The U.S. ambassador to the United Nations, Jessup, said publicly "we can see no justification for military action at this time".[13] Jessup was sharper in private, telling his Dutch colleague that this was "the biggest mistake by the Netherlands in its entire history".[14] The Republic had strengthened its standing in Washington by its suppression of the Madiun revolt.[15]

The Security Council called in late December for the cessation of conflict and the release of the Republican leaders. So little progress had been made that a resolution of 28 January 1949 had to call on the Netherlands in similar terms to ensure "the immediate discontinuance of all military operations", and "to release immediately and unconditionally all political prisoners arrested since 17 December 1948 and to facilitate the immediate return of [Republican] officials to Yogyakarta".[16] The Dutch resisted the Security Council resolutions, but their position steadily eroded both on the ground in Indonesia and in their relations with the United States.

After the meeting on 19 December, Hamengku Buwono walked back alone to the kraton. He had to consider his approach, now that the Republican leaders had been captured. Most of the earlier Dutch attacks had not directly touched Yogyakarta, although the blockade had imposed hardship and scarcities of all kinds. But now his own region had been attacked and occupied. In what looks in retrospect like a cleverly calculated political strategy, he resolved to isolate himself in the palace, refusing contact with Dutch officials, while running a clandestine government behind the scenes.

He ordered the closure of the palace gates, apparently to control admission and prevent the entry of Dutch spies, despite the presence of many refugees seeking shelter.[17] He subsequently allowed the Keban and Magangan buildings to be temporarily occupied by refugees until the situation was clearer.[18] He told senior officials, such as Honggowongso, that he would receive no one,[19] stating reasons of ill health.[20]

Prabuningrat was told to listen to Dutch emissaries' statements and messages and to report back, but to make no comment or response.[21] It was no doubt the latter stipulation which gave an impression of ambiguity which Dutch officials were to misinterpret. He refused to meet federalist emissaries such as Professor Husein Jayadiningrat and Sultan Hamid,[22] as well as Dutch officials like Resident Stok and local commander Colonel van Langen.[23] Hamengku Buwono and the Pakualam announced their resignations as head and deputy head of the Yogyakarta Special Region, respectively as of 1 January 1949, but as reports of the resignations only emerged around 20 January, the 1 January date may have been retrospective.[24]

Hamengku Buwono and his advisers had formulated local contingency plans in the case of a Dutch attack, and because of the growing tension, the Yogyakarta City government had already been running on a twenty-four-hour basis for some days.[25] While the phones were still working on the morning of 19 December, officials outside Yogyakarta were told to prepare to administer an illegal government. Hamengku Buwono and the Pakualam would stay in the city; civilian officials should remain in their areas and should try to avoid capture by the Dutch troops; they should expect regular visits from couriers — using code words — who would bring oral instructions and information from the city; and all provincial offices would remain closed indefinitely until orders were received from the Sultan.[26] The invisible government functioned with differing success in different areas; it was notably active in Sleman regency, featuring effective cooperation between the civilian regent (Projodiningrat) and the local military leaders, Colonel Jatikusumo and Lieutenant Colonel Suharto.[27]

The kraton began assisting the families of the arrested leaders, using its reserves of East Indies guilders. Many wives and families were left alone and without resources when virtually the whole Republican leadership was exiled,[28] but Hamengku Buwono's emissaries made regular visits, providing envelopes full of cash and keeping them apprised of developments.[29]

The head of Dutch economic administration, B.J. Mulder, admitted that of 10,000 public servants in the Special Region, only 150 were cooperating, and that these were doing so on the Sultan's orders, to ensure that basic services would still run at a minimum level.[30] These officials probably included a small group from the Social Affairs Department, who seemed ready to cooperate, something which Dutch officials were then regarding as a hopeful sign.[31] Some locals reported for work at the Dutch-run offices because they were short of food, but interest had quickly dwindled when the Sultan's attitude became known.[32]

Hamengku Buwono's strategy contained some risks. One risk emerged quickly as pamphlets were found in Yogyakarta accusing him of collaboration and criticizing him for not leaving with the TNI forces.[33] This could be rebutted by pointing out that he had met no Dutch officials, but as described below he was eventually obliged to speak out. Other risks were that the local population would tire of having no real government and of constant instability and guerrilla attacks, and would turn against him.

Indeed, many groups in the community asked him to provide leadership again.[34] He responded that he would consider resuming his position "if the people wished it".

The Dutch were another potential threat, but Hamengku Buwono banked on some measure of toleration from them, and realized that they hoped to win him over because his prestige in the region would make him a valuable ally. Even up to the first direct meeting with Dutch military and civilian officials in March, the Sultan's silence could be misinterpreted by the Dutch in self-serving ways. Kahin mentions that the slogan of the December 1948 attack was to "capture Yogyakarta and free the Sultan".[35] Apart from those colonial officials who after three years of revolution could not appreciate the wide appeal of *merdeka* ideas in Java, the more realistic ones had to cope with a largely uncomprehending government in The Hague and a totally uncomprehending Dutch public. The general elections of July 1948 had benefited the hardliners in the Catholic Party, which led to a more intractable Dutch attitude and contributed to the replacement of the relatively moderate Lieutenant Governor van Mook by the more intransigent Beel, now with the title of High Representative of the Crown.[36]

Flawed perceptions of the Sultan were complicated by misleading intelligence. In November 1948, Colonies Minister Sassen had quoted a local adviser as predicting that "just before or immediately after action taken by our side, the Sultan of Yogyakarta would take power in the Republic. This would make the appearance and consequences of our action much less unacceptable internationally."[37] Chief of Staff Maj Gen Buurman van Vreeden asserted baldly that "the Sultan is anti-Republican".[38]

Immediately after the attack, Colonies Minister Sassen proposed to Beel: "it is essential to have a Republican spokesman (for example the Sultan) indicate publicly as soon as possible that the Republic and the people reject foreign interference" (in the Indonesia question).[39] Despite his reputation for inflexibility,[40] Beel as the man on the spot had a greater grasp of reality and he curtly dismissed this idea as "totally illusory".[41] Sassen then suggested that the state of Central Java should be formed as soon as possible, "for example under the Sultan of Yogyakarta".[42] The head of the Dutch Foreign Ministry wrote that "it is of the greatest importance that figures such as Sukarno, Hatta, the Sultan of Jogja, Juanda,[43] Leimena and so on (among whom we must not be too choosy) should cooperate as soon as possible in the formation of the new 'Republican' Government".[44] Dutch officials believed that their triumph in capturing Yogyakarta was decisive, and the demoralized Republicans would have no choice but to cooperate.

Although the intelligence service was reporting that the Sultan's attitude "could not be ascertained",[45] Prime Minister Drees could report during his visit to Batavia in January, on advice from Sultan Hamid, that "It would be best if it can be arranged for Syahrir to join the interim government, that the Sultan of Jogja should take the lead in Central Java, … while Sukarno and Hatta remain out of action for the time being".[46]

In the meantime the guerrilla fighters were increasingly active. The first major attack in Yogyakarta city occurred as early as 29 December.[47] Further night attacks occurred on 9 January, 16 January,[48] and 4 February.[49] George Kahin personally witnessed the assault of 9 January, which penetrated very close to his hotel.[50] In early January, a Dutch visitor likened Yogyakarta to a city under siege.[51]

Beel reported to The Hague that "the Mangkunegoro and the Susuhunan of Solo are prepared to cooperate. This can however *not* be disclosed in the Security Council, as this could adversely influence the attitude of the Sultan of Jogja, whose cooperation is of preponderant importance because of his greater influence, but who has not yet positively declared his readiness to cooperate."[52] The report mentioned the planned visit to Yogyakarta by Sultan Hamid of Pontianak.

But Hamengku Buwono refused to meet his fellow Sultan. Drees commented: "The impression was that he was adopting a waiting attitude, because he first wanted to know what his position would be as an autonomous ruler, what would happen to the four leading figures of the Republic, what the position of the Republic would be and what the Security Council would do."[53] Some of these explanations seem realistic enough, but they still imply that his role as an autonomous ruler would be separable from the Republic.

The Dutch Cabinet continued to hope. Foreign Minister Stikker reported that: "It is conceivable that Central Java will come under the administration of the Sultan of Yogyakarta and other Republican ministers, such as Leimena, etc. … With some flexibility solutions can be found."[54]

HAMENGKU BUWONO DECLARES HIS POSITION

On 21 January, however, Hamengku Buwono and the Pakualam resigned as head and deputy head of the Yogyakarta region, respectively, criticizing the

Dutch attack and denying that they were cooperating with the occupation.[55] Hamengku Buwono's letter on the subject said:

> Reports in the press that I am cooperating with the Dutch are a lie.[56] I have resigned my office as head of the Yogyakarta Special Region.... I have done so because I cannot approve of the Dutch action towards our Republic. I cannot work to safeguard the peace and welfare of the people of Yogyakarta because of brutal actions of the Dutch towards the people — male, female, youth, and the people in general. They have been arrested without any due process; houses and villages have been burned down until nothing remains. This was done not only against the Indonesian people, but against Chinese as well. Their protests have been answered with: "Yes, we are at war. The people have to suffer ..." Although we have met with a great many difficulties, we will fight on from here. I am prepared to face any action the Dutch will employ towards me, but it is for the Dutch to understand that my attitude is a result of their actions.[57]

The letter was circulated clandestinely in Java and became known in Jakarta by early February.[58] It joined other important documents circulating among the population, including the texts of speeches by Sukarno and Hatta which were not broadcast on 19 December because the radio was seized by Dutch forces.[59] Thus, one month after the Dutch attack, Hamengku Buwono once again revealed his Republican sympathies. His letter lacks specific evidence for the grave claims of brutality, arbitrary arrests, house burnings, and the nonchalant dismissal of complaints about these actions; but sufficient facts exist to substantiate the charges. Kahin writes of "Dutch tactics which were alienating the Indonesian population as a whole even more widely from the Netherlands than before ... [such as] increasingly frequent machine-gunning ... of villages near the roads to make sure that no guerrillas were lurking there, with no apparent regard for the killing of unarmed civilians."[60] He refers to raids and looting of houses of non-collaborating Indonesians.[61]

Indonesian sources have plausibly interpreted the resignation as an effort to disclaim responsibility for local administration and thus make it more difficult for the Dutch to demand cooperation.[62] Meanwhile, at Friday prayers the Imam of the grand mosque in Yogyakarta read out Hamengku Buwono's message to "continue the struggle with undiminished courage, because the Javanese/Indonesian [sic] people must be free".[63]

A few days later, in refusing to meet two federalist leaders, Hamengku Buwono wrote to van Langen that he could not meet anyone "without first having the opportunity to talk with Sukarno, Hatta and other colleagues".[64] Army Commander General Spoor asked pertinently whether there remained "any sense in continuing to entertain these attempts to contact Hamengku Buwono".[65]

Dutch leaders were showing signs of concern, if not desperation, at their failure to bring any Republicans to their side. Prime Minister Drees reported that "none of the moderate Republicans, such as the Sultan of Jogja, seem prepared to engage in meaningful discussions.… The Republicans form a closed unity, [and] the Federalists have moved to a vacillating position".[66] Professor Romme, an important powerbroker in the Catholic Party, asked why the Sultan had "changed his attitude". Drees replied vaguely that "international interference had influenced this. Two other rulers had resumed their former rights under their political contracts with the Crown after the military action. If the Sultan were prepared to take the lead in Central Java this would have great influence in Indonesia."[67]

In this period, Dutch officials appear to have offered Hamengku Buwono the presidency of the planned Central Java federal state.[68] A confusing aspect of reports about this and similar claimed offers is the multiplicity of versions which have emerged in Indonesian and other secondary sources. According to Hamengku Buwono himself, the first offer was the governorship of Java and Madura and then the post of "Deputy Governor General" of the East Indies.[69] Another version has the Dutch offering the kingship of "Greater Mataram", recreating the kingdom of Sultan Agung;[70] then the Dutch allegedly offered large sums of money[71] and railway and shipping shares. Kahin's version[72] is that the approach was made in early February 1949 through Prabuningrat. In the absence of any response from the Sultan, they offered all of Central Java and East Java, followed by a third offer, adding the shipping and railroad shares. Although there is a baffling lack of supporting evidence in the Dutch archives, the unanimity about the offers among Indonesians in a position to know, including Hamengku Buwono himself, make it likely that offers of some kind were indeed made, though perhaps not as extensive as claimed by the Republicans.[73]

In the meantime, Hamengku Buwono had issued more detailed information and instructions through the "illegal" apparatus some time in late January or early February. The main points included:

- The Dutch will definitely leave Yogyakarta at some stage. The people must remain patient and united.
- Any places occupied by the Dutch should be evacuated by the local populace, to facilitate later attacks by the TNI.
- Any village heads or sub-district heads appointed by the Dutch should be abducted (or worse).[74]
- The people should refuse to use Federal currency and only use Republican currency (ORI).
- Food supplies should not be prevented from entering Yogyakarta city, so that the city population should not starve; only material particularly "required by the Dutch (eggs, vegetables, and medicines [sic])" should be withheld.
- Local government in the rural areas should be as autonomous as possible, and not depend on regional government financing. (During January regional civil servants had [somehow] been provided with four months' pay, to tide them over the crisis period.)[75]
- The bupati of Sleman was appointed as a Special Deputy Head of the Special Region, to manage the illegal government in areas free of Dutch control outside the city.[76]

On 22 February, Dutch soldiers raided the Kepatihan building and discovered some of the secret instructions.[77] Spoor[78] reported that Hamengku Buwono had "seriously compromised himself" by promulgating orders aimed at isolating Dutch troops through a "blockade system", spreading anti-Dutch rumours,[79] an order — written personally by him — to abduct or even assassinate two "NICA" village chiefs in Bantul who were cooperating with the Dutch,[80] an indication of his support for a holy war (*perang sabil*) by Muslim groups against the Dutch,[81] and the resolute continuation of the guerrilla struggle.[82] This compelling evidence prompted Chief of Staff Buurman van Vreeden to recommend exiling Hamengku Buwono outside Java.[83]

Hamengku Buwono was holding twice-weekly "Cabinet" meetings with those ministers still in Yogyakarta (Juanda, Kusnan and possibly Laoh) and several members of the KNIP, the Republic's parliament.[84] The meetings closely followed international developments, including events in the United Nations.[85] Hamengku Buwono was "providing monetary support to the resistance leaders, Lt Col Latief and Lt Col Suharto",[86] apparently amounting to nine million rupiah.[87] He also supplied paper to enable the clandestine printing of 80,000 Republican banknotes at Panggang village outside the city.[88] The Pakualaman too was in regular contact with the TNI, mainly through Prince Suryaningprang, whose house became a city headquarters for the guerrillas.[89]

By the end of February, Dutch officials were losing patience. Yogyakarta Resident Stok[90] suggested: "The Sultan must be advised that the Republic and its Government no longer exist and that the only central government is the Federal one.... We must of course face the possibility that the Sultan will give no answer, or will decline to recognise the contract of March 1940. If so, he should be deactivated and if necessary exiled or interned.... We must then look for another Sultan." This illustrates not only unwillingness to recognize that times had changed but also the rigidity characterizing the thinking which led to the attack in December 1948. The new Minister for Overseas Territories van Marseveen agreed that Beel could "occupy the Kraton and replace the Sultan" if the situation deteriorated.[91]

Stok's advocacy of deposing Hamengku Buwono recalls the removal by the Dutch of the Sultan's ancestor Hamengku Buwono II in the early nineteenth century and his exile during the British interregnum.[92] An attempt to exile the Sultan would have been politically dangerous, but the Dutch were apparently actively seeking a replacement. Some Indonesian sources admit that various members of Hamengku Buwono's family were tempted by Dutch promises,[93] and an intelligence report claimed that Puruboyo had expressed interest in becoming Sultan under the Dutch, leading to a serious rift with Hamengku Buwono.[94] However, the latter report has to be taken with a grain of salt — if there was a rift, it did not last long, as another report shows Puruboyo in April acting as the Sultan's intermediary in contact with an UNCI military observer.[95]

An account from the Sultan reveals the growing tension in Yogyakarta:[96]

> A week before 1 March I already knew that relations with the Dutch would soon erupt, because I had not so far received a single Dutch official. They were committing many provocations, the greatest of which was the raid on the Kepatihan building, which they had thoroughly looted. At the time I thought that if this must happen, well, I would commit a provocation of my own. So I summoned an UNCI observer [the United Nations Commission for Indonesia], an American called Hazelett,[97] who had previously indicated his wish to see me. He was received as openly and conspicuously as possible, so that anyone could see it. The attack

by our people occurred on 1 March at 6 am. I thought if they [i.e., the Dutch] were smart, they would use this attack as an excuse. I thought that my house would be next. And I was right.

THE GENERAL OFFENSIVE

Hamengku Buwono heard a broadcast referring to an important UN Security Council meeting scheduled for early March,[98] and contacted General Sudirman proposing a major daylight attack by guerrilla forces, to demonstrate internationally the continued potency of the Republic's military arm. Sudirman suggested that he contact the local commander, Lt Col Suharto. Around 14 February 1949, therefore, the Sultan received Suharto,[99] operational commander of the local TNI forces, who entered the palace disguised as a palace official.[100] They discussed a major counterattack, and Suharto devised an operational plan with a speed and efficiency which impressed Hamengku Buwono.[101] This was a momentous meeting as it turned out, because it was Hamengku Buwono's first contact with Indonesia's future second President; but it was unimaginable then that this humble young village man could eventually appoint Hamengku Buwono, immeasurably his social superior, as his Vice President.

At 6 a.m. on 1 March, therefore, in what was to become known as the *Serangan Umum*, or General Offensive,[102] several thousand TNI soldiers attacked Yogyakarta and fought their way on to the main street.[103] The level of Indonesian fatalities was very severe, variously estimated at nearly 200 to as many as 375.[104] The Dutch lost seven soldiers killed and fourteen wounded.[105] By early afternoon, Hamengku Buwono heard of reinforcements arriving from Magelang and suggested to Suharto that his forces withdraw.[106] The attack had a clear political purpose, being timed to coincide with the UN discussions, and being aimed at demonstrating the hollowness of Dutch claims that the Republic had been extinguished. The Dutch General Staff concluded that the attack revealed "central direction, probably from the kraton".[107]

The next day Dutch officials had a stormy meeting with Hamengku Buwono, at which Central Java Commander General Meijer tried to confront him with the evidence of his illegal activities. The Sultan was defiant; he had expected to be arrested and had even brought a bag of clothes.[108] The visitors recorded that he gave "evidence of considerable emotion", and his appearance — unshaven, wearing sandals — showed that he wished to "accentuate the involuntary nature of the meeting".[109] Such reception of guests was highly discourteous in Javanese terms.

He announced that he was abdicating as Sultan, telling the Dutch officials "I didn't ask you gentlemen to come to Yogyakarta."[110] In a declaration which became famous in Indonesian history, he asserted that he had decided to step down because of Dutch provocations, to which he "added two requests, first that he be left in peace, and second that if the Kraton were to be ransacked as had the Kepatihan building,[111] he would prefer to die first".[112] The meeting ended inconclusively, but Hamengku Buwono had reaffirmed his non-cooperative stand. His defiance of the Dutch, in the form of stories that he had told them that they would enter the kraton "over my dead body" became one of the legends of the Revolution.

Although the Serangan Umum probably does not deserve the mythical status it acquired in nationalist historiography, especially during Suharto's rule, it has rightly attracted the attention of historians. Republican claims to have "nearly captured Yogyakarta" can be discounted,[113] but the attack was taken very seriously by the Dutch authorities.[114] Although it was just one attack out of a series of incessant major and minor raids across Java, it was probably the boldest and symbolically the most significant, and played its part in convincing the outside world, the Federalists, and ultimately the Dutch that the nationalist movement could not be overcome.

One further perspective is to set the attack in military context. As we have seen, local forces had already launched several important night attacks on Yogyakarta city, the first as early as 29 December, only ten days after the Dutch had taken the city. From the viewpoint of local TNI commanders like Suharto who had already been involved in at least three major attacks, the General Offensive, although more complex, would have posed few novel operational problems, apart from the audacity of launching an attack in daylight with proportionately greater risks.[115]

THE JAVANESE KING

The dramatic meeting of 2 March 1949, which is so often taken as an example of the model behaviour of an Indonesian patriot, might also be seen as a case study in the behaviour of a Javanese prince. It illustrates the multi-faceted role which Hamengku Buwono played throughout his career, as simultaneously (inter alia) a feudal ruler, a modern politician, an Indonesian nationalist and a Javanese mystic. Much has been written[116] about Javanese

Revolution — The Dutch Attack and Aftermath

conceptions of power and kingship, and the Sultan's performance during this episode might be seen in these terms. We cannot go into this in much detail here, but some elements of the behaviour of an ideal Javanese king might be relevant. According to the literature on this subject, a Javanese king should weigh his words carefully because they cannot be taken back,[117] should prefer diplomacy to fighting,[118] and should understand the benefits of — and frequently practice — *tapa* (asceticism).[119]

During this episode, the Sultan could be seen in Javanese terms as first cutting himself off from the Dutch (and the world as a whole), performing meditation and self-abnegation (a form of *tapa*) in his Kraton, and gathering strength to repel the forces of evil. Stories about Indic princes are full of episodes where the subject retreats from the world (usually in a forest or on a mountaintop), builds up virtue and strength, and then emerges to confound and defeat his enemies.[120] By remaining incommunicado in his palace, the Sultan could be seen as exercising *tapa* in order to gain mystic knowledge of God's will.[121] By doing this, he did not abate any of his power.

In terms of the correct behaviour of an ideal Javanese king, the Sultan no doubt made a creditable job at his meeting with the Dutch officials on 2 March. Although allowing his agitation to be evident to the Dutch, he "repelled his base desires" (including anger), retained his self-control, and was able to make several cogent points. The statement, "I didn't ask you gentlemen to come to Yogyakarta", was especially telling. In refusing their demands and in successfully asking to be "left in peace" while remaining stiffly correct if not wholly polite, he approximated ideal behaviour.[122] His Javanese *halus*-ness contrasted with the *kasar* (coarse) behaviour of General Meijer. The Sultan made his arguments with the minimum of words, none of which he had to take back. It might be argued that in Javanese terms he subdued his enemy without fighting, the most convincing possible sign of his standing.

Another way of looking at this incident is in terms of the *wayang* shadow play. The Dutch could be seen as the Kurawas in the Mahabharata epic who had usurped the kingdom and had to be defeated by the noble Pandawas, i.e., the Republic.[123] Alternatively, they could be seen as the *bhuta* (ogres) or *raseksa* (giants) from *tanah sabrang* (lands across the sea), who by invading Yogyakarta had disturbed the kingdom's natural harmony.[124] The Sultan had been powerless to stop this, but it was his duty to do everything possible to secure harmony by restoring the *status quo ante*. Hence, he would surreptitiously aid the resistance fighters, refuse to meet the Dutch and thus deny them legitimacy (but retain face all round by feigning illness), and when brought to bay, would face them off — "I didn't ask you to come." The Republican light from the kraton continued to shine resolutely down on the Yogyakarta people, despite the corrupting disharmony brought by the *bhuta*.[125]

EFFECTS AND AFTERMATH

Three weeks after the General Offensive, a Dutch cabinet paper provides the clearest possible statement of the official attitude to Hamengku Buwono.[126] It outlined the problem with candour:

> If there is something which the Netherlands authorities had not expected, it is this — the Sultan of Yogyakarta has slipped through our fingers. It was known that he had established good relations with the Republic, that he had obtained a position in the Cabinet, but the Netherlands authorities had conceived this — apparently sincere — standpoint as a more or less forced compliance, convinced that the interests and objectives of the feudal aristocrat and the revolutionary-democratic or communist-inspired Republicans would clash with each other, and that no mutual understanding *could* exist between them. It was thus expected that if the Netherlands could overcome the Republic, this would be a great relief for the Sultan and that an agreement with him could be reached.

The paper complains of Hamengku Buwono's subversive activities, including the evidence in the captured papers which would have justified detaining him, but adds that the Netherlands had maintained "its lenient attitude up to now".[127] The paper concedes: "That the Sultan, unlike the other Javanese rulers, had been able to maintain his position vis-a-vis the Republic and had continued to be respected by the people, certainly demonstrated great statesmanship on the part of this relatively young man, who a decade ago was called to his princely throne from the Leiden University student body without any transition period."[128] Surprisingly, the paper adds: "The hope to achieve cooperation with him should nevertheless not yet be abandoned", claiming that, while remaining aloof, he had encouraged his brother Puruboyo and others to offer cooperation to the Netherlands government "because if matters had gone better for us and if the Republic had indeed been destroyed, he could [then] have shown willingness to cooperate, while in the meantime he could sound out the public reaction to the cooperation [offered so far]".[129]

Hamengku Buwono's report of the 2 March meeting soon became known to the leader of the Republican delegation, Mohammad Rum in Jakarta, and the rest of the Republican leaders.[130] One result of the Serangan Umum and other TNI activity was that it further daunted the federalists (the BFO). BFO representatives had visited the Republican leaders on Bangka and had been impressed by their confidence that the TNI could hold out and by their refusal to negotiate unless they could return to Yogyakarta. Then came the news that the TNI was bold enough to mount a daylight frontal assault on Yogyakarta city.[131] Influenced by the moderate East Indonesian leader Anak Agung, the BFO passed a resolution on 3 March calling for the return of the Republican leaders to Yogyakarta. This was a savage blow for Beel, who was not used to defiance from the federalists and whose "Beel Plan" was based on establishing a puppet government without allowing the Republicans to return to their capital. Although some of the federalists later wavered, Beel even considered resigning.[132]

Threats in the American Congress against aid to the Netherlands were rising. As early as February, the allies were pressuring the Dutch government to allow the return of the Republican leaders to Yogyakarta in accordance with the Security Council resolutions. By March the Dutch were conceding that the Republican government might be restored to Yogyakarta under certain conditions.[133] While Dutch officials were saying in February that they "would rather die than say yes",[134] by mid-March the Dutch-language press was reporting the idea of a "conditional return" of the Republican leaders.[135]

Representatives of the Indonesian Republic in New York publicized the Serangan Umum as widely and quickly as they could.[136] Although the effect of the news cannot be known with any precision, the knowledge that the Dutch were unable to pacify Java must have had some impression on UN delegates. Three weeks later[137] a resolution was passed in the Security Council which came to be known as the Canadian Resolution. Although the Republicans considered this as much too weak,[138] it did reinforce the January resolution.

Also significant was a change in the United States' attitude around this time. The State Department was describing Dutch (and French) colonial policies as follows:

> (1) anti-historical in direction; (2) an economic drain on and political liability for us; (3) a vain and insupportable extravagance for the Dutch

and the French; (4) a drag on the economic and military revitalisation of Western Europe ... (8) doomed to ultimate failure.[139]

The report added that the "principal leaders of the Republic ... were essentially men of moderation", and concluded that the United States' interest was "the creation of a sovereign Indonesian state which will satisfy the fundamental demands of militant nationalism".[140]

Facing strong criticism in Congress and threats to the Marshall Plan and the Atlantic Pact,[141] which were the cornerstones of U.S. foreign policy, Secretary of State Acheson told the visiting Dutch Foreign Minister that that Congress would not authorize military assistance to the Netherlands if the Indonesian question remained unresolved.[142] The Americans were uncertain that the threat had struck home, and they kept up steady pressure on the Dutch.[143] From this time on, it became evident that serious negotiations would have to recommence and that the Republican leaders would be restored to Yogyakarta.[144] The Sultan had an important role in arranging the latter enterprise.

On 20 March, UNCI officials paid their first visit to Yogyakarta since the Dutch occupation. Hamengku Buwono told them of his plans for the return of the Republican government; he was confident of maintaining security provided he had sufficient weapons and other equipment for the Republican police force, which remained intact outside the city and with which he was in constant touch.[145] He could take the responsibility for regional security at three days' notice.[146] As a first step, he would take control of the city of Yogyakarta and environs to a distance of about five kilometres.[147]

HOW "LOYAL" WAS HAMENGKU BUWONO?

Several reports have emerged over the years that Hamengku Buwono flirted with collaboration at this time or earlier, or at least made ambiguous statements which hinted at this. Dutch records contain references to a mysterious conversation between a brother of Hamengku Buwono and General Spoor in February 1948,[148] apparently in the context of plans to involve the Sultan in forming a state of Central Java. A related report describes the contact in February as a feeler from Hamengku Buwono to the effect that if the Dutch were to attack Yogyakarta, he (Hamengku Buwono) would "take power" in the Republic.[149] Read literally, such an approach looks like an invitation to the Dutch to launch an attack. The difficulty in assessing such reports is their vagueness. Since Dutch officials had a history of misinterpreting signals from the Republic and the Sultan, and if we assume that some kind of indirect contact indeed took place, the intention of one side may have been misunderstood by the other.

At various times in 1949, self-appointed intermediaries such as the republican official Hermani[150] and Sultan Hamid advised Dutch officials that Hamengku Buwono was, or had been, considering cooperating with them. Hermani told Resident Stok in February that though Hamengku Buwono was at present not cooperating with the Dutch, he privately favoured the policies of the new conservative PIR party (Partai Indonesia Raya; Greater Indonesia Party) which supposedly took a more cooperative line.[151] Later, in conversation with other Dutch officials, Hermani claimed that the Sultan "did not object to cooperation with the Dutch; on the contrary, the Sultan himself regards cooperation as a very real requirement for the reconstruction of an independent Indonesia and he shall, as far as his position allows it, be pleased to engage in such cooperation". A key point here is the meaning attached to the word "cooperation", i.e., did it mean "collaboration"?[152] In the circumstances at the time, clearly it did not.

Around August 1949, well after the crucial period, Sultan Hamid reported Hamengku Buwono telling him that the Dutch had erred in "not making him sign an instrument of surrender…, and in … not sending him into exile. Then he would have come over to the Dutch side."[153]

In both these cases, the nature of the sources generate some doubt about the information conveyed by them. After giving some credence to Hermani, the Dutch themselves came to question his general reliability,[154] and in any case, Hamengku Buwono's remarks as reported by Hermani are ambiguous. Various reasons exist to question Sultan Hamid's reliability,[155] and it seems improbable that in 1949, Hamengku Buwono would have trusted Hamid, whom he regarded as a Dutch puppet,[156] to the extent of making the remarks attributed to him, unless he was indulging his sense of humour.

One genuinely puzzling document along these lines is a report by Berkhuysen, Assistant Resident of Central Java, of a conversation with Prabuningrat on 11 April 1949, the day that Hamengku Buwono was making his first visit to Jakarta to start arranging the return of Sukarno and Hatta to Yogyakarta. Berkhuysen reports Prabuningrat as saying inter alia that: (a) the Sultan felt personally bound to Sukarno, but circumstances might arise where the bond could be loosened … (b) the Dutch (or perhaps the UN) should ask the Sultan which areas of Java he wished to take responsibility for … (c) as a result of such a process, the Sultan would "stand above the other Republican leaders".[157]

Prabuningrat possibly exceeded his instructions in some way, although there is no other known occasion when he did so. But neither the Dutch nor the UN appear in fact to have "asked the Sultan which areas of Java he would take responsibility for", so if the approach was really made in the terms presented here, no substantial response ever eventuated. Since the report relates to the period when the tide was visibly turning in the Republic's favour, Hamengku Buwono could hardly have been offering to come over to the Dutch side; but the reference to standing "above other Republican leaders" is surprising. The prestige of the civilian leadership, especially Sukarno, was clouded because they had tamely allowed themselves to be captured in December 1948; their standing among TNI leaders was low,[158] and alternative political leadership was perhaps being considered by Republicans in Yogyakarta in the absence of Sukarno and Hatta;[159] and notions of Hamengku Buwono's alleged ambition to supplant the leadership were even being mentioned as late as November 1949;[160] the circle around Hamengku Buwono may have had their own aspirations for their leader;[161] but this can only be speculation in the absence of more definitive evidence.

But another possible explanation for the phrase "standing above other Republican leaders" suggests itself. At this stage (mid-March), Hamengku Buwono was concerned to ensure that his word carried as much weight as possible in the confused circumstances of Central Java. The term "Republican leaders" may in fact have been referring only to local leaders in the area and not to the exiled Republican leadership on Bangka; and this approach to the Dutch may have been connected to Hamengku Buwono's request to Hatta around this time for a full-powers letter to enable him to negotiate with the Dutch as well as to strengthen his authority vis-à-vis other centres of power, including the military.[162]

Dutch intelligence reports indicated suspicions in military quarters that Hamengku Buwono wanted to be president.[163] These reports consistently claimed that Hamengku Buwono desired the maximum autonomy for his own region, as distinct as possible from the Republic.[164] Unfortunately, the reports, though often useful, are not always reliable or accurate, and they usually exaggerate any signs of dissension in Republican circles.

Nevertheless, if there was a push in some Republican circles to have Hamengku Buwono replace Sukarno, few Indonesians after the Revolution would have wished to admit it.

Claims that Hamengku Buwono was playing his own game are not consistent with his actual behaviour, including his close relationship with Hatta in particular.[165] His conduct in arranging the return of Sukarno and Hatta did not conform with an ambition to "stand above" the supreme leadership. An associate of Hamengku Buwono[166] says that he regarded Sukarno as the guarantor of Indonesian unity through his charisma and oratory, so this was why he was reluctant to move to supplant him when he might have done so.

COORDINATOR OF SECURITY

During March–April 1949, the question became not whether the Republican leaders would be restored to Yogyakarta, but under what terms and exactly when. This was formalized when the Rum–van Royen agreement was concluded on 7 May, to be followed by the Round Table Conference in The Hague. This meant a heavy defeat for hard-line Dutch officials, especially the military, weakened by Sassen's resignation in February, the evidence of an effective Republican insurgency, and defections among the Federalists. Beel resigned in mid-May; and a later blow was the sudden death of General Spoor from a heart attack on 25 May.[167]

Although negotiations continued, Hamengku Buwono, as Coordinator of Security and, later, Defence Minister, and already armed with full powers from Sukarno and Hatta,[168] made arrangements for the return of the leadership to Yogyakarta. Many problems remained, including how to ensure a peaceful withdrawal by the bitter and demoralized Dutch and colonial troops,[169] how to minimize vengeful actions by Republicans, and how to conciliate those armed groups and others who regarded the Round-Table process with suspicion and might not accept its results. Among the latter group could be numbered — most significantly — Armed Forces Commander in Chief Sudirman himself, who despite his grave illness, retained enormous prestige among the TNI and the people at large.

Hamengku Buwono was in a unique position as a senior Republican leader who could speak to Dutch commanders at any time but could also liaise — with some difficulty — with TNI leaders like Sudirman and Simatupang. From 11 April he had begun commuting to Jakarta in UN aircraft,[170] met senior Dutch and UN officials, and he visited Bangka in early June to confer with the interned Republican leaders.

The first visit to Jakarta involved a group including Juanda, Laoh, and Johannes Latuharhary.[171] The plan emerged that immediately after the mooted return of the Republican leaders to Yogyakarta, Sukarno would issue a ceasefire order. According to Hamengku Buwono, this would be obeyed as the TNI units were "intact" and operational. He remained confident that he could restore the civil government in Yogyakarta soon after the withdrawal of the Netherlands troops.[172] Under the Linggajati agreement, the Republic's ambit covered Java, Madura, and Sumatra, and if the Dutch-created negaras on those islands were to dispute this, plebiscites could easily settle the matter.[173] Republican assurance about their popular backing remained undiminished. Hamengku Buwono believed, too optimistically as it turned out, that he could easily reach an understanding with all left-wing groups in the Yogyakarta region.[174] He told the press that the presence of the Dutch was the main obstacle to the restoration of security in Yogyakarta.[175]

Hamengku Buwono, in his new capacity as Minister of State/Security Coordinator of the Republic of Indonesia,[176] told the joint committee on the return of the Republican Government which had been established under the Rum–van Royen agreement, that he needed arms and uniforms for his police.[177] The Dutch were prepared to provide uniforms but were most reluctant to arm Republicans. Complex negotiations ensued on the restoration of the railways, road repair, radio and air communications, and the exact terms under which an initial "suspension of arms" and then a full ceasefire would occur.[178] The process often faltered and was complicated by many incidents, including the arrest by the Dutch of two of Hamengku Buwono's brothers and of Republican officials who were re-establishing the Department of Defence in the Kepatihan building.[179] The Sultan accused the Dutch of mounting a scare campaign, as a result of which nearly 40,000 local people, many of them Chinese, were evacuated from the city to Semarang and elsewhere.[180] The evacuation was presumably an annoyance[181] and a humiliation for Hamengku Buwono, who had issued a statement guaranteeing the security of all who chose to stay.[182]

Dutch reports identified three main political groupings around Yogyakarta — a small group who supported the Sultan, larger groups also broadly supporting the Republic, as well as various leftist groups violently opposed to further talks with the Dutch.[183] The Dutch bias was to exaggerate Republican difficulties and indiscipline, arguing that the return of the Republican leadership would pose considerable security problems. Republicans responded that the presence of the Dutch themselves caused the security problems. But the situation in Central Java was undoubtedly confused, communications were slow and often cut, food was scarce, and outbreaks of disease were threatening.

Difficulties with dissident groups led to an order from Hamengku Buwono to round up and disarm non-cooperating militias.[184] Local commander Suharto, increasingly trusted by Hamengku Buwono, put considerable pressure on PKI-oriented groups, as well as some others, disarming them and in some cases even forcing them to flee into Dutch lines.[185]

In mid-May Hamengku Buwono officially reopened the Sultanate offices after a gap of nearly five months.[186] He predicted that, although difficulties with some communist groups might still occur, the Republic had sufficient reliable troops to guarantee a ceasefire in the Yogyakarta region. He had "summoned" Commander in Chief Sudirman, who — "although mentally and physically exhausted" — had enough influence to ensure the observance of a ceasefire order.[187] As noted, Sudirman was not to prove so amenable.[188] The first stage would be the takeover of all areas designated as Republican by the Renville agreement, and the withdrawal of Dutch troops from those regions.[189]

When in early June the Sultan met Sukarno and other Republican leaders on Bangka for the first time since the Dutch capture of Yogyakarta,[190] Sukarno was anxious about funding the leaders' return, but Hamengku Buwono quietly observed that he could contribute six million guilders to the process. Sukarno leapt up and embraced him.[191] This was probably as close as this relationship ever got.

In arranging the Dutch withdrawal, Hamengku Buwono originally designated the police to take over the town,[192] but after dissension involving not only the police but also the other senior commander in the area, Col Jatikusumo,[193] Suharto was entrusted with the task. This looks like a surprising victory for the young commander in facing off competition from other forces for the signal honour of reoccupying the Republic's capital city;[194] but from Hamengku Buwono's viewpoint it may well have been the most pragmatic solution. As we have seen, the police were short of arms, and Jatikusumo's force, being largely students from the Military Academy,[195] may have been less practised and capable than Suharto's brigade.[196]

On 9 June Hamengku Buwono issued an order to Republican troops to avoid contact with Dutch forces.[197] But the TNI were still very distrustful of the Dutch, were disposed to make few concessions, and threatened to attack if the Dutch did not withdraw on schedule.[198] Suharto as local commander refused to contemplate any sort of handover ceremony in Yogyakarta, arguing that the Dutch had never occupied Yogyakarta and there was thus no question of the TNI receiving the city back from them.[199]

In a phased withdrawal, Dutch and KNIL troops left Gunung Kidul on 24 June, Bantul on 27 June, Yogyakarta city on 29 June, and the last units left the principality on 30 June.[200] Thus, on 29 June 1949, the Dutch withdrew northwards from Yogyakarta city, and after a brief period TNI troops entered the city, maintaining a distance between the two, and witnessed by UNCI military observers and by Hamengku Buwono himself.[201] The last Dutch troops, having spent the night at Medari, left the Yogyakarta residency on 30 June, thus ending 200 years of Dutch claims on the principality.[202]

In a radio broadcast, Hamengku Buwono lamented the suffering experienced by many Indonesian families,[203] adding that the recovery of Yogyakarta was just one step in the independence struggle. Much work remained to be done and he called on a united people to help support the Republican Government. The Republic had regained only one part of its territory and would continue the struggle alongside the peoples of Pasundan, East Indonesia, Borneo, Sumatra and other regions. Citizens should act for the common good and not for selfish sectional interests. He added, "the Republic guarantees democratic rights, and everyone has the right to speak freely against everything being done by the state with which they do not agree". But freedom of speech should be exerted through legal channels. He threatened strong action against anyone endangering security.[204]

On 6 July 1949, amid jubilation, Hamengku Buwono greeted Sukarno, Hatta, and other figures at the airport. Despite predictions in the Dutch-language press of "terror and chaos" after the evacuation,[205] Yogyakarta remained peaceful, and the Dutch press had to admit, "We asked before 'Can the Sultan do it?' So far, indeed he has."[206]

Hamengku Buwono said that the city's southern suburbs had suffered badly during the war as they had seen virtually continuous fighting,[207] but the rest of the city was surprisingly undamaged. Prambanan village, near the ancient temple complex, was almost totally destroyed. Markets across the city were returning to normal as peace beckoned.²⁰⁸ Political leaders in Yogyakarta were now unconcerned about possible threats from communist groups outside the city.²⁰⁹ As many as a hundred alleged collaborators were arrested, and a committee to screen Republican civil servants and weed out collaborators was immediately formed.²¹⁰

The next step was to arrange the ceasefire, to be followed by a complete cessation of hostilities. Hamengku Buwono was reasonably confident that a ceasefire order would be obeyed, but the military leaders could not be taken for granted. Supreme Commander Sudirman was the hardest to convince, and Hamengku Buwono and other leaders, especially Sukarno, but also military figures like Nasution, Simatupang, and Gatot Subroto, had to exert all their powers to persuade him at last to return to Yogyakarta.²¹¹ The ceasefire was set for 11 August, but even in Central Java the military were intent on a demonstration; they launched a major attack on Solo on 10 August, one day before the ceasefire took effect.²¹² But from then on, despite many incidents and misunderstandings, and occasional clashes with the Dutch or between different nationalist forces, the ceasefire held reasonably well.²¹³

Although negotiations over the final transfer of sovereignty were proceeding in The Hague,²¹⁴ the Sultan, now Minister of Defence,²¹⁵ toured Java during August and Sumatra during September, contacting military leaders to discuss the ceasefire and inform them of the progress of the negotiations. Different situations required different approaches; he had good relations with TNI forces in Central Java, but other regions could be more problematic. The East Java commander Colonel Sungkono²¹⁶ — not an easy personality at the best of times — did not know Hamengku Buwono personally, but his fellow East Javanese Roeslan Abdulgani induced him to agree.²¹⁷ An earlier emissary, Darmasetiawan, had been shot at.²¹⁸ The Sultan's party toured West Java on bicycles, contacting Siliwangi commanders like Kemal Idris.²¹⁹ The visit to Sumatra proceeded without major incidents, Hamengku Buwono's personal prestige and acceptability seemed high in all areas,²²⁰ and public enthusiasm was evident in many localities.²²¹ He commented that the situation in Sumatra was easier than in Yogyakarta.²²²

In October Hamengku Buwono put a proposal to the last Dutch viceroy, Lovink, under which the Netherlands troops would concentrate in the main cities, with guaranteed lines of communication between the major deployments. This would help to separate the two opposing forces.²²³

He also warned urgently of serious tensions in East Java and the East Pasundan area in West Java.[224] In East Java the Republicans were alleging continuous provocations by the Dutch under the obstinate General Baay, who during October had arrested as many as "2000 TNI and Republican civil officers".[225] Lovink apparently saw Hamengku Buwono's proposal as an attempt to impose a Republican and "communist" regime in these areas, displacing the negaras.[226] Displaying an uncharacteristic lack of patience, Hamengku Buwono was so concerned at Lovink's refusal to take serious action that he issued a statement expressing fear of an "explosive situation",[227] and even mentioning the risk of a third Dutch military action. Even sympathetic foreign observers privately criticized him for an "ill-advised" action.[228] Some days later, however, Hamengku Buwono conceded to U.S. visitors that the situation had eased, and rebutted Dutch claims that extremists were getting out of hand, saying that the Republic remained in control.[229]

He toured Sumatra again in December, making various military appointments, including appointing Col Kawilarang as commander in Aceh, Tapanuli and East Sumatra.[230] He warned local Republicans against undertaking reprisals against collaborators.[231] Accompanied by Ali Budiarjo, Jatikusumo, and Nasution, he then toured Banjarmasin, Makasar, Den Pasar, and Bangkalan.[232] Nasution recorded the Sultan's wide acceptability among "feudal" officials and social groups in these regions.[233] The main difficulty arose in Makasar, where local authorities, officials of the strongest Dutch-created negara, rejected the deployment of TNI troops, saying that their own KNIL troops could guarantee security.[234]

The final act was the formal transfer of sovereignty at the end of the year. In a ceremony in Jakarta, Hamengku Buwono — as acting President of the new Republic of the United States of Indonesia (RUSI or RIS) — received the symbolic transfer of sovereignty from Lovink. Sukarno arrived in Jakarta triumphantly the next day. Meanwhile, a parallel transfer of sovereignty ceremony, involving Queen Juliana and Mohammad Hatta, had taken place in The Hague.

SUMMARY

The Indonesian Revolution was Hamengku Buwono's finest hour, so much so that the rest of his career, despite its distinction, looks almost like an anticlimax. His central conviction, that the time of colonialism was over, seemed to guide all his actions during 1949, and he was prepared to take high personal and political risks to justify it. He was playing for high stakes, because the Dutch had exiled some of his ancestors and considered doing the same to him. His judgement that, when it came to the point, they would not dare to do so, proved correct. Apart from the political risks, during the Revolution he had also survived serious physical risks to himself, in 1945, 1948, and 1949.

One of the aims of this study is to discern Hamengku Buwono's ideological stance and indeed what he stood for in his career. At the end of 1950, he was thirty-seven years old, and it could be assumed that his beliefs about politics and society were reasonably fixed by this stage. Since he rarely made any statement of ideology, we have to judge largely from his actions, of which there were many in the Revolution period.

The first obvious feature is a sturdy and obstinate anti-colonial nationalism. Despite the beliefs or hopes of the Dutch that Hamengku Buwono might come to favour the stability, comfort and privileges which they had afforded him during their rule, the evidence for this is faint indeed. Far more compelling is the evidence for his belief that the Dutch time was past, that it was time for Indonesians to take responsibility for their own future, and he could and should assist the process. This involved committing all his prestige, status, and political flair on the side of the Republic.

But there was a limit to his radicalism. His conflict with Amir Syarifuddin in late 1947, if Dutch intelligence reports are to be believed, and his attitude to the Madiun affair demonstrated his lack of sympathy for extreme social revolution, and his identification with the moderate nationalist viewpoint. In maintaining links with such varied leaders as Sukarno, Hatta, Sudirman, Nasution and Syahrir, he seemed to aspire to a middle-of-the-road status.

Closely allied with this was a conviction that the Indonesian people were firmly behind the Republic and that nothing the Dutch or others could do would alter this. He had evidence of the popularity both of the Republic itself and its leaders, and of his own personal popularity. Public enthusiasm was evident in a string of meetings and public events, the patriotism with which local youth flocked to join the militia, and the extent to which Yogyakarta society accepted his leadership. But he was realistic enough to know that others, especially Sukarno, commanded a wider and perhaps deeper allegiance among the Indonesian people as a whole.

His anti-colonialism was limited in another way, too. As Dutch intelligence had already discerned, Hamengku Buwono was pragmatically aware that Indonesia needed foreign expertise and investment in all fields, including defence and security. It followed that, although he had struggled determinedly against the Dutch during the Revolution, later as Minister of Defence in an independent Indonesia, he was quite prepared to accept the Netherlands Military Mission in Jakarta, because he was well aware of the deficiencies of the Indonesian armed forces. The xenophobia which motivated some Indonesian nationalists found little resonance with him. This pragmatic attitude, influenced no doubt by his knowledge of Europe, was reflected in his speech at the transfer of sovereignty when he said, "we gladly accept the assistance of other nations, particularly that of the Netherlands, which are skilled and experienced and imbued with the sincere wish to help our people".[235]

A further feature of his world view was a commitment to more democratic, representational forms of government, mixed in practice with a pragmatic employment of available tools of power. His efforts during 1946–48 confirm a sincere leaning towards progressive and more democratic political and social forms. As we will see, throughout his career he always seemed to represent a more inclusive and tolerant alternative to what was currently on offer, whether the Dutch or Japanese, the PKI, Guided Democracy or Suharto. The reputation he had gained during the Revolution remained curiously untarnished in later times, even after the 17 October 1952 affair, and was an important factor in his wide public acceptability in the dramatic days of the 1960s.

His commitment to democracy was not unqualified. His statements during the Revolution contain as many references to the need for unity as to democracy, and it was unclear at this stage what he would do if faced with a choice between the two. Calls for the abandonment of selfish sectional interests, such as he had made in 1949,[236] can easily become an impatience with minority rights. The difficulty presented by the many calls for unity in this period was how to answer the question, "unity on whose terms?" It would become clear later that for Hamengku Buwono, unity on Sukarno's terms became unacceptable.

Finally, what was his contribution to the Indonesian independence struggle? Nearly every commentator agrees that it was important, and some even argue that it was crucial. Some Indonesian contributors to *Tahta untuk Rakyat* asked what would have happened if Hamengku Buwono had not been there in 1949,[237] with the implication that the Republic's temporary defeat may have become a complete one without Hamengku Buwono's intervention. Counterfactual history is notoriously difficult to handle, and some historians dismiss it as useless speculation; historians cannot behave like scientists in a laboratory conducting an experiment with one set of ingredients, then mixing the batch anew and repeating it with one or two ingredients omitted.

But the proposition that the Republic would not have survived in 1949 without Hamengku Buwono seems hard to justify. Such judgments are essentially impressionistic, but the desire for independence appeared too innately powerful in Java and Sumatra for the Dutch attack to succeed, even if Hamengku Buwono's determined and subtle resistance had not been there. The Republic did not ultimately depend on the efforts and standing of any one individual, whether Sukarno, Hatta, Sudirman, Tan Malaka or Syarifuddin. A whole host of factors came into play in 1949, including the strong international revulsion against the Dutch, the large number of guerrilla fighters who were able to keep the countryside in constant uproar, and the discovery by the Dutch that their resources were insufficient to pacify the country.

Having said that, we could still reasonably argue that without Hamengku Buwono the Republic's task would have been considerably more difficult in 1949; that his strategy was a unique asset for the Republic; that his exploitation of the various factors involved — such as his own status and Dutch respect for it, his links with the various local power apparatuses, the favourable popular feeling for him and for the Republic, his financial support for the Republic at crucial times, the international power equation — was masterly; and that without him the process of restoring the Republican leaders to Yogyakarta and securing the ultimate ceasefire and transfer of sovereignty would have been more complex and time-consuming. Whether he (or anyone else) was indispensable, it is hard to see how he could have performed better.

Notes

1. There seem to have been only eight ministers present at first. These were Sukarno, Salim, Laoh, Juanda, Natsir, Kusnan, Ali Sastroamijoyo, and Hamengku Buwono — *Suluh Rakjat*, 25 April 1949.
2. He had been resting in the palace at this time under the care of Dr Sim Ki Ay — *Siasat* weekly magazine, Year 7, 20 December 1953, p. 6.

3. *TUR*, p. 70. Hamengku Buwono says that Sukarno confirmed this personally to him.
4. "Four Princes Letter" (cited here as *FPL*), p. 3, Arsip Daerah Yogyakarta no. 157. The "Four Princes Letter" is a fascinating joint account dated 21 June 1950, by three Sultanate princes and one Pakualaman prince (respectively, Pujokusumo, Suryobronto, Hadikusumo and Suryaningprang) of the illegal civilian government during the Dutch occupation.
5. Abrar Yusra, *Komat-Kamit Selosoemardjan* [The Murmurings of Selosumarjan], p. 163.
6. Hatta, *Mohammad Hatta, Indonesian Patriot, Memoirs*, p. 295.
7. Quoted for example in MvD/CAD, NEFIS 1948/1949, Bundle AA16, CMI doc no. 5797 of July 1949, *De terugkeer van de regering naar Jogja* [The Return of the Government to Jogja], pp. 28–29.
8. For Nasution's reaction, see Penders and Sundhaussen, *Abdul Haris Nasution*, p. 75.
9. Nasution, *Perang Kemerdekaan* [War of Independence], vol. 9, p. 171.
10. Ibid., p. 172.
11. The Dutch had broken Indonesian military codes and were thus aware of the exercises; another factor was their similarly sourced awareness of Sukarno's plans to visit India shortly, a plan which they wanted to forestall. Kahin, *Southeast Asia A Testament*, p. 88.
12. For example, NA 2.10.17, Procureur Generaal (henceforth "Proc Gen"), part 329, record of interrogation of head of the Indonesian Central Bank Margono Joyohadikusumo, 13 January 1949.
13. McMahon, *Colonialism and Cold War*, p. 262.
14. *Officiele Bescheiden Betreffende de Nederlands — Indonesische Betrekkingen*, vol. 17, p. 255 — Document 180, 20 December 1948 (See Bibliography for details of this series, referred to hereafter as *NIB*).
15. Reid, *Indonesian National Revolution*, p. 146, and McMahon, op. cit., p. 290.
16. *NIB*, op. cit., vol. 17, pp. 709–11.
17. Yusra, op. cit., p. 164.
18. "Belanda Serbu Jogja" [The Dutch Attack Yogyakarta], *Siasat* weekly magazine, Year 7, 20 December 1953, op. cit., p. 341.
19. NEFIS file 01709 of 2 May 1949, held in Dutch Foreign Ministry. Also Proc Gen, NA 2.10.17, Part 367, page dated 29 December 1948 headed *Afschrift I* ("Copy I").
20. As noted above, he *was* ill at the time of the Dutch attack, but not seriously. In mid-January, he refused to meet Professor Husein Jayadiningrat and Ir Muns, because he felt "neither physically nor mentally strong" — undated letter to Col van Langen in answer to latter's letter of 14 January 1949, MvD/CAD Bundle AA21, NEFIS 1949.
21. Kahin, in *TUR*, op. cit., p. 177. Prabuningrat was the principal but not sole

channel to the Sultan. *FPL*, op. cit., p. 6, says that Resident Stok's many requests for meetings were made to Honggowongso.
22. *TUR*, p. 75.
23. Requests by the military authorities to meet the Sultan began on the first evening after the attack — *FPL*, op. cit., p. 5.
24. MvD/CAD, NEFIS 1949, Bundle AA21, *De Toestand in Jogja* [The Situation in Jogja], 22 February 1949.
25. *FPL*, p. 3.
26. Ibid., p. 4.
27. Arsip Daerah Yogyakarta no. 165, records of joint civilian–military meetings during April–August 1949. A "T" brigade intelligence report dated 12 February 1949, in MvD/CAD, NEFIS 1949, bundle AA22, assessed that the Republican administration was especially effective in Sleman.
28. *TUR*, p. 213, note by Mrs Rahmi Hatta, wife of Mohammad Hatta; a similar story is told by Mrs Fatmawati Sukarno, in her *Catatan Kecil bersama Bung Karno, Bagian I* [A Few Notes on my Life with Bung Karno, Part 1], p. 75.
29. Fatmawati, ibid. Juanda was the main contact, but at times Bintoro too called on Fatmawati. According to another account, the families received fl 15 per week; van Kaam, *Vu* magazine, March 1984, NIOD 081591, "Natijd lists", p. 111.
30. Kahin in *TUR*, op. cit., p. 177. The Dutch became aware fairly soon of Hamengku Buwono's order to the civil servants — MvD/CAD, Bundle AA15, NEFIS Weekly Report, 24 January 1949, p. 9.
31. *NIB*, vol. 16, p. 278, doc 205, report from CMI director Somer, 22 December 1948.
32. Column in *Nasional* weekly, 22 March 1950. *FPL*, op. cit., p. 8 (part 4) admits that "some" Republicans agreed to cooperate because of fear or lack of food.
33. MvD/CAD, Hoofdkwartier Generale Staf (Headquarters General Staff) archive, Inv no. 695, *Samenvatting van gegevens betreffende de Sultan van Djokja* [Summary of Information on the Sultan of Yogyakarta], 18 April 1949, p. 1.
34. MvD/CAD, Bundle AA15, NEFIS Weekly Report, 24 January 1949, p. 9. Also MvD/CAD, Bundle AA21, CMI report by J.A. Gulden of 19 January, reporting a petition to the Sultan "to lead the people again".
35. Kahin, *Nationalism*, p. 176.
36. Reid, op. cit., p. 149.
37. Sassen to Stikker, *NIB*, vol. 15, p. 613, 29 November 1948. The adviser was Raden Abdulkadir Wijoyoatmojo, the most senior official of Indonesian ethnic origin on the Dutch side.
38. NA 2.21.036.01, Collectie Spoor, Inv no. 27, report by Buurman van Vreeden, 7 November 1948.
39. *NIB*, vol. 16, p. 238, Sassen to Beel, doc 161, 19 December 1948.

40. D. Lee, ed., *Australia and Indonesia's Independence, the Transfer of Sovereignty, Documents 1949*, p. 411, doc 399, Critchley to Burton, 14 May 1949.
41. *NIB*, vol. 16 op. cit., Beel to Sassen, doc 173, 22 December 1948, p. 249.
42. *NIB*, vol. 16, p. 264, doc 192, Sassen to Beel, 21 December 1948.
43. Ir Juanda was Indonesia's last prime minister. He was born in Tasikmalaya, West Java, in 1911. He studied engineering in Bandung, headed a Muhammadiyah school and then practised as an engineer during the 1930s, and joined the executive of Oto Iskandar Dinata's Sundanese political party from 1933 to 1942. He was Deputy Minister for Communications in Syahrir's second cabinet in 1946, and collaborated as a member of Hamengku Buwono's "secret cabinet" under the Dutch occupation in 1949. After the Revolution, he held various senior ministerial positions, rising to be Sukarno's Prime Minister in the early 1960s, dying in office in 1963. Sukarno became his own prime minister after this, and the position was never revived. Anderson, *Java in a Time of Revolution*, p. 418.
44. *NIB*, ibid., p. 327, doc 252, note of 24 December 1948 by Secretary General of Foreign Ministry Lovink.
45. Ibid., p. 278, doc 205, note by CMI director Somer, 22 December 1948.
46. Report by Drees on his visit, ibid., p. 613, doc 455, 15 January 1949.
47. Elson, op. cit., p. 31.
48. Suharto claims to have devised and led the whole series of attacks, not only the Serangan Umum of 1 March 1949 — Nasution, *Memenuhi Panggilan Tugas*, vol. 2A, p. 325.
49. SESKOAD, *Serangan Umum* [General Offensive], p. 196.
50. Kahin, *Nationalism*, op. cit., p. 395. See also Kahin, *Southeast Asia a Testament*, op. cit., p. 104.
51. *NIB*, vol. 16, attachment to doc 401, report of "4 January 1946" (sic — must mean 1949), by Teunissen (director, Java Bank) to his fellow directors.
52. Ibid., p. 619, Beel to Sassen, 10 January 1949.
53. Ibid., p. 648, doc 470, note by Drees, 11 January 1949.
54. *NIB*, vol. 17, p. 217, report by Stikker to Drees, 19 January 1949.
55. Kahin, *Nationalism*, op. cit., p. 413. Reid, op. cit., p. 153. Kahin gives the date of the letter as 21 January. It seems likely that the resignations were announced around 17 January (see following note) but backdated to 1 January.
56. It is unclear what these reports were. *De Locomotief* of Semarang, for example, only made its first reference to Hamengku Buwono since the Dutch attack on 26 January 1949, in reporting his resignation as district head (also *Sin Po* of the same date, quoted in *NIB*, vol. 17, op. cit., pp. 189–90).
57. Kahin, ibid. Dutch records contain a translation of a clandestinely circulated Javanese-language document which is similar but not identical to Kahin's version. Dated 17 January 1949, it states inter alia: "The Sultan and the

Pakualam have resigned as of 1 January because: (1) they cannot approve of Dutch actions against the Republic, and (2) they do not wish to cooperate with the Dutch; rumours that the Sultan is receiving Dutch officials are all lies; no local officials are cooperating with the Dutch; the people of Mataram should follow this example." Document of 17 January 1949 headed *De Stem van de Republiek* [The Voice of the Republic], in MvD/CAD, NEFIS 1947–49, Bundle AA22.

58. D. Lee, op. cit., p. 192, doc 190, Critchley to Department of External Affairs (DEA), 4 February 1949.
59. Kahin, ibid., p. 393.
60. Ibid., p. 412.
61. Ibid., p. 413n.
62. Department of Education and Culture, *Biografi Pahlawan Nasional Sri Sultan Hamengku Buwono IX* [Biography of National Hero Sri Sultan Hamengku Buwono IX], p. 45.
63. MvD/CAD, AA21, NEFIS 1949, page headed *De zegen en de reden van Z E de Sultan* [The Blessing and Message of the Sultan], dated 24 January 1949. The term "Javanese/Indonesian" in the text may be a quirk of NEFIS translation.
64. *NIB*, vol. 17, op. cit., p. 242, doc 156, Beel to Sassen, 26 January 1949.
65. Ibid., p. 242, n 3.
66. Ibid., p. 405, doc 242. Meeting of Commission of Nine (a special consultative group of Dutch government and parliamentary leaders), 3 February 1949.
67. Ibid., p. 410.
68. Kahin, p. 398, seemingly referring to the January–February period. Available supporting evidence for this approach is thin and emerges at what seems to be the wrong time period. U.S. reports, however, have one suggestive indication in a report of 27 April: "Referring story Sultan approached from Netherlands sources view taking over matters law and order Jogja residency, Van Royen said possible one or more approaches may have been made to Sultan some weeks ago [late March/early April?] when Netherlands officials Batavia hoped a *daerah* [region] might be formed out of that area". *Foreign Relations of the United States 1949*, vol. 7, Part 2, The Far East and Australasia [henceforth FRUS], p. 367, report by Consul General Livengood, 27 April 1949.
69. Hamengku Buwono in *Asiaweek* interview 1986, op. cit., p. 60. He added, "I said jokingly that I would talk about becoming Sultan of Indonesia." This seems to correspond to the content of the following NEFIS report: MvD/CAD, Bundle AA21, NEFIS 1949, CMI secret report no. 624 of 5 April 1949, headed SULTAN .
70. Reid, op. cit., p. 153.
71. *TUR*, p. 75, saying that this offer was made by an unnamed bank official.

Teunissen of the Java Bank visited in early January but his report of the visit does not mention such offers. *NIB*, vol. 16, p. 525n, attachment to doc 401, report by Teunissen of 4 January 1949.
72. Kahin in ibid., p. 178.
73. From December 1948 to March 1949, Dutch archives — including cabinet documents — are full of references to the need to contact the Sultan, to win him over, and to persuade him to accept a role in a new Central Java government, but with no reference to inducements — in *NIB*, vols. 16, see for example pp. 11, 238, 379, 525, 579, 613, 619, and 17 — pp. 24, 217, 587, 609. These volumes cover the period from December 1948 to the end of February 1949. T.K. Critchley (former Australian UNCI representative, personal letter to author, 20 May 2003) confirmed the common belief in Republican circles that these offers had been made. It seems unlikely that the Republicans would fabricate such a story and maintain it ever after if it was untrue.
74. *FPL*, p. 10. The words in the original are *kalau perlu harus diculik atau ...* i.e., "if necessary (they) must be kidnapped or ..." (Sinister dots in original).
75. Unmarried civil servants received fl 7-50 per week, while married ones received fl 15-00 per week during this period. Van Kaam, *Vu* magazine, NIOD 081591, Natijd lists, p. 108.
76. *FPL*, op. cit., pp. 9–11. See reference above to the effectiveness of the clandestine apparatus in Sleman.
77. "Belanda Serbu Jogja" [The Dutch Attack Jogja], in *Siasat* weekly magazine, Year 7, 20 December 1953, op. cit., ibid.
78. *NIB*, vol. 17, op. cit., Spoor to Beel, 24 February 1949, p. 672, doc 366.
79. Ibid. — This was described as a "whispering campaign".
80. Ibid. The word used was *disrobot*, meaning to kidnap (or perhaps kill).
81. The document (quoted in the previous chapter) was dated 1948. NEFIS material, e.g., NEFIS/CMI files held in Dutch Foreign Ministry, Inv no. 06909, 25 February 1949.
82. *NIB*, op. cit., vol. 17, p. 672n.
83. Buurman van Vreeden to Spoor, 26 February 1949, MvD/CAD, Bundle AA21.
84. *NIB*, vol. 17, op. cit., p. 673.
85. Ibid.
86. Ibid. Lt Col Latif Hendraningrat, a Siliwangi officer, was noted as commander of the Yogyakarta garrison in December 1948, in Yusra, op. cit., p. 159.
87. MvD/CAD, NEFIS files 1948–49, NEFIS weekly report no. 4, 10 February 1949, p. 7.
88. Gatot Mangkupraja, "The PETA: My Relations with the Japanese — A Correction of Sukarno's Autobiography", *Indonesia Magazine*, no. 5 (April 1968): 133.

89. Mangkupraja, ibid. Suryaningprang, was one of the Pakualam's main representatives — MvD/CAD, AA21, NEFIS 1949, van Langen report of 18 January 1949.
90. *NIB*, vol. 17, p. 671, n366.
91. *NIB*, vol. 18, p. 12, document 7, van Marseveen to Beel, 1 March 1949.
92. Ricklefs, *A History of Modern Indonesia*, pp. 108–9.
93. Romo Noordi Pakuningrat, interview 20 August 2002; Professor Selosumarjan, in an interview on 31 July 2002, confirmed that some of the "uncles" were considering cooperation with the Dutch.
94. MvD/CAD, NEFIS 1949, Bundle AA21, CMI document, report 1508 of 16 February 1949 from Captain Gulden to General Spoor; also ibid., report headed *Opvolger van de Sultan* [Sultan's Successor] of 14 February 1949, where Puruboyo is reported to be willing to replace Hamengku Buwono, "were he to resign".
95. MvD/CAD, Hoofdkwartier Generale Staf [Headquarters General Staff] archive, Inv no. 695, op. cit., *Samenvatting van gegevens betreffende de Sultan van Djokja* [Summary of Information on the Sultan of Yogyakarta], 18 April 1949, p. 2.
96. *TUR*, op. cit., p. 85, Hamengku Buwono's letter to Sujono of 26 March 1949.
97. Lt Cmdr Samuel Hazelett was an American UNCI military observer. Hamengku Buwono met him on 27 February "without the knowledge of the Dutch authorities" — MvD/CAD, Hoofdkwartier Generale Staf, Inv no. 695, cable of 28 February.
98. *Gelora Api Revolusi* [The Fire of Revolution], edited by C. Wild and P. Carey, interview with Hamengku Buwono, pp. 188 et seq.
99. *Asiaweek* interview, op. cit., p. 60.
100. "Prabuningrat document", an untitled and undated 3-page account of Hamengku Buwono IX's conduct in 1948 and 1949, written personally by Prabuningrat (early 1980s?), p. 2.
101. Wild and Carey, op. cit., p. 189.
102. The term *Serangan Umum* seems to have come into common usage for this specific attack some time after the Revolution, although the term was known in military parlance even before 1 March 1949 — see Nasution, *Perang Kemerdekaan*, vol. 10, p. 654 (p. 8 of report by Lt Col Zulkifli Lubis of 4 February 1949).
103. *Aneta News Bulletin*, 4 March 1949, p. 2.
104. Elson, op. cit., p. 38.
105. *Aneta*, 3 March 1949.
106. *TUR*, p. 79; *Gelora Api Revolusi*, pp. 190–91; and *Asiaweek* interview, 4 May 1986, vol. 12, no. 18, p. 60.
107. MvD/CAD, Hoofdkwartier Generale Staf, Inv no. 695, report of discussion at house of Col van Langen, 2 March 1949, p. 1.
108. Prabuningrat, op. cit., p. 2.

109. *NIB*, vol. 17, p. 18.
110. Ibid.
111. As noted, the administrative centre of the Kraton had been despoiled by Dutch troops on 22 February — *SO*, p. 89.
112. *NIB*, ibid.
113. Kahin makes this claim — op. cit., p. 411. But see Elson, op. cit., p. 36.
114. *NIB*, vol. 18, Beel cable to The Hague, 1 March 1949, p. 16. It was the only attack of the series mentioned above which caused Beel to send Spoor to Yogyakarta to investigate in person.
115. This paragraph is based on points made by David Jenkins, personal communication, August 2004.
116. See for example Anderson, Kumar, Ricklefs, Soemarsaid Moertono, and Moedjanto in the Bibliography. Others who have written on these and related subjects, but not cited here, include Schrieke, Berg, Veth, and Selosumarjan.
117. *Sabda pandita ora kena wola-wali* — Moedjanto, *Konsep Kekuasaan Jawa* (Javanese Concepts of Power), p. 145.
118. Kumar, *Java and Modern Europe*, p. 383.
119. Kumar, ibid., pp. 394–95 and p. 404.
120. The most famous mythical example is King Yudhistira in the *Mahabharata* epic, exiled with his brothers for fourteen years.
121. Moertono, op. cit., p. 40.
122. The importance of polite (*halus*) behaviour, even under pressure, is stressed in Javanese mores. See Anderson, op. cit., p. 44 and p. 50.
123. For the Dutch being cast as the Kurawas by Javanese wayang practitioners, see Dahm, *Sukarno and the Struggle for Indonesian Independence*, pp. 25–27.
124. Great store is set on harmony in the Javanese world view. See Anderson, op. cit., p. 51; or Quinn, *The Novel in Javanese*, p. 46.
125. See the various images of the light of power quoted above. Anderson provides the image of Javanese power as like a reflector lamp, p. 35, with more dazzling light in the centre, fading to a penumbra at the margin.
126. This appears to have been prepared for the Dutch cabinet meeting of 21 March 1949, headed *De Houding van de Sultan van Yogyakarta* [The Standpoint of the Sultan of Yogyakarta]. The cabinet paper is unsigned.
127. Hamengku Buwono's immunity caused resentment among the occupying forces — see the letter by KNIL intelligence officer Lt J.A. Bakker, undated, but written during 1949, in Proc Gen, op. cit., part 367, p. 10.
128. Cabinet paper, ibid.
129. Ibid., p. 2.
130. Hamengku Buwono also apparently sent a similar but briefer report to General Sudirman, complaining about being forced to receive the Dutch officials on 2 March — MvD/CAD, Hoofdkwartier Generale Staf, Inv no. 695, unsigned

CMI report headed "Activity of Military Observers (from an interview with Mr Juanda)."
131. Kahin, op. cit., p. 411. Elson is sceptical about the claims made (mainly by Indonesians and sympathetic observers like Kahin) about the effects of the Serangan Umum on the Dutch and on international opinion; but he does not dispute the effect on the Federalists — Elson, op. cit., p. 40.
132. See the useful introduction in D. Lee, op. cit., pp. xv–xvi.
133. For example, a letter of 8 March 1949 from Stikker to British Foreign Minister Bevin states "insurmountable objections" to the return, but then lays down a plan under which the return could be effectuated.
134. Lee, op. cit., p. 198, doc 196, Critchley to McIntyre, 8 February 1949.
135. *Het Dagblad*, 10 March 1949, front-page article entitled *Voorwaardelijk terugkeer van republikeinen naar Djokja?* [Conditional Return of Republicans to Yogyakarta?].
136. *SO*, p. 129, indicates that Sujatmoko called a press conference as soon as the news arrived. But Security Council records of 1949 contain no specific reference to it. See *UNSC Official Records 4th Year,1949, nos. 26–54*; *UNSC Official Records 4th Year nos 420–448*, 21 March–27 September; *UNSC Official Records 4th Year Supplements*; *UNSC Official Records 4th Year nos. 449–458* [October–December 1949].
137. Lee, op. cit., p. 324 (23 March 1949).
138. Kahin, *Nationalism*, op. cit., p. 413.
139. Document NSC-51 of 28 March 1949, quoted in McMahon, *Colonialism and Cold War*, p. 290.
140. McMahon, ibid.
141. McMahon, op. cit., p. 291.
142. Ibid.
143. Ibid.
144. The possible return of the Republican leaders to Yogyakarta was commonly mentioned in Dutch records from this time on. E.g., de Beus, op. cit., p. 103.
145. Lee, op. cit., p. 314, doc 305, Critchley to McIntyre, 21 March 1949.
146. Ibid.
147. NA 2.10.14, inv no. 4542, "Report of Visit by Deputy UNCI Leaders to Yogyakarta", 21 March 1949, p. 6. By early May, he was demanding the whole Yogyakarta principality "as a minimum"; Lee, op. cit., p. 386, doc 372, Critchley to DEA, 2 May 1949.
148. *NIB*, vol. 15, p. 573, doc 280, Sassen to Stikker, 3 November 1948. I have not been able to trace any direct report of the alleged conversation. February 1948 is covered by *NIB*, vol. 12 (pp. 660–844) and vol. 13 (pp. 1–120), which contain no reference to Hamengku Buwono.
149. *NIB*, vol. 15 op. cit., p. 613, doc 300, Sassen to Stikker, 7 November 1948.

See also the reference to Hamengku Buwono's being interested in "being a minister or President of an independent Indonesia" in MvD/CAD, Bundle AA21, NEFIS 1949, CMI secret report no. 624 of 5 April 1949, p. 1, headed SULTAN, reporting a conversation on circa 18 March between Hamengku Buwono and a UN representative, noted above.

150. P. Drooglever, "Sultan in Oorlogstijd" [Sultan in Wartime], p. 9, quoting a document in the Stok archive at the Nationaal Archief.
151. Drooglever, ibid. For details about the PIR, see Kahin, op. cit., pp. 324–25.
152. Drooglever, ibid. Once it had been established that the Republican leaders were to return to Yogyakarta, "cooperation" with the Dutch surely came to mean receiving their assistance in restoring Republican rule, i.e., it no longer meant "collaboration". *NIB*, vol. 18, doc 120, p. 185, Beel to van Maarseveen, 18 March 1949.
153. Drooglever, op. cit., p. 17, n 19.
154. *NIB*, vol. 18, Spoor to Beel, 30 March 1949, doc 175, p. 282, n 1 — marginal note by Koets, "Alas, the reliability of Hermani's reporting is not always 100%."
155. We saw above his inaccurately optimistic assessment of Hamengku Buwono's position in January 1949 — Drees report, *NIB*, vol. 16, p. 613, doc 455, 15 January 1949.
156. At Hamid's trial in 1953 (see next chapter), Hamengku Buwono said "I distrusted Hamid because of political differences". *Proces Peristiwa Sultan Hamid II* [The Trial of Sultan Hamid II, p. 98 and p. 100]. Although he was speaking here about events of 1950, it is highly likely that his distrust of most Federalists dated from the Revolution period. Republican distrust of Hamid began early — see *KR*, 3 April 1946.
157. Berkhuysen report, 11 April 1949, in *NIB*, vol. 18, p. 413.
158. "Military respect for civilian authority was gravely weakened during this period, with results that have been obvious ever since." Reid, op. cit., p. 155.
159. Dutch officials believed this — *NIB*, vol. 14, p. 573n. A report in May referred to a "secret plebiscite" among Republicans in Purwokerto in which Hamengku Buwono, Haji Agus Salim, and Syahrir emerged as the preferred leaders, in that order. MvD/CAD, Bundle AA22, NEFIS 1948–49, Purwokerto weekly report, 20–25 May 1949.
160. Lee, op. cit., Pritchett to DEA, 22 November 1949, p. 601, doc 531. Australian officials like Critchley and Pritchett were sceptical of Dutch claims of dissension in Republican circles.
161. One explicit claim to this effect occurs in a "Summary Report" by Berkhuysen under letter of 17 May 1949 from Col van Langen, claiming that the "Sultan's group" planned to hold "a meeting behind closed doors to call Sukarno and Hatta to account, … so that after about two months a referendum can be held

to restore Hamengku Buwono as Sultan and Supreme Leader". MvD/CAD, Kabinet Legercommandant, inv no 35, Summary Report of 16 May 1949, p. 1.
162. Lee, op. cit., Cutts to DEA, 14 April 1949, p. 378, doc 365. According to Suwarno (op. cit., p. 253), Hamengku Buwono had requested the powers from the Bangka leadership to make clear his authority vis-à-vis other local centres of power.
163. MvD/CAD, Bundle AA15, NEFIS 1949, NEFIS Weekly Report no. 7, 3 March 1949, p. 3.
164. Elson, op. cit., p. 33.
165. MvD/CAD, Hoofdkwartier Generale Staf, Inv no 695, report by Resident Stok, 30 March 1949, p. 5.
166. Interview, Sudarpo Sastrosatomo, October 2003.
167. Critchley described Spoor's political standpoint as "reactionary". Lee, op. cit., Critchley to Burton, 5 June 1949, p. 455, doc 428.
168. Suwarno, op. cit., p. 253. See above.
169. An imaginative and piquant account of the attack and occupation of Yogyakarta is provided in the novel *The Weaverbirds*, by Y.B. Mangunwijaya — "We gained control of Yogyakarta, seat of the republican camp. But what an anticlimax it was" (p. 125).
170. He insisted on using only UN aircraft and facilities, not Dutch. *FPL*, op. cit., p. 13.
171. For more information on these personalities, see Anderson, op. cit., p. 320; Kahin, p. 127 and p. 325; and Reid, op. cit., p. 39.
172. MvD/CAD, Bundle AA21, NEFIS 1949, secret report of 14 April 1949 headed *Besprekingen door de Sultan van Djokja in Batavia* [Sultan of Yogyakarta's Discussions in Batavia], by Captain Nelissen, p. 1.
173. Ibid.
174. MvD/CAD, NEFIS 1949, Bundle AA15, NEFIS Weekly Report no. 13, 14 April 1949.
175. Darmosugito, *Kota Yogyakarta 200 Tahun* [City of Yogyakarta 200 Years], p. 173.
176. Suwarno, op. cit., p. 252, gives the date of the appointment as Security Coordinator as 1 May 1949.
177. Lee, op. cit., p. 428, Critchley to Burton, 20 May 1949.
178. Ibid.
179. Ibid., Critchley to Burton, 10 June 1949, p. 458, doc 431.
180. A figure of 38,414 is given in NA 2.10.14, Algemene Secretarie, no. 4539, *Rapport van Sociale Zaken te Jocja betreffende de massa-evacuatie mei 1949* [Social Affairs Report on the Mass Evacuation from Jogja], p. 1.
181. Annoyance can be deduced from the following reported exchange between Hamengku Buwono and his Chinese doctor, Sim Ki Ay. When Dr Sim said

that many Chinese were afraid and wanted to join the convoys to Semarang, Hamengku Buwono said they were free to go if they wished; but their decision would "be noted" by the Yogyakarta people. Interview, informant no. 21, 22 August 2002.
182. NA 2.21,183.80, Collectie 301 Stok, parts 22–28, undated, but around late May 1949.
183. *NIB*, vol. 18, report by Spoor on situation between 20 and 26 April, p. 459, doc 282.
184. Elson, p. 40.
185. Elson, ibid.
186. NA 2.21.183.80, Collectie 301 Stok, parts 22–28, *Verslag Bespreking Commissie I* [Report of Commission I Meeting], 11 May 1949, p. 2.
187. MvD/CAD, NEFIS 1949, NEFIS Political Weekly Report no. 18, 20 May 1949, p. 2.
188. U.S. Consul General Livengood reported that Hamengku Buwono "stressed urgency getting agreement and restoration Jogja soonest. Thereafter ... simple to bring in Republican Military Commander Sudirman and staff". *FRUS 1949*, op. cit., p. 367, Livengood to State, 12 April 1949.
189. NEFIS Political Weekly Report no. 18, op. cit., ibid.
190. He visited Jakarta and Bangka between 10 and 15 June 1949. *De Locomotief*, 10 and 15 June 1949.
191. Djoeir Moehamad, *Memoar Seorang Sosialis* [Memoirs of a Socialist], pp. 307–8.
192. The original plan involved occupation of the western sector of Yogyakarta by the police Mobile Brigade and of the eastern sector by the Student Army and the Military Academy under Jatikusumo. NEFIS/CMI files in Netherlands Foreign Ministry, inv no. 07201.
193. Elson, p. 41.
194. Elson, ibid., pp. 41–42. Hamengku Buwono mentioned Suharto's role in an interview with *De Locomotief*, 22 June 1949.
195. One Dutch organization chart of the clandestine Republican government prepared in April does not mention Jatikusumo. Showing Hamengku Buwono as the head, it lists Suharto as Acting Regional Commander and TNI Commander.
196. Elson, ibid., p. 42, reports Hamengku Buwono saying after the reoccupation that Suharto's 600 troops lodged in the city were "well disciplined".
197. NIOD 081591, van Kaam, op. cit., p. 111.
198. MvD/CAD, NEFIS 1949, Bundle AA21, T brigade report no 1481, *Onderhoud met Bardasono* (Conversation with Bardasono), June 1949.
199. Elson, op. cit., p. 41.
200. Suwarno, op. cit., p. 256.

201. NA 2.10.14, Algemene Secretarie, Inv no 4539, UNCI Information Release, 1 July 1949. Hamengku Buwono joined UNCI personnel on the dividing line between the two forces — *Nieuwsgier*, 30 June 1949.
202. *De Locomotief*, 1 July 1949.
203. *De Nieuwsgier*, 2 July 1949; the report was headed "Jogja's Sultan Praises Terrorists"(!).
204. *Aneta News Bulletin*, Batavia, 2 July 1949.
205. *De Locomotief*, 17 May 1949, headline "Jogja fears Terror and Chaos".
206. *De Locomotief*, 16 July.
207. Attitudes to the Dutch in south Yogyakarta were openly hostile during the occupation — NA 2.21.036.02, part 125, Collectie Buurman van Vreeden, T. brigade report by Vosveld of 8 February 1949, entitled *Analyse van de Situatie in het Stadsgebied Djocja* [Analysis of the Situation in the City of Yogyakarta].
208. Lee, op. cit., Critchley to Burton, 8 July 1949, p. 488, doc 454.
209. Ibid.
210. NEFIS file 07201, held in Dutch Foreign Ministry, T brigade *Rapport over de Situatie in Djokjakarta* [Report on the Situation in Yogyakarta], undated, but probably early October 1949, p. 2.
211. Reid, op. cit., p. 161. Sudirman finally returned to Yogyakarta on 10 July. In a plea to Sudirman (probably in late June), Hamengku Buwono argued that the proposal was a "suspension of arms" rather than a full ceasefire. He added, "I had earlier proposed [the desirability of a ceasefire] order from you because I feared the situation being exploited by irresponsible groups to drive a wedge between us". Nasution, *Perang Kemerdekaan*, op. cit., vol. 10, p. 602.
212. Ibid. Nasution says he advised Republican leaders of military reservations about the negotiations. Hamengku Buwono had responded that there was really no alternative. Nasution, ibid., p. 556.
213. The prickliness of both sides led to the exaggeration of minor incidents, as when General Baay supposedly insulted Hamengku Buwono during a visit to Surabaya (*De Locomotief*, 7 September 1949).
214. The Round Table Conference commenced on 23 August and concluded on 2 November.
215. This appointment dates from the cabinet meeting of 13 July 1949, according to Suwarno, op. cit., p. 258.
216. The grim-faced Sungkono, the man who executed Tan Malaka in early 1949, was the most powerful TNI commander in East Java. Anderson, p. 162, p. 242, and p. 374.
217. At least that was Roeslan's version — interview, 7 August 2002.
218. Roeslan interview, ibid.
219. Ibid.
220. Nasution, *Memenuhi Panggilan Tugas*, vol. 2A, p. 203.

221. Kawilarang, *Officier in Dienst van de Republiek Indonesie* [Officer of the Republic of Indonesia], p. 144.
222. *Het Dagblad*, 28 September 1949.
223. Oey, Hong Lee, *War and Diplomacy in Indonesia*, p. 245.
224. D. Lee, op. cit., Pritchett to Critchley and DEA, 15 October 1949, op. cit., p. 569, doc 507.
225. Ibid., Pritchett to Critchley and DEA, 20 October 1949, p. 577, doc 512.
226. Van den Doel, *Afscheid van Indie* [Farewell to the Indies], p. 347.
227. *Statement by Republican Minister of Defence [Sri Sultan Yogyakarta]*, undated but probably 16 October 1949.
228. Ibid., Pritchett to Critchley and DEA, 17 October 1949, p. 571, doc 510. The comment was Pritchett's.
229. *FRUS 1949*, op. cit., p. 540, report by Consul General Beam after visit to Yogyakarta, 19 October 1949. Lovink had given the newly arrived Beam a frightening picture of a Republic dominated by extremists, fanatics, and resurgent communists — ibid., p. 538.
230. *Aneta*, 16 December 1949.
231. Kawilarang, op. cit., p. 144.
232. *Merdeka*, 26 December 1949.
233. Nasution, *Memenuhi Panggilan Tugas*, vol. 2A, op. cit., p. 206.
234. Ibid.
235. *Aneta*, 28 December 1949.
236. See report of broadcast in *Aneta News Bulletin*, Batavia, 2 July 1949, referred to above.
237. *TUR*, p. 133 — article by Moh Rum, "What would have happened to the Republic if Hamengku Buwono had not been there?" Also article by Moh Natsir ("'The 'Goalkeeper' of the Independence Struggle"), ibid., p. 197.

7

THE PROBLEMS OF INDEPENDENCE

Once Indonesian independence was internationally recognized, the fragile unity of the new United States of Indonesia (Republik Indonesia Serikat [RIS]) fractured in a variety of ways, including within the new armed forces as the central government strove to amalgamate the disparate elements of the TNI with the remnants of the KNIL, which had been fighting on the Dutch side only months before. The first challenge occurred within weeks.

On 23 January 1950, forces under the command of the notorious Raymond ("Turk") Westerling[1] briefly occupied Bandung, supposedly to protect the local regional *negara* of Pasundan.[2] Sultan Hamid approached Defence Minister Hamengku Buwono and offered to mediate, but Hamengku Buwono declined the offer because he distrusted Hamid.[3] An armed clash occurred the next day in the Kramat area of Jakarta between TNI elements and pro-Westerling forces.[4] The Hatta government got wind of a plot to attack the cabinet during a meeting in Jakarta either on the evening of the same day (24 January)[5] or on 25 January;[6] the meeting was held, but Hatta forestalled the attack by closing the meeting early.[7]

The putsch discredited the Pasundan federalists, but the entire federalist movement was compromised when Hamid's complicity became known.[8] He was arrested in April, accused of planning the attack on the cabinet and of ordering Westerling to kill Hamengku Buwono, Secretary-General of the Defence Department Ali Budiarjo and Armed Forces Chief of Staff Simatupang.[9] Hamid himself was to be wounded in the leg, to direct suspicion away from himself. He apparently believed that he himself would then be the obvious candidate to become the next Minister of Defence.[10]

Revelation of this outlandish plot ended Hamid's career, and he was jailed for over ten years,[11] acquiring a reputation in Indonesian history similar to Benedict Arnold in U.S. history. His autonomous territory of West Kalimantan was abolished, and the affair encouraged the move towards a unitary Republic of Indonesia. The involvement of former Dutch KNIL officers and KNIL deserters inflamed suspicions of the Dutch, enhanced by a statement in which Hamengku Buwono appeared to blame the Dutch high command.[12] The inability of Dutch officers to control their troops, and their inaction against Westerling before the coup despite Indonesian government pleas to restrain him, gave grounds for suspicion.[13]

In a succinct briefing on policy, Hamengku Buwono told the press that the Darul Islam rebellion in West Java was a political and a military problem and should be dealt with accordingly; that the RIS armed forces would be a national body composed of Indonesian citizens; as an example of the national-level approach being adopted, a battalion of Balinese troops would not be stationed on Bali because RIS army units could be stationed anywhere on Indonesian soil; and that the Defence Minister, and not local authorities, would decide the deployment of army units.[14]

The statement reflected the approach taken by the general staff, especially Simatupang and Army Chief of Staff Nasution. They took what might be regarded as a predictable position for a central government, namely that Indonesia needed professional, well-equipped and well-trained armed forces, which were nationally staffed, centrally directed and in which ethnic and tribal differences and locus of previous service — whether KNIL, Peta, or whatever[15] — counted for little. The collapse of federalism which occurred progressively throughout 1950 seemed to validate the vision of a united national armed forces.

However, the aims of the senior commanders did not include the creation of an apolitical military force; the army had always had a political role, and senior officers retained a great concern with political developments, particularly where military interests were affected.[16] The armed forces badly needed reorganization, and the country did not require such large and irregular forces after the Revolution had ended. Many forces became badly demoralized through lack of pay, loss of status once the struggle against the Dutch ended, and the disillusionment which followed the gaining of independence.[17]

Hamengku Buwono told the RIS Parliament on 11 March 1950 that the government would form a "rationally structured and appropriately sized army", adding "the government fully recognises the services of those soldiers and elements of the people who helped the army during the independence struggle. But it would be contrary to the national interest to induct into the army all those who participated in that struggle."[18]

Hamengku Buwono's unifying vision was attractive, but was bound to be challenged. The Indonesian army had not emerged as a united force in 1945, and many nationalist fighters claimed to have arisen from "the people", to owe their allegiance to a local commander, and to enjoy considerable autonomy. Many felt deprived of their share of the fruits of independence for which they had fought, and the less well-trained soldiers feared that the new professional army would have no place for them. It was thus understandable that the Defence Minister would face great difficulty in enforcing his ambitious plans.[19]

A series of regional crises were major distractions, apart from the persistent threat posed by Darul Islam, which was not finally defeated until 1962 (and indeed by some measures may not have been defeated even today).[20] The next challenge came from eastern Indonesia. The East Indonesian government, the strongest of the negaras, resented Hamengku Buwono's efforts to deploy TNI forces to Makasar; but by March, as other federal states were fading away, even that government came under pressure from pro-Republican demonstrations in Sulawesi demanding integration with the Republic.

The East Indonesians demanded authority over internal security, with the aim of excluding TNI forces from their region. Hamengku Buwono proposed a compromise, whereby security would be handled by a three-man committee chaired by a civilian, with, as members, a senior KNIL officer and Lt Col Mokoginta, the Sultan's appointed regional commander.[21] Mokoginta was of local ethnic origin and made some progress in establishing himself in Makasar, but this was interrupted when Captain Andi Aziz of the local KNIL attacked Republican forces and detained Mokoginta. The Indonesian government commented that both Andi Aziz and Sultan Hamid, who had just been arrested, feared "losing the influential position which they attained during and through Dutch rule in Borneo and East Indonesia".[22]

Fears of civil war arose as Hamengku Buwono threatened to deploy further TNI troops to quell the revolt. But tension eased after Hamengku Buwono telephoned the moderate East Indonesian leader Sukawati to advise him that the deployment had been postponed because Aziz had consented to come to Jakarta.[23] Sukawati had helped to persuade Aziz to do this.

Aziz's revolt had been encouraged by other East Indonesian figures, notably Minister of Justice Soumokil[24] who had opposed deployments of Republican troops to Makasar during Hamengku Buwono's visit in December 1949.[25] Aziz was arrested on arrival in Jakarta,[26] amid arguments about whether the government had deceived him. But Hamengku Buwono announced firmly that he had been arrested as a rebel who had surrendered unconditionally and that although the government had hoped for a peaceful solution, its patience had run out.[27] The arrest of Aziz did not end the trouble in Sulawesi, and several large clashes occurred before central government authority was established there.[28]

Moderate leaders like Sukawati were prepared to merge with the Republic, but anti-Jakarta feeling in Maluku erupted in a revolt by the Republic of the South Moluccas (RMS) led by Soumokil. The Indonesian government was disturbed by further suspicions of Dutch involvement, and Hamengku Buwono complained to the Dutch High Commissioner of a lack of support for Indonesia's territorial integrity.[29] Hatta and Hamengku Buwono, with Sukarno's encouragement, dispatched a force which largely quelled the revolt by July after bitter fighting.[30] On 17 August 1950, the unitary Republic of Indonesia was established, and the Hatta government handed over to the first cabinet of the new Republic, headed by the Masyumi leader Moh Natsir.

During 1950, Hatta as Prime Minister and Hamengku Buwono as Defence Minister set up Indonesia's first civilian intelligence service. They sent approximately ten young operatives in great secrecy to the United States for training with the CIA. Well after Hatta and Hamengku Buwono fell from power, the organization thus created became the Badan Pusat Inteligens (BPI — Central Intelligence Body), controlled by Subandrio, and immediately abolished when Suharto came to power. Some operatives retained close personal links with Hamengku Buwono, however, and clandestinely briefed him on developments well into the

1960s.³¹ This was evidently one reason that he remained well-informed and active on the political scene even when out of office between 1953 and 1959.

By the time the Hatta government ended, the programme of rationalization and reduction of army numbers had been only partially implemented. Nevertheless, Feith concludes:

> The Hatta cabinet at least made a big start with the task of rehabilitation. It accommodated large numbers of guerrillas in educational institutions of various kinds, many of them newly established. It set up a number of training centres to give short-term instruction in craft skills.... Inadequate as these measures were to deal with the problem in its entirety — and they were in a sense merely first steps — they did create a measure of confidence in the government's capacity to provide for ex-guerrillas.³²

During this period, Hamengku Buwono ably pressed the military's opinions and interests with the civilian cabinet and played a useful mediating role between the military leaders and those civilian politicians distrustful of military pretensions to power.³³ Thus, he reconfirmed his reputation for a sympathetic understanding of military problems and indeed must have seemed at the time the foremost civilian specialist on defence and security issues.

The army's willingness to intervene in politics when its own interests were affected was demonstrated when Hamengku Buwono, still caretaker Minister of Defence, wrote to Prime Minister–designate Natsir to advise him that his choice as Defence Minister, Abdul Hakim of Natsir's Masyumi party, was unacceptable to senior army officers.³⁴ At the inception of the Sukiman cabinet in April 1951, the army leaders pressed for Hamengku Buwono to return to the Defence portfolio; but, for the second time in his career, the Sultan declined the post, because he felt incompatible with the Sukiman cabinet.³⁵

Hamengku Buwono returned to the Defence portfolio under the Wilopo government in April 1952 in less favourable circumstances. The economy had suffered from the end of the Korean War boom, Indonesia had to repay heavy Indies debts from the 1949 Round Table Agreement,³⁶ and much disillusion was being felt with independence and with the growing climate of corruption, party factionalism, and an atmosphere of "moral crisis".³⁷ The Sukiman cabinet had faced revived conflict in South Sulawesi when former Republican commander Kahar Muzakkar had joined the Darul Islam rebellion,[38] and a battalion mutiny in Central Java had also led to defections to the Darul Islam.[39]

Broad ideological divisions among the elite were emerging fairly clearly, and Hamengku Buwono was becoming identified with Syahrir's socialists (the PSI) and the Natsir wing of the Masyumi. His main political friendships seemed to be with Hatta, Subadio (leader of the PSI fraction in the parliament), the PSI-oriented Ali Budiarjo, Subadio's brother Sudarpo, and (rather later) the leading young PSI intellectual Sujatmoko.[40] His links with the PNI were much weaker, although he served amicably with the moderate PNI figure Wilopo. These connections were therefore largely with the "administrators", contrasted with solidarity-makers like Sukarno, Sidik Joyosukarto of the PNI, Mohammad Yamin or Chaerul Saleh.[41] The differences became considerably sharper throughout 1952.

Nevertheless, the Wilopo cabinet began office amid hope for a new start. It announced its intention of lifting the state of emergency declared in several provinces by the Sukiman government, and Wilopo and Hamengku Buwono expressed willingness to free PKI cadres jailed the previous year.[42] The PKI was moving to a more moderate stance, and even announced its readiness to provide qualified support to the cabinet.[43] Great things were expected from Hamengku Buwono, who — it was hoped — would take a more aggressive line against the Darul Islam insurgency than his predecessor (the West Javanese politician, Sewaka), who was widely regarded as ineffective.[44]

But Hamengku Buwono soon encountered difficulties in resuming guidance of the reorganization process. The effort at rationalization was now even more badly needed because of the economic slump which forced the government into severe budgetary cuts. The ambitious plan to reduce the armed forces from 200,000 to 120,000 was consistent with careful budgeting, but would obviously be unpopular.[45] About half of the numbers to be dispensed with were soldiers who were prepared to resign or were of pensionable age; but many were to be dismissed as medically or otherwise unfit.[46]

The plans were bound to lead to much opposition among the soldiers, commanders and units affected. But genuine sympathy existed for them in some civilian political circles, and several grounds for resistance to the government's plans existed. On one level, negative oppositionism had become firmly entrenched in politics, and many opposition figures would use any available weapon to bring down a cabinet in which they had no spoils of power. The opposition included powerful and vocal forces, more or less corresponding to the "solidarity-maker" component of Indonesian political life. Allied against Hamengku Buwono's plans were most of the PNI (especially the important Sidik wing) because the faction of Prime Minister Wilopo was not dominant nor particularly typical in the party, as well as the PKI and other leftist groups, and many elements of the armed forces, especially most of the 80,000[47] or so slated for demobilization, and their commanders.

In this context, Feith described the phenomenon of "bapakism", where the commander regarded himself as the *bapak*, i.e., father, of his subordinates. (This would probably be called "patronage" or "patrimonialism" these days). Commanders, fearing loss of status, resisted both disbandment of their commands and central office attempts to transfer them to other duties or other regions.[48] To make matters worse, many such commanders had been demoted in the reorganizations.[49] Disquiet existed — or could be whipped up — at the presence of Dutch military advisers in the Netherlands Military Mission (NMM) in Jakarta, which was providing technical advice and training to the Indonesian Armed Forces. Finally, party political considerations ranged many forces against Syahrir's small but influential PSI party.

During Hamengku Buwono's period out of the Defence portfolio (i.e., the Natsir cabinet when he was Deputy Prime Minister, and the Sukiman period), the demobilization effort had largely stalled, although many efforts had been made to retrain surplus soldiers or offer alternative employment. The submission in July 1952 of four bills aimed at giving full effect to the demobilization brought matters to a head.

Meanwhile, and very importantly, the President was out of sympathy with the Wilopo government. He began receiving calls at the palace[50] from a disaffected officer called Col Bambang Supeno,[51] Inspector of Infantry, Army Headquarters, Bandung.[52] Supeno had already been campaigning for the removal of Nasution, whom he blamed for many of the ills besetting the organization. He advocated the replacement of Nasution by the prominent East Javanese figure, Colonel Bambang Sugeng.[53]

Supeno was called to a meeting at Simatupang's house in mid-July, where an angry confrontation took place. He thereupon sent a protest letter to the President, the Defence Minister and the Defence Committee of parliament.[54] Supeno expressed lack of confidence in the high command and accused his superiors of abandoning the ideals of the revolution. Nasution immediately suspended Supeno, gaining Hamengku Buwono's written support a week later.[55] This retrospective concurrence implies that

Nasution did not consult the minister beforehand, but at this stage both Hamengku Buwono and Nasution apparently regarded the matter as an internal personnel problem.

A further stormy meeting took place when Hamengku Buwono, Simatupang and Nasution called on Sukarno.[56] Simatupang in particular was furious at Sukarno's interference with the chain of command. Simatupang had already shown his willingness to deal forthrightly with civilian politicians in his approach to the Sukiman cabinet, and his earlier blunt rejection of a suggestion by Sukarno that the NMM be disbanded was no doubt a further cause of tension.[57] Hamengku Buwono told Sukarno that defence policy was his responsibility as Defence Minister, implying that the President should deal with him about it rather than directly with any single officer; but otherwise he seems to have allowed the military leaders to speak for themselves.[58] Simatupang said that the military leadership could not possibly perform their duties if the present situation persisted, while Nasution offered his resignation if the leadership was dissatisfied with him. Sukarno refused to accept the resignation, but otherwise gave little ground.[59]

The confrontation cannot have improved Hamengku Buwono's relationship with the President, and perceptions of a serious rift date from this period. Sukarno began dropping hints in his speeches of his distaste for certain aspects of government policy and behaviour.[60] The substance of the policy difference between Hamengku Buwono and Sukarno, regarded by some at the time as the "two strong men of Indonesia",[61] related to their competing concepts of the ideal role of the armed forces. The Sultan wanted a relatively "non-political army trained on western lines", whereas Sukarno and his allies preferred a militia on the revolutionary model, subject to political influence.[62]

Room for disagreement existed within the two broad viewpoints. The armed forces leadership would not want a totally non-political role, even if (possibly) that may have been the ultimate aim of civilian leaders like Hamengku Buwono, Wilopo, or Hatta. Within the peak military staff, especially Nasution, notions were circulating of the army as the guarantor of the Indonesian state and the ultimate arbiter of Indonesia's future, and such ideas (especially Nasution's later developed "Middle Way" proposal) were the precursors of Suharto's later dual function doctrine.[63] Sukarno's conception of the army as a politicized popular militia also had its ambiguities. If it should be political, what brand of politics should it favour? Sukarno seemed to assume that such a militia would automatically side with his brand of leftist Jacobin revolutionary fervour, but this could hardly be guaranteed.

Underlying all this was a very divergent assumption about the future direction of the Indonesian state. Hamengku Buwono, Hatta, Syahrir and the PSI leaders, but perhaps not the armed forces leadership, distrusted the more populist strains of politics which had arisen from the Revolution period. To put it simply, they thought the Revolution should now stop, and governments should be allowed to advance economic and social prosperity through cautious and responsible administration.[64] This thinking was anathema to Sukarno. He wanted soldiers with revolutionary dash, a romantically brave force ready to challenge all odds, not a sober, administratively correct, and technocratic armed forces.

A contentious public debate broke out in which the media divided on predictable lines; the pro-PSI and pro-Nasution press attacking Supeno (and by implication Sukarno), while the PNI and "solidarity-maker" media belaboured Hamengku Buwono and the armed forces leadership. Mohammad Yamin's *Mimbar Indonesia* and (especially) the pro-PNI newspaper *Merdeka*, led by the skilful political opportunist B.M. Diah, were particularly vehement, much more so than the PKI daily *Harian Rakjat*.[65] The most extreme critics were approximately the same group which had joined in the kidnapping of PSI leader Syahrir in the 3 July 1946 affair during the Revolution.[66]

Hamengku Buwono held several meetings with Supeno to find middle ground, but the effort was unsuccessful.[67] Debate in parliament went on for weeks, reaching a peak when Bebasa Daeng Malolo of the PRN (Partai Rakyat Nasional; National People's Party) faction absurdly called Hamengku Buwono "anti-national and pro-Dutch".[68] The more substantive opposition criticisms related to the many complaints in armed forces circles which the parliamentary committee had heard during recent regional tours, the claim that an officer of Supeno's rank should not have been suspended without the approval of the President, the incitement of suspicions of the NMM, and the allegation that the PSI was establishing a bridgehead in the armed forces[69] because leading figures including Hamengku Buwono were said to be too close to the PSI. Some criticisms were manifestly unfair, a few were reasonable, but their cumulative effect was powerful.

The armed forces leadership became increasingly impatient with the civilian parliament, because its criticism was often overblown, because they regarded civilian politicians as ignorant of military problems, and because they bristled at criticism from an unelected body including many politicians who had not been active in the nationalist struggle and in some cases (the federalists) had even opposed or hindered it. Nasution wrote, "The parliament arising from the Round Table Conference was two-thirds composed of former 'van Mook negaras'. We had defeated the 'time bombs' of Westerling, Andi Aziz, RMS and so on…. But this 'time bomb' was tougher."[70]

The extent to which the army leaders were preparing a coup in this period remains controversial. Feith states:

> Despite some conflicting evidence, it may be regarded as established that Colonel Nasution was engaged for several months before 17 October in working out plans for a type of military coup. It seems that his plans, to which the Minister of Defence and Maj Gen Simatupang were opposed, involved using the Siliwangi division…[71]

Sundhaussen[72] disputes this, on the grounds that Nasution had several times offered his resignation as Chief of Staff, he had appeared doubtful about the direct political action favoured by some of his radical subordinates,[73] and all of the Siliwangi officers interviewed by Sundhaussen denied knowledge of any coup plans.[74] Nasution, a former West Java commander, had extensive and intimate links with the Siliwangi.

Nevertheless, Nasution later admitted favouring a "half-coup" (*sic*) directed against parliament,[75] adding:

> it was never decided by the Army Chief of Staff, or by any meeting between the latter and the commanders, to LAUNCH A COUP D'ETAT, IN THE SENSE OF COMPELLING the President with threat of force. What is true is the use of maximum pressure, both through argumentation AND ALSO THROUGH INVITING SYMPATHETIC SOCIAL GROUPS to show their support.[76]

This disclaimer is full of ambiguities. What did he mean by a "half-coup"? Did it imply some sort of direct military action against certain parliamentarians? What was the difference between "compelling the president with a threat of force" and "the use of maximum pressure"? Does an invitation to "social groups" to show support indicate that he was behind the subsequent demonstrations? Feith says that Nasution had told Sukarno of his plans, which promised greater power for Sukarno himself; and Sukarno had been prepared to countenance the idea but had later backed off. But if Hamengku Buwono and Simatupang opposed Nasution on the point, as Feith reports, why was their opinion not decisive? The current state of our knowledge on these matters does not seem any better than was Feith's in the early 1950s.

On 24 September Baharuddin moved a motion of no-confidence in the Defence Minister. Confused debate followed in which two further important motions were put. The key motion, by the leftist PNI member, Manai Sophian, was amended several times, including an amendment at PKI (!) instigation to remove direct criticism of Hamengku Buwono, because of the need to avoid offence in Java.[77] Other critics conceded Hamengku Buwono's personal integrity while attacking his advisers and the army leadership for allegedly misleading him.[78] It called for "reformation and reorganisation of the leadership of the Ministry of Defence and Armed forces", for a national Defence Law, and for the establishment of "a special parliamentary commission to investigate administrative and financial fraud in the Ministry and Armed Forces".[79] While in final form the motion did not directly attack Hamengku Buwono, he let it be known that he would regard it as one of no-confidence. It may have appeared to him that the threat of resignation would defeat the motion.

On 1 October Hamengku Buwono made a speech to parliament, covering virtually point-by-point all the matters raised in the debate. One senses here a possible tactical mistake by Hamengku Buwono and his advisers. A point-by-point rebuttal risked, by its cumulative effect, giving credence to the notion that something was seriously wrong with the overall management and direction of the Defence Ministry, even if he convincingly rebutted every single point. Nevertheless, this looks like a sincere attempt to engage with the critics, and Nasution records the commanders' increased respect for Hamengku Buwono[80] because of his dignified defence of his policies and armed forces' interests, under intense provocation. His various statements of the time, including this one and briefer statements in May and on 15 October, avoided personal responses to his critics and concentrated in a restrained manner on the issues at hand.[81]

The speech[82] of 1 October covered various aspects of troop deployments which had been raised, the Kahar Muzakkar case, civil/military cooperation in restoring security, personnel policy in the Ministry, financial questions, the role of the Army Service Association, purchasing policy including denials of the critics' allegations of irregularities, and many other matters. In some cases, the wildness and inaccuracy of the criticism was clearly shown up.[83] The address reflected careful, rational administrative policymaking from a centralist perspective, with no attempt to engage in theatrics or point scoring, or to pander to revolutionary feeling. In short, this was an "administrator" speaking.

In a subsequent response[84] to his critics, on 10 October Hamengku Buwono answered further detailed charges, while admitting "I concede frankly that much improvement is still needed in the Ministry of Defence and the Armed Forces, as in all sectors of our country. Many criticisms have been made and I have tried to respond to them all.... Many mistakes have been pointed out and if the accusations were true I have admitted them. Where they were not true, I have explained the true state of affairs."

Hamengku Buwono's statements were factually based, but the opposition would not listen, and the Murba party announced that it was quite prepared to see the government fall.[85] However, the key to the vote was the attitude of the PNI,[86] and even more importantly, of the President. After a bewildering series of moves and countermoves in which the proposal surfaced that the Sophian motion should not be voted on, Sukarno called PNI leaders to the palace and insisted on a vote. The motion was passed on 16 October by 91 to 54.[87]

The next day a well-organized demonstration of about 5,000 men broke into parliament, amid cries of "Parliament is not a coffee shop", smashed up the cafeteria and marched around the city, displaying banners demanding the dissolution of parliament and the holding of elections.[88] They marched to the presidential palace, where army units appeared in force, placing machine guns pointing at the palace and the parliament building. Sukarno then addressed the crowd.[89] In one of his finest moments, he mollified them with promises of elections soon, chided them for wanting him to be a dictator, which is what he would become, he said, if he were to disband parliament, and sent them away. They cheered him and dispersed peacefully.

Buoyed up by this demonstration of his power, he received a deputation of army officers, including Nasution and many provincial commanders, who called apparently with the permission of Hamengku Buwono. They delivered a written statement,[90] complaining of parliament's behaviour, of the destructive and negative tone of much of the criticism, which (a veiled threat) could lead to "undesirable political and social consequences". They urged the President to form a new parliament "responsive to the people's wishes". No government of any political stripe could operate if the parliament's behaviour continued as it was.[91] They urged action against armed forces officers "who violated their duty to keep the secrets of the armed forces".[92]

The tone of the meeting was respectful, "like children going to their father".[93] But Sukarno gave them nothing, and it was evidently a mistake to have waited to make their representations till after he addressed the crowd. While saying he understood their complaints, he refused to endorse the statement, refused permission for it to be published, and was non-committal about the dissolution of parliament until he had consulted the cabinet. The only concession, if it was one, was that he then consulted Wilopo and Hatta, and they gained the parliament's agreement to go into recess for a period.[94]

The demonstration had been organized by the eccentric head of the army dental service, Dr Mustopo, who had strong links with the PSI, and by the Jakarta commander Col Kosasih. Some demonstrators were soldiers in civilian clothing, and this may go down in Indonesian history as the first major pre-arranged political demonstration (many more were to come), although the demonstration certainly reflected a strong strain of public feeling. Several PSI figures were also heavily involved.[95]

Army units arrested several opposition figures, including former Prime Minister Sukiman, Mohammad Yamin and Bebasa Daeng Lalo; declared a state of emergency in the capital; imposed a curfew; cut off Jakarta's communications; and closed several newspapers. But within a few days, the government had reversed all these measures. The cabinet then anti-climactically carried on much as usual, and it was for a while unclear to observers quite what had happened.[96] Hamengku Buwono did not resign as he had threatened, thereby losing some credibility, but eventually resigned on a related issue some months later. He issued no statement explaining his role or attitude to the events of 17 October, thereby, according to some observers, damaging his standing.[97]

Sukarno's behaviour in the affair was full of contradictions. He had encouraged Supeno's activities, despite the obvious disruption to military discipline. He encouraged the subsequent takeovers of regional commands by Warouw in Sulawesi and especially Sudirman in East Java.[98] But when offered Nasution's resignation in the meeting of 18 July and Hamengku Buwono's later, he had either refused or (apparently) given no response. Some observers believed that although Sukarno's motives in undermining Hamengku Buwono and the government were political because he disagreed with the government's policies, they were also partly personal in that he thought that the Sultan posed some threat to him.[99] Hints were dropped in the press about Sukarno's possible replacement — the *Times of Indonesia* published a version of the Joyoboyo prophecies in which the Leader was to be supplanted by a "Prince from Java".[100] Sukarno supposedly accused Hamengku Buwono of plotting to be President, and Hamengku Buwono, shocked out of his usual taciturnity, reportedly replied, "If I had wanted that I could have managed it long ago."[101]

Another personal motive may have lain behind Sukarno's attitude. The suspicion that Syahrir's PSI was behind the demonstrations would have affected his reactions, because his relations with Syahrir had been very poor since 1949.[102] Syahrir's influence on Hamengku Buwono, the presence of PSI ministers in the Wilopo government, and the evidence of PSI involvement in the demonstrations must have hardened Sukarno's resolve to defeat the 17 October forces.

The record of Hamengku Buwono's career does not in fact reveal large political ambitions. Admittedly, several times during his career claims were made of his ambition to carve out a wider role for himself, but his actual behaviour did not justify these judgments. Dutch reports in 1949 referred to his supposed ambitions to secure as autonomous a role as possible; suspicions of an intention to replace Sukarno in 1952 were voiced, even including one or two reports of his supposed "boundless ambition".[103]

But examination of his actual behaviour reveals rather a consistent loyalty to the mainstream leadership. In 1949, he stuck by the Republican leadership through the difficult days of the Dutch occupation, and, despite claims at the time, little solid evidence of any plan to replace Sukarno and/or Hatta ever emerged. In 1952, while some army figures may have plotted to overthrow the parliament, the evidence of an army plan to remove Sukarno himself is weak, and the lack of any evidence of Hamengku Buwono engaging in such plotting is even more glaring. It is even harder to discern any intention by Hamengku Buwono in 1966 to replace Sukarno; it is more credible that he joined the New Order out of a sense of duty. There is no hint of disloyalty to Suharto in the 1970s despite the evidently rising tension between the two men at the time.

This does not mean the total absence of ambition, and he may well have accepted the presidency if it fell to him, but he would not actively seek it out. The need to avoid any appearance of ambition or desire for power is well engrained in the Indonesian (or Javanese?) scale of values,[104] so that, for example, a book about Hamengku Buwono's son could be subtitled *Bukan Karena Ambisi* (Not Because of Ambition),[105] and Suharto always portrayed himself as becoming President by acclamation, rather than through personal aspiration.[106] A Javanese aristocrat acquires fame, distinction or high office because of innate merit (or *wahyu*), and does not need to exert enormous effort in achieving his aims. Heroes in the fights in the wayang are portrayed as winning almost without effort, because of their innate virtue derived from constant meditation.[107]

In the following months the "pro-17 October" forces lost engagement after engagement, as several regional commanders were removed by their subordinates, encouraged covertly by Sukarno. In Sulawesi, Gatot Subroto, a signatory of the 17 October statement, was overthrown by Lt Col Warouw, a local Sulawesi officer. In East Java, a group sent by Sukarno and led by Bambang Supeno encouraged Lt Col Sudirman to displace the local acting commander.[108] In South Sumatra, Lt Col Kretarto took over from Lt Col Kosasih. Real or alleged involvement in the 17 October affair was given as the rationale for these actions.

Hamengku Buwono and Nasution tried to persuade the rebel officers in the regions of the justice of the government's cause, but with scant success, except in South Sumatra where a compromise settlement was reached. Warouw in Sulawesi announced that he would meet Hamengku Buwono only if he was carrying a mandate from the President.[109]

But the most revealing episode was Hamengku Buwono's visit to Malang in East Java in November.[110] Although there was vague goodwill for him in East Java during the Revolution, he was not as well known as in Central Java. In speaking to senior officers of the Brawijaya command, he explained his irritation at the attacks in parliament, especially because many critics were former federalists.[111] Hamengku Buwono outlined the 17 October events in factual terms, though admitting that he had ordered "one officer in civilian clothes" [sic] to join the demonstrators. When asked whether he could have prevented the demonstration, he replied that the increasingly impassioned situation had got out of control, "and that he was too dejected (*moral kapot*)".[112] The demonstration was wrong, but he could not prevent it as the demonstrators came "from everywhere".

On the Manai Sophian motion, he commented that its demand for a national defence committee was unacceptable because it would obviate the need for a Defence Minister; the parliament would be better occupied in passing an election law as soon as possible. He excited local officers' scepticism by denying that the army had trained its guns on the presidential palace. Finally he said that Sukarno had demanded the dismissal of

Simatupang, Nasution and Ali Budiarjo, but that he had refused this and offered his resignation.[113] He did not persuade the rebel officers, who had already made up their minds.[114] On his return, he made a brief press statement implying that agreement had been reached with the East Java officers, but they quickly contradicted this.[115] It is unclear whether this was a genuine misunderstanding or a deliberate deception by the rebels.

In November, the government issued a statement about the events of 17 October,[116] describing the demonstration as a demand by "the people of Jakarta" for parliament's dissolution, but conceding that the Army's involvement needed explanation. The statement described the events of the day in familiar detail, adding that the senior armed forces personnel who called at the palace "opened their hearts to" the President, demanding the dissolution of parliament, but that Sukarno had refused. Wilopo had then told a similar group of callers that parliament could not be dissolved, and the creation of a new parliament had to be left to the government. These facts should therefore dispose of the allegation "that a seizure of power would have taken place on 17 October".[117] The government disapproved of the participation of "a few officers and members of the Armed Forces" in the demonstration, and of unauthorized manoeuvres by army units.[118]

A remarkable feature of the statement is that the Minister of Defence is not mentioned at all, and the list which it provides of participants at the crucial meeting with Sukarno does not include him, although both Hatta and Wilopo attended.[119] Not a single source offers any explanation of Hamengku Buwono's absence. His presence may have risked annoying Sukarno whom the army leaders wanted to win over, although one might think that the presence of Simatupang would also have been provocative.[120] Indeed there were reports that Simatupang deliberately arrived late in order to minimize provocation to Sukarno.[121]

Nasution publicly accepted responsibility for the events of 17 October,[122] resigned as chief of staff, and was replaced by a reluctant Bambang Sugeng. One reason for reluctance was that Hamengku Buwono refused his request to remove Simatupang as Armed Forces Chief of Staff.[123] Hamengku Buwono and Sugeng were thus not a compatible pairing, especially as Sugeng's appointment was seen as largely a move sponsored by Sukarno,[124] and matters came to a head when Sugeng agreed to confirm Warouw as commander in Sulawesi, legitimizing his local coup.

This was too much for Hamengku Buwono. The issue may have seemed narrow, relating only to Warouw's appointment; but it affected a wider point of principle, and the resignation may simply have reflected Hamengku Buwono's feeling that his position was untenable. Some concluded despairingly at the time, "If the Sultan cannot keep order, then no one can."[125]

His statement read in part:

> I believe that
> a) this decision of the cabinet is at variance with its statement of 22 November 1952 ... so that consequently there is no clear guideline for the public nor for the cabinet itself in settling the problems which we now face;
> b) I cannot approve of a procedure in which the government simply accepts a *fait accompli* presented to it.
> Only history will demonstrate which viewpoint is preferable, from the perspective of the true interests of the Republic of Indonesia and of the development of the Armed Forces as a healthy military organisation.[126]

In a radio broadcast in Yogyakarta,[127] Hamengku Buwono counselled the people to give priority to national and not party interests. He conceded that national unity had suffered badly during 1952 and, to overcome the present disunity, he called for a more businesslike[128] attitude to current problems. In a clear message directed at Sukarno and his allies, he added that all those "who called themselves our leaders, large or small", should learn self-control and avoid emotionalism.[129] Political parties should pursue their aims not to achieve power over others, but to solve the problems faced by the nation and people. Leaders had above all to dispense with a priori attitudes, prejudices and suspicions. Finally, he expressed the hope that the "bitter experience" of 1952 would convince all of the need to reconcile party interests with duty to the people and the nation. An implication of this statement was an evident dislike for narrow sectional and party politics.

Hamengku Buwono saw no reason why the whole government should fall because of him, and he persuaded the PSI ministers Sumitro and Lukman not to resign in solidarity with him, as previously planned.[130] An enfeebled government staggered on for the next six months, helped to survive by an opposition which saw some reason to allow it to do so while they got themselves organized.

In the next few years, feelings among all factions in the armed forces, whether pro–17 October or against it, congealed into a common distaste for civilian interference. This culminated in the meeting in Yogyakarta of February 1955, where the factions were reconciled, at least temporarily.[131] Hamengku Buwono had no role in this, but his return to office in 1966 perhaps owed something to widespread military perception of his understanding of their problems, but he never afterwards had any direct connection with military affairs.

SUMMARY

Hamengku Buwono's brief and restrained resignation statement and the 1953 new year statement implied considerable disappointment and even bitterness. From his viewpoint, he had been trying to put some order into the bloated armed forces, keeping firmly in mind the interests of Indonesia as a strong and united nation-state. All he had met with was sabotage from negative civilian politicians and selfish and narrowly based sectional interests within the army.[132] The climax must have been Sukarno's behaviour, and it would be not surprising if he saw Sukarno's encouragement of Supeno as a personal betrayal. Sukarno's outmanoeuvring of the army leadership on 17 October may also have looked like lip-service to democratic forms while subverting the government.

A more negative summation of the same facts would read as follows. Hamengku Buwono as the responsible minister should have known what was going on in the army, and should have nipped it in the bud. Although he had shown sympathy for military concerns, he should have drawn the line when real or implied threats to the President were planned. It is at least questionable for a Minister for Defence to allow his forces to menace the President by aiming their weapons at the palace. Even plans for a "half-coup" should not be acceptable, as the government statement of 22 November indicated.[133] In defence of Hamengku Buwono on these points, it could be urged that Indonesia was not a developed democracy, that as Minister of Defence he did not have the authority over the armed forces that a defence minister in, say, the United Kingdom would have, and it is hard to imagine any other Defence Minister being able to control the passions which were unleashed in the affair.

Hamengku Buwono and the armed forces leadership showed a lack of political acumen in not foreseeing the extent of opposition to their plans. Even though a programme of reductions in army numbers and the other ambitious reforms was patently necessary, the amount of pain inflicted on the forces was guaranteed to produce much public dissension. For someone of Hamengku Buwono's political instincts, this was a surprising failure. He and the armed forces leaders seem to have been so certain of the obvious correctness of their chosen path, and so sure that their opponents would be revealed as unprincipled opportunists (which many indeed were), that they underestimated the forces building up against them. It was rather more excusable that they did not foresee Sukarno's actions in the affair.[134]

Accounts of the affair (Feith, Sundhaussen, Nasution, Crouch, Salim Said) commonly refer to the activities of the senior armed forces figures and give little or no coverage to Hamengku Buwono's role. This is understandable to an extent, because Simatupang and Nasution were much more conspicuous than Hamengku Buwono. But as Minister of Defence he was a key actor in these events, and his comparative invisibility is rather reminiscent of A.J.P. Taylor's description of Lord Halifax in the 1930s: "Halifax had a unique gift. He was always at the centre of events yet managed somehow to leave the impression that he was not connected with them."[135]

Still, Hamengku Buwono's resignation statement has left the challenge open — what does "history" conclude about the affair? First, events of the following years may provide some guidance. The departure of the "big four" — Nasution in November 1952, Hamengku Buwono in January 1953, Ali Budiarjo[136] in April 1953, and Simatupang in late 1953 — severely weakened the armed forces as a unified body, and even the critics came to realize the disadvantages of this.[137] The encouragement given to regional "warlords" by Sukarno fostered a sentiment within the army that regional defiance of the centre was — if not permissible — at least possible if local leaders felt strongly enough or had local support; and this not only dissipated the impression of central resolution provided by the action against Westerling, Aziz and Soumokil, but fed into the regional revolts of the late 1950s.

Another effect of the 17 October affair was to deepen army distrust of civilian politicians. The civilian leader most clearly identified with the army had received a stinging rebuff. His successors, especially Iwa Kusuma Sumantri, the Defence Minister in the Ali government of 1953–55, engendered much dislike among the soldiers, and the success of the reconciliation meeting of 1955 owed much to their experience of that period.[138] By 1958, when Nasution became Defence Minister, the armed forces were happy to have one of their own in the position, and a civilian would become Defence Minister again only after Suharto's fall forty years later.

When civilian defence ministers of the 1950s are compared, despite the deficiencies of his period in the portfolio, Hamengku Buwono stands out,[139] not only in possessing a clear vision and plans for implementing it, but also in his ability to assemble a strong and effective team. Such a talented team was not to be seen in the Defence Ministry again, although some — in the New Order period — would be more powerful. After Iwa's controversial period in the portfolio, the habit arose for prime ministers to take the defence portfolio concurrently, which ensured high-level attention to military issues. None of the prime ministers was however seen as being especially close to the military.

Hamengku Buwono's career can be seen as punctuated by gallant resignations. His de facto resignation as potential Dutch viceroy in Yogyakarta in 1948 might be seen as the first. In the present case, he held on as long as he could until his position became untenable, but his departure was seen as an act of principle and his reputation for integrity remained untarnished.[140]

By the time the New Order emerged, senior army officers had not acquired any greater respect for civilian authority, and the civilian parliament's conduct in 1952 and Sukarno's subsequent behaviour contributed to their already low regard for civilian politicians. Political circumstances, especially the attitude of Sukarno, defeated Hamengku Buwono in 1952, but the result of the affair was a blow for the advancement of Indonesia as a whole and especially as a united country.

Notes

1. Westerling was hated and feared by Republicans for his terroristic counter-insurgency activities during the Revolution. See Reid, *Indonesian National Revolution 1945–50*, p. 107.
2. UNCI report on the incident, attached to a letter of 27 January 1950 from the Dutch UNCI representative A.H.C. Gieben, NA 2.10.14, Inv no. 4572.
3. *Proces Peristiwa Sultan Hamid II* [The Trial of Sultan Hamid II], by P.B. Persaja editorial team; p. 98 and p. 100. (Henceforth cited as "*Hamid*".) Testimony by Hamengku Buwono on 4 March 1953.
4. Ibid., p. 149.
5. Feith, *Decline of Constitutional Democracy*, p. 62. (Cited henceforth as *Decline* where necessary.)
6. The date of 25 January is specified in an Aneta report of 8 April 1950.
7. *Hamid*, testimony by Frans Najoan, p. 83.

The Problems of Independence

8. "Some time between January and April", when Hamid was arrested. Ibid., p. 102, testimony of Simatupang.
9. Najoan testimony at trial of Sultan Hamid, ibid., p. 83.
10. Leading federalist Anak Agung testified that Hamid wanted the Defence portfolio; ibid., p. 149. Westerling and Hamid both consistently denied Hamid's alleged involvement — see Moor, J.A. de, *Westerling's Oorlog*, p. 428, and pp. 480–82.
11. Hamid was released in 1958, but rearrested in 1962 amid a wave of arrests of opposition leaders. He was released again in 1965 and died on 30 March 1978.
12. Driessen and Koster, *De Westerling-Affaire* [The Westerling Affair], p. 15.
13. Feith, *Decline*, p. 63.
14. *Aneta*, 15 January 1950.
15. Ibid., p. 44.
16. See Feith, *Decline*, passim, but especially pp. 209–10.
17. One account of the state of affairs in West Java about the TNI's poor performance against the Darul Islam reads: "They don't like combat these days. Many of the soldiers are too ill. Maybe 20 percent of the army has tuberculosis. So the Sultan wants to demobilise many of them, but they are resisting. One officer, who came to read out a demobilisation order in Jakarta's name, was beaten up and chased away". F.J. Goedhart, *Een Revolutie op Drift* [A Drifting Revolution], pp. 95–96.
18. *DPR-RIS, Pertanjaan Anggota dan Djawaban Pemerintah* [RIS Parliament, Members' Questions and Government's Responses], p. 45.
19. Crouch, *The Army and Politics in Indonesia*, pp. 36–38.
20. Some modern-day Jemaah Islamiyah (JI) leaders had close family connections with former DI elements. See International Crisis Group, *Recycling Militants in Indonesia: Darul Islam and the Australian Embassy Bombing*, Asia Report no. 92, 22 February 2005.
21. Sundhaussen, *The Road to Power*, p. 56.
22. Ministry of Information statement, 11 April 1950, in NA 2.05.52, Part 277.
23. *Aneta*, 15 April 1950.
24. Feith, op. cit., p. 67.
25. Nasution, *Memenuhi Panggilan Tugas* [Obeying the Call of Duty], vol. 2A, p. 206.
26. Ibid., p. 68.
27. *Aneta*, 16 April 1950.
28. A commander prominently involved in these actions was Suharto, now confirmed in his rank of lieutenant colonel — Elson, *Suharto*, pp. 46–48.
29. Hamengku Buwono letter as Acting Prime Minister, of 23 May 1950, MvD/CAD, NEFIS 1950, bundle AA21.

30. Feith, ibid., pp. 70–71.
31. Informant no. 12, interview, 14 December 2004. An extraordinary feature of the initiative is that they kept the matter secret from the President. The informant, who was one of the operatives in question, believed that Hatta and Hamengku Buwono were very distrustful of communism and were uncertain of Sukarno's ultimate attitude to local communism. Kahin describes what may be a precursor to this episode (in 1948) in his memoir, *Southeast Asia, a Testament*, pp. 66–67. Also Conboy, *Intel*, pp. 22–23.
32. Feith, op. cit., p. 81.
33. Ibid., p. 209.
34. Ibid., p. 149. See also Salim Said, who says that Chief of Staff Simatupang, always a blunt and forceful soldier, told Natsir that his preference (whom he names as "Abdul Halim") was unacceptable to the army, which preferred Hamengku Buwono. Said, *Militer Indonesia dan Politik: Dulu, Kini dan Kelak* [The Indonesian Military and Politics: in the Past, the Present and the Future], p. 318.
35. Feith, ibid., p. 210.
36. The burden on post-independence governments is outlined by Kahin, *Nationalism*, p. 122.
37. Feith, ibid., pp. 222–23; the term used was *krisis achlak*.
38. Suharto was still in Makasar at this time and was involved in the struggle against Muzakar. Elson, op. cit., p. 48.
39. Feith, ibid., p. 214.
40. Nursam, *Pergumulan Seorang Intelektual, Biografi Soedjatmoko* [The Struggles of an Intellectual, a Biography of Sujatmoko], p. 192.
41. Feith, ibid., p. 113.
42. *Jawa Post*, 15 July 1952.
43. Feith, ibid., pp. 237–38.
44. NAA A1838, file 3034/2/1 pt 2, Australian Embassy (henceforth AE) Jakarta despatch no. 4/52 of 21 April 1952, p. 7.
45. Ibid., p. 249.
46. Ibid.
47. The figure envisaged in the 1953 budget alone was 60,000 soldiers, as well as 60,000 civil servants and 30,000 police. Feith, *Decline*, p. 248.
48. Ibid., p. 127.
49. Ibid., p. 248.
50. Nasution, *Memenuhi Panggilan Tugas*, op. cit., vol. 3, p. 27.
51. Col Bambang Supeno was a former Japanese-trained Peta officer, had served as an intelligence officer in East Java and as a head of the Chandradimuka Military Academy, and was a distant relative of Sukarno. Feith, p. 250.
52. NAA A1838, file no. 3034/12 pt 1, AE Jakarta memorandum to Canberra, 4 September 1952.

The Problems of Independence

53. Sugeng, who suffered from a lung infection (perhaps tuberculosis — see Nasution, ibid., p. 345), was thought to be sympathetic to the anti-Nasution forces and to *bapakism*, but he subsequently proved to be independent minded. *Commentaar op rapport nopens kolonel Bambang Sugeng* [Commentary on Report about Col Bambang Sugeng] of 18 December 1952, in Archief HNMM (Head of the Dutch Military Mission), NA 2.13.73, Inv no. 8, Bundle 3/15.
54. Feith, ibid., p. 253.
55. Nasution, ibid., p. 338. Letter of Hamengku Buwono of 22 July 1952. Nasution's action was seen as precipitate in some quarters (Penders and Sundhaussen, *Abdul Haris Nasution*, p. 83). By 22 July, Hamengku Buwono must have known of the political sensitivity of the matter, but would have decided to maintain his support of the army leadership.
56. Feith, ibid., p. 251.
57. NAA A1838, file 3034/2/1 pt 2, AE Jakarta cable of 16 January 1953.
58. Nasution, op. cit., vol. 3, p. 27. Sundhaussen (*The Road to Power*, p. 66) reports this statement rather differently: "The Sultan accepted all responsibility for the army reforms, thus tying the cabinet to the army leadership."
59. The two most detailed accounts of the meeting are given by Nasution (ibid.) and Sundhaussen (ibid.).
60. His reference in a speech to "the evil of (some parties) not respecting the authority of the state" was taken as directed at Hamengku Buwono. NAA A1938, file 3034/2/1 pt 2, memorandum AE Jakarta to Canberra of 18 July 1952.
61. NAA A1838, file 3034/12 pt 1, Australian Department of External Affairs, Canberra, note of 7 January 1953.
62. Ibid. Sukarno regarded himself as the Supreme Commander under the 1950 constitution, which he seemed to interpret to allow him to have direct access to senior military officers as desired. See *Commentaar* note quoted above, pp. 1–2. The Wilopo government wanted to keep Sukarno to the role of a limited constitutional president.
63. Crouch, op. cit., p. 24. Also Said, *Genesis*, pp. 132–33.
64. Cf Hatta's well-known statement that "a revolution should not last too long" — see Hatta's article of that title in Feith and Castles, *Indonesian Political Thinking*, p. 94.
65. *Merdeka*, June–October 1952 passim; and *Harian Rakjat* ditto.
66. Feith, "Toward Elections in Indonesia", *Pacific Affairs* 27, no. 3 (September 1954): 241n.
67. Yusril Djalinus et al., *Perjalanan Hidup A H Nasution* [The Life of A.H. Nasution], p. 85.
68. *Djawa Post*, 7 October 1952.
69. Feith, *Decline*, pp. 253–54.
70. Nasution, vol. 3, p. 168.

71. Feith, ibid., p. 262.
72. Sundhaussen, *The Road to Power*, p. 72.
73. Sutoko, Parman, and Kemal Idris were mentioned in this connection. Sutoko was one of Nasution's deputies, Parman was commander of the Jakarta garrison, and Kemal was commander of the Siliwangi (West Java) division.
74. Sundhaussen, ibid.
75. Nasution, op. cit., vol. 3, p. 169.
76. Ibid. Emphases in original.
77. Penders and Sundhaussen, op. cit., p. 83.
78. Aruji Kartawinata, quoted in Nasution, ibid., p. 45. Kartawinata was an open opponent of Nasution.
79. Feith, op. cit., p. 258.
80. Nasution, ibid., p. 169.
81. See, for example, *Risalah Perundingan DPR 1952*, session of 15 October 1952, p. 6097, (fiche 240, vol. 16, ANU).
82. Nasution, ibid., pp. 345–68. This appears to be a slightly edited version.
83. Ibid. — for example, he flatly denied allegations that PSI members Sudarpo and Wibowo were involved in defence purchases.
84. Nasution, op. cit., vol. 3, pp. 80–83.
85. *Jawa Post*, 7 October 1952.
86. Sundhaussen, op. cit., p. 68.
87. Feith, *Pacific Affairs*, "Towards Elections in Indonesia", op. cit., p. 241.
88. Ibid., p. 242.
89. Nasution prints the text of the speech — ibid., pp. 405–8.
90. Nasution, op. cit., p. 483.
91. Ibid.
92. Ibid. Since this point was aimed at Sukarno's protégé Supeno, it was not surprising Sukarno rejected it.
93. Sundhaussen, op. cit., p. 72.
94. Feith, *Decline*, p. 260.
95. Feith article, "Elections", op. cit., p. 243n. Hamengku Buwono was later quoted as saying that a Professor Jokosutono (University of Indonesia?) was involved in persuading students to join the demonstration. Nasution, op. cit., p. 428.
96. The Australian Embassy, for one, got it badly wrong at first, concluding "the Sultan solidly supported by the army commander and by a proportion of the cabinet,... has outwitted and at least temporarily cowed his opponents". NAA, A1838, file 3034/2/1 pt 2, AE despatch 9/52 of 20 October 1952.
97. NAA A1838, file 3034/2/1 pt 2, British Embassy Jakarta, Monthly Summary of November 1952, p. 1.

98. He even tried to undermine Nasution's base in the military, the Siliwangi, but the disaffected officer whom he encouraged to displace Siliwangi commander Kawilarang, rejected the idea. Sundhaussen, op. cit., p. 74.
99. See, for example, Goedhart, op. cit., p. 196.
100. Feith, *Decline*, p. 263n.
101. Sartono, *Seputar Yogyakarta dan Beberapa Tokoh Kepemimpinannya* [On Yogyakarta and Several of its Leading Personalities], Address on Receiving the Hamengku Buwono IX Award, typescript, 1995, p. 13.
102. On the Sukarno–Syahrir relationship, see Sukarno, *An Autobiography as told to Cindy Adams*, pp. 258–59. The dislike of Syahrir was certainly a motive in the opposition press — see the vehemence of the denunciations of the 17 October affair in *Merdeka* 1952–1953 passim, especially the anonymous article *Figuur Sultan* (by B.M. Diah?), 21 November 1952.
103. NAA A1838, file 3034/12 pt 1, AE Jakarta memorandum entitled "President Sukarno versus Defence Minister", 4 September 1952.
104. Sundhaussen, op. cit., p. 81.
105. Wasi Ismoyo, Sunaryo Purwo Sumitro, eds., *Sri Sultan Hamengku Buwono X: bersikap bukan karena ambisi* [Sri Sultan Hamengku Buwono X, Not Because of Ambition] (Yogyakarta: Biagraf, 1998).
106. On Suharto's real or pretended reluctance to become President, see Elson, op. cit., p. 158.
107. Anderson, "The Idea of Power in Javanese Culture", in his *Language and Power*, p. 51.
108. Sundhaussen, ibid., p. 75.
109. *Merdeka*, 21 November 1952.
110. Nasution, op. cit., annex 18, pp. 425–27. This is a reprinted report by an officer of the Brawijaya command and thus is a hostile account which has to be treated carefully. Some details seem accurate but others are dubious.
111. Ibid.
112. Ibid., p. 427.
113. Ibid., p. 429. That Hamengku Buwono was mistaken in trusting the rebel officers with a frank account of the affair is demonstrated by the leaking of details of their exchange to the opposition press — *Merdeka* editorial, 18 December 1952.
114. Ibid., p. 430.
115. Nasution, op. cit., vol. 3, pp. 182–83.
116. Department of Information, government statement of 22 November 1952.
117. Ibid., p. 1.
118. Ibid., p. 2.
119. Ibid., p. 1.
120. Ibid.

121. *Merdeka*, 31 December 1952.
122. *Merdeka*, 26 November 1952.
123. NAA A1838, file 3034/12 pt 1, British Embassy Press Summary 10 December 1952.
124. Sundhaussen, op. cit., ibid.
125. Bro, *Indonesia: Land of Challenge*, p. 90. Others were less charitable: "I have the impression that the Sultan has been extremely weak." Letter of F.J. Goedhart to J.D. Sie, 6 January 1953, NA 2.21.285, collection 570 F.J. Goedhart.
126. *Harian Indonesia*, 3 January 1953.
127. *Kedaulatan Rakjat*, 2 January 1953.
128. *Zakelijk*.
129. *Sentiment*.
130. NAA A1838, file 3034/2/1 part 3, UK High Commission (Kermode) "savingram" no. 7, 30 January 1953, p. 1.
131. Sundhaussen, op. cit., p. 80.
132. His disgust with national politics after this experience was evident. He was quoted as saying during the 1950s that "only fate" could bring him back to the national level. L.B.J. (President Johnson) national security files Asia/Pacific 1963–69, reel 8, Cornell University, CIA intelligence memorandum, 2 December 1965, p. 7.
133. Needless to say, the opposition press did not hesitate to make these points and more. *Merdeka* (3 January 1953) editorialized that Hamengku Buwono was a minister "with a very bad reputation"; he was presenting his resignation as a point of principle, but this was not really true.
134. Though see Sundhaussen, op. cit., p. 63, on the extent to which the Wilopo government, probably needlessly, offended Sukarno.
135. A.J.P. Taylor, *Origins of the Second World War*, 2nd ed., pp. 133–34.
136. Virtually all neutral commentators refer to Budiarjo as a very capable and reliable civil servant. E.g., interview, informant 2, 10 October 2003.
137. Sundhaussen, op. cit., ibid.
138. Ibid., p. 79.
139. The defence ministers of the period were Hamengku Buwono (1950–51), Sewaka (1951–52), Hamengku Buwono again (April 1952–January 1953), Iwa Kusuma Sumantri (Ali cabinet 1953–55), Burhanuddin Harahap (doubling as Prime Minister, August 1955–March 1956), Ali Sastroamijoyo (doubling as Prime Minister in his second cabinet, March 1956–March 1957), Juanda (doubling as Prime Minister, April 1957–July 1959). Thereafter, Nasution held the portfolio (sometimes called "National Security") in various cabinets until 1965.
140. NAA A1838, file 3034/12, AE Summary of World Broadcasts, 8 January 1953, p. 23.

8

THE END OF GUIDED DEMOCRACY AND THE RISE OF THE NEW ORDER

In the early 1950s, Hamengku Buwono told a foreign observer that "there are dangerous and troubled times ahead" because an alliance was forming between Sukarno and the PKI.[1] The 1950s was a decade of disappointment for Hamengku Buwono, as his PSI allies failed badly in the 1955 elections, left-wing forces — especially the PKI — gathered strength, and Sukarno moved towards more repressive policies, culminating in the inception of Guided Democracy in 1959.

Perhaps one minor consolation had been the performance in the 1955 election of the Gerinda party, the political successor to the PKN of the 1930s, which was the third-strongest party at the polls in the Yogyakarta Special Region. Hamengku Buwono had not endorsed it, but its identification with the kraton presented some kind of confirmation of the continued popular appeal of the Javanese nobility, including Hamengku Buwono himself. Although he paid more attention to the Yogyakarta principality, he remained Jakarta based and seems to have busied himself mainly with his many non-political activities such as his business interests, especially tourism,[2] the scouting movement and sports administration.[3]

In this period, he remained on the political sidelines, but despite the setback in 1952, some were still prepared to predict a national political future for him.⁴ As liberal democracy failed and regional revolts erupted, some of those who turned against Sukarno's leadership looked to the more moderate Sultan, whose name was usually coupled with that of Hatta as possible saviours of an increasingly problem-ridden nation. For reasons which have never been entirely clear, Hamengku Buwono was one Javanese leader who generated widespread trust in regions outside Java. His moderate reasonable image was part of the explanation; the residual respect in many areas in Sumatra, Bali and East Indonesia for feudal rulers may be another part. Within Java of course, Hamengku Buwono commanded an enormous amount of public faith and even reverence.⁵

Although in the 1950s Hamengku Buwono said little in public, it was evident that he disapproved of many of Sukarno's policies and actions. In private, he was particularly critical of Sukarno's relationship with the PKI and fearful of the possible consequences.⁶ Nevertheless, his attitude to the PKI was pragmatic, and at least locally in Yogyakarta itself he managed to establish a reasonable modus vivendi with them.⁷

In 1957, as regional dissatisfaction threatened to turn into open revolt, Hamengku Buwono was involved in a series of efforts at reconciliation.⁸ By early 1958, leaders of the PRRI/Permesta regional revolt called on Sukarno to bring Hatta and the Sultan into government again,⁹ as a condition for serious talks to end the conflict, and for a while this seemed a genuine possibility. Hopes rose as Sukarno held two rounds of talks with Hatta,¹⁰ and Hatta expressed interest in heading a government without communist participation.¹¹ Hamengku Buwono, who seems to have been constantly consulted, was optimistic that Sukarno would accept Hatta as prime minister. He even predicted Subandrio's removal from the foreign ministry and expected to rejoin the government, possibly as Defence Minister again.¹² Such an appointment would have reassured the rebels in Sumatra and may well have led to some process of reconciliation.

The incumbent prime minister, Juanda, always modestly pragmatic, was prepared to accept his replacement by Hatta. If Sukarno did not accept the plan, Hamengku Buwono feared even more trouble for Indonesia than it was currently experiencing.¹³ Unfortunately, these ambitious plans came unstuck largely because of Sukarno's reluctance, and the regional rebellions were settled by force.

In mid-1958 a further effort was made to involve Hamengku Buwono in government, and both Sukarno and Juanda were clearly expecting his cooperation, but at the last minute, and to Juanda's embarrassment, he told Sukarno that the cabinet list did not include sufficient figures with whom he could work.[14] This setback seemed to have been based on a genuine misunderstanding between the two parties. Neither Hatta nor Hamengku Buwono were to serve in any cabinet during this period.

The next year, in a reconciliation of sorts, at the instigation of Nasution,[15] Sukarno appointed Hamengku Buwono as head of Bapekan (*Badan Pengawas Kegiatan Aparatur Negara* — State Apparatus Supervising Board), a new body whose function was to exert some prudential supervision over government departments. The appointment carried nominal ministerial rank, but Sukarno immediately made it unworkable by turning it into a Nasakom body and appointing various PKI figures, including the veteran communist Semaun.[16]

THE BPK

In November 1963, Sukarno moved Hamengku Buwono to another supervisory body which (unlike Bapekan) was entrenched in the 1945 constitution but more oriented to financial questions, the *Badan Pemeriksa Keuangan* (BPK — National Audit Board). This too carried ministerial rank though having little real power, but it provided a useful vantage point from which to observe national politics and especially financial issues.[17]

However, any hope of effective operation of the BPK was sabotaged in early 1965 by Sukarno, who decreed that he himself would be the government's chief auditor.[18] Hamengku Buwono later said that he had consistently refused cabinet posts in the Guided Democracy era, despite much pressure to do so. He had preferred to remain outside cabinet and thus had accepted appointment as head of the BPK, but even there had faced disappointment when its reports on financial maladministration in government agencies had been ignored.[19]

During 1964 and especially 1965, speculation about the succession to Sukarno, whose health at times seemed to be failing, usually involved two main possibilities. The first envisaged a succession by left-wing or Sukarnoist forces, most often identifying Subandrio as the leading candidate, although PKI leader Aidit was regarded as a possibility. Alternatively, succession by an army regime was the most common choice, and the name most mentioned was Nasution's, but other predicted alternatives were either Hatta or Hamengku Buwono, supported by the army.[20]

The year of 1965 was a dangerous and fearsome one in Indonesian history.[21] Those like Hamengku Buwono who disliked Sukarno's rule and lamented the leftward drift of policy, constant economic decline, and the advance of the PKI became increasingly downcast by the trends of the time.[22] Hamengku Buwono's associates say that a major difficulty was to know who could be trusted and relied upon. Rumours of possible coups, whether from the right or left, of PKI death lists,[23] and fears of a breakdown of society became common. In many government organizations, including the BPK, the Nasakom ideology meant that PKI or left-wing PNI figures were often appointed to senior positions. For the managers of these organizations, this severely complicated operations because regular ideological conflict arose.[24]

Within the BPK itself, Hamengku Buwono appointed a team of experts to assist him in the work. This included experts on accountancy (Radius Prawiro), customs (Muchtar Usman), and finance (Hans Pandelaki, later a senior Finance Department official). To the extent possible, he sidelined the two PKI members of the BPK board and used to ignore the official guidelines and follow his own programme. One board member, Sukardan, was a moderate PNI figure who was a good speaker, so that he usually did most of the talking before the BPK board and at parliamentary hearings.[25] The limitation of the BPK's work was (and still is) that although it could audit government instrumentalities, any follow-up — including action against identified defalcations — was the responsibility of the law enforcement agencies, which commonly failed to act.

In this period, the formation of informal political groups of friends and trusted associates became a way of sharing notes and discussing developments without fear of unwelcome disclosure. Hamengku Buwono quietly formed a group which became known as "Seven Up"; the cover was their common hobby of cooking meals, and each month they would take turns at preparing a meal at their homes.[26]

The group included Hamengku Buwono, Selosumarjan, Radius Prawiro, General Ashari Danudirjo (already a Minister, he became Trade Minister in the first New Order government and later Ambassador in Tokyo), Air Marshal Ali Budiarjo (later Suharto's Minister for Information), Brig Gen Sugih Arto (later Attorney General), and Frans Seda (also a minister under Sukarno and later Finance Minister and Communications Minister in the New Order). General Surono later joined the group. The group's composition suggests Hamengku Buwono's continued interest in and informal involvement with armed forces affairs.

THE ATTEMPTED COUP

This is not the place to describe in detail the bloody events of 1 October 1965, nor the even bloodier aftermath, which destroyed the Indonesian Communist Party, led to the deaths of at least 100,000 people[27] and probably more, and eventually to the fall of Sukarno and Suharto's surprising emergence to untrammelled power. Suffice it to note that on the evening of 30 September/1 October 1965, raiding parties from the presidential guard killed seven of the eight most senior generals of the army. The most senior general, Nasution, escaped. The leader of the putsch, Lieutenant Colonel Untung, broadcast a statement from the "30 September Movement" claiming that he had foiled an attempted coup by a Council of Generals. By the end of 1 October, however, Army Strategic Reserve Commander Suharto had retaken all the major points, and the 30 September Movement was comprehensively defeated. Many questions about this affair remain unanswered and may never be answered.

Hamengku Buwono IX makes one obscure appearance in the drama.[28] Some time on 1 October,

> Suharto was in touch with the Sultan of Yogyakarta, with whom he discussed the idea of the Sultan's going to Bandung to set up a rival government there. The Sultan is reported to have advised Suharto against this idea until they had more definite information on Sukarno. The Sultan had a feeling that Sukarno just might be involved in the coup: he told Suharto that "the whole thing sounds like Sukarno to me". He realised that it would be a mistake to announce the formation of a rival government that might later seem to have been a move against Sukarno.

The source for the story is the U.S. intelligence body, the CIA, and no Indonesian source has ever confirmed it; several aspects of it are unclear. It is not explained how Suharto contacted the Sultan — did the Sultan come to Kostrad headquarters that morning?[29] More plausibly, did they exchange written communications or messages through intermediaries (perhaps Selosumarjan)? What was the CIA's source? Since it later appeared that the U.S. intelligence on the coup and especially on Suharto was quite poor, one would guess that the information came from the Sultan rather than from the military.[30]

A corroborating detail is the fact that at least one senior figure, Minister for Information Roeslan Abdulgani, was sent to Bandung as a security measure on 1 October.[31] At the time, Suharto was unsure of the precise targets of the coup plotters; a confusing factor had been the death of a security guard from the premises of Deputy Prime Minister Johannes Leimena, across the road from the house of General Nasution. The guard had been killed after investigating the commotion on the morning of 1 October, but his fate had understandably led to rumours that Leimena too had been a target. Suharto might therefore want to get important civilian officials into safety until the affair was sorted out.[32]

The story provides some fascinating insights. First, Suharto knew the Sultan sufficiently closely to seek his advice in a time of crisis. Second, the Sultan's political sense was sharp enough to counsel caution until Sukarno's position became clear. Third, Suharto took the advice. The plan to establish a government in Bandung was dangerous and could have caused chaos and even civil war, or at least more of both than ultimately happened.

The next events cast a grim shadow over the inception of the New Order. As mentioned earlier, at least 100,000 people were killed in a series of massacres of real or alleged PKI members or associates across the country, especially in Java and Bali.[33] This was a time of moral panic, and thousands of PKI members were jailed for many years. Only a very small proportion of the dead or imprisoned would have been aware of, or involved in, the 30 September Movement. Association with the PKI, a legal organization in 1965, was not a crime under the Sukarno government, but under the new regime it suddenly became one. Admittedly, the PKI had behaved provocatively at times, especially through the so-called *aksi sefihak*, the unilateral seizure of land in various locations in Java for distribution to poor peasants; but whatever the provocation, the reaction did not qualify as a proportionate response.

Elson has concluded that Suharto bore the central responsibility for the massacres, even if they became much worse than he had expected.[34] In considering the role of other major New Order figures, including Hamengku Buwono, the question arises whether they too had some level of responsibility. One answer would be that the civilians stayed carefully out of military affairs, that they had no power or authority to intervene, and that they would have been ignored or even removed if they had attempted to do so. But the question may be legitimately put — what did they do to moderate or alleviate the bloodshed?

The only extant statements by Hamengku Buwono related to his own region of Yogyakarta. In a radio address,[35] Hamengku Buwono outlined the events in Jakarta in factual terms, including the abduction and murder of the generals, the formation by the 30 September Movement of a Revolutionary Council "without the knowledge of Great Leader of the Revolution President Sukarno", and the defeat of the Movement by the "skill" of the army under Major General Suharto.

He emphasized Sukarno's condemnation of the Movement and his repeated calls for calm while further steps were taken against the perpetrators of the events of 30 September. Hamengku Buwono condemned the associated murders of the two Yogyakarta commanders and the movement's attempt to overthrow the legal government of the Special Region (which in some sense was *his* government), and called on the people of Yogyakarta to assist the armed forces in restoring security and order.[36]

Three weeks later, at a minor ceremony outside Yogyakarta city to mark the beginning of the tobacco harvest, Hamengku Buwono criticized foreign media reports which claimed that Java was a battlefield, whereas in the meantime routine activities like the present one were continuing.[37] Despite provocations, the people of Yogyakarta would continue their work as normal. Once again, he deplored the 30 September Movement as "counter-revolutionary" and referred to Sukarno's rejection of it and his condemnation of the murders of the generals. On the page where it reported Hamengku Buwono's statement, the same newspaper reported the "voluntary" dissolution of a communist party branch in Klaten regency, involving a reported 10,000 members.[38]

A striking feature of Hamengku Buwono's two statements is the lack of reference to the PKI, and the lack of any attempt to blame the PKI for the 30 September events.[39] To that extent, and through his references to Sukarno's condemnation of the 30 September Movement, Hamengku Buwono seemed implicitly to take a middle position, ignoring the army's contention that the PKI was definitely involved and giving Sukarno qualified support by pointing out his distancing of himself from the attempted coup, even though Hamengku Buwono must have known that this was grudging on Sukarno's part. The need to tailor his explanations to local sentiment in Central Java may have lain behind his gingerly treatment of Sukarno. He pointedly downplayed the seriousness of the disturbances, and although killings did occur in Yogyakarta and environs, it is not clear whether any had occurred at this early stage.[40] His first statement repeated calls for calm, but the advice to the people of Yogyakarta was not clear cut, and at no stage did he call directly for violence to cease. The counsel to assist the armed forces was ambiguous and might be taken as licence to pursue the PKI even further. Nevertheless, unlike many of the military leaders (especially Nasution) and some civilians, Hamengku Buwono was never on record calling directly for severe vengeance against the PKI.

KOTI

In November Sukarno appointed Hamengku Buwono as Deputy Supreme Commander for Economic Affairs[41] in KOTI (*Komando Operasi Tertinggi* — Supreme Operations Command), the organization originally created by Sukarno for the West Irian campaign but which had persisted as an important decision-making body[42] and which the armed forces regarded as a potentially useful centre of power.[43] Nasution was appointed to KOTI at the same time.[44] Seeing the need for regular consultations, Hamengku Buwono proposed to Suharto and Nasution that they hold monthly meetings at Nasution's house. One such meeting was held, but the arrangement was overtaken by yet another reorganization of KOTI by Sukarno,[45] and the possibility of a Nasution–Suharto–Sultan triumvirate faded, if indeed it had ever existed. The reorganization of KOTI was seen as an effort to put the economy to rights, and great hopes were held for it,[46] but observers were soon expressing disappointment.[47]

For some years, under the guidance of the gifted Colonel Suwarto,[48] commander of the army staff college in Bandung, contacts had been established between important armed forces personalities and a group of academics at the University of Indonesia, including Professor Wijoyo Nitisastro and other economists. It was thus natural that they became active as advisers of KOTI at this time, because they saw a possibility of its becoming a kind of "counter-government".[49]

SUHARTO–MALIK–SULTAN TRIUMVIRATE

In the period after the attempted coup, an informal and temporary triumvirate emerged consisting of Suharto, the Sultan, and Adam Malik. This was a period of dual government, shifting loyalties and much intrigue as the three men patiently worked to change government policy, to diminish Sukarno's influence, and eventually (although it is very unclear when this became the objective) to remove Sukarno altogether. At first, the triumvirate and their supporters met regularly at the house of Adam Malik or of Mashuri,[50] then a kind of informal cabinet (the so-called *kabinet ndelik*, or secret cabinet) would meet at the Sultan's office on the south side of Merdeka Square.[51] There the triumvirate would receive briefings from Ali Murtopo on efforts to end Confrontation against Malaysia, from the technocrats about new directions in economic policy, and from student leaders about current popular unrest and demonstrations in the main cities. Many leaders of the student action front KAMI[52] became habitués of the Merdeka Square office,[53] until the student movement faded from influence. Much was going on behind the scenes in this period, and a great deal will probably never be revealed.

Political triumvirates in history have been notoriously short-lived, and this was no exception. The Second Triumvirate of Antony, Octavian and Lepidus in the Roman Republic was an uneasy linkage between two powerful and well-armed rivals with a wealthy but not very influential patrician leader. Its existence merely staved off for a time the inevitable clash between the two equally matched and ambitious military leaders. The triumvirate of Stalin, Zinoviev and Kamenev in Soviet Russia in the 1920s was on the face of it a more even contest, as the men had worked together for years in the underground Bolshevik party, all shared a veneration for the dying Lenin, and none had direct links with armed force. But Stalin had steadily built up his support in the Bolshevik party machine, whereas the other two — though faithful and close followers of Lenin and far more ideologically authoritative — badly underestimated Stalin's personal ambition.[54] To them, the greatest threat was the popular Trotsky, whose status as the builder of the Red Army made him dangerous. One factor which both these cases had in common was that once the triumvirs had defeated their opponents, they then fell out amid bloody and tragic conflict.

The Indonesian triumvirs presented a different pattern, and they never publicly fell out, no doubt because the power equation was so different. Only Suharto had the potential of armed force behind him, although at first he was neither nearly as powerful nor as central to the army as he later became; but he led no civilian political organization, as the "functional organization" Golkar was only transformed into a political vehicle some years later. Both Hamengku Buwono and Adam Malik had strong credentials as civilian leaders, although neither had much organized political backing, probably one of the factors which made them acceptable to Suharto. From the beginning, they could not have seemed any threat; for the moment, the bigger threat was Sukarno if he succeeded in making a comeback, which at times over the next year seemed perfectly possible.

As the leader of the effort to promote economic recovery, the Sultan needed expert assistance. He found this in the group which became known collectively as "the New Order technocrats", or more informally "the Berkeley mafia", because several had obtained doctorates from that particular U.S. university. Prominent among these were a tightly-knit group from the Economics Faculty of the University of Indonesia, including Professor Wijoyo Nitisastro, Dr Emil Salim, Professor Ali Wardhana, Professor Mohamad Sadli, Professor Sarbini, Johannes Sumarlin, Dr Saleh Afiff, and Professor Subroto. Rather different were the handful of Dutch-trained economists like Drs Radius Prawiro and Drs Frans Seda; even more different was the senior economist and former regional rebel Professor Sumitro Joyohadikusumo, who reemerged from exile rather later.

As we have seen, several had become advisers to the army leadership as a result of their links with Col Suwarto. They formed special teams to advise the new Chairman of the Cabinet Presidium (Deputy Prime Minister Suharto) after March 1966. The Sultan made considerable use of the advice and reports of the Staff College's Economic Team in formulating his new economic policies.[55] Clearly Suharto was closely involved in approving and perhaps formulating the policies, but the details of the consultative process are rather obscure.

The technocrats were to become fixtures in successive New Order cabinets, occupying virtually all the economic portfolios at one time or another. Most of them became well known and highly respected among foreigners, especially those responsible for foreign policy, trade policy, foreign investment or economic aid. The figures who occupied senior positions in the National Planning Board (Bappenas) — such as Wijoyo, Salim and Afiff — made regular appearances at meetings of the Inter-Governmental Group on Indonesia (IGGI), the special international group of aid donors chaired by the Dutch.

In late 1965 or early 1966, Selosumarjan (probably at the instigation of Sujatmoko, whose help had been sought by Hamengku Buwono)[56] arranged, almost clandestinely, for Wijoyo and the others to meet Hamengku Buwono at his request.[57] Hamengku Buwono was aware that his 1930s-style Dutch economics was well out of date, and his new task of rehabilitating the Indonesian economy, imposed on him by the arrangement between the triumvirs, would require the best economists Indonesia could offer. At the meeting were the two Dutch-trained economists, Frans

Seda and Radius Prawiro, as well as the U.S.-trained group consisting of Wijoyo, Emil Salim, Mohamad Sadli, and Ali Wardhana.[58] Hamengku Buwono already knew Radius from his membership of the BPK and Seda through informal networks. Although clearly unhappy at the state of the Indonesian economy, Hamengku Buwono said little, but listened to the economists' ideas about how the economy might be rehabilitated.[59] Their expertise, and the clear ideas they had already developed,[60] impressed him, and he may have decided there and then that these were the people he needed. Awareness of their links with SSKAD would have been an additional recommendation.

Hamengku Buwono's influence seemed to be increasing from his vantage point in KOTI, although he could not prevent bad policy from being made. Fears of a Sukarno comeback emerged in December when at a KOTI meeting, Sukarno restated all his old positions, refused to ban the PKI, and was unwilling to reorganize government in ways proposed by the triumvirate.[61] Sukarno then launched a new economic policy which involved several drastic measures. These included attempts to control inflation and stabilize the rupiah through replacing old rupiah with new on a thousand-to-one basis (a "1,000 per cent devaluation") and through drastic price increases in fuel and public transport costs. Within weeks the policy failed, as rice prices increased dramatically and the rupiah sharply weakened.[62]

Renewed and massive student demonstrations strengthened the hand of the New Order forces during January and February 1966,[63] and Sukarno was forced to instruct his economic ministers to reconsider and to consult Hamengku Buwono and Suharto. Deputy Prime Minister Chaerul Saleh announced that prices would be lowered again, and that — "in accordance with a proposal from the Sultan" — the government would review currency policy, especially the circulation of old rupiah notes.[64] There was still considerable uncertainty in February 1966 about the ultimate outcome of the power struggle, until the decisive confrontation in March.[65]

At an important seminar organized at the University of Indonesia by the KAMI student organization,[66] the Sultan called for a "realistic" approach to Indonesia's economic problems. A successful economic strategy had to be based on the true circumstances of society. In a clear reference to Sukarno, he added that leaders should admit their mistakes, so that lessons could be drawn and future mistakes avoided. In a talk a few weeks later, he again hammered the theme of a "realistic" approach, in which the effect on the economy of non-economic factors was properly understood and accounted for.⁶⁷ In an address to a military audience the same week, read on his behalf by Selosumarjan, he emphasized the damage wrought by the dramatically increasing inflation levels. Development projects could not proceed because funding had suddenly become inadequate, existing infrastructure could not be maintained, and workers' wages and salaries could not keep up with the ever increasing prices of basic necessities.⁶⁸

These statements revealed how far his thinking had diverged from Sukarno. Their differences in 1952 had related to military policy; now his disquiet with Sukarno's economic policies was emerging publicly, although he did not criticize Sukarno directly. Indeed, throughout his entire political career he never made any direct public criticism of Sukarno, or of Suharto for that matter. But the call for leaders to "admit their errors" was, by Hamengku Buwono's standards, a fairly blunt reference to Sukarno, and reminiscent of his call after his resignation as Defence Minister in 1953 for "leaders, large or small, to learn self-control".⁶⁹ The statement about non-economic factors also revealed his conviction that politics had trumped economics for far too long.⁷⁰ He avoided quoting statistics or using technical economic terminology, presumably because he wished to explain current economic circumstances to the public in readily understandable terms.

The statements by him and others were part of a concerted effort by the New Order forces to publicize as widely as possible the true state of the Indonesian economy, which had been either ignored or dismissed as unimportant by Sukarno and his allies. This was a deliberate triumvirate strategy, counteracting Sukarno's claims that the Indonesian economy was in reasonable shape and those who doubted it were secret counter-revolutionaries.⁷¹ The Indonesian public had good reason for ignorance because relevant agencies such as the central bank (Bank Indonesia) had ceased publishing economic statistics.⁷² Perhaps the single most compelling evidence of the failure of Sukarno's economic policies, a phenomenon which could not be hidden, was that inflation had been rising at over 100 per cent per annum during 1963–65, and was to reach more than 1,000 per cent in one twelve-month period during 1965–66.

IN GOVERNMENT

On 21 February, a cabinet reshuffle brought Hamengku Buwono his first meaningful government post for thirteen years, as Coordinating Minister for Development, responsible for six economic ministries, including resources like oil and mining.[73] This looks like a tacit if belated admission by Sukarno that something needed to be done about the economy, but political events were acquiring a momentum of their own. Student demonstrations were gaining force, and public impatience was rising both with Sukarno himself and with Suharto's cautious approach to the President.

Following the drama of 11 March 1966, when Suharto received executive power from a thoroughly intimidated Sukarno[74] through the 11 March Order (*surat perintah sebelas Maret*, or "Supersemar") and became one of the six deputy prime ministers and the real power in the government, a new regime emerged. Days of bargaining[75] ensued as Hamengku Buwono[76] played an important role with Suharto in assembling a new cabinet which, while retaining some holdovers from previous governments, marked a substantial break with the past. After 11 March, Suharto had arrested over a dozen members of the previous government, including Subandrio, seen as the most likely successor to Sukarno only six months before.

The cabinet presidium changed from a membership of Subandrio, Leimena, Chaerul Saleh, Idham Chalid and Achmadi, to a membership of Suharto, Hamengku Buwono, Malik, Leimena, Roeslan Abdulgani and Idham Chalid. The latter three were regarded as Sukarnoists, and it had always been impossible to imagine the Muslim leader Idham Chalid and Leimena, the Ambonese Christian leader, ever challenging Sukarno. While Roeslan was also seen as a Sukarnoist, he was more independent or at least more flexible; he soon left the cabinet but, in an amazing feat of political survival still not fully explained,[77] he was able to re-emerge as the new regime's Ambassador to the United Nations, and later as the high priest of Pancasila ideology in the 1970s.

The emergence into prominent roles of personalities like the Sultan and Adam Malik would suggest that they were Suharto's choices, or at least that their appointments were the product of compromise between Suharto and Sukarno. Sukarno knew both men well, even though he had had serious differences with them; he had appointed them to ministerial posts in recent years. He could feel that they might moderate the forces which were building up to seek his removal. He must have known by this time that many in the armed forces were suspicious of his role on 1 October 1965 and were not certain that he would gracefully accept the drastic changes in policy that Suharto was forcing on him.

From Suharto's (and the army's) perspective, the reasons for wanting the Sultan and Malik in important posts were political and practical. Suharto was totally unknown in the wider world, but Indonesia desperately needed foreign sympathy, aid and investment. He required the higher profile of figures like the Sultan and Malik, who would provide the New Order with a public face. Both had for a long time been known to and respected by most foreigners with an interest in Indonesia. Hamengku Buwono, like Malik, represented stability, steady administration, and continuity with the early days of the Indonesian state.

Another factor was the domestic one, arising from the common assumption that Sukarno retained much support among the Javanese population in Central and East Java,[78] which were vital areas politically. This helps to explain Suharto's extremely cautious treatment of Sukarno, because his public humiliation might dangerously inflame an already unstable situation in Java. But Javanese supporters of Sukarno could well be mollified by the presence in the government of another respected Javanese leader and culture hero. Suharto originated from central Java, but he knew that he had nothing like the profile and standing of the Sultan.

Hamengku Buwono became Deputy Prime Minister for the Economy, Finance and Development, and was to hold similar positions until 1973. Malik became Foreign Minister, a post he was to hold for over a decade. For his part, Suharto became Deputy Prime Minister for Security and Defence and concurrently Minister for the Army. The triumvirate had thus taken over the cabinet presidium and had moved into the central position in government. Dr Leimena was the nominal chairman of the presidium,[79] but the real power lay elsewhere.

A *Kompas* editorial commented approvingly[80] that "the government as a whole had to win the people's approval because of the presence of personalities with desirable traits, ie, having a honest character, having a Pancasila mentality, as well as being capable in the area of work assigned to them". Hamengku Buwono was clearly one of the ministers *Kompas* had in mind.

Nevertheless, one might ask why he was chosen to take on the role of getting the economy to rights. He had studied some economics at Leiden University, but that was nearly thirty years before; he was not renowned as an economist, but rather his earlier ministerial roles in the 1940s and 1950s had been first as a minister of state and then in the defence and security areas. His activities as head of the BPK, while familiarizing him with the government's desperate financial plight and pervasive corruption,[81] were hardly a preparation for this weighty burden.

Those who served in government at the time explain this rather as the outcome of a pragmatic division of labour between the triumvirs.[82] Management of the armed forces, internal security and the restoration of public order were unambiguously Suharto's territory, which the other two would not enter. Malik was well known internationally, and with his engaging personality could easily become the external face of the new regime; his presence in the government also provided comfort (of a kind) to old-style nationalists of the revolutionary generation, even including the non-communist left.

This left Hamengku Buwono with the economy; his inclusion in the triumvirate was less related to any economic expertise than to his prestige across Java, the open secret that he regarded Sukarno's economic policies as disastrous, and his nationalist credentials. All three men had known each other since the Revolution. Hamengku Buwono had much cooperative association with Suharto during 1949, had probably met him when Minister of Defence in the early 1950s, but had only occasional contact since,[83] and the link was not close. He had probably known Malik from a distance during the Revolution and again when they served as ministers in the early 1960s, but without close contact; he would have been impressed by Malik's ultimately unsuccessful struggle as Trade Minister to resist PKI and leftist pressure against his pragmatic policies in 1964. No personal relationship among the three was particularly intimate, and they never seemed to meet outside work hours and the occasional semi-official social function.[84]

The bolder student leaders were already beginning to canvass the removal of Sukarno and were looking at possible candidates to replace him. When a student delegation asked Hamengku Buwono's opinion about Suharto as successor, he apparently replied by referring to Suharto's attitudes to business dealings and raising money.[85]

In his first press conference in his new capacity,[86] the Sultan was accompanied by all the ministers who reported to him (nine in all).[87] His area of responsibility included trade, finance, public works, mining and oil, the various industry portfolios, agriculture and transport. He emphasized the need to bring down inflation, which was reaching historically unprecedented levels, even compared with the Japanese period. Priority would be given to the rice economy and especially the price of rice in the markets. He announced a government austerity programme, which would include spending cuts and a careful inventorying of government assets, with the aim of establishing the true extent of government property and selling off unnecessary assets.[88]

Shortly thereafter, Hamengku Buwono drew on his experience in the BPK to promulgate an instruction requiring government departments and agencies to account more closely for their use of government funds.[89] He noted the BPK's conclusion that many agencies had not been using funds for the purposes for which they had been appropriated. Strict deadlines for departments and agencies to report on these matters were announced. He was now in a position to enforce the conclusions which — in the BPK days — he could only hope would be followed up. Hamengku Buwono's action parallelled similar efforts by Seda in the Finance Ministry and Radius Prawiro in the central bank (Bank Indonesia).[90]

Radius himself had a salutary experience of the way in which appointments were made at this time. He learnt of his appointment while watching television. In conversations with Sukarno, Suharto, and Hamengku Buwono, he had strongly advocated greater independence for the central bank, but with no notion that he himself might be a candidate for the position.[91] In this case at least, because of Hamengku Buwono's previous knowledge of Radius in the BPK, the appointment would probably have arisen on his recommendation. The same would probably apply to the appointment of Pandelaki (also previously of the BPK) to the State Budget position in the Finance Department. Hamengku Buwono's associates Frans Seda and General Ashari, who were promoted in the reshuffle, had already held cabinet positions and had independent links with Sukarno and probably with Suharto as well. Sugih Arto, also an associate of Hamengku Buwono, became Attorney General, but had his own direct links to Suharto, having been one of his assistants since November 1965.[92] Despite his various connections among the Indonesian elite, Hamengku Buwono never seems to have attempted to create his own political organization. This, coupled with a reputation for not indulging in intrigue, reinforced the public impression of his being above normal politics.

Political-Economic Statement

In mid-April 1966 came one of the most important public statements of Hamengku Buwono's career, the so-called political-economic statement, which set out the policies and priorities of the New Order, in many cases totally reversing previous policy. In its sobriety, factuality and lack of flourish, the tone was similar to his last speech to parliament as Defence Minister in October 1952.

He emphasized above all the desperate need to stabilize and rehabilitate the economy. He called on the political elite to adopt more modest lifestyles, adding that the government would henceforth give less emphasis to luxury goods. The focus was on the short-term programme over the next six to twelve months, aimed at having immediate effects on the economy. He foreshadowed a programme to reform and renew the government apparatus. He stressed once again the need to combat inflation which had accelerated in recent months.[93]

The scant areas of prosperity still existing in Indonesia were an illusion because they rested on the basis of debts which Indonesia could not repay. The debts now amounted to US$2.4 billion,[94] an amount which looks small by modern standards but which in the 1960s was very large. This candid admission of insolvency must have been a shock to those who believed the economy was still in reasonable shape. For years, Hamengku Buwono added, Indonesia had been importing staples through the use of short-term loans, on very disadvantageous terms. Indonesia's exports on the other hand had progressively declined every year since 1961, from US$750 million to US$450 million, a decline of over 30 per cent. Food production was not keeping up with the increase in population, and the transport infrastructure was inadequate.[95]

Hamengku Buwono stressed that the government had to combat the many vested interests which had grown up around the economy, including pervasive corruption, mismanagement and excessive bureaucracy.[96] He outlined the government's programme to rescue and rehabilitate the economy. The first requirement was an immediate austerity programme, covering all government departments. He instructed all departments to provide an inventory of their activities and establish priorities with a view to abandoning unproductive programmes. Second, government enterprises would have to be run henceforth on normal commercial lines. The tax system would be reviewed, and the government would strongly promote all economic projects which could yield badly needed foreign exchange. Measures would be taken to encourage the productive use of foreign exchange earnings; existing special permits for foreign exchange, based on non-economic criteria, would be withdrawn. Procedures for foreign and internal trade would be simplified, including in harbours and airports, to facilitate commerce rather than impede it. The government would give highest priority to industries aimed at satisfying basic needs, such as the clothing industry and products like fertilizer which would assist food production. Improvements in transport were essential and would be encouraged by facilitation of imports of commercial vehicles.[97]

Significantly, and in a very sharp departure from previous policy, Hamengku Buwono drew attention to the potential of private enterprise in the rehabilitation process; regulations which discouraged private business would be reviewed. Finally, he called on the people of Indonesia to exercise their right to supervise and criticize the implementation of government programmes. He himself would make no unrealistic promises; his only promise was to work hard and honestly for the country's welfare.[98]

The Australian Embassy reported that Hamengku Buwono's statement formed part of a campaign to "demolish the policies of the previous regime and condemn all those closely associated with it".[99] Most public reaction was also favourable. The *Kompas* columnist P.K. Ojong commented:[100] "After almost twenty years of working in journalism, we have rarely seen a ministerial statement which was so businesslike and sober. A statement so steady and self-aware,[101] so rational and realistic, raising the hope and surmise that now at last we are getting what we yearn for, namely: *Economic Leadership*.[102]… It was like an annual report by a business leader addressing his shareholders."

The latter comment aptly reflected the style of the new economic policies and indeed of the government generally. The time for brilliant oratory and manipulation of colourful symbols and slogans was ending. Hamengku Buwono's simplicity and even dullness suited the tone of the new era. The administrators had come into their own, but just at a time when the distinction between administrator and solidarity maker was losing its relevance. Different formulations were needed to describe the new power relationships and to categorize the differences and similarities among the new elite which would now rule Indonesia. Some scholars would draw attention to the strength and significance of patrimonial networks.[103] New Order critics would emphasize the role of military elites;[104] neo-Marxists would describe the new wealth accumulation which was about to occur.[105] The division into "solidarity makers" and "administrators" was beginning to look outmoded.

Hamengku Buwono's speech reflected awareness that the driving force of the raging inflation of the time was the government's uncontrolled budget deficit. Control of government spending was important in itself but it would

The End of Guided Democracy and the Rise of the New Order 257

also be a crucial anti-inflationary measure. The shift in government priorities was striking, giving emphasis to better financial controls, more commercial approaches among government-owned firms, the need for civil service reform, and a more open attitude to private enterprise. By implication, the latter point would mean a more accommodating approach to the local business sector which was dominated by ethnic Chinese, although at this stage the New Order could not afford to address the Chinese issue too openly, and some influential elements of the new regime were equivocal about the Chinese role or even hostile to it.[106]

The ideological implications of the address were profound. The move to a free-market approach flatly contradicted much of Sukarno's thinking. It was not absolute, as we will see, but the new policy necessarily meant a less dirigiste and control-oriented attitude to market forces. Another part of the programme, no doubt deriving more directly from Hamengku Buwono's concern with good governance, was the requirement to regain control of the government sector, by inventorying the exact range of government activities, eliminating unnecessary and wasteful activities, and improving financial controls.

Hamengku Buwono's address, the first major articulation of the New Order's economic policies, omitted several important factors, probably for reasons of space and priority. Issues like cooperatives, transmigration and population policy were not mentioned, although the New Order would later pay great attention to them. Nor was there any hint of Boeke-style dualism in the address. The alien Western-style capitalist sector had been badly battered by the nationalizations and economic decline of recent years, whereas the indigenous agricultural sector had been less affected by the economic decline, even though it was operating at a low level. To the extent that his earlier training was remembered, the idea of dualism was probably dismissed as irrelevant, and it certainly provided little guidance for action.

The period between the 11 March Letter of Instruction and the MPRS session of June 1966 featured regular student demonstrations and considerable tension. Sukarno had become a constitutional head of state after 11 March,[107] but he still had many supporters. It was also uncertain whether he would content himself with this role and adapt himself to new circumstances. During 1966, the triumvirs, or at least Suharto, gradually came to realize that Sukarno was untameable and that he would have to be replaced.

Sukarno retained personal links with prominent figures he had known for years, and on one occasion he took Adam Malik and Frans Seda on a visit to his Japanese wife, Ratna Sari Dewi. Dewi, known to speak frankly to Sukarno from time to time and not lacking political instinct, told Sukarno that the student movement represented an important element in public opinion, and he should pay attention to their demands. The argument grew so heated that Sukarno decided to leave. As they re-entered their vehicle, he said disgustedly, "She's been talking to Koko (i.e., Sujatmoko) and the Sultan again."[108]

PROJECTING THE NEW ORDER OVERSEAS

After plans were announced for Hamengku Buwono to lead an economic delegation to Japan, he himself faced a student protest when a large group of KAMI representatives met him at his office in Merdeka Square. The KAMI delegation contended that he should await the forthcoming MPRS session before committing Indonesia to economic undertakings abroad.[109] Not surprisingly, Hamengku Buwono, whose relations with the students were cordial, argued that the entire Indonesian people was pressing the government for a solution to the country's economic problems. He could not wait for the MPRS meeting, which might for some reason or other be postponed. The whole country was "sick", and the medicine available within Indonesia itself was not sufficient; he therefore had to seek foreign help urgently.[110]

This domestic pressure sharpened the requirement for the mission to produce tangible results, and Hamengku Buwono left Jakarta with the twin aims of convincing the Japanese of the government's sincerity in its new policies and its power to implement them, and of gaining immediate assistance.[111] On arrival, Hamengku Buwono told the media that Indonesia hoped to work with all relevant international organizations in its efforts to mend its economy. He mentioned especially the UN, the World Bank and the IMF.[112]

He briefed the Japanese Foreign Minister on Indonesia's grave economic plight and on the aid Indonesia was now receiving from other countries, especially the United States. He dismissed suggestions that aid from the United States would be a politically delicate matter in Indonesia.[113] The new government's priorities were rehabilitation of the infrastructure, especially communications and transport; as well as "foreign currency-earning projects and foreign currency-saving projects".[114]

He put as positive a gloss on politics as he could. Nasution, Suharto, Malik, and he himself were cooperating harmoniously. Sukarno could not be expected to change his views overnight, but he had agreed to peaceful resolution of the Malaysia dispute and at a recent meeting had accepted early recognition of Singapore. He seemed more tolerant of the planned entry (or re-entry) of Indonesia to international organizations, and Indonesia's return to the UN and IMF was already being seriously examined.[115]

Reflecting the main objective of his mission, Hamengku Buwono pressed for US$50 million in economic assistance for 1966 and US$150 million the next year, and a promise of this aid "before he left Japan". For political and no doubt personal reasons, he needed to be able to show results. The Japanese reaction was reasonably positive, but betrayed some muted disquiet at the Indonesian assumption that the world owed them a living.

Prime Minister Sato asked about Sukarno's title of "President for Life" and the Malaysia dispute. Hamengku Buwono foreshadowed the possible withdrawal of the title, adding that there was no such provision in the 1945 constitution, and by implication confirming the steep decline in Sukarno's standing. On Malaysia, he pointed out the President's agreement to the forthcoming talks between Malik and Tun Razak.[116] In a later meeting, Sato indicated that Japan could offer only $30 million in immediate aid.[117] Nevertheless, the Indonesians were pleased with the result, which Hamengku Buwono announced from Tokyo.[118] He had demonstrated that the new government's approach could deliver the goods.

In Manila, Hamengku Buwono reasserted his claims of political stabilization in Indonesia and predicted further improvements when the MPRS met. He added that major decisions were taken by a "nucleus cabinet" (i.e., the presidium), which had reached an understanding with Sukarno, although there was often "debate".[119] The net impression of Sukarno's position at this stage was that, while weakened, he was giving ground on important matters and could possibly stay on as a figurehead president.

On his return Hamengku Buwono told a Pancasila Day parade that Pancasila had to be defended, emphasizing the need for national unity under the banner of Pancasila. International respect for Indonesia was gradually being restored, and trade was recovering.[120] The government's trade policy focused on staple goods for the people and not on luxury goods for the elite.[121] The reference to Pancasila was one of the first indications of the new regime's preoccupation with the national ideology and the need to "restore" it after the alleged deviations from it by Sukarno and the PKI.

In a further report to parliament,[122] Hamengku Buwono repeated many of the same themes as before, but his emphasis on welcoming constructive criticism and suggestions from the parliament seemed to reflect not only a commitment to openness, but perhaps also some relief that he was facing a more cooperative parliament than he had previously seen in 1952. Although concerned at the continued high level of price inflation, he expressed the government's satisfaction that the rice harvest appeared relatively large. Indonesia faced severe shortages of foreign exchange, leading in turn to a lack of imported goods. The need for foreign aid and investment had induced the government to send a series of "technical and diplomatic missions" abroad, to seek rescheduling of debts as well as new credit, although the practical results of these missions would only be felt over the next twelve months or so.[123] He repeated the need to reorganize government-owned firms, to evaluate their activities, to review all contracts with foreign firms and to simplify and facilitate export procedures.[124]

Members' questions related to the government trading firms, the need to disband unproductive government agencies, trade matters in general, inflation levels, taxation and the government budget.[125] Hamengku Buwono's responses repeated the emphasis on regularization of government procedures, further encouragement to private traders and exporters, and a major public works programme to rehabilitate the infrastructure.[126] Many of the 1966 budgetary assumptions had been proven wrong, and the entire budget needed to be reviewed.[127]

During this period, Hamengku Buwono seemed to be an important triumvirate representative in parliament, especially where economic issues were discussed. The possibility that parliament would exercise a genuine supervisory and legitimizing role as a counterweight to government seemed real at the time, and the respect in which he was held contributed to cordial and productive relations with the parliament.

Hamengku Buwono's assertion that foreign investment might be both welcome and necessary had not been heard in Jakarta for many years. A corollary was the need for a much closer relationships with the main sources of international capital and investment, i.e., the United States, Japan and Europe, which Sukarno had done his best to spurn and provoke. A corresponding implication was a much lower priority for relations with communist countries, already less favoured for political reasons. The openness to foreign involvement in the economy accorded with the pragmatic acceptance of outside expertise which Hamengku Buwono had stood for since the early 1950s.

SUMMARY

The weakness of the civilian leaders vis-à-vis Suharto in power terms was not yet evident in 1966, and the appearance of a shared leadership, after the capricious individualism of Sukarno, had its attractions. At this stage few saw Suharto as the Octavian or Stalin of the Indonesian triumvirate. A civilian–military partnership could have a reasonably broad appeal, and Hamengku Buwono presented a reassuringly familiar element within this, especially in Java. But his real power remained quite limited and might be better classified simply as influence; while Suharto's was increasingly the decisive voice.

In public at least, therefore, the resurgent Hamengku Buwono appeared once again as an important leader of his country in a time of crisis. Under his guidance and with the advice of the experts around him, the populace could hope for an improvement in their daily lives. His economic programme, including several sharp reversals of previous policy, looked like a practical blueprint for recovery. Calls on the elite to adopt more modest lifestyles, which were constantly repeated throughout the New Order but which appeared increasingly hollow in view of the way the elite actually lived, looked sincere coming from the Sultan.

Alongside the promise of practical action was the abrupt change in style presented by the new leadership group. The new approach was worthy, colourless, and dull, but conveyed a strong determination to provide more effective government, and reverse previous styles of governance. Hamengku Buwono was an important part of this effort, his public reputation remained high and if anything had been greatly enhanced since the emergence of the New Order, and he engendered much trust in his reliability and integrity among the public. But private reservations about the true level of his influence and even about his leadership qualities were beginning to emerge, as will appear in the following chapter.

Notes

1. Brackman, "A Great Javanese, A Great Indonesian, A Great Human Being", *TUR*, p. 243.
2. On his involvement with Bali tourism, see Adrian Vickers, "Selling the Experience of Bali 1950–71", pp. 16–17.

3. Professor Hooker has suggested that this lifelong involvement indicates a concern and interest in nurturing and mentoring Indonesian youth. This seems probable, as a reputation for a concern for youth welfare would help to explain his good relations with the student movements in 1966.
4. NA 2.21.285, collection 570 F.J. Goedhart. Goedhart said: "Mark my words, against all predictions (especially in *Merdeka*), that the Sultan and his allies are finished as opponents of Sukarno and the PNI, I can only say: it can turn around!" Letter of 10 April 1953 to unnamed correspondent.
5. See NAA A1838/280, file no 3034/2/2/2 pt 4, Australian Embassy (henceforth AE) report, J. McMillan memorandum of 21 August 1957 following a tour of Java, p. 3, noting "the authority exercised in central Java and elsewhere by the Sultan of Yogyakarta who is held in reverential awe by people of all levels".
6. See the Brackman quote mentioned above, *TUR*, p. 243.
7. NAA A1838/404, file TS383/6/1 pt 2, AE Washington cable to Canberra, 12 February 1958, p. 3. Thanks to David Jenkins for drawing this to my attention.
8. For example, he was a member of the high-level Committee of Seven in the *Musyawarah Pembangunan Nasional* (Munap — National Development Consultation) in September 1957, which looked promising but eventually failed.
9. Feith, *Decline*, p. 586.
10. Ibid., p. 587.
11. NAA A1838/404, ibid., p. 2.
12. Ibid.
13. Ibid.
14. NAA A1838, file 3034/2/1/2 part 1, AE Jakarta situation report no. 44, 10 July 1958.
15. Nasution, *Memenuhi Panggilan Tugas* [Obeying Duty's Call], vol. 5, p. 257.
16. Ibid. The Bapekan period is very obscure. Hamengku Buwono's only recorded comment was made to George Kahin, whom he told that Bapekan was a potentially very useful instrument of government. Feith papers, MON 78, 1991/09/012, item 198, Kahin/Feith letter of 20 December 1960, p. 1.
17. "This experience would serve (Hamengku Buwono) well when the responsibility was at last his to find solutions." J.H. Sullivan, The United States and the "New Order" in Indonesia (PhD thesis, University microfilms, Michigan, 1970), p. 301.
18. Drs Radius Prawiro, interview 8 August 2002.
19. *SH*, 11 June 1971.
20. NAA A1838, file 30034/2/1/7, Department of State Bureau of Intelligence and Research paper "The Succession in Indonesia", 9 March 1964, p. 4.

21. "I found tensions building, the atmosphere poisonous". Hastings, *The Road to Lembang*, p. 20.
22. See Feith papers, MON 78 1991/09/033 item 552, "Sujatmoko very depressed".
23. Most anti-PKI or anti-Sukarno figures of the time assumed that the PKI would take revenge on their enemies if they got the chance. See Hughes, *The End of Sukarno*, p. 189. Supposed PKI death lists have often been mentioned over the years (including Hughes, p. 190), but no actual list has ever surfaced.
24. Interview, Sudarpo Sastrosatomo, 10 October 2003.
25. Drs Radius Prawiro, interview, 8 August 2002.
26. Interview, Drs Frans Seda, Jakarta, 9 August 2002.
27. The numbers killed in these events remain a contentious matter. A U.S. intelligence estimate of the time was 105,000, but with a high margin of error. See *FRUS 1964–68*, vol. 26, doc 162, Editorial Note, p. 340.
28. CIA Intelligence Report (H.L. Hunter), *Indonesia 1965, the Coup that Backfired*, Washington, 1968, p. 47.
29. Early that morning he and other BPK members had visited the parliament for a session with a parliamentary committee, but found no one in attendance — Radius Prawiro, interview, 8 August 2002.
30. The late Professor Selosumarjan could not confirm the report when I raised it with him — interview, 31 July 2002. Hughes in *The End of Sukarno*, p. 59, is the only other source I have found for this Suharto-Sultan contact on 1 October, adding the intriguing detail that "he [Hamengku Buwono] checked with Madame Dewi Sukarno, who declared that her husband was far from dead". Although Hughes is not always a reliable source, the fact that two sources exist for this story leads me to accept its veracity.
31. Interview with Roeslan Abdulgani, 30 September 2003.
32. Sukarno's family was also evacuated to Bandung. Rachmawati Sukarnoputri, *Bappakku Ibuku* [My Father and Mother], p. 165.
33. Works which deal wholly or partly with the wave of violence from October 1965 to early 1966 include Hughes, *The End of Sukarno*; Robert Cribb, ed., *The Indonesian Killings of 1965–66: Studies from Java and Bali*; Elson, *Suharto*; and the various biographies of Sukarno. See *Asian Survey*, vol. 42, no. 4, July/August 2002, especially Cribb, "Unresolved Problems of the Indonesian Killings in 1965–66". More polemical is Deirdre Griswold, *Indonesia the Bloodbath that Was*. In recent years, much attention has been given to alleged Western, especially United States', complicity in the killings. An article by Kathy Kadane in the *Washington Post*, 21 March 1990, is commonly quoted, particularly claiming that the U.S. Embassy handed over to the army a list of PKI members. See *FRUS 1964–68*, vol. 26, doc 185, Editorial Note, p. 386.
34. Elson, *Suharto*, p. 125.

35. This was apparently timed to mark the funerals of Yogyakarta commander Col Katamso and his deputy Lt Col Sugiyono, killed by 30 September Movement sympathizers in Yogyakarta. The two were buried on 22 October. Statement of 22 October by Hamengku Buwono entitled "Pidato Radio Sultan Hamengku Buwono IX, Kepala Daerah Istimewa Yogyakarta" [Radio Address by Sultan Hamengku Buwono IX, Head of Yogyakarta Special Region], Yogyakarta Special Region Information Service, Yogyakarta, 1 November 1965.
36. Ibid.
37. *Berita Nasional*, 11 November 1965.
38. Ibid.
39. Official records in Yogyakarta claim that local PKI leaders admitted the party's involvement in the 30 September Movement. This claim must be taken with reserve, because of the obvious possibility of duress. Yogyakarta Regional Archives, document no. 115, Yogyakarta Special Region Government, Department of Interior Political Bureau memorandum (signed by Bureau head Resonegoro), 14 April 1966, "G30S Influence on Government in Yogyakarta Special Region", quoting PKI leader Sujiono.
40. The Resonegoro document gives some figures of killings in Yogyakarta and Central Java. It claims few deaths in the Special Region compared with other areas, but the figures it provides are not comprehensive. It says : "Kulon Progo 12; Klaten 59; Solo 114; Boyolali 110; Jatinom/ Manisrenggo 86."
41. "This seemed to herald an army effort to take constructive action towards ameliorating the nation's severe economic problems." CIA memorandum of 5 February 1966, in the L.B.J. (President Johnson) national security files, Asia and Pacific 1963–69, Country File Indonesia, vol. 7, Cornell University, reel 8, p. 4, paragraph 13.
42. See the descriptions of major developments in KOTI in Crouch, op. cit., pp. 47–48 and pp. 54–55.
43. *Kompas*, 15 December 1965.
44. Ibid.
45. Nasution, op. cit., vol. 6 (*Kebangkitan Orde Baru* — The Rise of the New Order), p. 356.
46. NAA A1838, file 3034/2/1/8 pt 6, AE Jakarta memorandum by G. Miller, 26 November 1965.
47. LBJ (President Johnson) national security files (Cornell University), op. cit., reel 8, CIA intelligence memorandum, 5 February 1966, p. 4, paragraph 14.
48. Suwarto would probably have played an influential part in the New Order, if he had not been struck by cancer, dying in 1967. Elson, op. cit., p. 148.
49. Feith papers, Monash University archive, MON 78, 1991/09/079 item 1431, note of 3 February 1967 by Feith of conversation with "SS" (almost certainly Selosumarjan).
50. Interview, Sudarpo Sastrosatomo, 10 October 2003.

51. *Memori Jenderal Yoga* (Memoirs of General Yoga), p. 38. In 1965 and 1966, Hamengku Buwono regularly called on Seda at the latter's office to discuss developments and to concert action. Seda, *Simfoni Tanpa Henti* [The Endless Symphony], p. 218.
52. *Kesatuan Aksi Mahasiswa Indonesia* — Indonesian Students' Action Front.
53. As late as mid-1967, prominent student leaders like David Napitupulu and Cosmas Batubara were commonly seen there. Feith papers, MON 78, 1991/09/079, item 1431, conversation with "SS", 17 July 1967.
54. Isaac Deutscher, *Stalin, A Political Biography*, p. 273. "Neither [Zinoviev nor Kamenev] suspected him of the ambition to become Lenin's sole successor."
55. Panggabean, ibid., p. 356.
56. Interview, Sudarpo Sastrosatomo, 3 October 2003. Unlike the other account, in this version, Hamengku Buwono originally asked Sujatmoko's advice, leading to the meeting described by Informant 7, who was actually present.
57. Interview, informant 7, 2 August 2002. This informant thought the meeting occurred near the end of 1964, but this seems too early.
58. Interview, informant no 7, 2 October 2003.
59. Ibid.
60. Some of these ideas were expressed by Wijoyo as early as 1955, in a debate with Wilopo. Feith and Castles, *Indonesian Political Thinking*, p. 382 et seq.
61. *FRUS 1964–68*, vol. 26, p. 396, US Embassy cable of 2 February 1966.
62. NAA A1838, file 3034/2/1 pt 49, AE Jakarta "savingram" no. 4, 26 January 1966, p. 7.
63. *FRUS*, op. cit., ibid.
64. NAA, ibid.
65. The CIA released a report entitled "Paralysis in Indonesia" in February 1966 — *FRUS*, op. cit., p. 398n.
66. The "The Leader, The Man and the Gun" seminar, reported in *Kompas*, 11 January 1966.
67. *Kompas*, 1 February 1966.
68. *Kompas*, 4 February 1966.
69. *Kedaulatan Rakjat*, 2 January 1953. See Chapter 7.
70. *Persoalan ekonomi begitu berat dan politik telah menjadi Panglima*. [In 1965] "The economic problems were so bad, and politics was in command". Patmono, *Radius Prawiro*, p. 28.
71. Even after the March crisis, Sukarno mocked critics who claimed the economy was verging on collapse. NAA A1838, file 3034/2/1 pt 49, AE cable to Canberra of 14 April 1966.
72. The important Bank Indonesia Annual Report had ceased publication in 1960. The Central Statistics Bureau had ceased publishing its Statistical Pocketbook in 1963. See *Bulletin of Indonesian Economic Studies* (henceforth *BIES*), no. 11, October 1968, p. 108 and p. 111.

73. *Kompas*, 22 February 1966.
74. Elson, op. cit., p. 137.
75. M. Panggabean, *Berjuang dan Mengabdi*, p. 353.
76. Hamengku Buwono's role is mentioned in NAA A1838, file 3034/2/1 pt 49, AE Jakarta (Ambassador Shann) cable of 16 March 1966.
77. How Roeslan managed this remains something of a mystery. See Hastings, *The Road to Lembang*, p. 15.
78. See, for example, Green, *Indonesia Crisis and Transformation 1965–68*, p. 97.
79. *Kompas*, 28 March 1966. Roeslan said that when the proposed presidium list was presented to Sukarno, he rearranged the order of the names, because, he said, the oldest (Leimena) should be at the top. He made the alterations in his own hand, and Roeslan, noting that Sukarno's handwriting was on the document, whispered to Suharto, "Mas Harto, don't lose that list. It shows there's been no coup." Roeslan, interview, 30 September 2003.
80. *Kompas*, editorial, 28 March 1966, p. 3.
81. By the end of 1964, he seemed to have despaired about combating corruption. He told the Australian ambassador, "If I wanted to do that I would have to start with my own court." Feith note on conversation with Shann, 16 December 1964. Feith papers, MON 78, 1991/09/033, item 552.
82. Radius Prawiro, interview, 15 October 2003.
83. When Ho Chi Minh visited Yogyakarta in 1959, Hamengku Buwono and Suharto (as Central Java commander) met Ho at Yogyakarta airport. *KR*, 4 March 1959.
84. The three did not seem to share any leisure pursuits. Unlike Suharto, Hamengku Buwono did not play golf or go fishing. Hamengku Buwono's hobbies were cooking and photography; there is no record of Suharto cooking a meal or using a camera. Moreover, Hamengku Buwono was concerned to maintain a distance from the Suharto family — a hint of social contact between his son (the future Hamengku Buwono X) and the Suhartos led to a swift warning from Hamengku Buwono IX. Informant 5, interview, 22 August 2002.
85. Vatikiotis, *Indonesian Politics under Suharto: The Rise and Fall of the New Order*, p. 17. This reports Hamengku Buwono saying with a laugh "Is he [Suharto] still stealing?"
86. *Kompas*, 5 April 1966, p. 1.
87. Ibid.
88. *Berita Yudha*, 2 April 1966.
89. *Berita Yudha*, 15 April 1966.
90. Radius found a chaotic situation in Bank Indonesia following the Jusuf Muda Dalam era. Interview, Radius Prawiro, 2 August 2002. See *BIES*, no. 5, October 1966, "Survey of Recent Developments", p. 10.

91. Radius Prawiro, *Indonesia's Struggle for Economic Development, Pragmatism in Action*, p. 55 n.
92. Elson, op. cit., p. 134 and p. 145.
93. *Kompas*, 13 April 1966, p. 1.
94. Other accounts give a higher figure — Prawiro, ibid., p. 62, quotes a figure of US$3.133 billion.
95. *Kompas*, loc. cit.
96. Ibid.
97. Ibid., p. 2.
98. Ibid. Again the word "unrealistic".
99. NAA A1838, file 3034/2/1 pt 49, AE (Parsons) cable of 14 April 1966.
100. P.K. Ojong, *Kompasiana*, p. 99, article of 15 April 1966.
101. The Dutch word *zelf-bewust*.
102. The phrase *Economic Leadership* was in English.
103. Harold Crouch, "Patrimonialism and Military Rule in Indonesia", World Politics 31, no. 4 (July 1979): 571–87.
104. Refer to Cornell's *Indonesia* magazine throughout the 1970s and up to the 1990s.
105. The classic account in this vein is Robison, *Indonesia: The Rise of Capital*.
106. H.W. Arndt, "Survey of Recent Developments", *BIES*, no. 7, June 1967, pp. 9–10. Also the references to the Mashuri group's anti-Chinese attitudes, Feith papers, MON 78, 1990/09/079 item 1431, note of conversation with SS, 4 February 1967. Some technocrats were happy to diminish Chinese dominance — see NAA A1838, file 3034/2/1 pt 56, AE cable of 12 April, p. 2, re. Emil Salim's attitudes.
107. Rachmawati, op. cit., p. 199.
108. Interview, Frans Seda, 9 August 2002.
109. *Berita Yudha*, 21 May 1966.
110. *Berita Yudha*, ibid.
111. NAA, A1838, file 3034/2/1/8, pt 14, AE Tokyo report of 31 May 1966, recording a Gaimusho briefing. *Berita Yudha*, 10 May 1966 reports detailed plans for the forthcoming visit.
112. *Berita Yudha*, 26 May 1966.
113. For the Americans, the need not to complicate the army's task by making them look like Western puppets, and hence a hesitation to provide large amounts of aid, were themes in U.S. official thinking in the period. See *FRUS*, op. cit., passim — for example, p. 488, Vice President/Ambassador Green meeting of 17 February 1967.
114. NAA A1838, op. cit., p. 1.
115. Ibid., p. 2.
116. Ibid.

117. Ibid., p. 3.
118. *Kompas*, 31 May 1966. *Berita Yudha*, 30 May 1966.
119. NAA, A1838, file 3034/2/1/8, part 14, AE Manila/Canberra cable of 1 June 1966.
120. *Kompas*, 5 June 1966.
121. *Berita Yudha*, 6 June 1966.
122. *Djawaban Wakil Perdana Menteri Bidang Ekonomi, Keuangan dan Pembangunan Sri Sultan Hamengku Buwono IX* [Responses by Deputy Prime Minister for Economic, Financial and Development Affairs Sri Sultan Hamengku Buwono IX], Department of Information, 28 May 1966. The speech itself is dated 23 May.
123. Ibid., p. 4.
124. Ibid., p. 8 — decree of 20 May 1966.
125. Ibid., pp. 9–22.
126. His emphasis on public works no doubt reflected an interest dating back to the Japanese period.
127. Ibid.

9

HAMENGKU BUWONO IN THE NEW ORDER

After the political/economic statement of April 1966, Hamengku Buwono's standing was as high as it had ever been. His humiliation at the hands of Sukarno in 1952 was a distant memory and the discrediting of Sukarno's economic mismanagement looked like a belated vindication of Sukarno's long-standing critics. Hamengku Buwono occupied important posts in the New Order for the next twelve years, including the vice presidency from 1973 to 1977, but became, surprisingly, less and less prominent and influential. His public statements became fewer, Suharto consulted him less, and he seemed increasingly isolated from the decision-making process. The more senior his position became, the more obscure his role seemed to be. The probable reasons for this are outlined inter alia in this chapter.

The MPRS session in June 1966[1] reconfirmed the March Letter of Instruction (Supersemar), removed Sukarno's title of President for Life, rejected Sukarno's first attempt to explain his role in the 30 September Affair and demanded further information, reconfirmed Suharto's ban on the PKI, and approved the ending of Confrontation against Malaysia.[2]

The results of the session varied for each leading personality. Suharto's influence had clearly increased as Sukarno was cut down to size. Some observers thought, accurately as it turned out, that the popular Nasution had been sidelined, despite his elevation to the constitutionally important MPRS chairmanship. Malik kept in the background, but, having just negotiated the Bangkok agreement, his star remained bright. For Hamengku Buwono, the results were equivocal. Complaints were heard of a lack of dynamism, even accompanied by rumours that he might be removed in the next cabinet reshuffle.[3] The Australian Embassy reported, "The Sultan has fared less well [than Malik]. His personal status is still untouched, but there is obvious ill-ease [sic] at his lack of drive." Such comments were never made public but were beginning to be heard in private.[4]

Meanwhile, his reputation based on his conduct during the Revolution, his general air of being above politics, and his steady and sober image somehow made him almost unassailable in public discourse. The process seems to have been a gradual one, but by the late 1960s it became unimaginable that anyone could say or write in public anything critical of him. This may have been a part of the general tightening of government control and restrictions on freedom of speech as the 1960s became the 1970s, and as the 1966 generation's combination of youthful unrest, artistic license and strident criticism of the Old Order came to be seen as a false dawn, at least in terms of press freedom, freedom of assembly and freedom of expression. This may have been a factor, but the Sultan's invulnerability seems also to have derived from his genuinely high personal reputation, whatever was said in private.

Accounts by his colleagues of Hamengku Buwono's approach and role over the next few years vary somewhat, but they mostly describe him as a democratic chairman of the regular economic ministers' meetings,[5] generally seeking consensus which all could live with. Unlike Suharto, he was not disposed to give orders, but regularly brought discussion to heel with the Dutch interjection "Dus, hoe?" (So, what's our conclusion?)[6] On issues where a decision was needed, wise ministers would try to organize consensus through Hamengku Buwono before the session. Meetings of the full cabinet usually had important ceremonial significance, but decisions nominally taken at such meetings had invariably been agreed beforehand.[7]

One informant describes Hamengku Buwono's approach as deriving from concern with what would now be called good governance. His training in Indology at Leiden aimed at producing efficient middle-level administrators at the regency (*kabupaten*) or provincial level, in such areas as irrigation, roads, public administration, and village management. He thus had training at the microeconomic level but was weak at the macro level. Hence the technocrats filled the gap with their more up-to-date macroeconomic expertise.[8] Other informants, while paying tribute to his role as a public symbol of stable New Order administration, describe Hamengku Buwono as a figurehead[9] who faded steadily into the political background as Suharto gained more power and assurance, and into the economic background as the true leader in the area, Wijoyo, came discreetly to the fore.

All agree that Hamengku Buwono, like Malik and unlike Suharto, did not delve into the detail of economic facts and policies, leaving ministers to get on with their portfolios. Like Malik, he rarely spoke at the formal cabinet meetings.[10] They all refer to his unaffectedness and the ease with which he created an atmosphere of teamwork. He also played a role as a sympathetic confidant for civilian ministers and others facing military interference with their policies,[11] for example when Mohamad Sadli, then Minister for Mines, discovered to his distress that Suharto had decided to allow Ibnu Sutowo, head of Pertamina, to report directly to him, thus bypassing the minister.[12] The Pertamina crisis of 1974 was to show how correct the technocrats had been in advocating more careful supervision of Ibnu Sutowo.

Indeed, civilian cabinet ministers never had total control of their portfolios because of the "shadow government" which came to exist. "Economic generals" like Ibnu Sutowo and Logistics Board (BULOG) head General Achmad Tirtosudiro — and, increasingly, Suharto's own family — often got their own way in any clash of interests with a civilian minister. Many examples of this were to occur throughout the New Order period. Suharto could on occasion support the technocrats or protect them from military criticism,[13] but this was not guaranteed. Wijoyo's role was important, as he was usually called on to try to persuade Suharto in such cases.

On another occasion, Seda, as Minister of Finance, faced a dilemma when the new Acting President demanded his own special fund, apparently with limited accountability. Hamengku Buwono advised Seda to treat the request with great care and avoid giving Suharto any reason for a grudge against him.[14] Thinking at first that he might have to resign over the issue, Seda found that a special fund already existed which could be adapted for the purpose.[15] Hamengku Buwono's judgment that Suharto was a man who bore grudges was borne out repeatedly in future years, indicating that his instinct about people, as shown earlier in his assessment of Sultan Hamid, could be very acute.

At the same time, the government was continuing to seek as much foreign aid as possible. Hamengku Buwono and Malik both wrote to U.S. Secretary of State Rusk in July, urging the resumption of aid programmes and appending a list of urgently needed items to the value of US$495 million.[16] The United States could provide only limited aid at first because the Foreign Assistance Act forbade assistance to countries which expropriated U.S. assets without compensation,[17] although a measure of hesitation also existed for political reasons.[18]

Shortly thereafter, Suharto formed the new Ampera cabinet, where Sukarno's influence had been further weakened.[19] Suharto became chairman of the presidium, while Hamengku Buwono retained much the same responsibilities as before, with the title of First Minister for Economics and Finance. He may have felt some bemusement at the appointment as Information Minister of B.M. Diah, his former trenchant critic in 1952. By this stage, it appears that Suharto consulted others much more rarely than before about senior appointments.[20] An important further stage in the cooperation between the army and the technocrats was the second army seminar in Bandung in August 1966. The technocrats laid out their plans for economy recovery, greatly impressing Suharto. This resulted in due course in further programmes of economic reform.[21]

CONSOLIDATING EXTERNAL ECONOMIC RELATIONS

If Hamengku Buwono was regarded as rather passive, he could not be accused of inaction, as he travelled frequently and delivered regular statements to parliament. In August, he announced Indonesia's decision to join the IMF, adding that he would soon visit Europe and then attend an IMF meeting in the United States.[22] Hamengku Buwono and his party visited Europe in September[23] to seek new aid and to negotiate Indonesia's debts as part of the long and hard road to economic recovery and restoration of Indonesia's creditworthiness. In London, the British promised to play a constructive role in the forthcoming debt conference in Tokyo.[24] In the debt negotiations in The Hague, Frans Seda took the lead negotiating role, under Hamengku Buwono's general direction. The Indonesians knew so little about their own economy that they had to ask the Dutch what the debt level was and were shocked at the response.[25] The debt was two billion Dutch guilders, much higher than expected.[26]

The negotiations went well although hard bargaining was needed. Once the delegation had recovered from the shock of the true extent of the debts, Seda set about negotiating them down. His initial claim was a reduction to only 250 million guilders[27] with a zero interest rate.[28] When the Dutch offered 650 million guilders at 3 per cent over thirty years, Hamengku Buwono instructed Seda to accept.[29] They also reached an arrangement on former Dutch-owned estates.[30] Seda told the media that the mission had also gained increased credits from the Netherlands, to the amount of 66 million guilders, and had reached understandings with the British about future economic relations.[31] The Indonesians had every reason to be pleased with these outcomes and with the Netherlands' cooperative attitude.

Hamengku Buwono explained to Indonesian businessmen in Germany that elections, which were expected within two years, would not affect economic development.[32] Western countries understood Indonesia's severe economic problems, and the government's firm resolve to overcome them. Many countries had demonstrated this confidence by their willingness to extend emergency credits.[33]

Hamengku Buwono visited Tokyo from 19 to 20 September for a "Tokyo Club" meeting on debts, attended by the main Western creditor nations, including the United States and Japan (but not the Soviet Union, which was not invited).[34] The main Indonesian spokesman at the meeting, however, was Hamengku Buwono's former associate in the BPK, Hans Pandelaki, and the Indonesian statement to the meeting was in the name of Suharto as chairman of the presidium. No agreement on a debt moratorium was achieved, although it was recognized that Indonesia had no prospect of servicing the debt. Temporary deferment of payments was agreed, and substantive questions were postponed to a further meeting in Paris in December.[35] Hamengku Buwono subsequently received the Japanese Foreign Minister in late October and discussed preparations for the Paris meeting. They announced hopes for more positive results than had been achieved in Tokyo.[36]

In October he departed on another extensive visit, attending IMF and World Bank meetings in Washington, where Indonesia joined those organizations. He told a business audience in New York that Indonesia no longer regarded foreign capital as the "devil", but rather as a vital factor in rehabilitation and economic development.[37] A new law on foreign investment was being drafted, and the government was working hard to create a climate of trust and confidence in which foreign investment could flourish. Nevertheless, foreign investors should not concentrate solely on profits but should bear in mind the development needs of Indonesia itself.[38]

Hamengku Buwono reported to cabinet[39] that the mission had secured new credit amounting to US$180 million from various countries, while a further US$180 million was under discussion.[40] He then emphasized to parliament the urgency of the 1966 budget bills. The original 1966 budget had been drawn up on unrealistic assumptions, and hence supplementary bills had been devised, involving efforts to decrease spending and increase revenues. These would be followed very quickly by the draft 1967 budget, and hence parliament needed to act speedily to settle the 1966 supplementaries. Mismanagement had contributed to high inflation which the government was attempting to combat. He referred once again to the loss of international confidence in Indonesia, a process which the government was striving to reverse. The need to achieve this goal and the associated need to get the budget in order were intensified by the forthcoming meeting of creditor nations in Paris in November.[41]

PROMOTING THE NEW ECONOMIC POLICIES

A few weeks later Hamengku Buwono thanked parliament for its speedy approval of the government's programme to rejoin the IMF, World Bank and ADB, and of the recently concluded aid agreement with the Netherlands.[42] He emphasized the need to move away from the Old Order's attitude of ignoring economic problems, condoning corruption and believing that inflation was unimportant. The government had to improve the people's purchasing power, eaten away by years of inflation. It was accordingly acting to correct structural problems in the government apparatus, to promote the circulation of agricultural goods in general and export goods in particular, and to reform the management and financial structure of government-owned companies.[43] Pricing policy would change because the experience of past years demonstrated that setting prices for the products of government companies at far too low a level did not benefit the people as intended. The only beneficiaries were middlemen, or those with connections who could obtain the goods at the official price.[44] The government wished to encourage economic activity and not to control and restrict it. Accordingly, a programme of "debureaucratization and decontrol" would be carried out. The government would still attempt to guide and influence the economy in constructive directions, but using more indirect methods than before.[45]

This kind of critique of Old Order policies was becoming common in the press, and the emphasis on rehabilitating government agencies and improving management no doubt owed something to Hamengku Buwono's earlier training at Leiden. But the influence of the New Order economists was very evident, especially in the remarks on the unintended consequences of Sukarno's pricing policies. For years the idea of subsidizing prices for the common people, while superficially attractive, had registered dismal results, but the hamstringing of debate under Guided Democracy had never allowed economists to point this out. The New Order itself never eliminated the subsidies, but in the early years it did allow market forces to operate more freely.

Despite dissatisfaction in some quarters at Hamengku Buwono's performance, in late 1966 well-informed Indonesians were still uncertain about the succession to Sukarno. With Nasution's move to the MPRS, he was no longer regarded as the favourite for the succession. Stories even circulated that Hamengku Buwono might become the next president,[46] but it became clear in the next few months that Suharto would do so.

It is hard to recall now the tentativeness which surrounded perceptions of Suharto's leadership in the early years. His modest origins, his lack of education and narrow perspectives, and his shyness of public scrutiny[47] not only led many to underestimate him, but also fostered doubts about his confidence and capabilities outside of his restricted military environment. He looked like a man who needed all the support he could get from those who disliked Sukarno's rule and desired economic advancement and a more stable life. Accordingly, Hamengku Buwono, Malik, and especially the economic advisers actively encouraged and frequently briefed Suharto on a variety of matters. Hamengku Buwono for one was astonished at Suharto's ignorance of the wider world and of the broader arts of government.[48] An enormous briefing effort was put in train, notably when Suharto first went overseas as full President in March 1968.[49] But during this period Hamengku Buwono and the technocrats were themselves to be astonished at Suharto's grasp of their briefings, his retentive memory, and mastery of detail.[50]

In early 1967, Hamengku Buwono and the economic ministers reached an important new stage with the passing of the Foreign Investment Law, providing tax holidays for new investors, compensation in the event of a takeover, and the right to transfer profits. It permitted foreign investors to bring their own managerial staff, though with provisions for selecting and training suitably qualified Indonesians where possible.[51] The government also continued handing back foreign firms which had been nationalized under Guided Democracy.[52] These measures occurred under Hamengku Buwono's general supervision, but the prime drafter of the Investment Law was said to be Selosumarjan.[53]

One of the first signs of a lack of consultation with key New Order figures was the announcement on 22 February 1967 that Sukarno would relinquish all his powers to Suharto.[54] Neither Hamengku Buwono nor Malik seem to have been aware of this. The lack of consultation gives colour to the U.S. Ambassador's judgement at the time that the "Sultan of Yogyakarta is a nice man, but not too powerful."[55]

SUHARTO AS AN ACTING PRESIDENT

Suharto became Acting President in March 1967 after the MPRS session of that month.[56] The changing relationships within the new regime meant a progressive narrowing of access to Suharto, a growth in the power of his military staff, and the emergence of increased rivalry and tension between the military and civilian wings of government. Tensions within the new regime, not excluding sharp disagreements between Suharto and individual technocrats,[57] had already begun to surface but were always kept within bounds.

Suharto's staff, which seemed to be drawn upon by Hamengku Buwono and Adam Malik as required, was an amalgam of civilians and military men. The formal military structure was the SPRI (*Staf Pribadi Republik Indonesia* — Republic of Indonesia Private Staff), whose access to the Acting President was unquestioned. The head of SPRI was Alamsyah Prawiranegara, the tough Sumatran general who was then much feared but who gradually lost Suharto's confidence over the next few years.[58] The civilians resented Alamsyah's power[59] and his role in channelling funds to the army.

From early 1967, the Sultan and Malik saw Suharto less and less often, commonly only once a week at the Wednesday presidium meetings.[60] The civilians with regular access to the Acting President at this juncture were Mashuri,[61] who was an important link with the students and the CSIS[62] think tank but whose role steadily declined, and — of increasing importance and influence — Professor Wijoyo.[63]

The civilian advisers were divided into two broad groups, the political and the economic. The former were headed by Professor Sarbini, with Ali Murtopo as the contact with Suharto's military staff; the latter were headed by Wijoyo, with Sujono Humardhani in the equivalent role. At one stage, apparently Sarbini was to be designated as Hamengku Buwono's economic adviser, but Wijoyo successfully opposed this.[64] Sarbini's political group was later in effect taken over by Ali Murtopo, and Sarbini became a strong critic of Wijoyo's economic policies.

The fate of the economic group was different. With continued cordial relations with Hamengku Buwono and under Wijoyo's able leadership, they increasingly gained Suharto's confidence, and all eventually became ministers in economic portfolios in successive New Order governments. The technocrats worked well with Sujono Humardhani, whom they liked and even respected because of his unquestioned access to Suharto. His commercial activities[65] made them uneasy and at least one of them considered him corrupt,[66] but the relationship was considerably better than with Alamsyah and Ali Murtopo.

A rare disagreement between Hamengku Buwono and Wijoyo emerged in February 1967, when Hamengku Buwono expressed interest in a proposal for local interests to buy into foreign firms.[67] He was probably motivated by the need for Indonesians to be seen to share in the economic development that was in prospect. However, Wijoyo doubted whether this was practical because of Indonesian lack of capital, although a few local individuals or companies might have the needed capability. Wijoyo seemed to fear the emergence of another knot of privileged and rent-seeking military entrepreneurialism. It is unclear how the debate turned out, although in the longer term the local business sector, as Wijoyo evidently feared, became dominated by politically favoured entrepreneurs.

In the same month, Hamengku Buwono reiterated publicly the need for realism in facing up to Indonesia's economic problems.[68] The Old Order government had received no effective supervision from parliament, and accountability was badly lacking. Moreover, coordination between political and economic policies was deficient, leading to severe distortions. The New Order had achieved reasonable results so far, although there was a long way to go. It had rescheduled the debts, it had made progress in balancing the budget for 1967, and the gap was narrowing between the official and the black market exchange rates.[69] There is no little irony in some of these remarks about the progress of the New Order, which itself came to neglect parliamentary oversight of government policy and which allowed less and less public accountability in any real sense.

In February, the main aid donors met in Amsterdam and established the broad pattern for aid to Indonesia which would be maintained for many years in the future. The United States offered a broad commitment of one-third of the US$200 million required, and after some hesitation, the Japanese matched this. International confidence in the new regime was growing although, given the manifest and widespread economic problems, there was still much uncertainty.

In April, Malik secured an aid agreement with Japan for a new US$60 million credit. Briefing the Australian Ambassador on this,[70] Hamengku Buwono expressed considerable satisfaction at Malik's success. The traditionally difficult first three months of the year (the period of shortage known as the *paceklik* just before the main rice harvest) had safely passed. He predicted more agricultural employment from this time on, and the government — having clamped down on inflation — could stimulate economic activity without much risk, inter alia through allowing the money supply to increase by 25 per cent. The budget was running according to plan, expenditures were at appropriate levels, revenues rather higher than expected, and the government expected export performance to improve soon. The development budget would be focused on agriculture and rehabilitation of the communications infrastructure, still in a very poor state.[71] These remarks reflected a higher level of confidence than had been evident before in government circles. The news of the agreement with Japan, coupled with domestic developments, finally gave grounds to believe that the government was making progress. But the tone of the Sultan's comments also indicated how short-term the government's preoccupations were.[72] All were aware that the recovery remained precarious.

Hamengku Buwono made further criticisms of Old Order attitudes in a message to a naval audience, saying that Indonesia's economic problems had to be the top priority of government and that they could not be solved with empty slogans. The economy had been in such bad shape that the old mental habits could not possibly have rectified it. Only an economic programme based on realistic and rational principles could do the job.[73]

By mid-1967, hopes of further economic improvements were rising, and prospects for the crucial food sector looked quite favourable.[74] The Americans[75] concluded:

> Progress in domestic economic reform has been considerably greater than expected in August last year. An ambitious and reasonable effective stabilisation program was put in effect. The pace of wild inflation has been checked. Prices of major consumer items have levelled off. A stultifying jungle of licenses and controls has been swept away.

Nevertheless, stabilization brought its own problems, and government efforts to ease credit proceeded too slowly to satisfy demand. A commentator reported a chorus of alarm about perceived stagnation and even recession, although noting that it was perhaps a "case of disappointed expectations".[76] Industrial production seemed to have levelled off or even declined, but judgment on the point was difficult because of a lack of reliable statistics.

Hamengku Buwono could soon confirm to parliament that inflation was moderating, registering growth of 5 per cent per month. He added that prices would have risen even further if stabilization measures had not been taken. Compared with 1957, prices in 1967 were 3,600 times higher, but without the government's stabilization measures they would have been 1.5 *million* times higher.[77]

Installing the new Mines Minister[78] he again stressed the importance of foreign investment, adding that the outdated view of foreign investment as economic colonialism showed "inadequate confidence in our ability to preserve our sovereignty", whereas the Foreign Investment Act gave the government "the authority to maintain our independence". *Kompas* commented approvingly that foreign investment was a moral issue. "It is amoral if we let the people suffer longer only because we are unwilling to use foreign capital."[79]

THE TRIUMVIRATE FADES AWAY

An inconspicuous but important development the next week was the formal assumption by Suharto of presidium responsibility,[80] marking the end of the presidium as a political body. In other words, the triumvirate was definitely a thing of the past and the idea of a collective leadership was fading. Hamengku Buwono told parliament that Ministers were merely assistants to the President, adding that they were not a part of the government as in a parliamentary cabinet with a Prime Minister.[81] In making this statement, Hamengku Buwono was implicitly reaffirming his loyalty to the new President.

Informants who were ministers or advisers during this period rejected suggestions that the triumvirate was merely a cover for the assumption of power by a military elite headed by Suharto.[82] They contended that the triumvirate period featured a genuine sharing of power and responsibility between the three central figures, each with his own role. It was not evident in the early stages that Suharto would necessarily become President,

Suharto looked then like a constitutional democrat compared with Sukarno, and the economic problems were so serious that the partnership coped with periodic crises without giving much thought to long-term political succession or structures.

The triumvirate must be regarded as a success in terms of its broad objectives. In the approximately two-year period of its existence, it brought greater political and economic certainty to a chaotic situation, it reopened wider and more cooperative links with the outside world except communist countries, and it started the process of economic recovery.

Hamengku Buwono's role in the following years, however, became more and more enigmatic. His public statements became fewer as more prominent and higher-profile ministers, like Malik, Sumitro, Seda, Wardhana and (to an extent) Wijoyo, took centre stage.[83] He was consulted less as Suharto grew into the presidency, he seemed to be called upon to take fewer decisions, and faded into the shadows.

A few signs exist that he was not quite as inactive as might appear. An anecdote from a well-informed source provides a rare glimpse of him as a practising politician. In parliamentary discussion of the 1967 budget presented by Finance Minister Ali Wardhana, a "New Order radical" MP questioned Hamengku Buwono about military finances. Referring to the standard economists' doctrine that all government finances without exception should be stated in the official budget if the government were to keep proper control of its resources, he asked when military off-budget activities would be consolidated into the budget.[84] The Sultan immediately suspended the hearing, and taking the MP aside insisted that military funding was much too sensitive a matter to discuss in open session. In deference to Hamengku Buwono, the MP was prepared to let the matter rest.[85] Hamengku Buwono was well aware that Suharto was not prepared to interfere with military fundraising. But the failure of the New Order to regularize military finances perpetuated problems which remained unresolved well into the post-Suharto period.

Hamengku Buwono and Adam Malik visited Geneva for an important meeting with foreign investment houses and media leaders,[86] organized by James Linen, president of the Time-Life organization. The audience comprised captains of industry from European and North American countries. Both leaders made brief statements to an appreciative audience about Indonesia's new policies and its more welcoming approach to foreign investment, while Sadli and Salim provided detailed presentations and led the subsequent discussion.[87]

But a severe embarrassment for the New Order was emerging at the time. A renewed bout of inflation began in September, culminating in sharp increases in prices, especially of rice, reaching 39 per cent in the month of January 1967 alone. This setback in the rice economy was attributed to "domestic drought, world-wide shortage [of rice], and insufficient government stocks".[88] This provided an awkward background to Suharto's assumption of full power two months later.

During a series of visits to the regions,[89] Hamengku Buwono endeavoured to explain this development by saying that the reasons were "psychological", connected with baseless rumours about the "supposed failure" of the recent Amsterdam meeting.[90] The government had formed a special committee to tackle the availability and distribution of rice, which would contribute to solving the problem. He seemed to be arguing, not too convincingly in view of the price evidence, that the rice shortage was more appearance than reality, and of course the formation of a committee is a classic bureaucratic manoeuvre to create the appearance of action. In fact, with further shipments of rice and other foods, the problem was brought under control over the next few months. But the problem was a reminder that restoration of economic stability took time, and Wijoyo was to comment later that a fairly small mistake in scheduling food supplies could lead to a food crisis in the cities. An expert observer commented that the episode had "badly shaken public confidence".[91]

SUHARTO BECOMES FULL PRESIDENT

Suharto was sworn in as Indonesia's second president on 27 March 1968, and left for his first official overseas visits, to Japan and Cambodia. Hamengku Buwono was left in charge, but Suharto's caution about allowing anyone else even temporary authority was shown when the Sultan was not formally designated as "Acting President" (*Pejabat Presiden*), the title which Suharto himself had borne for the past year. The press reported[92] that Hamengku Buwono would be named Acting President, but on departure Suharto merely "passed on the carriage of his daily tasks as Head of State while he was abroad",[93] without mention of any formal title. A report on Suharto's return mentioned that the Sultan had been *pemangku jabatan Presiden*, i.e., "temporary holder of the office of President", again with no formal designation.⁹⁴ Despite the good personal relationship between the two men, Suharto would not give even the Sultan too much appearance of power.

In April, as price rises seemed to be moderating, the government took a difficult decision to increase petrol and kerosene prices, provoking a storm of protest. "There were student demonstrations, protest speeches in parliament, almost uniformly hostile press comment, demands for the dismissal of the Minister of Finance Drs Frans Seda, and widespread denunciations of the government's professorial economic advisers."⁹⁵ This was probably the lowest point reached by the technocrats, whose progressive move to high office and influence had seemed irresistible, but whose positions now seemed under threat. But following a mollifying speech to parliament by Hamengku Buwono, the storm passed.⁹⁶

Once again the government faced a querulous parliament, but a statement from Hamengku Buwono helped to persuade them, although it was in fact read for him by the Minister of Communications.⁹⁷ The statement emphasized the budgetary difficulties confronting the government if official prices were not increased.⁹⁸ The government needed to raise more funds for its routine budget from internal sources, and not be totally reliant on foreign funding. A "crippled" economy could only be cured by the application of remedial economic measures. Hamengku Buwono disclosed that the government had wanted to reduce the subsidies from the end of 1967, but "for various reasons" had thought it politic not to do so at the time. On the rice economy more generally, Hamengku Buwono predicted a shortfall of 1.2 million tons in the coming year, to be filled by imports.⁹⁹ It is hard to tell at this distance in time quite why this rather pedestrian speech should have won parliament over, but on this occasion the government again found the Sultan's standing an asset in its relations with the parliament.

The debate about the price increases reflected a recurrent theme in public discussion about economic policy over the entire history of modern Indonesia. Not only did these incidents confirm the difficulty of removing subsidies once they were in place, their innate wastefulness was very hard to drum into public consciousness. Over the years, government efforts to raise prices and eliminate official subsidies have always been tentative and sporadic, even during the height of Suharto's power, because of inevitably adverse public reactions.

The aid donors' meeting in Rotterdam in April 1968 failed to reach agreement on Indonesia's request for $250 million foreign exchange aid plus $75 million project aid. Hamengku Buwono announced after the meeting that the figure offered was only $270 million,[100] still a substantial amount. Indications of government disappointment may have contributed to public feeling in this period that the government was losing direction. Nevertheless, the World Bank intervened with a strong expression of support for Indonesia during a visit by the Bank president Robert McNamara, with promises of new credits.

Ekuin Minister

In June 1968, the Sultan became Coordinating Minister for Ekuin (*Ekonomi, Keuangan dan Industri* — the Economy, Finance and Industry) in the first Development Cabinet.[101] It was a sign of the gradual stabilization of politics after the constant changes of previous years that he was to hold this post with the same designation for the next four years. Several technocrats reached senior positions, including Ali Wardhana as Finance Minister, and, very controversially, the returned exile and former regional rebel Professor Sumitro as Trade Minister. Wijoyo became head of the National Planning Body (Bappenas) with Emil Salim as his deputy. In levels of professional expertise and ability, the Development Cabinet began to resemble the "working cabinet" (*zakenkabinet*) which Sukarno's critics had called for in earlier times.[102]

Suharto told the press, in much the same terms as Hamengku Buwono the previous year, that all ministers were ministers of state and all held the same status as "assistants to the president".[103] The period of office of a minister was not necessarily coterminous with that of the cabinet; the President could make changes to cabinet personnel as necessary. Suharto was not about to allow any minister to rise above his peers; this doctrine implied that Malik and the Sultan had no special standing beyond that conferred by their positions as coordinating ministers, thus emphasising even more clearly that the triumvirate was dead and buried. Suharto's remarks about terms of office reminded ministers that they owed their positions solely to his favour.

By late 1968, improvements in the economy were registering reasonably strongly.[104] Inflation was moderating, the rice price was stable, the highly active Trade Minister was moving to discourage inessential imports, the chronic foreign exchange shortage was allayed by better export performance and the conclusion of a further Japanese aid agreement, new programmes to encourage higher rice production were announced, and great attention was given to increasing fertilizer imports as well as enhancing local production capacity.[105]

Hamengku Buwono was able to draw public attention once again to declining inflation as the year advanced.[106] After the disaster of January 1968, where inflation had reached 39 per cent in one month, the monthly rate had dropped to about 6 per cent thereafter. This was still too high and the government would maintain its tight money policy. The New Order's first five-year plan was currently being formulated.[107] Under the title of *Rencana Pembangunan Lima Tahun* (Five Year Development Plan, or *Repelita*), this actually commenced in mid-1969 and was the first of a series of New Order development plans.

In the next three years, economic progress was strong. Inflation was brought under control, the debt issue moved towards settlement, the budget was regularized, significant aid and investment flows were secured, and a start was made in reducing the excessively large government sector. The government's announced intention of reducing public servants' numbers but paying them better was reminiscent of Hamengku Buwono's plans in 1940 for his own colonial-era public service.[108] By 1969, inflation had been reduced to zero, and focus was turned to means of further stimulating business activity, while the German banker Hermann Abs had been engaged to report on ways of restoring Indonesia's creditworthiness and reschedule the "Sukarno debt",[109] a process which concluded with a decisive conference in Paris in 1970, where debt arrangements were finally settled.[110]

Elections

Hamengku Buwono joined Golkar when it became the government's political vehicle and — along with Adam Malik and other New Order figures — was a candidate in Indonesia's first general elections in sixteen years, held in mid-1971. His decision to join Golkar was a departure for him because he had always been a "non-party" politician, but times had changed and it would have been most unusual for a prominent New Order figure not to join. In noting the Golkar candidacies, *Kompas* noted (with a hint of faint praise),

> The Sultan resembles a "Sphinx"; he is usually quiet but has charisma. As a long-standing national-level leader, he has the affection of the public, but always maintains his integrity.[111]

In Yogyakarta as the country approached the election campaign period, Hamengku Buwono again canvassed the issue of foreign debt, explaining that the government was incurring new debts because the poor state of the economy had forced it to.[112] Unlike its predecessor, the government would use the debt to benefit the Indonesian people. The countries which were supplying the capital were doing so on easy terms because of their confidence in the Suharto government. The government was improving administrative procedures, which had been very disorganized in the past, to the extent that the true dimensions of Indonesia's debt had been unknown. Only at the end of 1970 had the government ascertained the true level of Indonesia's foreign debt, enabling it to make repayments in an orderly fashion. In the meantime the government would utilize the newly available capital to increase production in all fields, especially in export industries.[113]

Hamengku Buwono joined the election campaign and, though overshadowed by the more newsworthy Malik, campaigned intensively for Golkar. At a ceremony to commemorate the restitution of Yogyakarta to the Republic in 1949, he said that no matter which party an elector chose, "we should always remember that we are one nation". It was only through united purpose that the people of Yogyakarta were able to expel the enemy at that time.[114] During a tour of East Java, he counselled against excessive emotionalism and point-scoring among the competing parties in the election.[115] He drew attention to the government's "pragmatic policies" and its attempts to rectify the economy without making inflated promises. Indonesia should elect representatives who could contribute constructively to the realization of the government's policies, which were the only practical way to achieve prosperity.[116]

He was more upbeat in a further stop in Yogyakarta, where he claimed that the government's economic policies were already registering successes and Indonesia had started on the road to wealth and prosperity. In contrast to the previous government, the New Order regime gave the highest priority to economic matters. He reiterated the sorry state in which the economy had been left, and therefore the need for time to overcome the many problems which existed. He had participated actively in the present government because it offered the prospect of lightening the heavy burden now borne by the ordinary Indonesian.[117] In Surabaya, he again belaboured the Old Order, drawing attention to its maladministration and carelessness with government funds, which he had become aware of during his period with the BPK. The Old Order's deficiencies had climaxed in the "betrayal" of the 30 September Movement, possibly the only time after 1966 that he referred to that event. Suharto's leadership was registering substantial progress in improving government administration and achieving economic development.[118]

Golkar won a convincing victory in the elections, which had however been so carefully stage-managed that the true extent of the government's popularity was difficult to discern. Hamengku Buwono was elected head of Golkar's twenty-man steering committee, which consisted of ten senior generals and some prominent civilians, including Malik, Wijoyo, Mashuri, and Radius.[119] The appointment may have been purely symbolic, because there is no further record of Hamengku Buwono's activities in Golkar until the next general elections in 1977.

Hamengku Buwono and the Economy

Hamengku Buwono's term as the minister responsible for the economy came to an end in late 1972, after nearly seven years. Despite the reservations and criticisms voiced in private and outlined above, his performance must be seen as a positive factor. It can be debated whether the credit for the stabilization and improvement in economic circumstances of the period (qualified though it needs to be in various ways) should be attributed primarily to the supreme leader Suharto or to the technocrats, rather than to Hamengku Buwono. Suharto took an increasingly detailed interest in the economy, and his government's economic successes came to be regarded as a kind of performance legitimacy for the entire regime. The technocrats — as noted earlier — were prominent and even essential in the process. Nevertheless, Hamengku Buwono was the minister with primary responsibility for the economy during the first six years of the New Order government, which by many indicators were the most difficult years, and thus deserves his share of the credit. His role seemed to be more of a spokesman, "front man", reassuring symbol and persuader, rather than a policy formulator or administrator.

The period between 1966 and 1972 was marked by an "amazingly rapid recovery".[120] In 1966 and 1967 when the priority was economic stabilization, growth rates were low, but thereafter the average was five per cent or above,[121] and such growth rates were maintained on average throughout the New Order period until the crash of 1998. GNP per capita in rupiah terms increased steadily throughout the entire period.[122] Industrial production, which was at times uneven during the New Order but normally on an upward trend, registered very strong growth in the early years, as industry, freed of regulatory shackles, was able to satisfy years of pent-up demand.[123] Agriculture showed less spectacular growth (and less profound dips), but did rebound strongly after the years of drought in 1968 and 1972.[124] The various measurements of poverty did not show great change in these years, but certainly did not get any worse, and over the period of the New Order as a whole, absolute poverty declined quite substantially.[125] By any standards the overall economic record in these years was remarkable.

THE VICE PRESIDENCY — IN OFFICE BUT NOT IN POWER

Speculation was increasing that Suharto would fill the post of Vice President, vacant since Hatta's resignation in 1956. Frans Seda raised the matter with Suharto some time in 1972,[126] canvassing the names of Adam Malik, Idham Chalid the NU leader, and Hamengku Buwono. In characteristic fashion, Suharto gave no reaction to the first two names, but on mention of the Sultan he questioned whether a combination of two Javanese would be acceptable in the outer islands. Seda, as an East Indonesian (born in Flores), said that indeed he *had* thought this, but the Sultan was different, because although he was a Javanese king, as a "person" he was a "non-Javanese".[127] Suharto agreed that he could tell the Sultan, who he then called on at the Ekuin office. Hamengku Buwono expressed surprise and asked about the conditions of the appointment. Seda said the matter should be discussed direct with Suharto.[128]

In discussion with Suharto, Hamengku Buwono supposedly suggested that he should identify and prepare ideas for the further democratization of Indonesia, Suharto agreed, and on this basis the Sultan accepted the appointment.[129] The story then becomes much less clear, and perhaps only Suharto and Hamengku Buwono knew the full details of the understandings they reached. If indeed, Hamengku Buwono attempted to advance democracy, there is little or no evidence for it,[130] and he would most likely have made little headway, given that Suharto's understanding of the central concepts of democracy was very limited, and the 1950s period of "liberal democracy" was regarded with horror by senior generals like Suharto. Hamengku Buwono's campaigning for Golkar contributed to the

New Order's semblance of electoral democracy, but that is not the same thing as promoting democratic rights in general.[131]

The institution of the Vice Presidency was a mystery to all at this stage, and it was unclear what functions a Vice President would or should have. The only clear guideline was the specification in the 1945 constitution that the Vice President must succeed the President if the latter dies, resigns or is incapacitated.[132] Whatever undertakings Suharto may have given, considerable doubts must have existed whether the vice presidency would have much meaning, bearing in mind that no clear responsibilities were specified in the constitution, and the Vice President controlled no departments of state, nor did he have any formal control over or responsibility for other ministers. But Hamengku Buwono decided to accept the appointment, leading to a frustrating and unproductive five years, during which his well-known patience was tested to the limit. As Vice President, he received very little responsibility and no power. He was restricted to ceremonial functions where he delivered a series of anodyne speeches.[133] This was the period when a foreign ambassador could describe him as a "political nonentity".[134]

It was during the period as Vice President that a major change occurred in Hamengku Buwono's private life. One of his four wives having previously died, he married the wife he loved best, Nurma Musa from Bangka island, commonly known as "bu Norma", who received the title of Princess Nindyokirono. This disrupted Hamengku Buwono's relations with his close associate Selosumarjan and also caused some disturbance in the kraton, apparently based on Norma's status as a commoner and some aspects of her background, including her previous service on Sukarno's staff and her forthright personal style. She certainly presented a great contrast with the modest and inconspicuous kraton wives. From this time on, Hamengku Buwono spent more time at his modest palace in Bogor (Shwarnabumi), rather than elsewhere.

In the 1977 election, Hamengku Buwono again campaigned dutifully for Golkar. In his speeches, which varied little in each place,[135] he recounted that he had joined Golkar before the 1971 election, because first he believed in the "Golkar concept" which had led to very beneficial national development; and second, he trusted the leadership of President Suharto. Golkar had indeed won in 1971, and although some issues and problems still existed, "we must continue to believe in our own capabilities". On a similar occasion in Semarang, he formally handed over to the Central Java

Governor a relief cheque following recent local flooding, while advocating a vote for Golkar because of the economic development the government had brought.[136] Public reaction to him in his home area of Central Java, though orchestrated by local authorities, seemed to have an element of genuine enthusiasm.[137]

In one of his few speeches of any substance, Hamengku Buwono warned against conflicts of interest and corruption in official circles.[138] He pointed to the need to avoid the "commercialization of government offices", both in the implementation of development projects and in revenue-receiving instrumentalities. Clearly basing his concerns on his earlier experience with the BPK, he called for more careful supervision of government financial controls by relevant agencies. He emphasized better priority-setting and more careful management of government property and equipment, drawing attention to the key role of the inspectors-general in the various government agencies. This reflected a long-standing personal preoccupation, but such lofty sentiments were undermined by the lack of serious government action against corruption as the new regime consolidated its power and neutralized its critics.

Most of his public speeches had much less weight than this one. Still widely respected and even revered in some quarters, he acted out an increasingly burdensome symbolic role. He appears to have come to realize that Suharto wanted him purely as window-dressing, to soften the New Order's image and provide some further appearance of a military–civilian partnership in government. He remained perfectly loyal in public, and his dissatisfaction only emerged by implication near the end of his term. During the term as Vice President and especially after, he seemed to fill his time more and more with ancillary activities which he had long been involved in, such as the tourism industry, his quite extensive but not uniformly successful business interests,[139] sporting organizations and the scouting movement.[140]

The Rift with Suharto

As the 1970s advanced, the relationship between Hamengku Buwono and Suharto gradually cooled. The full reasons for this, given the reserved nature of both men, will probably never be known. By all accounts they rarely had face-to-face meetings, usually needing a third person to be present.[141] Reconciliation — if it happened at all — would have to take place through intermediaries, and this never occurred. We do have one story of an effort by Mrs Tien Suharto to restore the relationship. Around 1976 or 1977, she told a cabinet minister of her concerns about the visible distance between her husband and Hamengku Buwono, and asked what could be done.[142] But this appears to have been too late. At that stage apparently, Suharto had not met his Vice President for an incredible nine months, part of the reason being that Hamengku Buwono had been ill.

Some indications of the reasons for the rift can be discerned. The first aspect relates simply to power; Hamengku Buwono may have expected that Suharto would give him a clear role and responsibilities and consult him as in the triumvirate days. His loyalty to Suharto and service to the New Order government had been demonstrated continuously since 1965. The Sultan was no threat to Suharto, having no independent power base beyond the minor one of the Yogyakarta principality. But Suharto was not a man to share power, and he distrusted anyone who gave signs of becoming too powerful or too popular. A host of former allies — Nasution, Sarwo Edhie, Kemal Idris, General Sumitro, Mohamad Yusuf, Benny Murdani — had found this out, or would do so. The only relationship with which he was comfortable as his confidence grew was that of superior to subordinate. He was visibly uneasy in the face of large semi-independent organizations which he could not directly control, he therefore had very equivocal relations with the leaders of such bodies as the NU and Muhammadiyah, and he became highly repressive towards the media.

Although he had been able to work reasonably harmoniously with Suharto since 1965, for his part Hamengku Buwono nevertheless had some doubts about Suharto from the beginning[143] and shared with the technocrats a distaste for the more sinister and politically manipulative style of the political generals such as Ali Murtopo.[144]

To issues of personality was added a series of incidents. On three known occasions, major decisions were taken in which he felt he, as a senior minister or as Vice President, should have been consulted or informed. We have already seen that he and Malik had probably been unaware of the final nudging of Sukarno from the presidency in early 1967. On another occasion, Hamengku Buwono, when Vice President, learnt through the press of a sharp increase in official fuel prices.[145] On another, at a routine meeting, Hamengku Buwono showed Suharto a foreign press report sharply critical of Suharto's family's growing business interests, intending to discuss the government's reaction.[146] Suharto's expression turned sour, he got up and left the room. After several minutes' wait, an adjutant entered and told Hamengku Buwono that the meeting was over. This humiliating incident played a part in convincing Hamengku Buwono that he could no longer have a productive relationship with Suharto.[147]

Former ministers who served in government at the time endeavour to explain away some of these incidents. For example, one said that information about price rises was usually held very closely — often restricted to the President, Finance Minister, and a few key officials — and non-advice to the Vice President would not be too surprising in such a case.[148] Hamengku Buwono may well have suffered from the absence of protocols of automatic consultation, formal or informal, surrounding the vice presidency, bearing in mind that it was — in effect — a new institution.

Another provocation arose from history. Early in his presidency, Suharto had instituted increasingly elaborate commemorations of the Serangan Umum of 1 March 1949. This was accompanied, as noted earlier, by more and more vainglorious claims about his own role. The high points of this effort were the construction on a major crossroads in Yogyakarta of a prominent monument with heroic statues and a series of bas-relief carvings; a pyramidal building called "Yogya Kembali", also in Yogyakarta, containing photographs, relics, and other mementoes; and the production of the feature film *Janur Kuning* ("Yellow Coconut Leaves"), which emerged in 1979, just after Hamengku Buwono's retirement. The effect of all this was virtually to blot out Hamengku Buwono's role, to the extent that, although he was shown as sympathetic to the Republic and to the military, his role in instigating the offensive was ignored. Another effect was the subtle denigration of the role not only of Hamengku Buwono but of all civilians in the independence struggle.[149] Hamengku Buwono said nothing in public about these developments and even gracefully joined in inaugurating the Yogya Kembali monument in 1973; but in private, his irritation was evident to his associates.[150] Annoyance about this among Yogyakarta people was to emerge after Suharto's fall in several publications challenging Suharto's version of events.[151]

A further source of tension was a matter of enormous personal sensitivity to Suharto, his own parentage. Some time in the mid-1970s, Hamengku Buwono confirmed to his associates his belief that Suharto was illegitimate, being the son of a former minor palace official who had divorced Suharto's pregnant mother in order to marry a better-connected woman.[152] But Suharto was certainly not — as one rumour had it — the illegitimate half-brother of Hamengku Buwono himself. Hamengku Buwono must have known how sensitive this information was, but assumed that it would remain within his private circle. Apparently, it did not.[153] Yet the exact effect of the incident on Suharto is debatable, and whatever the offence, it did not prevent him from wanting Hamengku Buwono to take a second term as Vice President.

Few of these issues are the stuff of statesmanship, but personal tensions can arise from objectively minor irritations between political actors and can then have political effects. For instance, the animosity between Sukarno and Syahrir has been partly attributed to the personal domestic tensions which arose between them when incarcerated together by the Dutch on Bangka Island in 1949.[154] What is clear is that by the end of 1977 Hamengku Buwono had had enough.

Meanwhile, Suharto had gone on running the country. The period was marked by such events as the Malari crisis in 1974,[155] the first oil shock of the same year which temporarily benefited Indonesia, the Pertamina crisis of 1975, the invasion and annexation of East Timor in late 1975, and the 1977 elections. A reason for scepticism about both Hamengku Buwono's performance as Vice President and about the vice presidency itself is the lack of evidence for any meaningful role for him in these major events and crises, apart from campaigning for Golkar in the elections.

Suharto took much persuading that Hamengku Buwono would refuse the further term as Vice President that Suharto was willing to offer. He actually had to write three times to Suharto reinforcing the point.[156] Adam Malik was hurriedly drafted as the successor,[157] although both the NU leader Idham Chalid[158] and General Surono[159] had been mentioned as possible candidates.

Most of the technocrats were alarmed at Hamengku Buwono's resignation and several tried to dissuade him. One told him that it was always unwise in politics to resign unless forced to, and that it was necessary to have a civilian in the vice presidency to balance Suharto.[160] Another approached him but, appreciating that the words of a king cannot be taken back, desisted when told that he had already sent his resignation letter.[161] The civilians naturally wanted another civilian in an important post, they were used to Hamengku Buwono and they feared his replacement by a general who would be less sympathetic to their concerns. A civilian vice president would always hold out the possibility that Suharto's eventual successor would not be another general.

After Hamengku Buwono's retirement, an acquaintance challenged him about his relationship with Suharto,[162] arguing that Hamengku Buwono, as an important leader in the Revolution and a cabinet minister long before Suharto came on the scene, should be able to correct Suharto when he did something wrong. Couldn't he talk to Suharto and point out the problems with his rule? Hamengku Buwono, implicitly accepting that criticisms of Suharto were justified, replied that Suharto would say to any critic, "How dare you criticise me? I saved the country in 1965; you wouldn't be here if I hadn't acted then. Without me, the country would fail." So, Hamengku Buwono concluded, Suharto was deaf to counsel.[163]

Hamengku Buwono presented his departure publicly as arising from his state of health, especially his declining eyesight, which was a reason for the brevity of his vice presidential speeches. But he left sufficient ambiguity to allow suspicion that this was not the whole story.[164] The daily *Kompas* stirred the waters by publishing a photograph of Hamengku Buwono driving his own car alongside a report that he had resigned for health reasons.[165]

Hamengku Buwono remained distant from politics after his retirement, but one curious episode was his flirtation with the possibility of joining the LKB (*Lembaga Kesadaran Berkonstitusi* — Institute of Constitutional Awareness), promoted by the distinguished journalist Mochtar Lubis. After initially expressing interest, Hamengku Buwono backed off, on the ground that such an association would amount to open confrontation with Suharto, which — as a Javanese — he was reluctant to engage in so soon after leaving politics. The episode both confirmed Hamengku Buwono's disenchantment with Suharto and also his caution (to the point of timidity) about opposition politics.[166]

Ever since Hamengku Buwono's term of office, and reinforced by the experience of Suharto's later vice presidents, the vice presidency has had a negative reputation. A story in Jakarta in 2004 was that Jusuf Kalla, having just been elected Vice President on Susilo Bambang Yudhoyono's ticket, asked surviving former vice presidents (presumably Sudharmono, Try Sutrisno and perhaps Habibie, and probably not Megawati) about their experiences, receiving very discouraging responses. Kalla was reported in early 2005 as saying that, although he accepted Yudhoyono's primacy, he did not wish to be a do-nothing vice president "like all his predecessors".[167]

SUMMARY

In such an anticlimactic and disappointing manner did Hamengku Buwono's political career come to an end. In assessing the period, we have to bear in mind not only that the role of the non-technocrat civilians was increasingly circumscribed as Suharto settled into power, but also that Suharto needed them less. Even Malik came to be surrounded with staff whose loyalties did not rest with him, and though he remained conspicuous as both Foreign Minister and then Vice President, he was less influential than many senior generals,[168] although his public relations skills made him, at least in some judgements, a more effective Vice President than Hamengku Buwono.[169]

This was Hamengku Buwono's third and final "gallant resignation". Since the resignation was made ostensibly on health grounds, it led to no public rift with Suharto, and the Yogyakarta Special Region remained untouched and Hamengku Buwono remained its head. Despite the lack of colour and profile of his period as Vice President, he retained an undiminished public reputation for integrity and probity, as well as an amazing degree of public respect and affection. The fact that he had never seemed to have any real role or responsibilities as Vice President seemed to make no difference. The enthusiastic public reaction to his carefully focused reminiscing about the past in 1980[170] seemed to confirm the continued public regard for him, at least in Yogyakarta.

We thus confront the central paradox of his later career — what turned the "forceful"[171] Sultan of the Revolution period into the low-profile figurehead of the 1970s? He was perhaps enacting a known and accepted role of some Javanese leaders, being important more for what he was than what he did. A Javanese king exerts power simply by being and not by doing. He might also be seen as the kind of political leader who delegates responsibility to ministers whom he knows to be competent, and then leaves them to their tasks. On the face of it, this apparent change might be an example of an personality altered by circumstances,[172] but there are possible political explanations for the change, as outlined below.

From one perspective, he was behaving prudently by not provoking Suharto in any way. Over the years, a few senior figures succeeded in leaving office despite Suharto's unwillingness to lose them, and the pattern in each case was similar. The person involved would usually have given good service without any major dissension with Suharto, and without having carved out — or tried to carve out — any power base of their own. They would have been reasonably conspicuous in government, but never excessively popular. They would have some plausible excuse for leaving government office. The successful departures from office of Professor Sumitro, Frans Seda and Hamengku Buwono all fitted this pattern.[173]

From a related perspective, Hamengku Buwono's mediocre performance as Vice President concealed one vital factor. By his careful reserve and caution and his public loyalty to Suharto, he had ensured his own political survival as head of the Yogyakarta region, that of his principality and of his dynasty, in the New Order period. Indeed, it may have been this consideration which acted as a brake on any impulse to challenge Suharto.

In February 1988, he proposed to the Pakualam that, because of their age, they both should abdicate and leave their titles to their successors.[174] The Pakualam agreed but asked for time to build a new dwelling on the outskirts of the Pakualaman kraton. Under well-established kraton custom, an abdicated king could not continue to live in the palace. Hamengku Buwono's intention seems to have been to ensure his son's succession as Sultan; but perhaps it was also aimed at strengthening his son's prospects of becoming Governor of the Special Region on the joint departure of Hamengku Buwono IX and the Pakualam. If Suharto had wished to intervene in the matter, he would presumably have found it more difficult to do so while Hamengku Buwono was still alive. Hamengku Buwono's plan miscarried because he died later in 1988, and the twin abdications did not take place. The Pakualam, evidently feeling released from his undertaking by Hamengku Buwono's death, carried on until his own death a decade later.

Hamengku Buwono had thus achieved the amazing feat, against all odds, of fulfilling his first and second duties as a king — not only to preserve his kingdom but also to preserve his dynasty — without doing violence to his allegiance to the Republic. It is unclear whether the actual result, whereby his son succeeded him as Sultan and even ultimately as Governor, was a long-held plan in Hamengku Buwono's mind, or whether it was an outcome achieved through exploiting a late opportunity. What is clear is that Hamengku Buwono had kept his options open, despite the public perception that at heart he was opposed to feudalism and despite the fairly widespread public impression that he would be the last Sultan.[175]

Notes

1. Elson, pp. 142–44.
2. On 11 August 1966, the formal signing of the Bangkok Accord in Jakarta ended Confrontation.
3. NAA A1838, file 304/2/1, AE Jakarta "savingram" (special report) of 7 July 1966, p. 3.
4. The bluntly spoken lawyer and MP, Adnan Buyung Nasution, told an Australian embassy official that Hamengku Buwono was "useless in his present job, but served a purpose as a focal point in Jakarta for Central and Eastern Javanese". NAA A1838, 3034/2/1, pt 49, Barnett record of conversation of 26 June 1966.
5. Interview, Mohamad Sadli, 7 August 2002.
6. Ibid.
7. Ibid.
8. Interview, informant 7, 2 October 2003.
9. Mohamad Sadli, personal communication, 5 December 2004.
10. "The other two [Hamengku Buwono and Malik] don't do much or say much." Feith papers, MON 78, 1991/09/079 item 1431. note of 1 March 1967, source "DJ".
11. Interview, Mohamad Sadli, 30 September 2003.
12. Interview, informant 8, 5 August 2002. Another anecdote related to the disconsolate Sunan of Solo who reported to Hamengku Buwono that Suharto had taken a sacred trident (*trisula*), an important heirloom of the Solo kraton. Hamengku Buwono replied (not very consolingly) that he should not worry, because if Suharto did not deserve the item, he would not be able to keep it. Frans Seda, interview, 9 August 2002.
13. He did defend the technocrats from strong and direct criticism by Ali Murtopo at one stage. Interview, informant 7, 2 October 2003.
14. "Hati2 sama pak Harto. Jangan sampai ada dendam." Interview, Frans Seda, 9 August 2002.
15. Interview, Frans Seda, 9 August 2002. Seda's Director-General of Finance, Maj Gen Piet Haryono, found the solution.
16. L.B.J. (Johnson) national security files (reel 9, no. 11393, p. 233), Cornell University, White House memorandum to W.W. Rostow, 9 July 1966, p. 1.
17. *FRUS*, op. cit., p. 401n, note of meeting between Secretary Rusk and Ambassador Green, 14 February 1966.
18. See earlier note.
19. Elson, p. 144.
20. Frans Seda, interview 9 August 2002, believed that Suharto may have consulted Adam Malik about cabinet appointments at this time, but not Hamengku Buwono.

21. Elson, pp. 149–50.
22. *Kompas*, 27 August 1966.
23. *SH*, 26 August 1966 and 6 September 1966.
24. *Harian Kami*, 13 September 1966.
25. Interview, Frans Seda, 8 August 2002.
26. The Indonesian press was quoting a figure of fl 1.2 million "of which the Dutch were demanding only fl 950 million". *SH*, 6 September 1966.
27. *BIES*, October 1966, p. 3.
28. Interview, Frans Seda, op cit.
29. Ibid.
30. *BIES*, no. 7, June 1967, p. 30.
31. *SH*, 13 September 1966.
32. *SH*, 4 October 1966. Elections in fact only occurred in 1971.
33. Ibid.
34. *BIES*, no. 5, October 1966, H.W. Arndt, "Survey of Recent Developments", p. 1.
35. Ibid.
36. *Kompas*, 27 October 1966.
37. *Kompas*, 6 October 1966. The audience was the Far East American Council of Commerce and Industry.
38. Ibid.
39. Ibid., 17 October 1966. This report contained a photograph of a smiling and confident triumvirate, with Suharto in the centre as Presidium Chairman. By contrast, during this period, *Kompas* regularly printed an unflattering photograph of Sukarno in mid-speech, with mouth open.
40. *Indonesian Observer*, 17 October 1966.
41. Ibid., 25 October 1966.
42. Ibid., 1 November 1966.
43. Ibid.
44. Ibid.
45. Ibid.
46. A1838, file 3034/2/1 pt 53, AE conversation with prominent businessman Julius Tahija, op. cit., 22 October 1966. Tahija added that Hamengku Buwono, "while no economic genius, was well respected".
47. He took much persuading to hold his first press conference in early 1967 — Feith papers, op. cit., MON 78, 1991/09/079 item 1431, "SS" note of 6 April 1967.
48. Interview, informant no. 8, 31 July 2002.
49. Ibid.
50. Interview, Radius Prawiro, 2 August 2002.
51. *BIES*, no. 6, February 1967, H.W. Arndt, "Survey of Recent Developments", pp. 13–14.

52. Ibid.
53. Sullivan, op. cit., p. 333.
54. Feith papers, MON 78, 1991/09/079, note of conversation with "Al F(riendly)" [sic], 21 March 1967. I must admit some speculation here. The note in the Feith papers says that "Malik and the Sultan didn't know of the 20/2 document till it was announced on 22/2", without specifying precisely which document it refers to. But the only (extremely) significant announcement on 22 February was the announcement about Sukarno.
55. *FRUS*, op. cit., p. 484, doc 229, Vice President Humphrey conversation with Green, Washington, 17 February 1967.
56. Elson, pp. 156–58.
57. This largely relates to the forthright Sumatran Emil Salim, who was said to have had three "rows" with Suharto over dealings with "shady" businessmen. Feith papers, op. cit., MON 78, 1991/09/079 item 1431, SS note of 21 October 1967. The note adds "Suharto could not sleep for a week" because of worries about the rice problem.
58. The immediate apparent cause of their cooling relationship was the impression he gave to Suharto, on his first overseas visit as full President in March 1968, that he could expect large amounts of aid from the Japanese, an expectation which was not fulfilled. Elson, op. cit., p. 167.
59. Feith papers, MON 78, 1991/09/079 item 1431, note sourced to "Juwono", 17 May 1967, where Feith describes the civilian attitude as "hatred".
60. Ibid., note sourced to "DJ", 1 March 1967. The triumvirate "used to meet daily, then less frequently, now only once a week at Wednesday presidium meetings".
61. Ibid., note of 7 September 1967 (no source).
62. Center for Strategic and International Studies.
63. Ibid., note of 25 May 1967 (no source).
64. Feith papers, ibid., note of 4 February 1967, sourced to "SS". "Wijoyo very cross when Sarbini picked as Sultan's economic adviser, took attitude 'it's him or me'."
65. See for example Feith papers, MON 78 1991/09 item 1431.
66. Feith papers, op. cit., item 1431, "SS" quoting Emil Salim, 15 December 1967.
67. Ibid., note of 4 February 1967, no source.
68. Interview with O.G. Roeder, *Far Eastern Economic Review*, 9 February 1967, p. 196.
69. Ibid.
70. NAA A1838, file 759/3/4 pt 2 ("barcode 552101"), AE cable (Loveday) of 11 April 1967.
71. NAA, ibid.

72. Finance Minister Seda was said to have "collapsed under the strain" in the first few months of 1967. NAA A1838, file 3034/2/1 pt 56, AE cable of 12 April, conversation with Emil Salim, p. 1.
73. *SH*, 13 April 1967. Again, the word "realistic".
74. *BIES*, no. 7, June 1967, H.W. Arndt, "Survey of Recent Developments", p. 14.
75. *FRUS*, op. cit., p. 516, State Department briefing paper, 4 August 1967, for NSC meeting of 9 August.
76. *BIES*, op. cit., ibid., p. 7.
77. *Kompas*, 11 July 1967.
78. *US Embassy Press Review*, 19 October 1967, p. 5, quoting report in *Djajakarta* daily.
79. Ibid., 25 October 1967, p. 4.
80. *Kompas*, 19 October 1967.
81. *Kompas*, 21 November 1967.
82. For example Radius Prawiro, interview, 15 October 2003.
83. See for example *Kompas* in 1971, where the civilian minister most often mentioned is Malik, followed by Wardhana, Sumitro, and Wijoyo.
84. Interview, informant 16, 8 August 2002. The MP had consulted Hatta and former Finance Minister Syafruddin Prawiranegara on the questions he might ask.
85. Ibid. See Elson, op. cit., p. 151, and passim, on Suharto's sensitivity to the issue of military funding.
86. *Kompas*, 19 October 1967.
87. Interview, Mohamad Sadli, 30 September 2003.
88. *BIES*, no. 10, June 1968, H.W. Arndt, "Survey of Recent Developments", p. 2.
89. *Kompas*, 20 January 1968, reporting a visit to North Sumatra.
90. The results of the Amsterdam meeting were in fact disappointing. "SS" told Feith that the meeting was a "flop", though the level of aid obtained was reasonable; the main stumbling block was strong criticism from donor countries about corruption. Feith papers, MON 78, 1990/09/079 item 1431, note of 10 December 1967.
91. *BIES*, ibid., p. 1.
92. *Kompas*, 27 March 1968.
93. Ibid., 28 March 1968.
94. Ibid., 5 April 1968. NAA A1838, file 3034/2/1 pt 59, AE "savingram" no. 14 of 29 March 1968, p. 2, reports Hamengku Buwono as holding "the executive [sic] of daily affairs of the Presidency".
95. *BIES*, ibid., p. 9. According to this, his speech was delivered on 8 May, but the *Kompas* report on the statement is dated 22 May, as reported below.

96. *BIES*, ibid.
97. NAA A1838, file 3034/2/1, pt 59, AE "savingram" of 17 May 1968, p. 4.
98. *Kompas*, 22 May 1968.
99. Ibid.
100. *BIES*, op. cit., p. 13.
101. *Kompas*, 7 June 1968.
102. Ibid. The *Kompas* report in fact used this term.
103. Ibid.
104. *BIES*, no. 11, October 1968, H.W. Arndt, "Survey of Recent Developments".
105. Ibid., p. 19.
106. *SH*, 2 August 1968. Message to the Development Economy Conference, Jakarta.
107. Ibid.
108. See Chapter 3.
109. See U.S. assessments in National Archives of USA, Kissinger memorandum to President Nixon, "Jakarta Visit: Your Meetings with President Suharto", 18 July 1969, p. 6.
110. Prawiro, op. cit., p. 66.
111. *Kompas*, 16 January 1971.
112. *Merdeka*, 25 May 1971.
113. Ibid.
114. *Suluh Marhaen*, 28 June 1971.
115. *SH*, 24 May 1971.
116. Ibid.
117. *SH*, 26 May 1971.
118. *SH*, 11 June 1971.
119. *Kompas*, 8 October 1971.
120. Hill, *The Indonesian Economy*, p. 3.
121. Ibid., p. 12, figure 2.1.
122. Ibid., p. 13, figure 2.2.
123. Ibid., p. 12, figure 2.1.
124. Ibid.
125. Forty per cent of the population were estimated as living in poverty in 1976; by 1987, this had fallen to 20 per cent. *BIES*, 25/3, December 1989, J.A.C. Mackie and Sjahrir, "Survey of Recent Developments", by p. 5.
126. Interview, Frans Seda, 13 October 2003.
127. See Seda's *Simfoni Tanpa Henti* [The Never-Ending Symphony], p. 218, for a more detailed account of what he said to Suharto, emphasizing Hamengku Buwono's popularity outside Java.
128. Interview, Frans Seda, op. cit.
129. Ibid.

130. There is no evidence whatever in the Hamengku Buwono Vice Presidential Archive in the Arsip Nasional (National Archives) in Jakarta.
131. The only policy-related document in the Vice Presidential Archive (doc no. 626) in Hamengku Buwono's name is an eight-page paper dated April 1973 and headed "Pedoman Pembinaan Kesejahteraan Rakyat" (Guidelines for the Promotion of the People's Welfare). This states that the President had designated the area of people's welfare as a special duty of the Vice President. I have found no other evidence relating to this.
132. Clause 8 of the 1945 Constitution.
133. Department of Information, *Himpunan Pidato Wakil Presiden Hamengku Buwono IX* [Collection of Speeches by Vice President Hamengku Buwono IX], Jakarta, 1979. Copy seen at Leiden University Library. This is apparently unavailable in Australia. No speech in this collection is any longer than four pages, and no announcement of any significance appears in them.
134. Woolcott, *The Hot Seat*, p. 132.
135. *SH*, 29 March 1977.
136. *SH*, 25 March 1977.
137. For example ibid.; and also *SH*, 28 March 1977.
138. *SH*, 21 March 1977.
139. Robison, *The Rise of Capital*, published in 1986, contains still the most detailed description of these interests.
140. See for example, *SH*, 27 February 1973 and 20 July 1977, and *AB*, 16 January 1976 on sports management; *SH*, 12 December 1972; and *SH*, 3 June and 1 July 1974, and *AB*, 2 March 1979, on scouting. Hamengku Buwono was the Indonesian IOC member from 1967 to 1972.
141. Interview, Frans Seda, 9 August 2002.
142. Interview, Frans Seda, 9 August 2002. This role taken by Tien Suharto may be unfamiliar to those more used to stories of her venality and interference in commercial matters. But Elson (op. cit., p. 306), while outlining her money-raising activities, especially through foundations of various kinds, draws attention to her skills as a "networker and strategist".
143. Vatikiotis, *Indonesian Politics under Suharto: The Rise and Fall of the New Order*, p. 17.
144. Interview, Mohamad Sadli, 20 September 2003.
145. Interview, informant 8, 31 July 2002.
146. Ibid.
147. Ibid.
148. Interview, Radius Prawiro, 15 October 2003.
149. For a report of a discussion of this issue, with reference to *Janur Kuning* and two other films on similar themes, see article in *Kompas*, 11 November 1999.
150. Interview, Frans Seda, 9 August 2002.

151. One (fairly poor) example was Tataq Chidmad et al., *Pelurusan Sejarah Serangan Oemoem 1 Maret 1949* [Correcting the History of the General Offensive of 1 March 1949] (Yogyakarta: Media Pressindo, 2001).
152. Suharto's real father is described variously as a palace batik maker, or a kraton official who carried royal parasols in processions, and was said to be a descendant of Hamengku Buwono II. Interviews, informant 10, 24 November 2004; and Frans Seda, 9 August 2002. It is unclear whether the Sultan really had any inside information on this. See Elson for an account of Suharto's birth.
153. Hamengku Buwono's comments had leaked out into public discourse by the early 1990s — see Vatikiotis, *Indonesian Politics under Suharto* (1994), p. 10.
154. Legge, *Sukarno*, p. 236.
155. The only (intriguing) indication of a role for Hamengku Buwono in the affair is provided by Djoeir Moehamad, in *Memoar Seorang Sosialis* [Memoirs of a Socialist], pp. 310–11, who records that the Sultan resisted military attempts to round up former PSI members, including Djoeir himself.
156. Elson, p. 225. Elson's source was unimpeachable, but no informant could tell me where the three letters were, and some who knew Hamengku Buwono well were unaware of the existence of more than one letter. None of the letters can be found in the Hamengku Buwono Vice Presidential Archive at the Arsip Nasional, Jakarta. According to a description of one of Hamengku Buwono's resignation letters, it said (1) he did not want to be Vice President again, (2) he could serve best outside the government, and (3) he could report to Suharto as an ordinary member of society. Informant 8, interview, 31 July 2002.
157. Elson, ibid., pp. 225–26. Also see Feith papers, MON 78, 1990/09/038 item 623, note of 4 March 1978.
158. Elson, ibid.
159. Feith papers, loc. cit., note of 29 December 1977.
160. Interview, informant 7, 2 October 2003.
161. Interview, Frans Seda, 22 October 2003.
162. Interview, informant 16, 8 August 2002.
163. Ibid. When interviewed for the book *Tahta untuk Rakyat*, Hamengku Buwono said that talking to Suharto was like "talking to a brick wall". Informant 19, 2 December 2004.
164. In farewell remarks to cabinet, he said that he wished to provide "greater and more effective service to the nation and people. This I can only do if I am freed from the restrictions surrounding the office of Vice President." *Kedaulatan Rakyat*, 13 March 1978.
165. Interview, Radius Prawiro, 8 August 2002.
166. Jenkins, *Suharto and His Generals*, pp. 103–4.
167. Kalla, press interviews, February 2005. Quoted in G.J. Forrester, *The Private Diary of Geoff Forrester on Indonesia's Turbulent Decade 1996–2005*, p. 176.

168. For example, Malik was publicly known to favour resumption of diplomatic relations with China, but was long prevented from doing this by military resistance — Elson, op. cit., p. 226.
169. Woolcott, loc. cit.
170. *Tempo*, no. 2, June 1980, pp. 6–7.
171. Reid, *Indonesian National Revolution*, p. 65.
172. Inga Clendinnen, "In Search of the Actual Man Underneath", public lecture, ANU, 4 May 2004.
173. Seda told Suharto that ten years as a minister was enough. Interview, Frans Seda, 13 October 2003. Professor Sumitro said that he wished to allow his son to enter business (which, he said, had not been possible for conflict-of-interest reasons while Sumitro was a minister) and to return to university teaching, his original career — *Sumitro Djojohadikusumo, jejak perlawanan Begawan Pejuang* [Sumitro Joyohadikusumo, The Path of the Veteran Activist], p. 203.
174. Interview, informant 5, 22 August 2002.
175. For example, the column by Herry Komar in *Tempo*, 15 October 1988. But earlier when asked directly about the succession, Hamengku Buwono IX had avoided the issue — "I don't know. It depends on decisions made up there" [pointing to heaven]. *Tempo*, 11 December 1971, p. 16.

10

CONCLUSIONS

The issues surrounding the biography genre canvassed in Chapter 1 included the connections between biography on the one hand and power and ideology on the other, and the question of the genre's legitimate boundaries. Problems of biography included claims that it was elitist, that it could obscure the wider picture by focussing on one individual, and that the impression of coherence given by narrative could cloak the true chaos and discontinuities of a subject's life. On Asian subjects (and indeed any subjects from a different culture), the main issues related to the need to bridge cultural gaps and the difficulties in doing so. We also examined the claimed advantages of biography in revealing connections between apparently disparate elements of history and in providing a new and perhaps unique perspective on well-known events. I attempt here to select some of these issues for further discussion in the context of Hamengku Buwono's life.

In the present case, perhaps "the text has constituted the life" and this work has created a power relationship with the subject, his family, or Indonesian historiography as a whole. But as noted previously, if power exists everywhere, this tells us little. Nevertheless, it is advisable to try to meet the assertion that the writing of Asian history by foreigners represents an attempt to exert hegemony in some way, imposing an alien discourse and set of prejudices on an exotic culture. Is the present study part of such an effort? Since this is the first study in English about this historical Indonesian figure, will it hold the field and present to the readers (such readers as it may have) a misleading, patronizing or distorted picture of the subject, uncorrected by more knowledgeable Indonesian (or other) commentators? How does a historian answer such charges?

The first part of a possible answer has to be a careful attention to the facts and sources, and it is here that the opinions of professional historians quoted in Chapter 1 become relevant. Historians are dealing with "something real", with the central distinction "between historical statements based on evidence and those which are not".[1] This account of Hamengku Buwono's life is intended to rest firmly on the available sources, allowing them to lead where they may.[2] The intention may not have been fulfilled, but if the adduced facts and judgments can be shown to be accurately based on the available evidence, this is a partial answer, but only partial, to the criticism outlined above.

Needless to say, a desire for accuracy and careful weighing of sources is insufficient in itself. Also needed, as the literature reminds us, is an awareness of our own prejudices and preconceptions; in attempting to present an account based on the evidence, have the facts been selected or interpreted according to a conscious or unconscious political or discursive bias? A biographer intent on building up Hamengku Buwono as a hero or an unswervingly patriotic Indonesian nationalist might be biased towards finding only evidence confirming these identities; a different slant would be taken by a biographer trying to debunk these propositions; one who disliked Javanese feudalism might stress the injustices and anomalies that can arise from social stratification based on accidents of birth; a foreigner might tend to include (or be biased towards including or even over-emphasizing) more negative and critical aspects of the evidence. In the present case, it will already be clear that the availability of evidence has influenced the presentation in some respects; for example, more evidence of Hamengku Buwono's achievements and activities during the Japanese period would have been welcome but was not available; the absence of intimate detail about his relationship with Suharto in the New Order also affected what could be presented in the relevant chapters. Thus, the sources can impose their own patterns, as they would in any biography. But more to the current point, some obvious biases emerge from this account: a sympathy for the subject, perhaps amounting to the desirable empathy discussed earlier, though trying not to portray him in a heroic vein and not avoiding criticism where it seems warranted; a wish — perhaps not fully realized — to give at least some attention to groups sometimes neglected in accounts of the period; a sceptical attitude towards nationalist accounts of Indonesian history (and towards nationalist accounts of any kind), and a distrust of uncorroborated reminiscences by historical figures well after the events they describe.

Furthermore, we must bear in mind the extent to which language subtly constructs and reconstructs the facts presented, their selection, and the analysis and conclusions reached. Can historians transcend the limitations imposed by their discourse? While it may seem impossible to do so, perhaps a more relevant and practical question is whether this study contributes to knowledge and debate about Hamengku Buwono's period of history, and whether it helps to explain his career in the various contexts in which he operated. Each generation undertakes its own historical reassessments, and as a number of observers[3] have remarked in recent years, this is a suitable time to review Indonesian historiography in general, and what is recorded here, about this significant political figure, may help in this.

Another possible answer to the criticism mentioned earlier is to insist on the universality of history, and to argue that the methods of historical biography (to the extent that they *can* be uniform) would be applied to a biography of any political figure in any country, and are not specific to any particular country. But are these methods, as some in the postcolonial school have argued, merely Western methods and "Western ways of thinking, categorising and evaluating",[4] and not universal at all? However, many of the postcolonial school have recognized that they themselves have become part of the Western Academy, and their thinking has in turn become part of global academic discussion. It is thus at least debatable whether there is anything peculiarly "Western" or "Eastern" about the competing views, approaches and methods on which the debate about life-writing focuses. In the present case, instead of asking "can the subaltern speak?",[5] we are asking "can the Sultan speak?" It is for the reader to judge whether the available sources (including previous accounts of Hamengku Buwono's life) have been constructively used to allow him to "speak" in a reasonably informative and comprehensive manner, while bearing in mind all the caveats noted earlier about the distance between the "textual Sultan" and the real one.

PROBLEMS OF BIOGRAPHY

The drawbacks of biography outlined in Chapter 1 included allegations of elitism. In one sense, biographical writing about a man born to the aristocracy, who rises to be Vice President of Indonesia, is ineluctably elitist. He associated throughout his life with princes, governors and members of the Dutch royal family; with Japanese generals and the Japanese prime minister; and with presidents, cabinet ministers, and ambassadors. Yet if Hamengku Buwono's performance in office influenced, for good or ill, the fate of his people in Yogyakarta and in Indonesia as a whole, an account of his life can tell us something about less-privileged layers of society. I devoted some space therefore to outlining economic developments at various periods in Yogyakarta and Indonesia (quite apart from the evident need to recount Hamengku Buwono's experience as the leading economic minister in the early New Order), including what is known about levels of poverty; as well as referring — to the extent permitted by the sources — to Hamengku Buwono's role vis-à-vis minority groups such as the Chinese, or out-groups such as the PKI and (in the *siap* period in 1945–46) the Dutch and Eurasians.

We must also consider whether a report of Hamengku Buwono's life, by presenting a continuous and linked narrative, distorts the true picture by artificially smoothing out the discontinuities and vicissitudes of his experience. In one way, such a result may be unavoidable, if anything readable is to be written. But the abrupt changes in Indonesian political history, the tumult and instability of the period, and the ups and downs of Hamengku Buwono's own career may guarantee that his life could not seem to be, and could not be presented as, a smooth progression in any particular direction. Similarly, where themes appear in his life, such as the need for political survival, the level (or otherwise) of his attachment to democratic principles or Javanese aristocratic norms, and the way in which he responded to challenges from major political actors, these occurred in such constantly changing circumstances that an appearance of unruffled consistency was impossible. What continuity and consistency there was in Hamengku Buwono's life was hard-won and by no means inevitable.

ADVANTAGES OF BIOGRAPHY — THE CASE OF HAMENGKU BUWONO

Do studies of this type provide a "centrally linking text" as claimed by the proponents of biography?[6] If biographies are "centrally linking texts", they can illuminate continuities between one period and another, perhaps point out elements in common and surprising connections between periods of sharp discontinuity, and provide unexpected information about political and social contexts of the subject's life. Hamengku Buwono's career exhibits an example of unusual continuity, especially in Indonesian circumstances. If a list were made in 1940 of the top twenty Indonesian figures in official positions, followed by a similar list in 1975, the only name in common between the two would be Hamengku Buwono IX.

But perhaps more instructive continuities are available. The most obvious is — as canvassed earlier — the improbable and precarious political survival of hereditary Yogyakartan kingship, although (as also noted before) both Sukarno and Suharto themselves at the height of their powers became Javanese kings in some senses. (As I explore later, some — but by no means all — of their modes of behaviour fitted the profile of Javanese kingship.) These are examples of a further continuity, the widespread persistence in Indonesia of traditional modes of thought and behaviour, but this has been remarked upon often enough to require no further comment.[7]

A perhaps less obvious aspect of continuity is the institutional one. To what extent can the Sultanate of Yogyakarta be regarded as an institution? Indonesia has a very erratic record in creating, preserving and strengthening institutions, and many believe that a crucial deficiency in Suharto's legacy was his near-total failure to build up and empower important institutions of state. No real institutional history of Indonesia has ever been written, no doubt because of the formidable problems of conceptualizing the discontinuities involved. The institutions left behind by the Dutch included notably the *pamong praja*, all the kingdoms and other princely entities, the feeble Volksraad, the KNIL, a body of law and a judiciary, an education system split between official schools and the indigenous system, and news media which was split between the Dutch-language press and the (largely Indonesian-language) vernacular. None of these proved especially robust over the next forty years. The bureaucracy and some elements of the education system and ex-KNIL armed forces survived best, though hardly any institution avoided major traumas and shocks. The Yogyakarta sultanate's bureaucracy was one of the very few institutions in Indonesia, however, where it would have been possible to work from the late 1930s to the 1970s (except for the crisis of 1948–49) in reasonably predictable conditions and under reasonably known rules. Such a judgement must be immediately qualified by trying to imagine what it was like to be in any of the following categories in the Yogyakarta *pamong praja*: anti-Japanese (if such there were) in 1942; Republican in 1949; or PKI or even leftist in 1965.

Nevertheless, the majority of civil servants in the Special Region might well have had a more predictable career in the period than elsewhere in the archipelago, under Hamengku Buwono's general aegis. This is not to say that the Yogyakarta public service was any more admirable or effective than elsewhere (by many judgements it was quite poor), but to the extent that stability and continuity constitute public goods and to the extent that it was possible to provide them in Indonesia's highly fractured modern history, Hamengku Buwono provided them.

In terms of intellectual continuity, Hamengku Buwono's contribution is slighter and harder to discern. He belonged to the now vanished generation of Dutch-trained statesmen and administrators, and became familiar with a series of "Indology" colonial teachings which many Republicans came to regard with suspicion. The virtues of steady administration and rule-based decision-making suffered an eclipse under Guided Democracy, but it is at least arguable that Hamengku Buwono's approach to public office in 1966 reflected elements of his earlier training, overshadowed though it soon was by the more up-to-date neoclassical economics of the technocrats. Of the themes for which he became known in these years, the most salient was the need for "realistic" policy processes, more orderly and predictable bureaucratic decision-making, the abandonment of revolutionary slogans and solidarity-making oratory, the need for leaders to "admit mistakes" (meant for Sukarno, but it may well also have applied to Suharto), and the avoidance of conflict of interest and exploitation of public office.

Image and Language

At the inception of the New Order, Hamengku Buwono was part of a marked change in public discourse, largely led by Suharto, affecting both image and language. In terms of image, the contrast with Sukarno was very pronounced. Among the triumvirate of the early New Order, only Adam Malik had claims to Sukarno-like charisma, and his lively and adroit persona provided a public flair which the other two lacked. Suharto, as noted, was an unknown quantity. He shunned the public eye in the early months and was a plodding public speaker. As for Hamengku Buwono, his grey image reflected the new style of government business — pragmatic, worthy and business like.

Hamengku Buwono's speeches at the time, including the political-economic address, were uninspiring and colourless, but they avoided all the rhetoric of Guided Democracy with which the younger generation was becoming impatient. Words and phrases like "revolution", "Nasakom", *banting stir* (turn the steering wheel, by implication to the left), "New Emerging Forces", and "socialism" were never found in Hamengku Buwono's speeches and were heard less and less as the New Order gained strength. Dull and sober economic terms like "development", "inflation", "rehabilitation", "foreign exchange", "infrastructure", "foreign investment", and "private enterprise" were increasingly heard, reflecting the change in priorities of the new regime. Hamengku Buwono's contribution to this change should not be ignored. Overall (unlike Sukarno) he left few memorable phrases with his countrymen, apart from his statement to the Dutch occupiers in 1949 that he would prefer to die before they entered the kraton. The accompanying remark, "I didn't ask you gentlemen to come", also deserves to be better known.

Asian Biography

As Hill admitted,[8] in writing about Mochtar Lubis, he created a "textual Mochtar" which he contrasted with the unattainable "real Mochtar". In this case, we must contemplate a "real Sultan" and a "textual Sultan". The real Hamengku Buwono in all the complexity of his career, the public and the private aspects of his life, and the twists and turns of his important relationships with figures like Sukarno, Suharto, Nasution and Malik presumably cannot be grasped *in toto*. Witnesses, including Hamengku Buwono himself, are missing, personal memories may be unreliable, archival material may contain misleading evidence or important gaps, and the biographer's judgements may go astray in any number of ways.

But, if the biography theory outlined in Chapter 1 is to be heeded, the "textual Sultan" produced here can usefully clarify and link up aspects of modern Indonesian history, including the role of the Javanese kratons, the ways in which different kinds of Indonesian identity were constructed, the way in which prominent figures like Hamengku Buwono negotiated the Sukarno and Suharto regimes, and even the role in Indonesian politics of competing versions of nationalist history. More broadly, the requirement to set the events of a life in the context of the times and in the context of the subject's major human relationships may give new insights. To give a few examples, Hamengku Buwono's perspective (or more precisely a "Hamengku Buwono-centric" perspective) on his complex relationships with Sukarno and Suharto has not previously been outlined in any detail, to the extent that detail is available; and the account of Hamengku Buwono's role at various times in dealing with the Indonesian military may also be useful. The account of his role in the Revolution as a whole, and not only in the crucial year of 1949, may add to the available body of knowledge about that critical period. I would thus argue for the usefulness in historiography of new and unfamiliar perspectives, as many historians (some influenced by postmodernism) now argue for the validity of much more radically unfamiliar approaches and subject matter.

None of the factors mentioned here seem to vary from the issues and challenges raised by the biography genre in general and do not seem to be specific to biographies of Asian figures. A perhaps more Asia-related issue canvassed in Chapter 1, however, was how the writer may try to mediate the cross-cultural gap. Thus, ideas of Javanese kingship and the influence of traditional patterns of thought on broader Indonesian political behaviour have been referred to from time to time. I have mentioned earlier (and attempt to summarize below) the ways in which Hamengku Buwono conformed with traditional Javanese ideals of kingship. I also drew a contrast between the traditional exemplar and a "modern Western-educated leader"; a conceptual continuum can perhaps be established, in which Indonesian leaders would lie somewhere between the theoretical "extreme traditionalist" and the "extreme modern Western". Hamengku Buwono could be placed reasonably close (but not too much so) to the "Western" end of the continuum. Another issue relates to the ways in which Indonesian approaches to politics in general can be explained, and Hamengku Buwono's various roles can illustrate aspects of these, as outlined below.

HAMENGKU BUWONO — CONCLUSIONS

Hamengku Buwono was a politically astute, non-ideological pragmatist who cleverly used his ascribed status as Sultan not only to support the Republican cause during the Revolution, but also to ensure his own political survival and, ultimately, to preserve his principality. Although not particularly creative politically, he showed a fine political touch at several key moments throughout his career. No doubt can exist about the sincerity of his commitment to Indonesian nationalism from about 1944 onwards, and his comparative silence on the subject before then can be explained (or explained away) by the demands of political circumstances at the time. But he had a subtle understanding of the prevailing power equation at each period, apparently more instinctually than intellectually formulated. In the 1940s he realized, from his observation of the mood of his own people and probably also from his travels around Java in 1945, that the Japanese had successfully galvanized public opinion and that colonialism could never be restored. At the same time, he knew that Japanese power was irresistible for the time being, and that he could best serve his people by remaining on reasonably good terms with the occupiers while quietly attempting to alleviate the worst of the occupation's effects. While his public works programme, especially the Mataram canal, was beneficial in its own right, its supposed subsidiary aim of restricting the numbers of *romusha* taken away from Yogyakarta had questionable success.

His biggest risk and greatest triumph occurred in 1948 when he judged that the Dutch attack could not possibly succeed. The spectacle of a pampered feudal ruler siding with red Republicans was a shock to the Dutch, but they should have examined more closely Hamengku Buwono's statements and actions during 1944–48. Even if individual exercises like the formation of the local militia or the invitation to the Republican government to move to Yogyakarta could be (mis)taken as judicious opportunism, the sum total of his actions before the second Dutch attack left little doubt of his ultimate loyalties. The perceived ambiguity of his responses to Dutch approaches in early 1949 can be attributed largely to Dutch self-serving eagerness to seize on any hopeful signs. Their need to deal through intermediaries no doubt complicated the task, but such misunderstandings may owe something to the well-known propensity even of experienced Westerners to misinterpret polite Javanese nods and half-smiles as agreement with what is being said, rather than as merely an indication that the hearer understands what is being said.[9] The other shock was the adroitness with which Hamengku Buwono exploited his various advantages to resist Dutch inroads after December 1948. As discussed elsewhere, it may be here that we see a minor example of an individual making a difference in history. The Republic would almost certainly have triumphed without him, but his presence eased the task.

Probably Hamengku Buwono's greatest failure was his underestimation of the forces opposing his defence reforms in 1952. He had assembled an impressive team of military leaders and civilians in the Ministry of Defence, but the obvious need to rationalize the armed forces and centralize its leadership seems to have blinded him and his advisers to the potential of the fierce resistance which built up. The involvement of Sukarno in the opposition meant that henceforth the personal relationship between the two men became highly ambiguous, despite the later ostensible reconciliation. The broader implications of the episode included a profound and long-lasting military distrust of civilian interference. Hamengku Buwono himself emerged from this bitter experience with honour intact and with a reputation for sympathy with military problems which no doubt enhanced his acceptability to the military elite — especially Suharto — which came to power in 1966.[10]

In the New Order period, although he may initially have hoped for a collective leadership, he was well aware that military power was growing and he took care never to antagonize the military leaders. His actual political beliefs during the period became increasingly obscure, because many of Suharto's policies and actions seemed to run counter to what Hamengku Buwono originally stood for. In his career he seemed better at resisting doing things which he did not want to do than at carrying through desired programmes or policies against opposition. I have suggested that his relative passivity and caution during the period can best be explained by the need for his own political survival and that of his dynasty, as well as his business interests. It was very much in his interests to remain titular head of the Yogyakarta Special Region and to retain the special status of that region, even after stepping down as Vice President. It was nevertheless a delicate operation to leave office while not offending Suharto by provoking him beyond his willingness to tolerate the continuance of the Yogyakarta political status quo. Critics may allege that he should have shown more resolution or courage during this episode, but there was more at stake than may have appeared on the surface. Elson has indicated that Hamengku Buwono deliberately gave Suharto very late notice of his resignation, to cause the maximum inconvenience,[11] and no doubt too to provide an oblique indication of his displeasure with the lack of role or influence which Suharto had given him.

Hamengku Buwono's departure was by this stage purely symbolic; having little power, his presence merely perpetuated an increasingly misleading public impression that the regime remained an equal partnership of military and civilians. His replacement by Adam Malik continued the symbolism without changing the power equation. After Malik's departure, Suharto paid even less attention to the appearance of a civilian–military partnership, and all his subsequent vice presidents were military men until the appointment of his last deputy, Habibie, in 1998.

Power

In terms of the power typologies mentioned at various times earlier, Hamengku Buwono presents an unusual case, because he seemed to have real power only at certain times of his career. During the Dutch and Japanese periods, his actual day-to-day power in his region seems to have gradually increased, especially after the handover of certain government functions by the Japanese in 1944, if indeed the handover was a genuine one.[12] It was in this period that he best fitted the Weberian concept of traditional power, especially in the experimental reform period of 1946–48 when his word seemed unchallenged within his own region. But his power was very much restricted *to* his own region, and he could only be said to have exemplary influence in wider national circles at the time. In telling the visiting Dutch official Idenburg in 1948 about his role, especially that he was only a Minister of State with limited responsibilities, he seems to have given the unvarnished truth.

In the period as Defence Minister after independence, his power as a minister in a collective government was limited, bureaucratic, and increasingly challenged, but the most useful typology at the time seems to be the dichotomy of Feithian administrator and solidarity-maker, both because of the pragmatic policies Hamengku Buwono attempted to carry out, and because of the company he kept. His antagonists at this period were virtually a roll call of the solidarity makers, as Feith remarked. By contrast, Hamengku Buwono's identity as a traditional leader seems of less relevance in assessing the period, and it seemed almost irrelevant to his unsuccessful attempts to enforce his policies. Although his opponents levelled most of their criticism at Nasution, they seemed to treat Hamengku Buwono essentially as just another politician, whatever his prestige may have been in Java.[13]

In the New Order period, the explanatory power of Feith's dichotomy weakened, partly because a new military elite arose and more so because the solidarity makers virtually disappeared as a meaningful separate category. Hamengku Buwono's power in the early New Order period probably conformed best with the Weberian category of bureaucratic power, with a thin veneer of traditional power. In the later years of the New Order, it is questionable whether he had any real power at all. Certainly, there are very few indications that his word carried much weight when important decisions were taken. The evidence that does exist, as outlined in the previous chapter, indicates that Suharto often failed to consult his Vice President.

One alternative dichotomy in these years was the distinction between the military and the civilian leaders, and a possible role for Hamengku Buwono at the time was as the chief civilian leader. His failure even to attempt to take such a role may qualify perceptions of him as a strong personality, but it may also have derived from a calculation that such an aspiration was risky. The role of Leading Civilian would have invited perceptions of a separate power base and of incipient rivalry with Suharto.

In fact throughout the New Order period, no civilian, except perhaps Malik when Vice President, ever really emerged as the Leading Civilian, and Malik was a loner who built no political coalitions or power base of his own, and could not have been regarded as powerful even at this time. Indeed, except for the very special case of Suharto's own family, few civilians had real power under the New Order, as distinct from influence. Wijoyo was identifiably the leading technocrat for a long period, but he carefully restricted himself to the provision of economic advice, kept his public profile as low as possible, and circumspectly avoided an overtly political role. The successful civilians during the New Order period remained only too aware of the reality of military power. The few civilians who allowed their distaste for Suharto's regime to emerge in public, such as T.D. Hafas, Adnan Buyung Nasution, Yap Thiam Hien, Sri Bintang Pamungkas and civilian members of the main dissident group, the Petition of 50, found themselves harassed, prevented from travel and in some cases jailed. Only near the end of Suharto's rule, when it became possible to imagine that the New Order might not last much longer, did civilian leaders like Megawati, Abdurrahman Wahid and Amien Rais establish anything like a clearly independent or oppositionist position, but this involved a delicate balancing act at times.

IDENTITIES — SULTAN AND JAVANESE LEADER

We have referred from time to time to Hamengku Buwono's role as a Javanese ruler, and the complex of ideas and values surrounding such a role. According to the literature, an ideal king has the mandate of heaven, or *wahyu*, cannot take back his words, commands the seen and unseen worlds, subdues his enemies without fighting, "is honoured by other countries",[14] and is always restrained and courteous. Hamengku Buwono had the divine wahyu through birthright, was notably reticent and courteous in public, never displayed public (and rarely private) anger, measured his words and rarely had to take them back, gained respect from other countries, and dutifully propitiated the unseen world by observing many of the traditional customs of the Yogyakarta royal house. It is arguable that in his dramatic confrontation with General Meyer on 2 March 1949, he defeated his enemy without fighting.

But although he resembles the ideal Javanese king in some respects, individuals only conform to an ideal to the extent permitted by their character and opportunities. The requirement not to take back one's words might have suited someone who was naturally inclined to taciturnity. More aggressive and publicity-conscious Javanese, both rulers and others, could easily call on other models to justify their actions; if models were sought in the *wayang*, men like Sukarno[15] could point to the truculent *ngoko*-speaking wayang character, Bima, while Javanese women had a corresponding model in Arjuna's active and outgoing wife, Sri Kandi.

A further problem is that some other parameters of the ideal ruler are vague or omit a great deal. What happens if the Javanese king cannot subdue his enemy without fighting, and the exemplary grandeur of his kingdom does not lead to automatic submission by rival kings? He will then presumably make war, and the ideal way of gaining foreign allegiance must apparently be abandoned. Such constraints did not perceptibly hold back the aggressively expansionist Sultan Agung, yet he is regarded as the greatest of all Javanese rulers. Moreover, how is the wahyu gained? It is not always gained by birthright, and Javanese history is full of stories of shifting wahyu. The requirement of a king not to take back his words could also lead to widely varying results; in the case of more dogmatic characters than Hamengku Buwono, it might encourage an intractable and obstinate king to pursue harsh or repressive policies in an inflexible manner.

Hamengku Buwono may have represented some of the virtues of the ideal monarch, but in the reforms in the principality during 1945–48, his period as Defence Minister during the early 1950s, and during the New Order period, he behaved much more like a modern Western-educated leader than a traditional Javanese prince. After 1950, he was away from his own Javanese surroundings, he was trying in these cases to establish modernizing reforms against some opposition, especially in

1952, and although his very presence implied an appeal to traditional Javanese authority and behaviour, his statements — perhaps surprisingly — contained no attempts to draw on or exploit atavistic modes of political discourse. They are always sober, factual and lacking in rhetoric. References to the wayang or even to the ancient glories of Majapahit or Mataram are missing, a conspicuous gap in comparison with the speeches and writings of Sukarno or Yamin. Neither did he refer in his public statements to his renowned forebear, Diponegoro, nor to other illustrious ancestors, nor to classical Javanese literature. In this respect, he was less traditional in his thinking than Sukarno. Suharto too on occasion quoted from classical Javanese writings.[16]

Javanese Leaders — Sukarno, Suharto and Hamengku Buwono

Hamengku Buwono and Indonesia's first two presidents were all Javanese, but their personalities and policies were so widely varied as to raise further caveats about any notion of a typical Javanese leader. There were however some features in common. Sukarno was said to be "in many respects a modern version of a Hindu-Javanese ruler",[17] while both he and Suharto surrounded themselves with many trappings of Javanese kingly status and mystical power, to the extent of acquiring magical *pusakas*,[18] consulting *dukuns*[19] and visiting pilgrimage sites. All of these actions are regarded in Java as normal attempts to concentrate power at the centre in the person of the ruler; all forms of power, whether temporal, spiritual or mystical, are essentially the same and the ruler must assemble as much of any kind of power as possible.

Like Javanese princes from time immemorial, both Sukarno and Suharto found it difficult to distinguish between the public and the private sphere, so that associates of various kinds (as well as, in Suharto's case, family members)[20] could enrich themselves at public expense. These two Javanese "princes" had no colonial administrators to advise a strict division between government funds and the civil list, although Suharto had the technocrats to play a similar role. As for Hamengku Buwono, while he tended his own business interests and investments with varying success,[21] he did not seem to indulge in the influence-peddling and rent-seeking for which Suharto (or at least his family) became notorious, although the business success which he did have was undoubtedly aided at least partly by the natural advantages of high office.[22]

Hamengku Buwono was different from the first two presidents in a more obvious way, in that his birth status already imbued him with much of the charisma, *kesaktian* and traditional power of the Javanese ruler. He had no need to gather pusakas because he already had them; he occasionally employed dukuns, but this was not as frequent an activity as it was with Suharto. He believed in *wisik* inspiration, observed all the rituals of the Yogyakarta royal house, and sought mystical sacralization of major events and major decisions, through use of pusakas and holy water.[23] A further difference from both of the first two presidents however was that he seemed to see little need for particular accretions of mystical power beyond his own realm. But in his quiet way, he also resisted attempts to intrude upon his Yogyakarta fiefdom. We have already mentioned his resistance to any idea of a dynastic marriage with the Suharto family, a policy continued with some difficulty by his son,[24] and he reportedly objected to a proposed purchase of land near the Yogyakarta kraton by a Suharto family member.[25]

Nor, unlike Sukarno and Suharto, did he seem enthusiastic about seeking wider temporal power. Early in his career, admittedly, he sought more authority from the Dutch, and gained more responsibility from the Japanese as the occupation proceeded, but neither of these processes looked like a grab for power. Rather, they seemed to be an attempt to secure what was his right and proper inheritance as Sultan. Beyond that, especially during the New Order, he seemed to be that rarest of politicians, one who wanted less power rather than more. His period as Defence Minister in the early 1950s and in the New Order appeared to derive as much from the training of a well-schooled Indology graduate to render good bureaucratic service as they did from Javanese tradition or Indonesian nationalist fervour. Direct statements of Hamengku Buwono's overall ideals and objectives are rare in his career, but a commitment to service can be discerned in both his statement to Governor Adam in 1940 that he was becoming Sultan out of a sense of duty and his promise in April 1966 to work hard to restore the Indonesian economy. In the 1950s and 1960s, Hamengku Buwono knew that Indonesia's tiny educated elite was stretched thin and that the country needed all its available trained administrators. We have already noted the Indology-derived frame of mind, discerned by the technocrats, which he brought to the New Order. Thus, Hamengku Buwono's teachers at Leiden, unacknowledged mentors like Governor Adam, and even adversaries like Idenburg or Stok, may have acquired an unexpected vindication.

When a book was published in 1980 about Sutan Syahrir, it contained a brief but unique contribution from Hamengku Buwono,[26] and his description of Syahrir — virtually the only public comment by Hamengku Buwono on any other Indonesian leader — included some interesting points. Hamengku Buwono pays tribute to Syahrir's patience, calmness in crisis, and intellectual sharpness. His ability as a negotiator and his ability to discern the best strategy for the Republic were conceded by the Dutch and most other foreigners, and he was an effective representative of the Republic in international forums. The Linggajati agreement was, in Syahrir's judgment, the best that Indonesia could achieve at that stage, as a stepping stone to full independence. But, according to the Sultan, many Republican leaders and others could not accept the agreement because it did not deliver "100 percent of the aims of the national revolution", and part of the reason for this problem was Syahrir's remote intellectuality and his difficulties in communicating with the common people. Therefore, although Syahrir attained great acclaim in international circles because of his penetrating, clear and realistic evaluations, his domestic influence was less because the people "could not appreciate as deeply and as clearly as he the problems which he faced". These judgements seemed to reflect common opinions about Syahrir, who was always said to be highly intellectual but lacking the common touch.

Hamengku Buwono evidently believed that he himself did not share the latter deficiency with Syahrir and that his own connection with his people remained strong. He believed that unlike Syahrir he himself was able to communicate clearly and effectively with the people. He had some grounds for this; for whatever reasons, throughout his career he never seemed to lose the innate affection which the common people, especially in Java, seemed to have for him, although he must have seemed fairly distant in the latter stages.[27] His public statements, while dull and uninspiring, were almost always couched in relatively simple terms and were easily comprehensible to the public. It can be claimed that unlike Sukarno or Suharto at the end of their careers, the link with the common people was never quite broken.

Identities — Hamengku Buwono as Politician

An impression of being apolitical, or of standing above politics, is a fine asset for a political actor, and Hamengku Buwono possessed this asset. But he was nevertheless a politician, and his awareness of the political winds was often acute. During the Revolution this extended not only to such well-known decisions as the formation of the Laskar Rakyat and the invitation to the government to move to Yogyakarta, but also issues like the need to avoid seeming too close to unpopular out-groups like the Ambonese while providing (or at least allowing) aid to them, the need for a local civilian intelligence service, the need — when resigning as Defence Minister — to make clear that it was on a point of principle, and the desirability of keeping on good terms with the military, especially in 1965, including averting attempts to examine military funding too closely. In the early 1950s Hamengku Buwono was quick to discern the dangers of the Sukarno–PKI alliance; in the 1960s he somehow[28] managed to become part of the new triumvirate to rule Indonesia. Even after retirement in 1978, his public reminiscing about his negotiations with the Dutch governor, his several interviews about historical matters, especially the General Offensive, and his participation in the festschrift *Tahta untuk Rakyat* may not have been aimed solely at setting the historical record straight; a further objective could well have been to reaffirm his public support, especially in Yogyakarta, and thereby shore up his position vis-à-vis Suharto. These carefully restricted reminiscences may have been an indirect reminder to Suharto that he, Hamengku Buwono, knew a great deal about Suharto himself, including the inception of the New Order.[29]

Identities — Hamengku Buwono as an Indonesian

C.W. Watson has outlined the importance of Indonesian nationalism to the sense of identity of most of the subjects of his book,[30] some of whom were contemporaries of Hamengku Buwono. Anyone born in the Indies between, say, 1884 (the birth year of Haji Agus Salim) and 1924 (the birth year of Suharto) had to confront and negotiate the cognitive challenges posed by the emergence of Indonesian identities, on top of, and in some cases in conflict with, existing ethnic, religious or regional identities.

We earlier raised the question of Indonesian identity as it applied to Hamengku Buwono. While he seemed to have little difficulty in reconciling the various identities he had or acquired and was perhaps an archetypically syncretic Javanese in this, it cannot be assumed that "becoming Indonesian" was an entirely simple process even for him. As we have argued in previous chapters, his identity as an Indonesian may not have been evident to him or others in his early years, and his education provided him very distinctly with all the elements of a Dutch-oriented aristocratic Javanese identity in a colonial context. The possibility of an Indonesian identity for himself and for many others, if felt, had to be repressed even up to the Japanese occupation. His successful assumption of an Indonesian identity in the 1940s widened the still rudimentary concept of what an Indonesian was and perhaps helped the survival of some other elements of traditional nobility, at least in Java. Although the other Javanese kratons did not survive politically, they at least survived physically, and princes like the Sunan and Mangkunegoro were left in possession of their palaces. The Javanese kratons also retained some degree of cultural and social cachet through all the political stresses of these times, and this too may partly derive from Hamengku Buwono's prestige.

In the meantime, the Hamengku Buwono clan retained influence and much public respect, so that Hamengku Buwono himself could be regarded as a natural nominee for the vice presidency, and his son could eventually succeed him as Sultan and Governor of the Special Province. Like most modern Javanese, the kraton family would contend that they had always had both Javanese and Indonesian identities, but, as argued earlier, the Indonesian identity of the Javanese nobility (and not only them) is a relatively recent construct.[31]

WHAT ULTIMATELY DID HAMENGKU BUWONO STAND FOR?

Hamengku Buwono leaves a positive but in some ways ambiguous legacy in political terms. What might be termed the physical legacy — the Yogyakarta principality — remains a principality and a Special Region within the Indonesian Republic, sixty years after the Republic was proclaimed. The survival of the arrangement, long after the abolition of similar entities in other ex-colonies like India, is a remarkable phenomenon, and is a tribute to the continued strength of the kingship myth in Java, as well as to the lingering renown of Hamengku Buwono IX himself.[32] The arrangement has come under challenge in recent years, and proposals for review led to an acrimonious debate in Yogyakarta during 2003–4, which reached no definitive outcome, followed by a further sharp debate in 2010, culminating in the new Law on Specialness (Undang2 Keistimewaan) in late 2012, which for the time being preserved the connection between the kraton and executive power in the Special Region.

In the meantime, Hamengku Buwono's son remained concurrently Sultan and Governor of the Special Region, a result which would no doubt have pleased and even surprised his father. As became evident during the debate on the matter, many of the Yogyakarta people still believed in their region's "specialness" (*keistimewaan*) and — by implication — their own unique status, but it is hard to imagine how the special arrangements for one province can survive indefinitely, in the face of persistent calls for greater democracy and more representative public institutions. Suharto had appointed the Pakualam, long-standing Acting Governor, as full Governor after Hamengku Buwono IX's death in 1988, a development which made clear that the governorship did not automatically devolve on the Hamengku Buwono family. It was only on the death of the Pakualam some years later that public sentiment forced the appointment of Hamengku Buwono X as Governor, and even then it was not a foregone conclusion. The local legacy of Hamengku Buwono IX's long reign can be expected to come under more challenge as time goes by, especially if his successor encounters political difficulties.

On the other hand, as the past sixty years have shown, the conservative loyalty of many Yogyakartans to "their Sultan" is not to be underestimated. This factor may perhaps reveal something about Indonesian identity in what might be regarded as the heartland of Indonesia. Does the persistent strength of feudal loyalty, at least in Yogyakarta, reflect not only the tenacious power of the Javanese kingship myth, but also some weakness in the more recent Indonesian nationalist myth? The Javanese have been familiar with the concept of loyalty to their kings for much longer than the notion of loyalty to a faceless Republic. (Of course the Republic was never faceless, rather Indonesians transferred their reverence for kings from the old royalty of the Javanese kratons to the new leadership represented by Sukarno and then Suharto.) But the automatic answer to this question from Indonesians, once again, would be that many Indonesians retain both their regional ethnicity *and* their identity as Indonesians, even if the exact balance between the two remains in some question. Firm conclusions are not possible here, but we merely pose the question whether Hamengku Buwono's success was partly due to sensitive exploitation of the unacknowledged but potentially important space between the two identities.

The most obvious enduring feature of Hamengku Buwono IX's broader political legacy was his role as a resolute nationalist in the anti-

Dutch struggle, which became the bedrock of his subsequent impeccable reputation. Events since then have challenged the "project of Indonesia" in a variety of ways, because much of the initial gloss has worn away from militant Indonesian nationalism, which has been increasingly troubled by ethnic conflict, Islamic religious radicalism, regional revolt, and the perception that the common people have not benefited as expected from nationalism's promises.[33] Nevertheless, a large majority of Indonesians would still regard Hamengku Buwono as one of the esteemed founders of the modern Indonesian state. After heroes like Sukarno, Hatta, Syahrir, Sudirman, and Tan Malaka, his name would probably be listed in the second rank of the 1945 generation alongside such figures as Haji Agus Salim, Simatupang, Malik, Nasution, Yamin, and so on. He is the only traditional Indonesian ruler to have attained this status, symbolized not only by the survival of the principality but also by such honours as a state funeral in Yogyakarta in 1988, attended by an estimated 200,000 people, and the naming of a major highway in Jakarta after him.

In ideological terms, Hamengku Buwono's legacy, when assessed across his entire career, is harder to define. Apart from his anti-colonial nationalism, he came to prominence originally as a progressive reformer, merging villages into more practical units, insisting that more representative institutions be formed across the province, channelling the energies of youth into his new militia, maintaining productive links with many Republican leaders, and providing land for Indonesia's first indigenously created university. The reforms became a model for other regions, and his first role in national government included providing advice to other regions on how best to manage their affairs.

But in later years, he seemed content to allow Yogyakarta to decline into stagnation, as he moved to Jakarta and left the province to the Pakualam.[34] No informant could name a single progressive reform originating and undertaken in the principality in all the years between 1950, when Hamengku Buwono first left Yogyakarta for national politics, up to the late 1970s when his career ended. The important reforms and changes which occurred under the New Order, including the spread of the Bimas agricultural extension programme, the distribution of new high-yielding rice varieties, the tightening of nationwide administrative controls and the strong increases in kabupaten funding, were entirely exogenous. The Yogyakarta bureaucracy at the time became known as unresponsive and backward-looking, and Yogyakarta remained one of the poorer areas of

Indonesia, rather similar to its status under the Dutch in the 1930s. Yet it could be urged that the Special Region did benefit from the overall economic liberalization and progress of the New Order years for which Hamengku Buwono IX bore much responsibility, and economists have noted that despite continuing serious poverty, marked improvements in several important human welfare indicators occurred in the Yogyakarta region during the 1970s and 1980s.[35]

In economic terms, Hamengku Buwono leaves a less equivocal impression. The Indonesian economy under his general tutelage from 1966 to 1972 registered impressive progress, reinforcing his image as a man for a crisis; stability was restored and inflation curbed, Indonesia's creditworthiness was bolstered, the debt question moved towards settlement, many choking regulations were removed, and Indonesia made large strides towards catching up (at least in economic terms) with the modern world. As Adam Malik moved Indonesia into greater international acceptability, Hamengku Buwono helped to launch the economy on a much stronger growth path, where it was more closely integrated into the world economy, and benefited enormously from inflows of international capital and expertise. Much of the many criticisms which could be made of the style of economic growth of the time, including the shadow economy where vested interests could often win out against good policymaking, involved areas where the civilians had only influence and no power. If a criticism could be made of Hamengku Buwono here, it was that he never seemed an advocate for his technocrats and never seemed to battle within the government for them or for sound economic policy; that role was left to the technocrats themselves, especially the persuasive Wijoyo. But Hamengku Buwono was a quite effective advocate for government policy in the public arena, with foreigners and in parliament.

A remaining issue is his persistent image as a democrat, bearing in mind that descriptions of him almost invariably use that word. As shown in the reforms during the Revolution, his instincts certainly seemed to point towards a desire for greater representativeness, and his reputation for inclusiveness was a factor in the PRRI rebels' naming him, along with Hatta, as a necessary element in a government of reconciliation. His reputation in this regard might be qualified by the 17 October 1952 affair, where he came to be associated with forces pressing for the dismissal of the parliament. Whether or not the appointed parliament of the time was unrepresentative, the fact remained that those forces appeared to be seeking the overthrow of a major representative institution. He may possibly have been directly involved with the efforts to disband parliament, he may alternatively have not been kept informed or perhaps was carried along by his wilder allies, but it is hard to see the episode as confirmation of his democratic credentials.

It was during the New Order that Hamengku Buwono's identity as a democrat came under most question. There seemed at the beginning every reason for him to join the new regime, as it dismantled Guided Democracy, brought a new wave of more representative forces to prominence (with the conspicuous exception of leftist forces), freed up the economy and restored cordial relations with much of the world. A refreshing sense of new possibilities and new departures arose, fuelled by the emergence of a vigorous younger generation, for which Hamengku Buwono's sympathy was evident.

But, as we have seen, the promise of greater pluralism and a more liberal political environment gradually disappeared. As the New Order government gained strength, the obvious falsity of its claims to democratic credentials must have made Hamengku Buwono at least uneasy as he campaigned for Golkar in the 1971 and especially the 1977 elections. Already in 1971, the full power of the government was brought into play on the Golkar side, the political parties were increasingly manipulated and weakened, and the PNI in particular was deprived of much of its civil service base by the new doctrine of "mono-loyalty", under which civil servants had to vote as the government told them. The doctrine of the "floating mass", whereby the ordinary villager was carefully insulated from party politics, seemed a direct contradiction of the objectives of Hamengku Buwono's reforms of the 1940s, which seemed intended to bring government closer to the people. Later, the successive crackdowns on dissidents during such incidents as Malari in 1974, the invasion of East Timor in 1975, and the wave of arrests of student leaders in early 1978 may arguably have been security matters in which civilian ministers were not involved, but as Vice President the Sultan had at least some symbolic responsibility.

It could thus be argued that, in terms of the principles for which Hamengku Buwono supposedly stood, his involvement with the New Order grew into a mistake and contradiction as time wore on. But if we examine the timing of his departure, we can see reasons for his hanging on for as long as he did. By 1973, when he became Vice President, the

New Order had made substantial gains in political stability and economic progress, but the struggle for sustained economic growth and prosperity had only just commenced and was clearly not yet won. Having accepted the vice presidency, he probably felt an obligation to see his term through, even if he disapproved of government behaviour in some cases and disliked Suharto's growing repressiveness and lack of consultation. He would have felt some residual loyalty to Suharto, whose rule had benefited him and his clan[36] in a variety of ways during the New Order, whatever the later tensions. For the reasons advanced earlier, leaving the government was an exercise that had to be managed carefully, and if he left before his five years were up, many more questions would be raised by the media than if he completed the term, and the risk of serious offence to Suharto was all the greater.

Hamengku Buwono retained through his career a less repressive and more moderate image than either Sukarno or Suharto. Up to the present era, he could be, and was, described as the epitome of "political decency".[37] He was the perennial middle-of-the-road alternative, mentioned quite early as a possible president even in the Sukarno period, to the extent that Sukarno became suspicious of him.[38] Under the New Order, Hamengku Buwono became the guarantee that, if Suharto disappeared from the scene for some reason, the country would be in steady and reliable hands. Even if he was regarded as a rather inactive figure, the ability to attract teams of effective officials which he demonstrated through his career provided some assurance that credible and moderate policies would be followed.

Nevertheless, much of the enormous and laudatory press coverage about Hamengku Buwono after his death in 1988[39] could be interpreted not only as praise for the deceased but also as indirect criticism of the living. The strong emphasis on Hamengku Buwono's credentials as a democrat was a reminder that the New Order was not particularly democratic. When the media lauded Hamengku Buwono's decency, humility, and closeness to the people, the reader was subtly invited to contemplate Suharto's increasing repressiveness, arrogance and abuses of power. No praise (or more rarely blame) of any political leader written during the New Order period can be read without considering whether other meanings were intended. This is not to say that the praise of Hamengku Buwono was insincere, but politically inhibited commentators could often insert an additional layer under the surface meaning of their remarks.

Finally, in the long-term historical context of Javanese traditional leadership, Hamengku Buwono IX was certainly the ablest ruler the Javanese royal houses had produced since Hamengku Buwono I (which admittedly is not saying too much). His illustrious ancestor Diponegoro may still be revered as a precursor of Indonesian nationalism, but his revolt was as much against his own family as against the Dutch.[40] By contrast, Hamengku Buwono IX's contribution to his country, while it has its dubious aspects, especially in the vice presidency period under Suharto, looks positive. Partly by steady and at times innovative administration, partly by displays of resolution at key moments, and partly by choosing the right time to give up power and position, he retained an enduringly favourable reputation in the minds of the Indonesian people.

Notes

1. Hobsbawm, *On History*, p. viii.
2. In some cases, the sources led in possibly negative directions. For example, Hamengku Buwono's admirers may not welcome the revelation that the young Dorojatun's favourite teacher became a Nazi fellow traveller, although this — of course — is no reflection on Dorojatun.
3. Reid, in *Sumatra*, p. 226, on the way Islamic movements in the early twentieth century are no longer regarded merely as precursors of Indonesian nationalism, but are valid objects of study in their own right; van Klinken, "The Battle for History after Suharto", *Critical Asian Studies* 33, no. 3 (2001); Curaming, "Towards Reinventing Indonesian Nationalist Historiography", *Kyoto Review*, March 2003.
4. Watson, *Of Self and Nation*, p. 234.
5. Ibid. The original phrase comes from Gayatri Spivak, "Can the Subaltern Speak?", in *Marxism and the Interpretation of Culture*, edited by Nelson and Grossberg. Needless to say, this comparison is rather strained. The subaltern school tries to give a voice to the previously voiceless, whereas in his career, Hamengku Buwono had much greater scope to speak, if and when he had chosen to do so.
6. Alexander, "Biography: A Case for the Defence", in *National Biographies and National Identity, a Critical Approach to Theory and Editorial Practice*, edited by McCalman et al. See Chapter 1.
7. E.g., Legge, "Sukarno: Traditional or Modern Leader?", in *Self and Biography*, edited by Wang Gungwu, pp. 171–84. For a highly negative judgment by an Indonesian of some traditional patterns of behaviour, see Mochtar Lubis, *Manusia Indonesia*.

8. Quoted in Chapter 1 — David Hill, "Objectifying Mochtar Lubis", in *Indonesian Political Biography: In Search of Cross-cultural Understanding*, edited by Angus McIntyre, p. 273.
9. As an example of such an episode involving Suharto and a visiting Australian minister, see Woolcott, *The Hot Seat*, pp. 266–67.
10. The claims made by Parera for Hamengku Buwono as a moderating influence in civilian/military relations seem, however, to be rather overdrawn; certainly they would only apply to a few episodes in his career. Parera, "Ketokohan Sri Sultan Hamengku Buwono IX, Reformator Budaya dan Perintis Orde Baru" [The Leadership of Sri Sultan Hamengku Buwono IX, Cultural Reformer and Forerunner of the New Order], *Prisma* magazine (Jakarta) 20 (1991): 61–62.
11. Elson, *Suharto*, p. 225.
12. This was certainly the belief of Selosumarjan (interview, 31 July 2002). But as noted in Chapter 4, others were more sceptical.
13. Except perhaps for the one curious episode where the opponents changed the wording of the critical motion to avoid direct criticism of Hamengku Buwono himself — see Chapter 7.
14. Feith and Castles, *Indonesian Political Thinking*, p. 181.
15. Legge, ibid., p. 23.
16. Anderson, "Cartoons and Monuments", in his *Language and Power*, p. 184, referring to a Suharto speech quoting from works of Mangkunegoro I. On Suharto and traditional Javanism, see Pemberton, *On the Subject of Java*.
17. Legge, *Sukarno*, p. 10.
18. Suharto was said to have obtained an important pusaka from a temple in Bali — see Feith papers 079 1431, source Tan Soen Houw (10 September 1967), — "before the MPRS session Suharto asked Anak Agung [former Indonesian foreign minister Anak Agung Gede Agung, prince of Gianyar] for a treasured *pusaka* to ensure MPRS went well. AA reluctant, but eventually agreed."
19. For Sukarno's possession of *pusaka*s and use of *dukun*s, see also Legge, ibid., p. 12 and p. 385. Suharto was the fourth-ranked member of a mystical sect headed by a certain Sudiyat, in which Sujono Humardhani was said to be the second-ranked member. See Feith papers, 079 1431, "Top Policy Makers and Suharto Circle", note of 24 January 1967, "Suj[ono] 2 steps higher in *kebatinan* than PH [Pak Harto]." An important threshold question in considering these practices is their actual effect on political behaviour. Did a dukun's advice ever materially alter a major political decision? Hamengku Buwono claimed that *wisik* influenced him, but did it merely reinforce a decision already made?
20. Elson, op. cit., p. 196. Sukarno was not said to be personally acquisitive, and the end of his rule was unaccompanied by revelations of large salted-away fortunes, as has happened in many other similar cases in the Third World; but the trial of Jusuf Muda Dalam in 1966 revealed how economic and financial

Conclusions

privileges accrued to his associates, including his mistresses — Hughes, *The End of Sukarno*, p. 269.
21. His chief business setback was the failure of his bank in 1980 after he left office.
22. One (possible) example of rent-seeking behaviour is however hinted at by Vickers in "Selling the Experience of Bali 1950–71", p. 16, relating to the takeover of Balitour in 1960. <http://pandora.nla.gov.au> (accessed 10 August 2005).
23. His use of holy water when he had decided to accept the vice presidency is attested by a family member, informant 5, interview, 22 August 2002.
24. An application to marry one of Hamengku Buwono X's daughters by Hutomo Mandala Putra ("Tommy") Suharto, later to be jailed for instigating the murder of a judge, was declined in the early 1990s.
25. Informant 8, interview, 5 August 2002.
26. Rosihan Anwar, ed., *Mengenang Sjahrir* [Remembering Syahrir], pp. 6–7.
27. In 1945, he had made extensive tours of the villages of the Yogyakarta region; in the next forty years, he never did this again. But up till the vice-presidency period (where security requirements limited contact with the public), he continued his long-standing habit of driving his own car alone and giving lifts to members of the public.
28. As noted earlier, the absence in the literature of accounts of how the triumvirate was first formed, and on whose initiative, is one of the curiosities of Indonesian history.
29. "I know much". Hamengku Buwono at his seventieth birthday celebration, *Kata Sambutan Sri Sultan Hamengku Buwono IX*, typescript, Jakarta, 12 April 1982, p. 2.
30. *Of Self and Nation*. Watson's subjects included Tan Malaka, the Muslim literary figure Hamka, and the senior colonial official Akhmad Jayadiningrat.
31. Hobsbawm, "Nations are historically novel entities pretending to have existed for a very long time." Ibid., p. 357.
32. Although a curious phenomenon since Suharto's fall has a been a resurgence in the role and profile of a number of previously eclipsed royal and semi-royal families across the archipelago.
33. See the gloomy comments by senior figures like Selosumarjan, Sudarpo, and Julius Tahiya in an article by John McBeth, "Why did we fail?", in *Far Eastern Economic Review*, 1 August 2002, pp. 46–49.
34. Cover page of *Tempo* magazine, 11 December 1971 and accompanying article — "Kenapa Kota Jogja Mati?" [Why is Yogyakarta City Dead?], pp. 13–20. An anonymous source was quoted in the article as saying "Jogjakarta is dead, killed by the Pakualam", ibid., p. 13.
35. Mubyarto, *Sistem dan Moral Ekonomi Indonesia*, pp. 218–19. This included various

public health indicators, especially women's health, and women's educational levels and workforce participation. On poverty levels in general, see *BIES* 25, no. 3 (December 1989), "Survey of Recent Developments", by J.A.C. Mackie and Sjahrir, p. 5.

36. The expanding New Order economy gave many opportunities to business groups, including Hamengku Buwono's own business empire. Some of his family members played out useful careers in that empire, within the kraton in Yogyakarta or elsewhere, in the context of the steady economic progress established under Suharto. On Hamengku Buwono's business interests, see Robison, *Indonesia: The Rise of Capital*.

37. *Jakarta Post* editorial, "On Political Decency", 31 January 2002.

38. As noted in an earlier chapter, Hamengku Buwono had been mentioned as a possible future President as early as 1949 — *Hidup* daily, 29 April 1949, MvD/CAD, bundle AA21, NEFIS 1949.

39. Scores of press articles were collected in such collations as *Sri Sultan, Hari — Hari Hamengku Buwono IX* [Sri Sultan, The Days of Hamengku Buwono IX], by the Tempo editorial team; CSIS editorial team, *Inilah Mati yang Paling Hidup* [The Death that is really Alive]; and Sugiono M.P., *Sang Demokrat Hamengku Buwono IX* [The Democrat Sultan Hamengku Buwono IX].

40. "Nowhere in his 'memoirs' ... does the prince [i.e., Diponegoro] speak of getting rid of the Dutch", Anderson, "Politics of Language and Javanese Culture", in his *Language and Power*, op. cit., p. 200n.

BIBLIOGRAPHY

Notes:
1. Items are listed in alphabetical order of name of author or editor. Many Indonesian/Malay names do not contain a recognizable "surname", so I have adopted the practice of using the first occurring name (e.g., Tataq Chidmat, Ariffin Omar) as the name for alphabetical purposes, unless the name is so well known that this would be obviously wrong (e.g., Mohammad Hatta), or where other guidance (e.g., a Batak marga name such as Mochtar Lubis) is available.
2. Works by government departments with no named author are usually in the order of the first letter of the first word of the name. I have tried to avoid the designation "anonymous" except where no other choice seems available.

Books

Abdulgani–Knapp, Retnowati. *A Fading Dream, The Story of Roeslan Abdulgani and Indonesia*. Singapore: Times Books, 2003.

———. *Soeharto: The Life and Legacy of Indonesia's Second President*. Singapore: Marshall Cavendish, 2007.

Abeyasekere, Susan. *One Hand Clapping: Indonesian Nationalists and the Dutch, 1939–1942*. Clayton, Victoria: Centre of Southeast Asian Studies, 1976.

Abrar Yusra. *Komat — Kamit Selosoemardjan* [The Murmurings of Selosumarjan]. Jakarta: Gramedia, 1995.

Abu Hanifah. *Tales of a Revolution*. Sydney: Angus and Robertson, 1972.

Adam, Lucien. "De Autonomie van het Indonesisch Dorp" [The Autonomy of the Indonesian Village]. PhD thesis, Melchior, Amersfoort, Leiden University, 1924.

———. "Zeden en Gewoonte en het daarmede Samenhangend Adatrecht van het Minahassische Volk" [Customs and Usages and the Associated Adat Law of the Minahasa People]. *Bijdragen tot de Taal- Land- en Volkenkunde*, no. 81 (1925): 424–75.

———. (Written when Governor of Yogyakarta), "In Memoriam Sultan Hamengku Buwono VIII", 4 November 1939, *Koloniaal Tijdschrift*, no. 24 (1940): 1–3.

Aidit, D.N. et al. *PKI, korban perang dingin: sejarah Peristiwa Madiun 1948* [The PKI, Victim of the Cold War: the History of the Madiun Affair 1948]. Jakarta: Era, 2001 (reissue).

Alamsjah, Sutan Rais. *Sepuluh Orang Terbesar Sekarang* [The Ten Greatest Indonesians Today]. Jakarta: Bintang Mas, 1952.

Alexander, Peter F. "Biography: A Case for the Defence". In *National Biographies and National Identity, a Critical Approach to Theory and Editorial Practice*, edited by McCalman et al. (q.v.). Canberra: Humanities Research Centre, Australian National University, 1996, pp. 75–93.

Allen, G.C. and Audrey Donnithorne. *Western Enterprise in Indonesia and Malaya*. London: Allen and Unwin, 1962.

Alvermann, Donna. "Narrative Approaches". *Handbook of Reading Research*, vol. 3, reprinted in Reading Online website — <http://www.readingonline.org/articles/handbook/alvermann> (accessed 22 June 2005).

Andaya, Barbara Watson and Leonard Y. Andaya. *A History of Malaysia*, 2nd ed., Basingstoke, Hampshire: Palgrave, 2001.

Anderson, Benedict A. *Java in a Time of Revolution: Occupation and Resistance, 1944–1946*. Ithaca, NY: Cornell University Press, 1972.

———. *Some Aspects of Indonesian Politics under Japanese Occupation 1944–1945*. Cornell: Cornell Interim Reports Series, Modern Indonesia Project, 1961.

———. *Language and Power*. Ithaca, NY: Cornell University Press, 1990. Includes the essay "Javanese Ideas of Power", first published in 1972.

———. "The Languages of Indonesian Politics". *Indonesia*, no. 1 (1966): 85–119.

Angelino, A.D.A. de Kat. *Colonial Policy*, abridged and translated by G.J. Renier, 2 vols. The Hague: Nijhoff, 1931.

Anonymous. "The Conquest of Java Island, March 1942" <http://www.geocities.com/dutcheastindies/java.html> (accessed 9 June 2004).

Appleby, Joyce O. *Liberalism and Republicanism in the Historical Imagination*. Cambridge, MA: Harvard University Press, 1992.

Ariffin Omar. *Bangsa Melayu, Malay Concepts of Democracy and Community 1945–50*. Kuala Lumpur: Oxford University Press, 1993.

Arniati Prasedyawati Herkusumo. *Chuo Sangi-in, Dewan Pertimbangan Pusat pada Masa Pendudukan Jepang* [The *Chuo Sangi-in*, The Central Advisory Body during the Japanese Occupation]. Jakarta: PT Rosda Jayaputra, 1982.

Arndt, H.W. *A Course through Life*. Canberra: Australian National University, 1985.

———. *The Economic Lessons of the 1930s*. London: Cass, 1943.

———. *Asian Diaries*. Asia Pacific Monograph no. 2. Singapore: Chopmen, 1987.

———. "Survey of Recent Developments". *BIES*, no. 7 (1967): 9–28.

Arsip Daerah Istimewa Yogyakarta [Yogyakarta Special Region Archives], *Daftar Pertelaan Arsip-Arsip Penting* [List of Important Archive Reports], Pemerintah

Propinsi Daerah Istimewa Yogyakarta, Kantor Arsip Daerah (Yogyakarta), 1997.
Asiaweek. Interview with Hamengku Buwono IX, "A Sultan Remembers", 4 May 1986 (vol. 12/18), pp. 58–60.
Atmakusumah, A., ed. *Tahta untuk Rakyat* [A Throne for the People]. Jakarta: Gramedia, 1982. A basic source on Hamengku Buwono IX, with some key documents and interviews.
Aziz, M.A. *Japan's Colonialism and Indonesia*. The Hague: Nijhoff, 1955.
Badan Musyawarah Musea Daerah Istimewa Yogyakarta — BMM DIY [Consultative Body of Yogyakarta Museums], *Sejarah Perjuangan Yogya Benteng Proklamasi* [The History of Yogyakarta as the Bastion of the Proclamation]. BMM DIY, 1984.
Ball, Desmond and Helen Wilson, eds. *Strange Neighbours, the Australia — Indonesia Relationship*. Canberra: Allen and Unwin, 1991.
Beale, Derek. "History and Biography". Inaugural Lecture by the Professor of Modern History, University of Cambridge. Cambridge: Cambridge University Press, 1981.
Benda, Harry Jindrich. *The Crescent and the Rising Sun, Indonesian Islam Under the Japanese Occupation, 1942–45*. The Hague: Van Hoeve, 1958.
Bennett, Bruce et al., eds. *Crossing Cultures, Essays on Literature and Culture of the Asia-Pacific*. London: Skoob Books, "c1996".
Beus, J.G. de. *Het Laatste Jaar van Nederlands — Indie* [The Last Year of the Netherlands Indies]. Rotterdam: Donker, 1977.
Bijl de Vroe, C.L.M. *Rondom de Buitenzorgse Troon, Indisch Dagboek* [Around the Buitenzorg Throne, Indies Diary]. Haarlem: Fibula van Dieshoeck, 1980.
Blumberger, Petrus. *De Nationalistische Beweging in Nederlandsch Indie* [The Nationalist Movement in the Netherlands Indies]. 2nd ed. with Foreword by Harry Poeze. Dordrecht: Foris, 1987. Original published in 1939.
Boomgard, Peter and Ian Brown, eds. *Weathering the Storm, The Economies of Southeast Asia in the 1930s Depression*. Leiden: KITLV Press and Singapore: Institute of Southeast Asian Studies, 2000.
Boomgard, Peter and A.J. Gooszen, eds. *Changing Economy in Indonesia*, vol. 11, *Population Trends 1795–1942*. Nijhoff, The Hague, nd.
Booth, Anne, W.J. O'Malley and Anna Weidemann, eds. *Indonesian Economic History in the Dutch colonial Era*. New Haven, CT: Yale University Southeast Asia Studies, 1990.
Bosdriesz, Jan and Gerard Soeteman. *Ons Indie voor de Indonesiers* [Our Indies for the Indonesians]. The Hague: Moesson, 1985.
Bourchier, David and John Legge, eds. *Democracy in Indonesia, 1950s and 1990s*. Clayton, Victoria: Monash University, 1994.
Bro, Marguerite Harman. *Indonesia: Land of Challenge*. New York: Harper, 1954.
Broome, Richard, ed. *Tracing Past Lives: The Writing of Historical Biography*. Carlton, Victoria: History Institute, 1995.

Brown, Colin. *A Short History of Indonesia: The Unlikely Nation?* Chiang Mai: Silkworm Books, 2003.

———. *Australia and Indonesia, Towards More Stable Relations?* Tokyo: Seikei University CAPS Discussion Paper Series 20, 1989.

Bruggen, M.P. van and R.S. Wassing, eds. *Djokja Solo, Beeld van de Vorstensteden* [Jogja Solo, a Picture of the Princely Cities]. Purmerend, Netherlands: Asia Maior, 1998.

Brugmans, I.J., ed. *Nederlandsch-Indie onder Japanse Bezetting: gegevens en documenten over de jaren 1942–1945* [Netherlands Indies under Japanese Occupation, Information and Documents for the years 1942–45]. Frankfurt: Wever, 1960.

Budiman, Arief, ed. "State and Civil Society in Indonesia". Monash Papers on Southeast Asia, no. 22. Melbourne: Monash University, 1990.

Buss, Claude Albert. *Asia in the Modern World: A History of China, Japan, South and Southeast Asia*. 1964.

Caldwell, Malcolm and Ernst Utrecht. *Indonesia — An Alternative History*. Sydney: Alternative Publishing Cooperative, 1979.

Carr E.H. "What Is History?" 2nd ed. with a new introduction by Richard J. Evans. London: Palgrave, 2001.

Catley, Robert and Vinsensio Dugis. *Australian — Indonesian Relations Since 1945: The Garuda and the Kangaroo*. Ashgate, 1995.

CIA (Central Intelligence Agency). *The Coup That Misfired*. Washington, 1968.

Chamamah Suratno et al., eds. *Kraton Jogja, the History and Cultural Heritage*. Yogyakarta: Yogyakarta Kraton and Indonesian Marketing Association, 2002.

Champion, Rafe. "A Humanistic Response to High Theory in Literature". In *Review of Rethinking Theory*, edited by Miller and Freadman, pp. 173–83, nd. <http://www.the-rathouse.com/RC_FreadmanMiller.html> (accessed 12 July 2005).

Chandler, David. "Writing a Biography of Pol Pot". In *Tracing Past Lives, the Writing of Historical Biography* (q.v.), edited by Broome, pp. 75–94.

Christie, Clive. *A Modern History of Southeast Asia: Decolonisation, Nationalism and Separatism*. London: Tauris Academic Studies, 1996.

Clements, Kevin, ed. *Building an International Community: Case Studies*. Canberra: Allen and Unwin in association with Peace Research Centre, ANU, 1994. Contains a few pages by T.K. Critchley on the UN Good Offices Committee in Indonesia, 1947–49.

Clendinnen, Inga. "In Search of the 'Actual Man Underneath'". Public Lecture on Biography, 4 May 2004, Australian National University.

Collins, Larry and Dominique Lapierre. *Freedom at Midnight, How Britain Gave Away an Empire*. London and New Delhi: Collins, 1987.

Comite voor Tri Windu Mangkunegoro. *Supplement op het Gedenkboek Tri Windu*

Mangkunegoro [Supplement to the Volume Commemorating Mangkunegoro's Three Windus]. Solo: Comite voor Tri Windu Mangkunegoro, 1940.

Conboy, Ken. *INTEL, Inside Indonesia's Intelligence Service*. Jakarta: Equinox, 2004.

Cowan, C.D. and O.W. Wolters, eds. *Southeast Asian History and Historiography: Essays Presented to D.G.E. Hall*. Ithaca, NY: Cornell University Press, 1976.

Cribb, Robert. "Political Dimensions of the Currency Question 1945–47". *Indonesia*, no. 31 (1981): 110–41.

———. "Unresolved Problems in the Indonesian Killings of 1965–1966". *Asian Survey* 42, no. 4 (2002): 550–63.

———, ed. *The Late Colonial State in Indonesia — Political and Economic Foundations of the Netherlands Indies 1880–1942*. Leiden: KITLV Press, 1994.

———, ed. "The Indonesian Killings of 1965–1966, Studies From Java and Bali". Monash Papers on Southeast Asia no. 21. Clayton, Victoria: Centre of Southeast Asian Studies, Monash University, 1990.

Cribb, Robert and Colin Brown. *Modern Indonesia: A History Since 1945*. London: Longman, 1995.

Crouch, Harold. *The Army and Politics in Indonesia*, rev. ed. Ithaca, NY: Cornell University Press, 1988.

———. "Patrimonialism and Military Rule in Indonesia". *World Politics* 31, no. 4 (1979): 571–87.

CSIS Editorial Team. *Inilah Mati yang Paling Hidup* [The Death that is Most Alive]. Jakarta: CSIS, 1988. Collection of Press Clippings About Hamengku Buwono IX.

Curaming, Rommel. "Towards Reinventing Indonesian Nationalist Historiography". *Kyoto Review*, March 2003 <http://kyotoreview.cseas.kyoto-u.ac.jp/issue> (accessed 15 June 2005).

Dahm, Bernard. *Sukarno and the Struggle for Indonesian Independence*, translated by Mary Somers Heidhues. Ithaca, NY and London: Cornell University Press, 1969.

Darmosugito. *Kota Jogjakarta 200 Tahun* [City of Yogyakarta 200 Years]. np: Yogyakarta, 1956.

Delden M. van. "Orde in de Chaos? De internering in en evacuatie uit de Republikeinse kampen" [Order in Chaos? The Internment in and Evacuation from the Republican Camps]. In *Het Einde van Indie*, edited by Wim Willems and Jaap de Moor, pp. 188–207.

Denoon, Donald and Philippa Mein-Smith, with Marivic Wyndham. *A History of Australia, New Zealand and the Pacific*. Oxford: Blackwell, 2000.

Departemen Sosial. *Riwayat Hidup Singkat dan Perjuangan Sri Sultan Hamengku Buwono IX* [A Brief Account of the Life and Struggle of Sri Sultan Hamengku Buwono IX]. Jakarta: Departemen Sosial, 1990.

Departemen Pendidikan dan Kebudayaan [Department of Education and Culture].

Biografi Pahlawan Nasional Sri Sultan Hamengku Buwono IX [Biography of National Hero Sri Sultan Hamengku Buwono IX]. Jakarta, 1989.

Deutscher, Isaac. *Stalin, a Political Biography*, 2nd ed. London: Oxford University Press, 1967.

Dewan Perwakilan Rakjat Republik Indonesia (Indonesian Parliament). *Risalah Perundingan 1952* [Records of Proceedings 1952]. Vols. 1–10. Jakarta: Pertjetakan Negara, 1952.

Di, Feng and Dang Fang Shao. "Life Writing in China (1949–93)". *Biography* 17, no. 1 (1994): 42–52.

Diamond, Jared. *Guns, Germs and Steel: The Fates of Human Societies*. New York: Norton, 1997.

Dijk, Kees van. "The Threefold Suppression of the Javanese". In *The Late Colonial State in Indonesia* (q.v.), edited by Robert Cribb, pp. 270–85.

Dirks, N.B. "Castes of Mind". *Representations*, no. 37 (1992): 56–78.

Djajadiningrat-Nieuwenhuis, Madelon. "Noto Soeroto — His Ideas and the late Colonial Intellectual Climate". *Indonesia*, no. 5 (1993): 41–72.

Djelantik, A.A.M. *The Birthmark: Memoirs of a Balinese Prince*. Hong Kong: Periplus Editions, 1997.

Djoeir Moehamad. *Memoar Seorang Sosialis* [Memoirs of a Socialist]. Jakarta: Yayasan Obor Indonesia, 1997.

Doel, H.W. van den. *Afscheid van Indie* [Farewell to the Indies]. Amsterdam: Prometheus, 2001.

Dorling, Philip and David Lee, eds. Three volumes on *Australia and Indonesia's Independence 1945–50*. Canberra: DFAT, 1998, forming vols. 11 (*Diplomasi — Documents 1947*), 13 (*The Renville Agreement*) and 15 (*The Transfer of Sovereignty*) *of Documents on Australian Foreign Policy, 1937–49*. Australian Govt. Pub. Service, Canberra, 1994–98.

Drake, Christine. *National Integration in Indonesia*. Honolulu: University of Hawai'i Press, 1989.

Driessen, Desiree and Rolf Koster. *De Westerling-Affaire* [The Westerling Affair]. Amsterdam: University of Amsterdam, 1998.

Drooglever P.J., ed. *Indisch Intermezzo, Geschiedenis van de Nederlanders in Indonesie* [Indies Intermezzo, History of the Dutch in Indonesia]. Amsterdam: De Bataafsche Leeuw, 1991.

———. *De Vaderlandse Club, Totoks en de Indische Politiek* [The Fatherland Club, Dutch Colonials and Indies Politics]. Franeker: Wever, 1980.

———. "Sultan in Oorlogstijd" (Sultan in Wartime, Sultan Hamengku Buwono IX and the Occupation of Yogyakarta 1948/49), Public Lecture, Catholic University of Nijmegen, 15 May 1996.

Echols, John and Hasan Shadily. *Kamus Indonesia Inggeris*. 3rd ed. Jakarta: Gramedia, 1992.

Edy Budijono. "Romusha: Korban Politik dan Pemerasan Tentara Pendudukan Jepang di Yogyakarta Tahun 1943–45" [Romusha, Political Victims and the

Exploitation by the Japanese Occupation Army in Yogyakarta 1943–45]. Undergraduate Thesis, University of Jember, 1996.

Elms, Alan C. *Uncovering Lives: The Uneasy Alliance of Biography and Psychology.* New York: Oxford University Press, 1994.

Elson, Robert. *Suharto, A Political Biography.* Cambridge: Cambridge University Press, 2001.

———. "Tragedy of Modern Indonesian History". Inaugural Lecture, Brisbane: Griffith University, 1998.

Elton, Geoffrey. *The Practice of History.* 2nd ed. with an afterword by Richard J. Evans. Oxford: Blackwell, 2002.

Ensiklopedi Nasional Indonesia [Indonesian National Encyclopedia], vol. 17 (U–Zw). Jakarta: Cipta Adi Pustaka, 1991.

Epenhuysen-Tuckerman, Ingeborg van. "Een Jaar in een Paleis" [A Year in a Palace], *Moesson* (1989): 12–13.

Epstein, William. *Contesting the Subject, Essays in the Post-modern Theory and Practice of Biography and Biographical Criticism.* Indiana: Purdue University Press, 1991.

Epton, Nina. *Magic and Mystics in Java.* London: Octagon Press, 1974.

Evans, Richard J. *In Defence of History.* London: Granta, 1997.

Fabricius, Johan. *Dipanegara, (De Java — Oorlog van 1825 tot 1830)* [Diponegoro, The Java War of 1825–30]. The Hague: Uitgeverij Leopold, 1977.

Fasseur, Cees. *De Indologen, Ambtenaren voor de Oost 1825–1950* [The Indologists, Officials for the East 1825–1950]. Amsterdam: Bakker, 1993.

Feith, Herbert. *The Decline of Constitutional Democracy in Indonesia.* Ithaca, NY: Cornell University Press, 1962.

Feith, Herbert and Lance Castles, eds. *Indonesian Political Thinking.* Ithaca, NY: Cornell University Press, 1970.

———. "Towards Elections in Indonesia". *Pacific Affairs* 27, no. 3 (1954): 236–54.

Florida, Nancy. *Writing the Past, Inscribing the Future, History as Prophecy in Colonial Java.* Durham, NC: Duke University Press, 1995.

Foreign Relations of the United States 1949, Vol. VII, Part 2, The Far East and Australasia. Washington: State Department, 1976. Cited as *FRUS*.

Forrester, G.J./Monfries, J.E. *The Private Diary of Geoff Forrester on Indonesia's Turbulent Decade, 1996–2005,* edited with an Introduction by John Monfries. Lewiston, New York: Edwin Mellen, 2011.

Forster, Harold. *Flowering Lotus.* London: Longmans Green, 1958.

Fox, J., R.G. Garnaut, P.M. McCawley, and J.A.C. Mackie, eds. *Indonesia: Australian Perspectives.* Canberra: Australian National University, 1980. Includes various essays with the collective title of *Indonesia: Dualism, Growth and Poverty.*

Friend, Theodore. *The Blue-Eyed Enemy — Japan against the West in Java and Luzon 1942–1945.* Princeton, NJ: Princeton University Press, 1988.

Furnivall, J.S. *Netherlands India: A Study in Plural Economy.* New York: Cambridge University Press, 1944.

Gatot Mangkupraja. "The PETA: My Relations with the Japanese — A Correction of Sukarno's Autobiography". *Indonesia* magazine, no. 5 (1968): 130–42.

Geertz, Clifford. *The Religion of Java*. Chicago: University of Chicago Press, 1976. First published in 1960.

———. *The Interpretation of Cultures*. New York: Basic Books, 1973.

George, Margaret. *Australia and the Indonesian Revolution*. Melbourne: Melbourne University Press, 1980.

Geyl, Peter. *Encounters in History*. London: Collins, 1963.

Glendinning, Victoria. "Lies and Silences". In *The Troubled Face of Biography* (q.v.), edited by Hornberger and Charmley, pp. 45–62.

Goedhart F.J. *Een Revolutie op Drift* [A Drifting Revolution]. Amsterdam: van Oorschot, 1953. An account of Indonesia in 1952. This is a follow-up to his book under the pseudonym of "Pieter t'Hoen" below.

———. ("Pieter t'Hoen"). *Terug uit Jogja* [Return from Jogja]: Amsterdam: Stichting Het Parool, 1947.

Goodwin, Barbara. *Using Political Ideas*. 2nd ed. Chichester: Wiley, 1987.

Grant, Bruce. *Indonesia*. Melbourne: Melbourne University Press, 1964.

Green, Marshall. *Indonesia: Crisis and Transformation*. Washington: Compass, 1990.

Griswold, Deirdre. *Indonesia: The Bloodbath that Was*. New York: World View, 1975.

Groen, P.M.H. "Dutch Armed Forces and the Decolonisation of Indonesia: The Second Police Action 1948–1949; A Pandora's Box". *War and Society* 4, no. 1 (1986): 86–102.

Hadi Soewito, Irna. *Rakyat Jawa Timur Mempertahankan Kemerdekaan, vol. I* [The People of East Java Defend Independence, vol. I]. Jakarta: Grasindo, 1994.

Hadiwijono. *Man in the Present Javanese Mysticism*. Baarn: Bosch and Keuning, 1967.

Hamengku Buwono X. *Bercermin di Kalbu Rakyat* [Reflecting the Heart of the People]. Yogyakarta: Kanisius, 1999.

Hastings, Peter. *The Road to Lembang, A Retrospect 1938–1966*. Australians in Asia Series no. 5. Brisbane: Griffith University, 1990.

Hatta, Mohammad. *Mohammad Hatta, Indonesian Patriot, Memoirs*, edited by C.L.M. Penders. Singapore: Gunung Agung, 1981.

———. "Colonial Society and the Ideals of Social Democracy". In *Indonesian Political Thinking* (q.v.) edited by Feith and Castles, pp. 30–34.

Hefner, R. and R. Horvatich, eds. *Islam in an Era of Nation States*. Honolulu: University of Hawai'i Press, 1994.

Heijboer, P. *De Politionele Acties* [The Police Actions]. Haarlem: Fibula-Van Dishoeck, 1979.

Helsdingen, W.H. van. *Op Weg naar Nederlandsche-Indonesische Unie* [On the Way to the Netherlands — Indonesia Union]. The Hague: van Hoeve, 1947.

Hertog Joyonegoro, B.R.H. "Ngayogyakarta Hadiningrat". Microfiche text of lecture to Lembaga Javanologi, Yogyakarta, 1987 (Seen at National Library of Australia).

Hill, David T. "The Objectification of Mochtar Lubis: Personalizing the Process of Biography". In *Indonesian Political Biography: in search of cross-cultural understanding* (q.v.), edited by A. McIntyre. Clayton, Victoria: Monash University Centre of Southeast Asian Studies, 1993, pp. 263–89.

Hill, Hal. *The Indonesian Economy*. 2nd ed. Cambridge: Cambridge University Press, 2000.

Himpunan Pidato Wakil Presiden Republik Indonesia 1973–78 [Collection of Speeches of the Vice President of the Republic of Indonesia]. (Percetakan Negara?, Jakarta, 1979?) (Copy Seen at Leiden University Library. Unobtainable in Australia).

Hobsbawm, Eric. *On History*. London: Abacus, 1998.

Holden, Philip. "Lee Kuan Yew, A Man and an Island: Gender and Nation in Lee Kuan Yew's 'The Singapore Story'", *Biography* 24, no. 2 (2002): 401–16.

Holroyd, Michael. "How I Fell into Biography". In *The Troubled Face of Biography* (q.v.), edited by Eric Hornberger and John Charmley. Macmillan, 1989, pp. 95–104.

Hoogstraaten, M.G. *Nederlanders in Nederlands — Indie, een schets van de Nederlandse koloniale aanwezigheid in Zuid — Oost Azie tussen 1596 en 1950* [The Dutch in the Dutch East Indies, a Sketch of the Dutch Colonial Presence in Southeast Asia between 1596 and 1950]. Zutphen: Thieme, *c.*1986.

Hornberger, Eric and John Charmley, eds. *The Troubled Face of Biography*. Macmillan, 1989.

Hughes, John. *The End of Sukarno*. London: Angus and Robertson, 1968.

Hughes-Freeland, Felicia. "A Throne for the People: Observations on the Jumenengen of Sultan Hamengku Buwono X". *Indonesia*, no. 51 (1991): 129–52.

Idenburg, P., ed. *Ten Years of Japanese Burrowing in the Netherlands East Indies, official report of the Netherlands East Indies Government on Japanese subversive activities in the archipelago during the last decade*. Batavia: Netherlands Information Bureau, 1942?

Inden, Ronald. "Orientalist Constructions of India". *Modern Asian Studies* 20, no. 3 (1986): 406–23.

Indisch Verslag (Verslag van Bestuur en Staat van Nederlands — Indie) over Het Jaar 1937 [Indies Report, Report of Government and State of Netherlands Indies]. The Hague, 1939.

Indonesia Marketing Association. *Kraton Jogja: The History and Cultural Heritage*. Yogyakarta: Yogyakarta, Karaton Ngayogyakarta Hadiningrat, 2002.

International Crisis Group. *Recycling Militants in Indonesia: Darul Islam and the*

Australian Embassy Bombing. Asia Report no. 92, 22 February 2005 <http://www.crisisgroup.org/home/index.cfm>.

———. *Indonesia's Presidential Crisis*. Asia Briefing, no. 6, 21 May 2001, Internet version of report, same website.

———. *Politics of Financial Reform in Indonesia*, 2001, Internet version, same website.

Ismuwanto, R. Hery and Moh Ali Pitoyo. *Katalog Arsip2 Penting Keraton Ngayogyokarto* [Catalogue of Important Archives in the Yogyakarta Kraton]. Yogyakarta: Kantor Arsip Daerah Istimewa Yogyakarta, 1997.

Jaquet, L.G.M. *Minister Stikker en de Souvereiniteitsoverdracht aan Indonesie* [Minister Stikker and the Transfer of Sovereignty to Indonesia]. The Hague: Nijhoff, 1982.

Jenkins, David. *Suharto and His Generals*. Cornell Monograph Series no. 64. Ithaca, NY: Cornell University Press, 1984.

Jenkins, Keith, ed. *A Post-Modern History Reader*. London: Routledge, 1997.

Jolly, Margaretta. *Encyclopedia of Life Writing*. 2 vols. London: Dearborn, 2001.

Jones E.L. "A Framework for the History of Economic Growth in Southeast Asia". *Australian Economic History Review* 31, no. 1 (1991): 5–19.

Jones J.D.F. *Storyteller, the Many Lives of Laurens van der Post*. London: Scribner, 2002.

Jong L. de. *Het Koninkrijk der Nederlanden in de Tweede Wereldoorlog, Nederlands-Indie* [The Kingdom of the Netherlands in the Second World War, Netherlands Indies] (2 vols.). Leiden: Nijhoff, 1984.

Kaam, Ben van. "Een Vorstelijke rebel, Nederlandse vergissing van 35 jaar geleden" [A Princely Rebel, a Dutch Mistake of 35 Years Ago]. *Vu* magazine 13, no. 3 (1984): 107–15; copy of article seen at NIOD, reference number NIOD 081591, Natijd lists.

Kadane, Kathy. "U.S. Officials' List Aided Indonesian Bloodbath in '60s". *Washington Post*, 21 May 1990.

Kahin, George Mc T. *Nationalism and Revolution in Indonesia*. Ithaca, NY: Cornell University Press, 1961. First published in 1952.

———. *Southeast Asia, A Testament*. London: Routledge, 2003.

———. "Some Recollections and Reflections on the Indonesian Revolution". *Indonesia*, no. 60 (1995): 1–16.

———. "The Sultan and the Dutch". In *Tahta untuk Rakyat* (*TUR*; q.v.), edited by Atmakusumah, pp. 175–78.

Kanahele, George. "The Japanese Occupation of Indonesia — Prelude to Independence". PhD thesis, Cornell University, Ithaca, NY, 1967.

Kaplan, Joseph. "Writing a Biography of Gore Vidal" <http://www.randomhouse/boldtype> (accessed 14 June 2005).

Kartini, Raden Ajeng. *Letters of a Javanese Princess*, translated by Agnes Louise Summers. New York: Norton, 1976.

Katoppo, Aristides, ed. *Sumitro Djojohadikusumo, jejak perlawanan begawan pejuang* [Sumitro Joyohadikusumo, The Path of the Veteran Rebel]. Jakarta: Pustaka Sinar Harapan, 2000.

Kawilarang, A.E. *Officier in Dienst van de Republiek Indonesie* [Officer in the Service of the Republic of Indonesia]. Breda: Warung Bambu, 1994.

Kermode, Frank. *Pleasing Myself*. London: Allen Lane, 2001.

Khoo, Boo Teik. *Paradoxes of Mahathirism, an Intellectual Biography of Mahathir Mohamad*. Kuala Lumpur, New York: Oxford University Press, 1995.

Kies, Charles. *Wat de Meeste nederlanders niet Weten omtrent Nederlandsch-Indie* [What Most Dutch People Do Not Know about the Netherlands Indies]. Deventer: van Hoeve, 1946.

Kitley, Philip, Richard Chauvel, and D.G. Reeve, eds. *Australia di mata Indonesia* [Australia in Indonesian Eyes]. Jakarta: Gramedia, 1987.

Klerck, E.S. de. *History of the Netherlands East Indies* (2 vols.). Rotterdam: Brusse, 1938.

Klinken, Geert Arend van. "Migrant Moralities, Christians and Nationalist Politics in Emerging Indonesia, a Biographical Approach". PhD thesis, Griffith University, 1996.

———. "The Battle for History after Suharto". *Critical Asian Studies* 33, no. 3 (2001): 323–50.

Koorn, F. "Herinneringen aan de Eerste HBS-B in de jaren dertig and veertig" [Memories of the First HBS-B in the Thirties and Forties]. In *Haarlem Jaarboek 1997* [Haarlem Yearbook 1997], edited by F. Koorn. Archief Kennemerland, 1997, pp. 121–25.

Kossmann-Putto, J.A. and E.H. Kossmann. *The Low Countries, the History of the Northern and Southern Netherlands*. Flanders (Belgium): Flemish-Netherlands Foundation Stichting Ons Erfdeel, 1987.

Kratoska, P.H. *The Japanese Occupation of Malaya*. Sydney: Allen and Unwin, 1998.

Kroef, Justus Maria van der. *Indonesia after Sukarno*. Singapore: Asia-Pacific Press, 1971.

Kumar, Ann. *Java and Modern Europe, Ambiguous Encounters*. Surrey: Curzon, 1997.

———. "Java — A Self-Critical Examination of the Nation and its History". In *The Last Stand of Asian Autonomies: Responses to Modernity in the Diverse States of Southeast Asia and Korea, 1750–1900*, edited by Anthony Reid. New York: St. Martin's, 1997, pp. 315–39.

Kwantes, R.C. *De Ontwikkeling van de Nationalistische Beweging*, vol. 4 (1933–1942) [The Development of the Nationalist Movement]. Groningen: Tjeenk Willink (the last of four volumes published during 1975–82).

Lambert, C.J. "Post-Modern Biography". *Biography* 18, no. 4 (1994): 305–15.
Larson, G.D. "Prelude to Revolution, Palaces and Politics in Surakarta, 1912–1942". PhD thesis, Northern Illinois University, 1979.
Lebra, Joyce, ed. *Japan's Greater East Asia Co-Prosperity Sphere in World War II, Selected Readings and Documents*. Kuala Lumpur and New York: Oxford University Press, 1975.
Legge, J.D. *Sukarno, a Political Biography*. Harmondsworth: Penguin Books, 1973.
———. *Indonesia*. Englewood Cliffs, NJ: Prentice-Hall, 1964.
———. "Sukarno: Traditional or Modern Leader?" In *Self and Biography*, edited by Wang Gungwu. Sydney: Sydney University Press, 1975, pp. 171–84.
Leur, J.C. van. *Indonesian Trade and Society: Essays in Asian Social and Economic History*, translated by J.S. Holmes and A. van Marle. The Hague: W. van Hoeve, 1955. Part of a series of *Selected Studies on Indonesia*, produced by an editorial committee chaired by W.F. Wertheim.
Lieblich, Amia. "Untitled review of Elms' *Uncovering Lives*". *Biography* 18, no. 3 (1995): 264–65.
Lindblad, J.T. "Van Javasche Bank naar Bank Indonesia" [From Java Bank to Bank Indonesia], p. 34 <http://www:tseg.nl> (accessed 29 November 2005).
Lindsay, Jennifer, R.M. Sutanto, and Alan Feinstein, eds. *Kraton Yogyakarta: Katalog Induk Naskah2 Nusantara no. 2* [Yogyakarta Kraton: Main National Catalogue of Documents no. 2]. Jakarta: Yayasan Obor Indonesia, 1994.
Loveard, Keith. *Suharto, Indonesia's Last Sultan*. Singapore: Horizon Books, 1999.
Lubis, Mochtar. *Manusia Indonesia Sebuah Pertanggunganjawab* [Indonesian Man, Taking Responsibility]. Jakarta: Yayasan Obor Indonesia, 2001. Reprint of 1977 publication.
Luns, Joseph. *Ik Herinner Me* (I Remember). Leiden: A.W. Sijthoff, 1971.
Lyon, Margot L. "Mystical Biography". In *Indonesian Political Biography* (q.v.), edited by Angus McIntyre, pp. 215–42.
MacDougall, J. "Technocrats as Modernisers, the Economists of Indonesia's New Order". PhD thesis, University of Michigan, 1975.
Mackie, J.A.C. and Sjahrir. "Survey of Recent Developments". *BIES* 25, no. 3 (1989): 5–26.
———. "The Concept of Dualism". In *Indonesia: Australian Perspectives*, edited by Fox, Garnaut, McCawley, and Mackie. Canberra: Australian National University, 1980, pp. 291–315.
Madiya. "Peranan Keraton Yogyakarta dalam Menghadapi Agresi Belanda Kedua" [The Role of the Yogyakarta Kraton in Facing up to the Second Dutch Aggression]. Undergraduate thesis, IKIP, Yogyakarta, 1993.
Malik, Adam. *Mengabdi Republik* [Serving the Republic]. 3 vols. Jakarta: Gunung Agung, 1978.
Mangunwijaya, Y.B. *The Weaverbirds*, translated by T.M. Hunter. Jakarta: Lontar Foundation, 1991.

Marcus, Laura. *Auto/Biographical Discourses*. Manchester: Manchester University Press, 1994.
Masyuki and Sutrisno Kutoyo. *Sejarah Revolusi Kemerdekaan di Daerah Istimewa Yogyakarta* [A History of the Independence Revolution in the Special District of Yogyakarta]. Yogyakarta: Proyek Inventarisasi dan Dokumentasi Kebudayaan Daerah, 1985–87.
Mathews, W.R., ed. *Indonesia Report, the Collected Dispatches of the American Correspondents who died in Bombay India 12 July 1949, on Return from a Tour of Indonesia*. Tucson: Arizona Daily Star, 1949.
May, R.J., ed. *Between Two Nations, the Indonesia-Papua New Guinea Border and West Papuan Nationalism*. Bathurst, NSW: Robert Brown, 1986.
McCalman, Iain, ed., with Jodi Parvey and Misty Cook. *National Biographies and National Identity: A Critical Approach to Theory and Editorial Practice*. Canberra: Humanities Research Centre, Australian National University, 1996.
McCoy, A.W., ed. *Southeast Asia Under Japanese Occupation*. Newhaven: Yale University, Southeast Asia Studies Monograph series no. 22, 1980.
McIntyre, Angus, ed. *Indonesian Political Biography: In Search of Cross-Cultural Understanding*. Clayton, Victoria: Monash University Centre of Southeast Asian Studies, 1993.
———. "Foreign Biographical Studies of Indonesian Subjects: Obstacles and Shortcomings". In *Indonesian Political Biography: In Search of Cross-Cultural Understanding* (q.v. above), edited by McIntyre, pp. 291–315.
McMahon, Robert. *Colonialism and the Cold War, the United States and the Struggle for Indonesian Independence*. Ithaca, NY: Cornell University Press, 1981.
McVey, Ruth. "The Case of the Disappearing Decade". In *Democracy in Indonesia, 1950s and 1990s*, edited by Bourchier and Legge. Clayton, Victoria: Monash University, 1994, pp. 7–29.
Merrill, Dana. *American Biography, Its Theory and Practice*. Portland, ME: Bowker, 1957.
Meulen, Daniel van der. *Hoort Gij de Donder Niet?* [Do You Not Hear the Thunder?]. Franeker: Wever, 1977.
Mintz, Jeanne. *Mohammad, Marx, and Marhaen*. New York: Praeger, 1965.
Miyoshi Shunkichiro. "The Japanese Policy Towards the Sultans' Autonomous Regions". In *The Japanese Experience in Indonesia: Selected Memoirs of 1942–45* (q.v.), edited by Reid and Okira. Athens: Ohio University Center for International Studies, Center for Southeast Asian Studies, 1986.
Moedjanto, G. *Kasultanan Yogyakarta dan Kadipaten Pakualaman* [The Sultanate of Yogyakarta and the Pakualaman Court]. Yogyakarta: Kanisius, 1994.
———. *Konsep Kekuasaan Jawa* [Javanese Concepts of Power]. Yogyakarta: Kanisius, 1987.
———. "Perjuangan Hamengku Buwono IX dan Peranannya dalam Pembangunan Nasional" [The Struggle of Hamengku Buwono IX and His Role in National

Development]. Lecture at Museum Benteng, Yogyakarta, 30 July 1998. Also in Sulistya, Suryanta Pamuji, and Budi Sanyata, eds. *Reformasi dan Pembangunan Bangsa* [Reform and National Development]. (q.v.).

Moertono, Soemarsaid. *State and Statecraft in Old Java*. Cornell Modern Indonesia Project Monograph Series. Ithaca, NY: Cornell University, 1968.

Moor, J.A. de. *Westerling's Oorlog*. Amsterdam: Balans, 1999, pp. 428, 480–82.

Mrazek, Rudolf. *Sjahrir, Politics and Exile in Indonesia*. Ithaca, NY: Studies on Southeast Asia, Cornell University, 1994.

———. "The United States and the Indonesian Military". PhD thesis, Czechoslovak Academy of Sciences, Dissertations Orientales series, Prague, 1978.

Mubyarto and Ace Partadireja. "An Economic Survey of the Special Region of Yogyakarta". *Bulletin of Indonesian Economic Studies*, no. 11 (1968): 29–43.

———. *Sistem dan Moral Ekonomi Indonesia* [The System and Moral Aspects of the Indonesian Economy]. Jakarta: LP3ES, 1988.

Munslow, Alun. *Deconstructing History*. London: Routledge, 1997.

———. "What History Is". In *History in Focus: The Nature of History*. October 2001 <http://www.history.ac.uk/ihr/Focus/Whatishistory/munslow6.html> (accessed 4 November 2005).

Nadel, Ira Bruce. *Biography: Fact, Fiction and Form*. London: Macmillan, 1984.

Nasution, Adnan Buyung. "The Aspiration for Constitutional Government in Indonesia, a Socio-legal study of the Indonesian Konstituante, 1956–69". PhD thesis, University of Utrecht, Koninklijke Bibliotheek, The Hague, 1992.

Nasution, A.H. *Sekitar Perang Kemerdekaan Indonesia* [On the Indonesian War of Independence]. 11 vols. Bandung: Penerbit Angkasa, 1978.

———. *Memenuhi Panggilan Tugas* [Answering Duty's Call]. 10 vols. Jakarta: Gunung Agung, 1983–84.

National Library of Australia. *Indonesian acquisitions list, Daftar pengadaan bahan Indonesia*. Canberra. Series published quarterly. Also available at <http://www.nla.gov.au/asian/pub/ial/>.

Natsir, Mohammad. "'Penjaga Gawang' Perjuangan Kemerdekaan" [The 'Goalkeeper' of the Independence Struggle]. In *Tahta Untuk Rakyat* (q.v.), edited by Atmakusumah, pp. 197–99.

Nayono, Ki. "Meneladani Sikap dan Tindakan Sri Sultan Hamengku Buwono IX dalam Perjuangan Nasional Bangsa Indonesia" [Emulating the Attitude and Actions of Sri Sultan Hamengku Buwono IX in the National Struggle of the Indonesian People]. 6-page typescript, lecture, 30 July 1998, at Monumen Yogya Kembali, Yogyakarta. Also included in Sulistya et al., referenced below.

Niel, Robert van. *The Emergence of the Modern Indonesian Elite*. The Hague and Bandung: van Hoeve, 1960.

———. "The Legacy of the Cultivation System". In *Indonesian Economic History* in the Dutch Colonial Era (q.v.), edited by Booth et al. New Haven, CT: Yale University Southeast Asia Studies, 1990, pp. 69–90.

Nimpuno, Raden. "Het Begrip 'Koningin der Nederlanden' voor de Inheemsche Bevolking van NOI" [The Perception of the 'Queen of the Netherlands' among the Native Population of the Netherlands East Indies]. *Indische Gids* 2, 1939, pp. 881–92.

Nishijima, Shigetada. "Testimony — Indonesian Independence and Revolution". In *The Japanese Experience in Indonesia: selected memoirs of 1942–1945* (q.v.), edited by Reid and Okira. Athens: Ohio University Center for International Studies, Center for Southeast Asian Studies, 1986, pp. 259–273.

Nordholt, H.G.C. Schulte. *De-colonising Indonesian Historiography*. Working Papers in Contemporary Asian Studies no. 6. Lund: Centre for East and South-East Asian Studies, Lund University, 2004.

Nortier, J.J. *De Japanse Aanval op Nederlands Indie* [The Japanese Attack on the Netherlands Indies]. 2 vols. Rotterdam: Donker, 1988.

Noto, Soeroto. *Kesultanan Yogyakarta* [The Sultanate of Yogyakarta]. Yogyakarta: Department of Education and Culture, 1986 (reissue).

Nugroho, Notosusanto. *Tentara Peta* [The Peta Army]. Jakarta: Gramedia, 1979.

Nursam, M. *Pergumulan Seorang Intelektual, Biografi Soedjatmoko* [The Struggle of an Intellectual, the Biography of Soedjatmoko]. Jakarta: Gramedia, 2002.

O'Brien, Patrick. "An Engagement with Postmodern Foes, Literary Theorists and Friends on the Borders with History". A review of the Routledge series of postmodern readers <http://www.history.ac.uk/ihr/Focus/Whatishistory/obrien.html> (accessed 6 September 2005).

O'Connor, Ulick. *Biographers and the Art of Biography*. Dublin: Wolfhound, 1991.

Oey, Hong Lee. *War and Diplomacy in Indonesia*. Townsville: James Cook University, 1981.

Ojong, P.K. (Auwjong, Peng Koen). *Kompasiana: esei jurnalistik tentang berbagai masalah* [Kompasiana, Journalistic Essays on Various Problems]. Jakarta: Gramedia, 1981.

O'Malley, William J. "The Pakempalan Kawulo NgaYogyakarta: An official report on the Yogyakarta People's Party of the 1930s". *Indonesia*, no. 26 (Oct 1978): 111–58.

———. "Indonesia in the Great Depression: A Study of East Sumatra and Yogyakarta in the 1930s". PhD thesis, Cornell University, 1977.

———. "Second Thoughts on Indonesian Nationalism". In *Indonesia: The Making of a Nation*, edited by J.A.C. Mackie. Canberra: Research School of Pacific Studies, Australian National University, 1980, pp. 601–14.

Osborne, Milton. *Southeast Asia, an Introductory History*, 8th ed. St Leonards, NSW: Allen and Unwin, 1995.

Pakpahan, G. *1261 Hari dibawah Sinar Matahari* [1261 Days under the Flag of the Rising Sun]. Jakarta: Marintan Djaya, 1979.

Panggabean, Maraden. *Berjuang dan Mengabdi* [To Strive and Serve]. Jakarta: Pustaka Sinar Harapan, 1993.
Parera, Frans Meak. "Ketokohan Sri Sultan Hamengku Buwono IX, Reformator Budaya dan Perintis Orde Baru" [The Leadership of Sri Sultan Hamengku Buwono IX, Cultural Reformer and Forerunner of the New Order]. *Prisma*, Jakarta, 1991, no. 20, pp. 41–80.
Patmono. *Radius Prawiro — Kiprah, Peran dan Pemikiran* [Radius Prawiro, Progress, Role and Philosophy]. Jakarta: Grafiti, 1998.
Paulus, J., ed. *Encyclopedie van Nederland Oost Indie* [Encyclopedia of the Netherlands East Indies], vol. 1. Batavia: Nijhoff, 1917.
Pemberton, John. *On the Subject of "Java"*. Ithaca, NY: Cornell University Press, 1994.
Pemerintah Propinsi Daerah Istimewa Yogyakarta. *Undang2 Dasar Negara Republik Indonesia, Amanat makloemat No 1–19* [Republic of Indonesia Constitution, Decrees 1–19]. Yogyakarta, nd.
Penders, C.L.M. and Ulf Sundhaussen. *Abdul Haris Nasution, a Political Biography*. St Lucia: University of Queensland Press, 1985.
Persadja (Persatuan Djaksa-djaksa Seluruh Indonesia, All-Indonesia Prosecutors Association). *Proces peristiwa Sultan Hamid II* [The Trial of Sultan Hamid II]. Djakarta: Fasco, 1955.
Phillips, Walter. "Historians, Biography and History". In *Tracing Past Lives, The Writing of Historical Biography* (q.v.), edited by Broome. Carlton, Victoria: History Institute, 1995, pp. 5–19.
Picard, H.W.J. *De Waarheid over Java* [The Truth about Java]. The Hague: van Hoeve, 1946.
Pijper, G.F. *Studien over de geschiedenis van de Islam in Indonesia, 1900–1950* [Studies on the History of Islam in Indonesia 1900–1950]. Leiden: Brill, 1977.
Pluvier, Jan. *Indonesie: Kolonialisme, Onafhankelijkheid, Neo-kolonialisme* [Indonesia: Colinialism, Independence and Neocolonialism]. Nijmegen: SUN, 1978.
Poeze, Harry. *In het Land van de Overheerser, Indonesiers in Nederland 1600–1950* [In the Land of the Overlord, Indonesians in the Netherlands 1600–1950], vol. 1. Dordrecht: Foris, 1986.
Polomka, Peter. *Indonesia since Sukarno*. Ringwood, Victoria: Penguin, 1971.
Pompe, S. "A Short Review of Doctoral Theses on the Netherlands Indies Accepted at the Faculty of Law of Leiden in the Period 1850–1940". *Indonesia*, no. 56 (October 1993): 67–98.
Post, Laurens van der. *The Admiral's Baby*. New York: Morrow, 1996.
Post, Peter and Elly Touwen-Bouwsma. *Japan, Indonesia and the War: Myths and Realities*. Leiden: KITLV Press, 1997.
Prabuningrat, B.R.H. "Prabuningrat document", an untitled and undated 3-page typescript account of Hamengku Buwono IX's conduct in 1948 and

1949. Published in abbreviated form in Nasution, *Memenuhi Panggilan Tugas* [Answering Duty's Call], vol. 2A, 1984, pp. 346–47.

Pramoedya Ananta Toer, Koesalah Soebagyo Toer, and Ediati Kamil, eds. *Kronik Revolusi Indonesia* [Chronicles of the Indonesian Revolution]. Multi-volume series, each volume labelled "1945", "1946", etc. Jakarta: Gramedia, 1999. Cited as *KRI* in the text.

Prawiro, Radius. *Indonesia's Struggle for Economic Development, Pragmatism in Action*. Kuala Lumpur: Oxford University Press, 1998.

Purwokusumo, Sudarisman (Soedarisman Poerwokoesoemo). *Daerah Istimewa Yogyakarta* [The Special Region of Yogyakarta]. Yogyakarta: Gajah Mada University Press, 1984.

———. *Kasultanan Yogyakarta* [The Sultanate of Yogyakarta]. Yogyakarta: Gajah Mada University Press, 1985 (reissue of thesis written in 1939).

———. *Tanggapan atas Disertasi berjudul "Perubahan Sosial di Yogyakarta"* [Reaction to Dissertation entitled "Social Change in Yogyakarta"]. Yogyakarta: Gajah Mada University Press, 1984.

———. *Sebuah Tinjauan tentang Pepatih-Dalem* [A Note on the Patih]. Yogyakarta: Proyek Javanologi, 1981.

———. *Biografi dan Perjuangan Sri Sultan* [Biography and the Struggle of the Sultan]. Yogyakarta? 1986? Unobtainable.

———. *Peranan Beberapa Tokoh Wanita di Puro Pakualaman* [The Role of Several Leading Women in the Pakualaman Palace]. Yogyakarta: Proyek Javanologi, 1985?

———. *Sumpah Pemuda dan Javanologi* [The Youth Oath and Javanology]. Yogyakarta: Proyek Javanologi, 1984.

Quinn, George. *The Novel in Javanese, Aspects of Its Social and Literary Character*. Leiden: KITLV, 1992.

Rachmawati, Sukarnoputri. *Bapakku Ibuku* [My Father and Mother]. Jakarta: Garuda Metropolitan Press, 1984.

Rahardjo, Suwandi. *A Quest for Justice, The Millenary Aspirations of a Contemporary Javanese Wali*. PhD thesis, Australian National University, 1985.

Ratmanto, Aan. *Mengawal Transisi, Sri Sultan Hamengku Buwono IX dan Pemeritnahan Transisi Republik Indonesia di Yogyakarta* [Beginning the Transition, Sultan Hamengku Buwono IX and the Transitional Government of the Republic of Indonesia]. Yogyakarta: Atap Buku and Mata Padi Presindo, 2012.

Regeeringsalmanak 1941 voor Nederlandsch Oost Indie [Government Almanac for the Netherlands East Indies], pt. 2. Batavia: Landsdrukkerij, 1941.

Reeve, David. *Golkar of Indonesia, an Alternative to the Party System*. Singapore/ New York: Oxford University Press, 1985.

Reid, Anthony. *The Indonesian National Revolution, 1945–50*. Hawthorn, Victoria: Longman, 1974.

———. *An Indonesian Frontier, Acehnese and Other Histories of Sumatra*. Singapore: Singapore University Press, 2005.

―――. "From Briefcase to Samurai Sword". In *Southeast Asia under Japanese Occupation* (q.v.), edited by A. McCoy. Southeast Asia Studies Monograph series no. 22. Newhaven: Yale University, 1980, pp. 16–32.

Reid, Anthony and Oki Akira, eds. *The Japanese Experience in Indonesia: Selected Memoirs of 1942–1945*, with assistance from Jennifer Brewster and Jean Carruthers. Athens: Ohio University Center for International Studies, Center for Southeast Asian Studies, 1986.

Reid, Anthony and David G. Marr, eds. *Perceptions of the Past in Southeast Asia*. Singapore: Heinemann, 1979.

Richards, P.D. *Asia Emerges: History of Japan, China, Indonesia, India*. South Melbourne: Nelson, 1994.

Ricklefs, M. *A History of Modern Indonesia, 1300 to the Present*. Macmillan, 1981.

―――. *Yogyakarta in the Time of Mangkubumi, 1749–1792: A History of the Division of Java*. London: Oxford University Press, 1974.

―――. *The Seen and Unseen Worlds of Java, 1726–49, History, Literature and Islam in the Court of Pakubuwana II*. Sydney: Allen and Unwin and University of Hawai'i Press, 1998.

―――. *Modern Javanese Historical Tradition: A Study of the Original Kartasura Chronicle and Related Materials*. London: SOAS, 1978.

Robison, Richard. *Indonesia – The Rise of Capital*. Sydney: Allen and Unwin, 1986.

Robson, Stuart, ed. *The Kraton – Selected Essays on Javanese Courts*, with an introduction by Stuart Robson, translated by Rosemary Robson-McKillop. Leiden: KITLV Press, 2003.

Roeder, O.G. *The Smiling General*. Jakarta: Gunung Agung, 1969.

Roem, Moh. "Apa yang akan terjadi Dengan Republik Jika Tidak Ada Hamengku Buwono IX?" [What Would Have Happened to the Republic If Hamengku Buwono Had Not Been There?]. In *Tahta untuk Rakyat* (q.v.), edited by Atmakusumah et al., pp. 133–41.

Rollyson, J. "Biography Theory and Method, the Case of Samuel Johnson". *Biography* 25, no. 2 (2001): 363–75.

Rosihan Anwar, ed. *Mengenang Sjahrir* [Remembering Syahrir]. Jakarta: Gramedia, 1980.

―――. *Against the Currents, a Biography of Soedarpo Sastrosatomo*, translated from Indonesian by Tunggul Siagian. Jakarta: Pustaka Sinar Harapan, 2003.

Saggs, H.W.F. *The Babylonians*. London: Folio, 1999.

Said, Edward. *Orientalism*. London: Penguin, 1995.

Said, Salim. *Genesis of Power – General Sudirman and the Indonesian Military in Politics 1945–49*. Singapore: Institute of Southeast Asian Studies, 1992; and Jakarta: Pustaka Sinar Harapan, 1992.

―――. *Militer Indonesia dan Politik: Dulu, Kini dan Kelak* [The Indonesian Military and Politics: In the Past, the Present and the Future]. Jakarta: Pustaka Sinar Harapan, 2001.

Saltford, John Francis. *UNTEA and UNRWI: United Nations Involvement in West New Guinea During the 1960's*. PhD thesis, University of Hull, April 2000.

Sape, G.M., ed. *Asian History and Civilisation*. Manila: IBON Foundation, 1999. A neo-Marxist history in school textbook form.

Sartono, Kartodirdjo. *Indonesian Historiography*. Yogyakarta: Kanisius, 2001.

———. "Seputar Yogyakarta dan Beberapa Tokoh Kepemimpinannya" [Yogyakarta and Several of its Leading Personalities]. Address on Receiving the Hamengku Buwono IX Award, typescript, 1995.

Sato, Shigeru. *War, Nationalism and Peasants, Java under the Japanese Occupation*. New York: Sharpe, 1994.

Sayidiman. *Mengabdi Negara sebagai Prajurit TNI* [Serving the Nation as a TNI Officer]. Jakarta: Pustaka Sinar Harapan, 1997.

Schoffer, Ivo. *History of the Netherlands*. Amsterdam: de Lange, 1973.

Schouten, Ted. *Dwaalsporen Oorlogsmisdaden in Nederlands- Indie 1945–49* [Tracing War Crimes in the Netherlands Indies 1945–49]. Zutphen: Alpha, 1995.

Sears, Laurie, ed. *Autonomous Histories, Particular Truths: Essays in Honour of John R.W. Smail*. Center for Southeast Asian Studies monograph no. 11. Madison: University of Wisconsin, 1993.

Seda, Frans, ed. *Simfoni tanpa henti: ekonomi politik masyarakat baru Indonesia* [The Endless Symphony — The New Indonesian Political and Economic Community]. Jakarta: Yayasan Atma Jaya and PT Gramedia Widiasarana, 1992.

Selosumarjan (Selosoemardjan). *Social Change in Jogjakarta*. Ithaca, NY: Cornell University Press, 1962.

———. "In Memoriam: Hamengkubuwono IX, Sultan of Yogyakarta". *Indonesia*, no. 47 (1989): 115–17.

———. "The Kraton in Javanese Social Structure". In *Dynamics of Indonesian History*, edited by Soebadio and du Marchie Sarvaas. Amsterdam and New York: North-Holland, 1978, pp. 225–39.

SESKOAD. *Serangan Umum* [General Offensive]. Bandung: SESKOAD, 1985.

Shiraishi, Takashi. *An Age in Motion, Popular Radicalism in Java, 1912–1926*. Ithaca, NY: Cornell University Press, 1990.

Siegel, James. *Solo in the New Order, Language and Hierarchy in an Indonesian City*. Princeton, NJ: Princeton University Press, 1986.

Silverstein, Josef, ed. *Southeast Asia in World War II, Four Essays*. New Haven, CT: Yale University, 1966.

Simatupang, T.B. *Report from Banaran*, translated by Ben Anderson and Elizabeth Graves. Ithaca, NY: Cornell University Press, 1972.

Singarimbun, Masri. *Reflections from Yogya, Portraits of Indonesian Social Life*. Yogyakarta: Galang, 2003.

Smail, J.R.W. "On the Possibility of an Autonomous History in Southeast Asia". *Journal of Southeast Asian History* 2, no. 2 (1961): 72–102.

Smithies, Michael. *Yogyakarta, Cultural Heart of Indonesia*. Singapore/New York: Oxford University Press, 1986.

Snooks, G.D. *The Laws of History*. London: Routledge, 1998.

Soe, Hok Gie. "Simpang Kiri dari Sebuah Jalan" [The Left Turn in the Road], MA thesis, Universitas Indonesia, Jakarta, 1969.

Soebadio, Haryati and du Marchie Sarvaas, Carine A., eds. *Dynamics of Indonesian History*. Amsterdam and New York: North-Holland, 1978.

Soebagijo, I.N., ed. *Wilopo 70 Tahun*. Jakarta: Gunung Agung, 1979.

———. *Sri Sultan Hamengku Buwono IX*. Surabaya: Panjebar Semangat, 1952.

Soeharto, Dr R. *Saksi Sejarah, Mengikuti Perjuangan Dwitunggal* [Historical Witness, Joining the Struggle of the Duumvirate]. Jakarta: Gunung Agung, 1982.

Soeharto. *Soeharto — Pikiran, Ucapan dan Tindakan Saya* [My Thoughts, Words and Deeds], as told to G. Dwipayana and Ramadhan K.H. Jakarta: PT Citra Lamtoro Gung Persada, 1989.

Soejatno, Kartodirdjo. *Revolution in Surakarta 1945–50: A Case Study of City and Village in the Indonesian Revolution*. PhD thesis, Australian National University, Canberra, 1982.

Soempono Djojowardono. *Kraton dan Daerah Istimewa Yogyakarta* [The Palace and the Special District of Yogyakarta]. Yogyakarta: Lembaga Javanologi, typescript, nd.

Soewito, Dra Irna H.N. Hadi. *Rakyat Jawa Timur Mempertahankan Kemerdekaan, Vol. I* [The People of East Java Defend their Independence Vol. I]. Jakarta: Gramedia, 1994.

Southall, Ivan. *Indonesian Journey*. Melbourne: Lansdowne, 1966.

Southgate, Beverley. *History: What and Why, Ancient, Modern and Post-Modern Perspectives*, 2nd ed. London: Routledge, 2001.

Spivak, Gayatri. "Can the Subaltern Speak?" In *Marxism and the Interpretation of Culture*, edited by Nelson and Grossberg, 1988, pp. 271–316.

Springborg, Patricia. *Western Republicanism and the Oriental Prince*. Cambridge: Polity, 1992.

Stanley, A.P. *The Life and Correspondence of Thomas Arnold, D.D., Late Head-Master of Rugby School, and Regius Professor of Modern History in the University of Oxford*, 5th ed. London: Fellowes, 1845.

State Department [United States]. *Foreign Relations of the United States 1949, Vol. VII, Part 2, The Far East and Australasia* [cited as *FRUS*]. Washington: State Department, 1976.

Steijlen, Fridus, ed. *Memories of "The East"*. Leiden: KITLV Press, 2002. A compilation of interview summaries from the Oral History Project Collection.

———. *Memories of the East*, CD-ROM. Leiden: KITLV, 2002; a special CD-ROM providing longer Dutch-language summaries of the interviews in the book mentioned above.

Steinberg, D.J., ed. *In Search of Southeast Asia: A Modern History*. Sydney: Allen and Unwin, 1987.

Strauss, Paul. "The Washington Post and the Indonesian Crisis". MA thesis, American University, Michigan, 1968.

Subadio, Sastrosatomo. *Perjuangan Revolusi* [The Revolutionary Struggle]. Jakarta: Pustaka Sinar Harapan, 1987.

Subadiyah, Purnami. "Penetrasi Politik Kolonial Belanda di Yogyakarta" [Dutch Colonial Penetration in Yogyakarta]. Undergraduate thesis, IKIP Semarang, 1997.

Subagio, Reksodipuro et al., eds. *Wilopo 70 Tahun* [Wilopo at 70]. Gunung Agung, 1979.

Sudarmanto, Y.B. *Jejak-Jejak Pahlawan, Dari Sultan Agung hingga Sultan Hamengku Buwono IX* [The Path of the Heroes, from Sultan Agung to Sultan Hamengku Buwono IX]. Jakarta: Grasindo, 1992.

Sudomo, Sunaryo, ed. *Buku Petunjuk Propinsi Daerah Istimewa Yogyakarta* [Guidebook for the Special Province of Yogyakarta]. Yogyakarta: Hubungan Masyarakat Propinsi Istimewa, nd, 1982?

Sugiono, M.P. *Sang Demokrat Hamengku Buwono IX, Dokumen Setelah Sri Sultan Mangkat* [The Democrat Sultan Hamengku Buwono IX, Documents Published after Sri Sultan's Death]. Jakarta: Yayasan Budi Luhur, 1988.

Sukarno. *An Autobiography as Told to Cindy Adams*. Hong Kong: Gunung Agung, 1966.

Sukarno, Fatmawati. *Catatan Kecil bersama Bung Karno, Bagian I* [A Few Notes on my Life with Bung Karno, Part 1]. Jakarta: Dela-Rohita, 1978.

Sulak, Sivaraksa. "Biography and Buddhism in Thailand". *Biography* 17, no. 1 (1994): 2–20.

Sulistya, Suryanta Pamuji, and Budi Sanyata, eds. *Reformasi dan Pembangunan Bangsa* [Reform and National Development]. Yogyakarta: Museum Benteng Yogyakarta, 1999. Contains articles by G. Moedjanto. "Perjuangan Hamengku Buwono IX dan Peranannya dalam Pembangunan Nasional"; and Ki Nayono, referenced elsewhere.

Sullivan, J.H. "The United States and the New Order in Indonesia". PhD thesis, Michigan, 1970.

Sundhaussen, Ulf. *The Road to Power, Indonesian Military Politics 1945–1967*. Oxford: Oxford University Press, 1982.

Suratmin. *Amanat Seri Paduka Ingkang Sinuwun Kangdjeng Sultan Hamengku Buwono IX dan Amanat Seri Paduka Kangdjeng Gusti Pangeran Adipati Ario Paku Alam VIII Tanggal 5 September 1945 dalam Lintasan Sejarah Perjuangan Bangsa Indonesia* [The Decree by HH Sri Sultan Hamengku Buwono IX and HH Sri Pakualam of 5 September 1945 in the History of the Struggle of the Indonesian People]. 12-page typescript. Yogyakarta: Balai Kajian Sejarah dan Nilai Tradisional Yogyakarta, 1998.

Sutherland, Heather. *Making of a Bureaucratic Elite: The Colonial Transformation of the*

Javanese Priyayi. Singapore: Heinemann, ASAA Southeast Asia Publications Series, 1980.

Sutrisno, Kutoyo. *Sri Sultan Hamengku Buwono IX, Riwayat Hidup dan Perjuangan* [Sri Sultan Hamengku Buwono IX, His Life and Struggle]. Jakarta: Mutiara Sumber Widya, 1996.

Suwandi, Rahardjo. *A Quest for Justice, the Millenary Aspirations of a Contemporary Javanese Wali*. Leiden: KITLV Press, 2000.

Suwarno. P.J. *Hamengku Buwono IX dan Sistem Birokrasi Pemerintahan Yogyakarta 1942–1974, Sebuah Tinjauan Historis* [Hamengku Buwono IX and the Bureaucratic System of the Yogyakarta Government 1942–1974, A Historical Review]. Yogyakarta: Penerbit Kanisius, 1994.

Swantoro, P. *Dari Buku ke Buku, Sambung Menyambung Menjadi Satu* [From Book to Book, Connecting up to Form a Unity]. Jakarta: KPG and Tembi, 2002.

Swift, Ann. *Road to Madiun: The Indonesian Communist Uprising of 1948*. Ithaca, NY: Cornell Modern Indonesia Project, Southeast Asia Program, Cornell University, 1989.

Tarling, Nicholas. *Southeast Asia: A Modern History*. Melbourne: Oxford University Press, 2000.

———. *A Sudden Rampage, the Japanese Occupation of Southeast Asia, 1941–45*. London: Hurst, 2001.

Tataq Chidmad, Sri Endang Sumiyati, and Budi Hartono. *Pelurusan Sejarah Serangan Oemoem 1 Maret 1949* [Correcting the History of the General Offensive of 1 March 1949]. Yogyakarta: Media Pressindo, 2001.

Taylor, A.J.P. *Origins of the Second World War*, 2nd ed. New York: Fawcett Premier, 1964.

Taylor, Jean Gelman. *Indonesia, Peoples and Histories*. New Haven, CT: Yale University Press 2003.

Tempo Team. *Sri Sultan, Hari – Hari Hamengku Buwono IX, Sebuah Presentasi Majalah Tempo* [Sri Sultan, the Days of Hamengku Buwono IX, A Presentation by *Tempo* magazine]. Jakarta: Yayasan Karyawan Tempo, 1988. A collection of press articles.

Thayer, Carlyle. "Australian Perceptions and Indonesian Reality". Lecture to New Zealand Institute of International Affairs Dunedin branch, 1988.

't Hoen, Pieter. See F.J. Goedhart.

Thongchai Winichakul. *Siam Mapped, a History of the Geo-Body of a Nation*. Honolulu: University of Hawai'i Press, 1994.

Tim Pemburu Fakta (several authors). *Siapa Dalang Prabowo?* [Who was Prabowo's Puppeteer?]. Jakarta: Yayasan Karyawan Matra, 2001.

Tino, K. *Hamengkubuwono IX, dari serangan umum 1 Maret sampai melawan Suharto: benarkah Hamengkubuwono IX anggota CIA?* [From the General Offensive of 1 March to opposing Suharto: Was Hamengkubuwono IX really a member of the CIA?]. Yogyakarta: Navila Idea, 2012?

Tjokropranolo. *General Sudirman, the Leader who Finally Destroyed Colonialism in*

Indonesia, edited by Ian MacFarling, translated by Libby Krahling, Bert Jordan and Steve Dawson. Canberra: Australian Defence Studies Centre, 1995.
Townsend, Lucy. "The Biographer as Sleuth: Using the Concentric Circle Method". *Biography* 16, no. 1 (1993): 19–25.
Tridgell, Susan. "Understanding Selves through Modern Western Biography: Insight, Illusion or Particularity?" PhD thesis, Australian National University, 2002.
———. "Doing Justice to the Generations: Ray Monk's *Bertrand Russell*". Paper delivered at the International Conference on Life-Writing. Melbourne: La Trobe University, 15–19 July 2002.
United Nations Security Council Official Records 4th Year, 1949, nos. 26–54. New York: United Nations, 1950.
United Nations Security Council Official Records 4th Year, 1949, nos. 420–448, 21 March–27 September. New York: United Nations, 1950.
United Nations Security Council Official Records 4th Year, 1949, Supplements. New York: United Nations, 1950.
United Nations Security Council Official Records 4th Year nos. 449–458 [October–December 1949]. New York: United Nations, 1950.
Vandenbosch, Amry. *The Dutch East Indies*. Berkeley: University of California Press, 1944.
Vanvugt, Ewald. *Het Dubbele Gezicht van de Koloniaal* [The Two Faces of the Colonial]. Haarlem: In de Knipscheer, 1987.
Vatikiotis, Michael. *Indonesian Politics Under Suharto: The Rise and Fall of the New Order*. London: Routledge, 1998. (Also revised edition of 1994.)
Verhoeff, H.G. "De Herziening van de Politieke Verhouding tot de Vorstenlandsche Zelfbesturen" [Review of the Political Relationship with the Autonomous Princely States]. *Koloniale Studien 1940* 24 (1940): 109–55.
Vervoorn, Aat. *Re Orient, Change in Asian Societies*. 2nd edition. Melbourne: Oxford University Press, 2002.
Vickers, Adrian. "Selling the Experience of Bali", on <http://pandora.nla.gov.au> (consulted on 10 August 2005).
Vitacchi, Tarzie. *The Fall of Sukarno*. New York: Praeger, 1967. Has some unsourced references to the Sultan not reported elsewhere.
Viviani, Nancy. "Australian Attitudes and Policies Towards Indonesia, 1950–1965". PhD thesis, Research School of Pacific Studies, Australian National University, 1973.
Wal S.L. van der, Drooglever, P.J., and Schouten, M.B., eds. *Officiele bescheiden betreffende de Nederlands–Indonesische Betrekkingen 1945–50* [Official Documents on Dutch–Indonesian Relations 1945–50], vols. 1 to 28. The Hague: Nijhoff. Cited as *"NIB"*. Series published during the 1970s and 1980s.
———, ed. *Besturen Overzee* [Governing Overseas]. Franeker: Wever, 1977.
Wallace, Helen. "Social and Cultural Interaction Between the Japanese and the Indonesians in Java 1942–1945". PhD thesis, Monash University, 2002.

Wang Gungwu, ed. *Self and Biography, Essays on the Individual and Society in Asia*. Sydney: Sydney University Press, 1975.

Watson, C.W. *Of Self and Nation, Autobiography and the Representation of Modern Indonesia*. Hawaii: University of Hawai'i Press, 2000.

Westerkamp, Rudolf Frederik. *Yogyase Roddels* [Yogya Gossip]. A 14-page personal memoir in typescript, by the former private physician of Hamengku Buwono VIII and Hamengku Buwono IX during 1939–1942. Written for his family around 1983.

Westerling, Raymond. *Challenge to Terror*. London: Kimber, 1952.

White, B.N.F. "Towards a Social History of Economic Crises: Yogyakarta in the 1930s, 1960s and 1990s". In *Indonesia in Transition: Rethinking "Civil Society", 'Region' and 'Crisis'*, edited by H. Samuel and H. Schulte Nordholt. Yogyakarta: Pustaka Pelajar, 2004, pp. 195–225.

Wild, Colin and Peter Carey, eds. *Gelora Api Revolusi* [The Turbulent Fires of Revolution]. Jakarta: Gramedia, 1986. Contains the text of a unique BBC interview with the Sultan about the Serangan Umum in 1949.

———. *Born in Fire*. Ohio University Press, 1988. An English-language version of the above book.

Willens, Wim and Jaap de Moor, eds. *Het Einde van Indie, Indische Nederlanders tijdens de japanse bezetting en de dekolonisatie* [The End of the Indies, Eurasians during the Japanese Occupation and the Decolonization Period]. The Hague: Sdu Uitgeverij Koninginnegracht, 1995.

Woodman, Dorothy. *The Republic of Indonesia*. London: Cresset, 1955.

Woodward, Mark. *Islam in Java, Normative Piety and Mysticism in the Sultanate of Yogyakarta*. Tucson: University of Arizona Press, 1989.

Woolcott, Richard. *The Hot Seat, Reflections on Diplomacy from Stalin's Death to the Bali Bombings*. Sydney: HarperCollins, 2003.

Yamin, Mohammed, ed. *Risalah Sidang Badan Penyelidik Usaha2 Persiapan Kemerdekaan Indonesia (BPUPKI) dan Panitya Persiapan Kemerdekaan Indonesia (PPKI), 28 Mei–22 August 1945* [Proceedings of the Body for the Preparation of Indonesian Independence and of the Committee for the Preparation of Indonesian Independence], 3rd ed. Jakarta: Sekretariat Negara, 1998.

Yusril Djalinus, Stanley, Adi Prasetyo and Toriq Hadad, eds. *Jenderal Tanpa Pasukan, Politisi Tanpa Partai, Perjalanan Hidup A H Nasution* [General without Troops, Politician without a Party, the Life of A.H. Nasution]. Jakarta: Grafitipers, 2002.

Interviewees
    The late Professor Dr Mohammad Sadli
    The late Drs Radius Prawiro
    The late Dr Roeslan Abdulgani
    The late Drs Frans Seda
    Professor Dr Emil Salim

General Ashari Danudirdjo
Dr Salim Said
Pak Atmakusumah Astraatmadja
The late Pak Soedarpo Sastrosatomo
The late Pak Rosihan Anwar
Dr Adnan Buyung Nasution
G.B.P.H. Pakuningrat
Princess Nindyokirono Hamengku Buwono IX
Pak Mashud Wisnusaputra
The late Professor Dr Selosumarjan
The late Professor Dr Wijoyo Nitisastro
Pak Aristides Katoppo
Mrs Ratmini Soedjatmoko

Archives and Official Sources

Australia
National Archives of Australia
    Citations are "NAA", followed by series number and file number.
    Department of Foreign Affairs files 1945–1970.
    Australian Embassy Jakarta files, 1945–1970.
National Library of Australia (NLA)
    Indonesian Acquisitions list, 1971–76.
    Private papers of Professor Herbert Feith — consulted with kind permission of Mrs Betty Feith. The papers have yet to be fully catalogued.
Monash University, Melbourne
    Papers of Professor Herbert Feith. These are broadly those papers connected with his official life as a lecturer at the University, while the papers in NLA are generally more of a private nature, but there is an overlap. These papers are identified with a series number, MON 78, an accession number 1991/09, and an item number.
Other
    Overzicht van de Inlandsche en Chineese Pers (Summary of Native and Chinese Press, produced weekly) 1919–30 and 1939–40, on microfiche at National Library of Australia and Menzies Library, ANU.

Dutch Archives and Official Publications
Nationaal Archief (National Archives — NA), The Hague, Netherlands
    Dutch colonial archives, including Verbaal files, official Ministry of Colonies (Ministerie van Kolonien) archives, intelligence files, and many personal archives. Citations from the Nationaal Archief normally start with the letters "NA" followed by an identification number, the name of the archive, and often also by an inventory number, e.g., "NA 2.10.17, Procureur Generaal Archive,

Part 367". Personal archives usually have such numbers supplemented by a personal name, e.g., "Collectie Spoor".
- *Memories van Overgave*, 2.10.39, handover reports by Dutch officials in the regions prepared for their successors. (Bafflingly, the copies in the Menzies Library at ANU on microfilm — apparently supplied to ANU some time in the 1970s or earlier — were censored versions, all of the political sections of the *Memories* being expunged. NA in The Hague has the uncensored versions.)
- Ministerie van Kolonien geheim Archief (Ministry of Colonies Secret Archives), 2.10.36.013, on microfiche.
  - including Mailrapporten (mail report series 1901–52, and secret mail report series AA, 1914–52).
- Archief Ministerie van Kolonien — Londen (Ministry of Colonies Archives, London) 1940–46, 2.10.45.
- Commissariat van Indische Zaken (Commissariat of Indies Affairs), 2.10.49.
- Personal archives of Minister Welter (2.21.175), General Spoor (2.21.036.01), E.M. Stok (2.21.183.80), Buurman van Vreeden (2.21.036.02), Tjarda van Starkenborgh Stachouwer (2.21.183.83), P.J. Idenburg (2.21.281.02), Lovink (2.21.281.02), F.J. Goedhart (2.21.285), Gesseler Verschuir (2.21.069), van Mook (NA 2.21.123).
- Archief Procureur Generaal (Archive of the Prosecutor General), 2.10.17.
- Algemeene Secretariaat (General Secretariat), 2.10.14.
- Personeelsdossiers (Personal dossiers), 2.10.36.10.

Nationaal Instituut voor Oorlogsdocumentatie (NIOD — National Institute for War Documentation), Amsterdam

Mainly dedicated to the Dutch experience during the Second World War. I consulted the material about the Indies/Indonesia — *Indonesie Collectie* (NIOD index Volumes 4A, 4B, 4D, 5, and 12 — diaries), which includes vast amounts of material about the internment camps; but also has Japanese-period documents, some material from the late Dutch period, RAPWI documents, and many documents relating to war crimes investigations. Almost all NIOD documents have six-figure identification numbers and are identified by those numbers preceded by "NIOD", e.g., "NIOD 076323". Other methods of accessing information include the name card index and the *trefwoord* (keyword) index. Apart from those mentioned, other useful categories include the Natijd lists, and Collectie K.A. de Weerd.

Foreign Ministry Library

Holdings of Netherlands Indies Intelligence Organisation (NEFIS) files, not yet handed over to the Nationaal Archief. These have their own series of five-figure identification numbers, e.g., 06915.

Bibliography

Centraal Archievendepot (Central Archives Depot [CAD]), Ministry of Defence, Rijswijk
Sources derived from this depot are cited as "MvD/CAD" followed by available identification numbers. This vast and valuable resource contains many NEFIS files, but these are poorly indexed.
- NEFIS files — normally indexed in bundles with AA numbers e.g., "AA21". Each bundle contains a series of folders labelled (uninformatively) with vague titles such as "NEFIS 1948–49". These are the largest holdings of NEFIS files.
- Hoofdkwartier Generale Staf (Headquarters General Staff) archive. These have a three-figure inventory number, e.g., "invnr 695".
- Kabinet Legercommandant (Cabinet of the Army Commander) archive. These have two-figure inventory numbers, e.g., "invnr 35".

Instituut voor Militaire Geschiedenis (IMG) (Institute of Military History), Alexander Barracks, The Hague
Cited as "IMG" followed by identification numbers. This contains duplicates of many files photocopied from holdings in the CAD, Nationaal Archief and elsewhere, including NEFIS files.

Archief Kennemerland, Haarlem
Records of HBS-B Haarlem, from the 1930s. Residence records.

Leiden University Library
Leiden University student enrolment records, 1934–40.

Indonesian Official Sources
Indonesian Government Official Archives (Arsip Nasional Indonesia), Jakarta
Foreign researchers need a research visa to examine and photocopy documents; but visitors without such a visa may normally be permitted to examine document inventories (only).
Vice Presidential Archive of Hamengku Buwono IX (1973–78).
Personal Archive of Roeslan Abdulgani.

Widyo Budoyo (Yogyakarta Palace Archives), Yogyakarta
Holdings are documented in two main index books: Lindsay, Jennifer; Sutanto R.M.; Feinstein, Alan, eds., *Kraton Yogyakarta: Katalog Induk Naskah2 Nusantara no 2* [Yogyakarta Kraton: Main National Catalogue of Documents no 2], q.v.; Ismuwanto, R. Hery; and Pitoyo, Moh Ali, *Katalog Arsip2 Penting Keraton Ngayogyokarto* [Catalogue of Important Archives in the Yogyakarta Kraton], q.v. Holdings of documents of political and historical interest are, however, relatively scanty.

- Permission to view files and other holdings as catalogued in these books is sought individually; permission is usually granted.
- Other holdings consulted include *Kan Po* 1942–45, *Pelopor Yogyakarta* 1973–78.
- Two large scrapbooks of press clippings from the period 1938 to 1944. These include clippings about Yogyakarta events from print media such as *Surabaiasch Handelsblad* (Surabaya) and *Mataram* (Yogyakarta). Citations from the scrapbooks give details of the newspaper articles cited but add the abbreviation KPC ("Kraton Press Clippings"), because many of these seem to be unobtainable in Australia.

Arsip Daerah Istimewa Yogyakarta (DIY) (Yogyakarta Regional Archives)
Documents in this archive carry their own three-figure identification number, e.g., 157, sometimes with an additional letter e.g., 115R. Holdings are indexed in Pemerintah Propinsi Daerah Istimewa Yogyakarta, *Daftar Pertelaan Arsip2 Penting* (list of Important Archives) Kantor Arsip Daerah DIY, nd (q.v.). Entry to the archive is possible for foreign researchers, but photocopying of documents is normally not permitted.

United States
LBJ (President Lyndon Baines Johnson) National Security Files, 1962–69, on microfilm at Cornell University.

Foreign Relations of the United States (*FRUS*) series (q.v.), available in ANU library and NLA. Some volumes available on the Internet.

National Archives and Records Administration (NARA) Washington — home page on Internet. http://www.archives.gov/

Newspapers, Magazines and Journals
Almanak Leidsch Studentencorps (Leiden Student Corps Almanac) 1932/33–1939/39, Leiden University, Leiden.
Aneta Bulletin, Jakarta, 1945–50.
Api Merdeka (Yogyakarta monthly, Indonesian language), March 1946–December 1946.
Asia Raya (Japanese-era Jakarta daily, Indonesian language, Jakarta), April 1942–September 1945.
   Almanak Asia Raya 1943 and 1944.
Asian Survey, University of California, Berkeley, 1961–67.
Berita Republik Indonesia 1945–50 (Indonesian language, Jakarta — official publication of Indonesian government during Revolution).

Bibliography

Biography magazine, East–West Center, Honolulu, from 1993 to 2005.
Bulletin of Indonesian Economic Studies (BIES), 1965–78. From special CD-ROM issued by Indonesia Project, ANU.
Dagblad, Het (Jakarta daily), 1946–49.
Djawa magazine, Yogyakarta 1940 (Dutch language).
Djawa Baroe, 1942–45 (Japanese era Jakarta daily, Indonesian language).
Gids der Rijksuniversiteit Leiden (Leiden University Guide) for the years 1932/33–1938/39.
Harian Rakyat (PKI (Communist Party) daily, Indonesian language), Jakarta, 1951–52.
Indische Gids (Indies Guide, Batavia, Dutch- language monthly) — 1912, 1914, 1919, 1920, 1921, 1938, 1940, and 1941.
Indologenblad, 1932/33–1939/39, Indology faculty, Leiden University, Leiden.
Indonesia (magazine, four issues per year), Cornell Modern Indonesia Project, Ithaca, NY, 1966–2000.
Indonesian Observer, Jakarta (English-language daily), 1966.
Javasche Courant, October–December 1939 (1940 et seq not available at ANU).
Kan Po, Official Japanese Military Government publication, Indonesian-language bi-weekly, Jakarta, 1942–45.
Kedaulatan Rakjat (Yogyakarta daily, Indonesian language) — 1945–48. Also Jakarta research assistants examined KR 1950–56 and 1962–63, 1978–80.
Koloniaal Tijdschrift (Colonial Magazine, Batavia, Dutch-language magazine), 1939–41.
Koloniale Studien (Colonial Studies, Batavia, Dutch-language magazine), 1939–41.
Kompas (Jakarta daily, Indonesian language), 1965–69. Also examined by Jakarta research assistants: 1970, 1971, 1972, and 1988.
Leidsch Universiteitsblad (Leiden University Journal), 1932/33–1939/39, Leiden University, Leiden.
Locomotief, De (Semarang daily, Dutch language), 1912, 1939–41 and September 1947 to June 1950.
Merdeka (Jakarta daily, Indonesian language), 1945–52 and 1971–72.
Merdeka Mingguan weekly magazine, 1948–61, examined by Jakarta research assistants.
Moesson magazine (Dutch-language monthly), Amsterdam, 1980–2003.
Nieuwsgier (Dutch language Jakarta daily), 1949.
Patriot weekly, Yogyakarta (?) (Indonesian language), 1945–49, examined by Jakarta research assistants.
Pelopor Jogja (Yogyakarta daily, Indonesian language), November 1973–December 1974.
Sedya Tama (Yogyakarta daily, Indonesian/Javanese), 1939–42.

Siasat magazine (Indonesian language), 1950, 1952, 1953, 1955, 1957, examined by Jakarta research assistants.
Sinar Harapan (Jakarta afternoon daily, Indonesian language), 1966, 1971–72.
Sinar Matahari (Japanese-era Yogyakarta daily, Indonesian language), April 1942–September 1945.
Soeara Asia (Japanese-era daily, Indonesian language), Surabaya, 1942–September 45.
Tapol Bulletin, London, August 1973 (vol. 1, no. 1), to February 1978.
Tropisch Nederland [Tropical Netherlands], vol. 11 (1938–39).

Abbreviations of Names of Important Sources
In some cases, reports are so commonly cited that their names are abbreviated in the footnotes. The following is a list. Full descriptions of these are provided above.

AE	Australian Embassy, Jakarta — relates to reports from the Embassy cited in documents at the National Archives of Australia (NAA — q.v.)
AR	*Asia Raya*, the Japanese-era Jakarta daily
CMI	Reports by Centrale Militaire Inlichtingsdienst (Central Military Intelligence Service), the former NEFIS
East	Steijlen, Fridus, ed., *Memories of "The East"*, KITLV Press, Leiden, 2002
East CD-ROM	A CD-ROM in the Dutch language containing more extensive versions of the interviews contained in *Memories of the East*. Copies of the CD-ROM are available at KITLV and NIOD, and elsewhere.
FPL	The "Four Princes Letter" (my coinage), an interesting 15-page local account of the Sultan's illegal government during the Dutch occupation in 1948–49.
IMG	Instituut voor Militaire Geschiedenis (Military History Institute), Ministry of Defence, The Hague
IPO	*Overzicht van de Inlandsche en Chineese Pers* (Summary of the Native and Chinese Press), produced from 1918 to 1942, microfiche, ANU
KPC	Kraton Press Clippings 1937–44 (my coinage) — see above
KR	*Kedaulatan Rakyat*, Yogyakarta daily newspaper, Indonesian language, 1945–49
KRI	*Kronik Revolusi Indonesia*, Indonesian language, a multi-volume chronology of events during the Revolution (see above)
MR	Mailrapport — the series of "mail reports", official colonial

	documents. These are always marked by a number followed by the year, e.g., MR 83/40. The ones quoted here are from the holdings at the Menzies Library, ANU.
MR geh/	Secret mail reports. "Geh" is short for *geheim* i.e., secret, followed by a similar serial number.
MvD/CAD	Centraal Archievendepot, Dutch Ministry of Defence, Rijswijk
NA	Nationaal Archief (National Archives), The Hague. Most of this material carries an identification number given by the Archief, e.g., NA 2.10.178, sometimes with a further identification e.g., "Collectie Stok".
NAA	National Archives of Australia, Canberra. Citations are NAA, followed by series number and file number.
NEFIS	Reports by Netherlands Forces Intelligence Services — later CMI q.v.
NIB	The valuable series of published Dutch official documents from the Revolution period, *Officiele Bescheiden Betreffende de Nederlands — Indonesische Betrekkingen 1945–50*. See above. (I examined vols. 1 to 19.)
NIGIS	Netherlands Indies Government Information Service, English-language radio monitoring reports prepared in Melbourne during the Japanese occupation. Most of the reports used here were obtained from the CAD and also carry the CAD bundle identification numbers.
NIOD	Nederlands Instituut voor Oorlogsdocumentatie (Netherlands Institute for War Documentation), Amsterdam. Formerly called RIOD.
Risalah	*Risalah BPUPKI*, edited by Mohammed Yamin (see above)
SA	*Suara Asia*, the Japanese-era Surabaya daily, Indonesian language
SM	*Sinar Matahari*, the Japanese-era Yogyakarta daily, Indonesian language
SO	*Pelurusan Sejarah Serangan Oemoem*, book published in 2000 to contest the Suharto version of events in March 1949 — see above
TUR	*Tahta untuk Rakyat*

Known Sources Which Were Unavailable

Sudarisman Purwokusumo, *Sultan Hamengku Buwono IX*. Yogyakarta, 1986?
Tashadi, ed. *Sejarah Revolusi Fisik di Daerah Istimewa Yogyakarta*. Jakarta, Depdikbud, 1995.

Index

11 March Order (Supersemar), 251, 257, 269
17 October 1952 affair, 2, 6, 113, 198, 222, 225–31, 324
30 September Movement, 243–45, 264, 269, 286

A

Abdul Hakim, 217, 234
Abs, Hermann, 284
Aceh War, 41
Achmadi, 251
Achmad Tirtosudiro, 271
Adam, Governor Lucien, 99, 103–4, 122, 166, 318
  born, 88
  negotiations with, 69–78
Adam Malik, 1, 21–22, 246–47, 251–53, 258–59, 270–72, 275–76, 278, 280, 283–87, 290, 292, 294, 296, 298, 303, 309–10, 313, 315, 323–24
ADB (Asian Development Bank), 274
"administrators", 5, 113–14, 157, 161, 218, 224, 256, 286, 309, 314
advisory council, *see* Dewan Penasihat (advisory council)
Aidit, 241
Alamsyah Prawiranegara, 276–77
Ali Budiarjo, 196, 214, 218, 228, 231, 242
Alimin, 157
Ali Murtopo, 247, 276–77, 290, 296
Ali Sastroamijoyo, 171, 199, 238
Ali Wardhana, 248–49, 280–81
American Republic, 136
Amir Syarifuddin, 97, 143, 148, 150, 156, 159, 172, 197, 199
  PKI member, as, 157
Anak Agung, 144, 187, 233, 328
Anderson, Ben, 142, 166, 206
Andi Aziz, 215–16, 222, 231
Antara, 140
anti-Chinese riots, 97, 171
"aristo-democracy", 33, 87
Army Service Association, 223
Army Staff Command College, *see* SSKAD
Army Strategic Reserve (Kostrad), 243
army youth auxiliary (Seinendan), 110
Arnold, Benedict, 214
asceticism, 65, 185
Ashari Danudirjo, 242, 254
"Asia for the Asians", 99
Asian Development Bank, *see* ADB
Asiaweek, 96, 158
Atlantic Charter, 140, 149, 164, 188
Autonomy of the Indonesian Village, The, thesis, 146
auxiliary police (Keibodan), 110

B

Baay, General, 196, 211
Baharuddin, 223
Bale Agung (Supreme Council), 32, 76, 91, 93, 121
Bambang Sugeng, 219, 228, 235
Bambang Supeno, 219, 221, 225, 227, 230, 234, 236
Bank Indonesia (central bank), 200, 250, 254
"bapakism", 219, 235
Bapekan (Badan Pengawas Kegiatan Aparatur Negara), 241, 262
Bappenas (Badan Perencanaan Pembangunan Nasional), 248, 283
BB (Barisan Banteng), 147–48
Bebasa Daeng Malolo, 221, 225
Beel, Louis J.M., 177–78, 182, 187, 191
"Beel Plan", 187
Berg, C.C., 41
Berkhuysen, 189, 208
"Berkeley mafia, the", 248
BFO (Bijeenkomst voor Federale Overleg), 144, 187
Bijleveld, Governor, 47, 72, 90
Bimas agricultural programme, 323
Bintoro, Prince, 44, 69, 116, 120, 142, 161, 201
see also Raisulngaskari
biography
advantages of, 307–9
Asian, 310–11
cross-cultural, 5, 16, 19
elitist, as, 14, 304, 306–7
image and language, 309–10
one-dimensional, 19
political, 9
problems of, 306–7
subgenres of, 10
text, as, 12
theory of, 13

black magic, 31
black market, 105, 277
"blockade system", 181
Boeke, J.H., 41, 43–44, 57, 257
BPI (Badan Pusat Inteligens), 216
BPK (Badan Pemeriksa Keuangan), 241–42, 249, 252, 254, 263, 273, 286, 289
BPK (Badan Pengawas Kerajaan), 100
BPUPKI (Badan Penyelidik Usaha2 Persiapan Kemerdekaan Indonesia), 44, 88, 104, 116–18, 122, 125, 131, 133, 137
Breda Military Academy, 39
Broekman, Mourik, 38
"budget chaos", 30
Budi Utomo, 31–32, 116, 131
Bukan Karena Ambisi (*Not Because of Ambition*), book, 227
BULOG (Badan Urusan Logistik), 271
Bureau for Princely Territories, *see* BPK (Badan Pengawas Kerajaan)
Burhanuddin Harahap, 238
Burma–Siam railway, 107

C

Canadian Resolution, 187
capitalism, 31, 43, 69, 146
Catholic Party, 177, 180
Central Advisory Council (Chuo Sangi-in), 104, 119, 122
central bank (Bank Indonesia), 200, 250, 254
Central Intelligence Agency, *see* CIA
Central Intelligence Body, *see* BPI
Central Java federal state, 180
Central Java, plague in, 31
Chaerul Saleh, 218, 249, 251
Chandler, David, 16
Chinese issue, 257
Chinese support, 155, 170
Chinese Red Cross, 45

Chuo Sangi-in (Central Advisory Council), 104, 119, 122
Churchill, Winston, 15
CIA (Central Intelligence Agency), 216, 243
Cipto Mangunkusumo, 31
Cohen, A.E., 49
Colijn, Hendrikus, 33, 49, 67–68
colonialism, 43, 51, 85, 98, 196, 198, 279, 312
colonial war, 154
Committee for the Preparation of Indonesian Independence, *see* PPKI
Committee to Investigate Preparations for Indonesian Independence, *see* BPUPKI
communism, 49, 157, 234
communist death squads, 158
Communist Party of Indonesia, *see* PKI
"concentric circles method", 21
Confrontation, against Malaysia, 247, 269
constitutional monarchical system, 120
corruption, 217, 252, 255, 266, 274, 289, 299
Council of Generals, 243
Council of the Indies (Raad van Indie), 72
Council of Youth Leaders, 154
coup, 158, 214, 222, 228, 230, 243–46
Cribb, Robert, 92, 263
Critchley, Tom, 173, 204, 208–9
cross-border smuggling, 105
CSIS, think tank, 276
cultural relativism, 18

D

Daendels, Governor General, 63, 102
Dahler, P.F., 117–18
Danurejo, Prince, 104, 119, 125, 132
Darmasetiawan, 195
Darul Islam, 214–15, 218, 233
death lists, 242, 263
'decentred self', 13
Defence Law, 223
"Defender of the Faith", 66
de Graaf, H.J., 41
de Jonge, Governor General, 33, 46–47, 49, 67
de Jong, Josselin, 41
democracy, and republicanism, 136
Department of Home Affairs, 134, 138
Depression, of 1930s, 62–63
de Saussure, Ferdinand, 12
"despairing pessimism", 43
Development Cabinet, 283
Dewan Penasihat (advisory council), 75–76, 91, 119, 159
Diah, B.M., 221, 272
Diponegoro, Prince, 77, 113, 317, 327, 330
divide-and-rule tactics, 64, 68
Divine Soul, 65
Dorojatun
    born, 28–29
    contacts with Dutch elite, 47–49
    father, 28, 60, 65, 85
    mother, 30–31
    school years, 29, 36–45
    student council, involvement in, 45
    succession, 72–73
    see also Hamengku Buwono IX
Drees, Prime Minister Willem, 178, 180
Dutch attack, 153–56, 160, 173–99
Dutch colonial army (KNIL), 96, 123, 144, 194, 196, 213–15, 308
Dutch Colonies Ministry, 150
Dutch East Indies Company (VOC), 63, 66

Dutch rule, paternalism of, 71, 89
dynastic rights, 79

E
East Timor, annexation of, 292, 325
economic dualism, 43
"economic generals", 271
Eerste Europese Lagere School B (Lower European Primary), school, 36
elections, 48–49, 75, 227, 239, 284–86, 292, 325
elitism, 14, 306
Elson, Robert, 16, 207, 210, 244, 263, 301–2, 313
Emergency Government, 173
emotionalism, 229, 285
Ethical Policy, 46, 67, 71–72
Evans, Richard J., 12
executive monarch, 120

F
family principle, 68–69
fascism, 49
"fascist Republic", 149
Federal Consultative Assembly, *see* BFO
Federal currency, 181
feudalism, 113, 132, 172, 295, 305
"fiefdom", status of, 79
First World War, 31, 49, 82
Five Year Development Plan, *see* Repelita
"floating mass", doctrine of the, 325
Foreign Assistance Act, 272
Foreign Investment Law, 275–76, 279
"Four Princes Letter", 200
Frans Seda, 242, 248–49, 254, 258, 265, 271–73, 280, 282, 287, 295, 299, 303
freedom of speech, 48, 194, 270
free-market approach, 257

Frobel school, 36
Funabiki, H., 100, 125
"functional groups", 68, 147

G
Gadjah Mada University, 152
Gandhi, biography, 9
Gapi, nationalist organization, 83
Garebeg celebration, 80
Gatot Subroto, 157, 195, 227, 248
General Offensive (Serangan Umum), 6, 183–84, 291, 320
  effect and aftermath, 186–88
Gerinda, 34, 239
Gerindo, 83
German occupation of the Netherlands, 83
Geyl, Pieter, 19
Giyanti Agreement, 63
Goldman, J., 49
Golkar, 151, 247, 284–89, 325
gotong royong (cooperation), 146–47
government, concepts of, 67–69
"Great Man" biography, 8, 11
guerrilla, 97, 160, 174, 176, 178–79, 181–83 199, 217
Guided Democracy, 1, 68, 146–47, 198, 239, 241, 275–76, 309–10, 325

H
Haarlem Lyceum, 38
Hadikusumo, Prince, 200
"half-coup", 222, 230
Hafas, T.D., 315
Halifax, Lord, 2, 231
Hamengku Buwono I, 51, 119
Hamengku Buwono II, 63, 182
Hamengku Buwono VII, 28, 36, 52, 79
Hamengku Buwono VIII, 28–30, 32, 36, 47, 49–51, 59–60, 70–71, 78–79, 111, 121

Index

Hamengku Buwono IX
  business interests, 239, 253, 289, 313, 317, 330
  children, 84
  Coordinator of Internal Security, as, 157–59, 171, 191–92
  coronation, 80–82
  "democrat", as, 2, 48, 325–26
  economy, and, 286–87
  characterizations of, 3
  Deputy Supreme Commander for Economic Affairs, as, 246
  Dutch, under the, 82–84
  incognito, travelling, 142–43, 166
  Indonesian, as, 320–21
  Javanese leader, as, 317–19
  militia and the army, and, 141–44
  Military Governor, as, 155
  ministerial role, 150–51, 156, 191–92, 195, 198, 216–17, 219–20, 231, 238, 241, 250–52, 272–73, 283–84, 316
  national government, role in, 150–56
  political contract, issues with, 73–78
  political-economic statement, and, 254–58
  politician, as, 319–20
  private life, 5, 84, 129–30
  relations with the nationalists, 112–15
  republic state, and, 133–38
  resignation, 175–76, 178–79, 203, 225, 232, 250, 292, 294, 313, 320
  rift with Suharto, 289–93
  tours, 111–12
  Vice President, as, 287–89
  wives, 84, 130, 284
  see also Dorojatun
Hamengku Buwono X, 51, 84, 111, 322, 329
Hamengkunagoro, 28, 51, 77

Hamid II, Sultan, 36, 39, 47, 144, 175, 178, 189, 208, 213–15, 233, 272
Hangabehi, Prince, 35, 48, 52
  see also Pakubuwono XI
Harada, General, 100
Harian Rakjat, newspaper, 221
Hatta Kikan, 98
Hatta, Mohammad, 40, 47–48, 51, 97, 98, 106, 113, 116, 133, 135, 137, 145–46, 156–59, 162, 173–74, 177–80, 189–91, 194, 196–97, 199, 213, 216–18, 220–21, 225–26, 228, 234, 240–41, 287, 299, 323
Hatta, Rahmi, 201
Hayam Wuruk, 65–66
Hazelett, Samuel, 182, 205
Hermani, 189, 208
Hertog, 46–47
Hill, David, 17
history theory, 13
Ho Chi Minh, 266
Hokokai, *see* Jawa Hokokai
holy war (*perang sabil*), 154, 181
Honggowongso, 141, 161, 173, 175, 201
Hoogere Burger School (HBS), 37–38
Hurgronje, Snouck, 41, 67
"hyper-relativism", 12

I
Ibnu Sutowo, 271
IBRD (International Bank for Reconstruction and Development), *see* World Bank
Idenburg, P.J.A., 153, 155, 314, 318
Idham Chalid, 251, 287, 292
IGGI (Inter-Governmental Group on Indonesia), 248
Imamura, Commander in Chief, 101, 125, 126
IMF (International Monetary Fund), 258–59, 273–74

In Defence of History, book, 12
Indies Association, 46
Indies Conference, 45
individualism, 68, 146, 261
"Indology", 37, 39, 40–41, 45–46, 49–50, 270, 309, 318
Indonesia
  debt, 255, 272–73, 277, 285, 324
  independence, preparations for, 115–18
  monarchy, and, 117–18
  new economic policies, 274–76
  proclamation of independence, 133–34
"Indonesia", as a term, 114, 130
Indonesian advisers (*sanyos*), 119
Indonesian Communist Party, see PKI
Indonesian National Army, see TNI
Indonesian Nationalist Party, see PNI
Indonesian parliament, 83–84
Indonesian People's Army, see TRI
Indonesian Republic, 137
Indonesian Socialist Party, see PSI
Indonesian Students' Action Front, see Kami
Indonesian Students Association, see Roepi
Indonesian Trade and Society, 42
inflation, 105–6, 249–50, 253, 255–57, 260, 274, 278–79, 281, 283–84, 310, 324
Institute of Constitutional Awareness, see LKB
Inter-Governmental Group on Indonesia, see IGGI
International Bank for Reconstruction and Development, see World Bank
International Monetary Fund, see IMF
"international occupation law", 97
internees and minorities, 140–41
Iwa Kusuma Sumantri, 231, 238

J
Janur Kuning, film, 291
Japanese
  "burrowing", 35
  occupation, 34, 36, 61, 78, 85, 95–120
  regulations, 105–6
  relations with the, 99–105
Jatikusumo, Prince, 110, 143, 176, 193, 196, 210
Java
  "indirect" rule in, 100
  revolts in, 32
Javanese
  concept of power, 34, 64, 185
  kingship, 308
  mysticism, 16, 64–65, 68, 184–85
Javanese King, elements of ideal, 184–86, 315–16, 322
"Jawa Baru" (New Java), 114, 130
Jawa Hokokai (Java Service Association), 111, 116, 128–30, 134, 138, 163
Jawa, magazine, 71
Jayadiningrat, Husein, 175, 200
JI (Jemaah Islamiyah), 233
Joyoboyo myths, 97, 102, 226
Juanda, 177, 181, 192, 199, 201–2, 238, 240–41
Juliana, Queen, 47, 196
June 1946 affair, 148
Just King (Ratu Adil), 29, 35

K
Kahar Muzakkar, Abdul, 116, 217, 223
Kahin, George, 157, 178
Kalla, Jusuf, 293
KAMI (Kesatuan Aksi Mahasiswa Indonesia), 247, 249, 258
Kartodipuro, Prince, 35, 50
Kasimo, 33

Katamso, Colonel, 264
Kawilarang, Colonel, 196, 237
Kedaulatan Rakjat, newspaper, 148
kedaulatan rakyat (people's sovereignty), 136, 139
Keibodan (auxiliary police), 110
Kemal Idris, 195, 236, 290
Kempeitai, 103, 109, 138–39, 164
Keynes, John Maynard, 44
Ki Bagus Hadikusumo, 116, 118, 131
Kido battalion barracks, 139
Ki Hajar Dewantoro, 30, 68–69, 116
king and religion, 65–66
"King of Indonesia", 35
KNI (Komite Nasional Indonesia), 139, 144, 148, 152, 181
KNID (Komite Nasional Indonesia Daerah), 138, 142, 144–45, 148
KNIL (Dutch colonial army), 96, 123, 144, 194, 196, 213–15, 308
KNIP, *see* KNI
Koiso, Prime Minister, 101, 115, 134
Kompas, 252, 256, 279, 284, 293, 297
Kooti Jimukyoku, 100–101, 125
Korean War, 217
Kosasih, Colonel, 225, 227
Kostrad (Army Strategic Reserve), 243
Kota Baru events, 138–40
KOTI (Komando Operasi Tertinggi), 246, 249
kraton army, 75, 77, 90
Kretarto, Lt Col, 227
Krom, N.J., 41
Kusnan, 181
Kustilah, Raden Ayu, 28
Kusumoyudo, Prince, 35–36
Kyai Joko Piturun, kris, 60

L
Laoh, 181, 192
Laskar Rakyat Mataram (Mataram People's Militia), 141–42, 159, 161–62
Latief Hendraningrat, 181, 204
Latuharhary, Johannes, 192
Leiden University, 37–39, 41, 45–46, 70–71, 142, 186, 252
Leidsche Corps, 142
Leimena, Johannes, 177–78, 244, 251–52
"liberal democracy", 287
"life-writing", theory about, 5
Linen, James, 280
Linggajati Agreement, 144, 151–53, 192, 319
"linguistic turn, the", 12
literary theory, 13
LKB (Lembaga Kesadaran Berkonstitusi), 293
Logistics Board, *see* BULOG
Lovink, Viceroy, 195–96

M
Madiun affair, 157–60, 175, 197
Mahabharata, Indic epic, 66, 185
"Mahabharata, The", thesis, 41
Malaysia, Confrontation with, *see* Confrontation against Malaysia
Malari crisis, 292, 325
Malino conference, 144, 149
Manai Sophian, 223–24, 227
Mangkubumi, Prince, 28, 51, 63, 80
Mangkunegaran, 35–36, 64, 126, 137, 148
Mangkunegaran Legion, 90, 102, 104
Mangkunegoro, 32, 63, 66, 80, 83, 85, 87, 94, 101–3, 110, 117, 121, 159–60, 178, 321
Mangkunegoro II, 87
Mangkunegoro III, 87
Mangkunegoro V, 131
Mangkunegoro VII, 32, 100, 126, 131
Mangkunegoro VIII, 131

March 11 Order, *see* 11 March Order (Supersemar)
Marshall Plan, 188
Marxism, 69
Mashuri, 246, 267, 276, 286
Masyumi, 131, 158, 216–18
Mataram Canal, public works project, 107–8, 111–12, 150, 312
Mataram, kingdom of, 63, 135
Mataram People's Army (Tentara Rakyat Mataram), 142
Mataram People's Militia (Laskar Rakyat Mataram), 141–42, 159, 161–62
McIntyre, Angus, 18
McNamara, Robert, 283
Meijer, General, 183, 185, 316
Merdeka 100%, 147
"merdeka ideals", 150
Merdeka, newspaper, 221
"Middle Way", 220
military codes, 200
Military Government, 101, 104, 110, 115–16, 119, 124, 132
Mimbar Indonesia, newspaper, 221
Ministry of Colonies, 39, 47
Misbach, Haji, 31
Mochtar Lubis, 17, 293, 310
Modoo, Adriana, 123
Mohamad Sadli, 248–49, 271, 281
Mohamad Yusuf, 290
Mokoginta, Lt Col, 215
monarchical system, 120
monetarism, 44
monetary policy, 105
"mono-loyalty", doctrine of, 325
Mozes, *see* Hamid II, Sultan
MPRS (Majlis Permusyawarahan Rakyat Sementara), 257–59, 269, 276
Muchtar Usman, 242
Muhammadiyah, 31, 131, 167, 202, 290

Muhammad Saleh Werdisastro, *see* Saleh, Mohammad
Mulder, B.J., 176
Murba party, 224
Murdani, Benny, 290
"Murder of Captain Francois Tack on 18 February 1686, The", thesis, 41
Muso, 157, 158
Mustopo, 225

N
Nadel, Ira, 13
Nahdlatul Ulama (NU), 290
Nakamura, General, 139
Nakayama, Colonel, 100, 124, 25
"Napoleon of Indonesia, the", 3
Nasakom, 241, 242, 310
Nasution, Abdul Haris, 1, 6, 21, 156, 158–60, 195–97, 214, 219–25, 227–28, 231, 235–38, 241, 243–44, 246, 259, 269, 275, 290, 310, 314–15, 323
National Audit Board, *see* BPK (Badan Pemeriksa Keuangan)
nationalism, 5, 19, 31, 35, 47, 49, 51, 81, 114–15, 153, 188, 197, 311, 320, 323, 327
National Planning Board, *see* Bappenas
National Socialist Movement, *see* NSB
Natsir, Mohammad, 174, 216–19
Nazi, 56, 327
NEFIS (Netherlands Forces Intelligence Service), 155, 170–72
Netherlands
    German occupation, under, 83
    economic background, 37–38
Netherlands Indies Civil Administration, *see* NICA
Netherlands Military Mission (NMM), 198, 219–21

Neutrale Europese Lagere School (Upper European Primary), 36
"New Biography", 8–9
New Java ("Jawa Baru"), 114, 130
New Order, 4, 21, 23, 44, 62, 69, 146, 226, 232, 242, 244, 248–50, 252, 254, 256–57, 269, 271, 275–77, 280–81, 284–88, 290, 295, 305, 307, 309, 313–16, 318, 320, 323–26
  projecting overseas, 258–61
NICA (Netherlands Indies Civil Administration), 140, 181
Nindyokirono, Princess, 85, 288
Not Because of Ambition (*Bukan Karena Ambisi*), book, 227
Notokusumo, 64
Notonegoro, 116, 141, 161
Noto Suroto, 33
NSB (Nationaal Socialistische Beweging), 47, 56
"nucleus cabinet", 259
NU (Nahdlatul Ulama), 290
Nurma Musa, *see* Nindyokirono, Princess
Nyai Roro Kidul, Goddess of the South Seas, 64

O

Office of Sultanate Affairs, *see* Kooti Jimukyoku
"Occidental", 42
October 17, 1952, affair, 2, 6, 113, 198, 222, 225–31, 324
Ojong, P.K., 256
Old Order, 170, 270, 274–75, 277–78, 285–86
On the Study of Indonesian History, 42
"one-dimensional biographies", 19
Organization for the Recovery of Allied Prisoners of War and Internees, *see* RAPWI
"Oriental", 42

"Orientalism", 16, 18–20
ORI (Oeang Republik Indonesia), 181–82
Oto Iskandar Dinata, 82, 202
Our Struggle (*Perjuangan Kita*), booklet, 140

P

Pakualaman House, 64, 68, 100
Pakualam Legion, 83, 103
Pakualam VII, 48, 111
Pakualam VIII, 48, 100, 111
Pakubuwono II, 63
Pakubuwono III, 63
Pakubuwono X, 35, 101
Pakubuwono XI, 85, 100
Pakubuwono XII, 52, 131
palace rivalries, 31
pamong praja, 148, 308
pan-Asianism, 99
pan-Malay nation, 116
Panatagama, title, 66
Pancasila ideology, 251–52, 259
Pandawa brothers, 66
Pandelaki, Hans, 242, 254, 273
"Pantheism and Monism in Javanese Suluk literature", thesis, 41
Parindra, nationalist party, 35, 83
Parman, 236
Patih, role of, 74–77, 99, 102
"patrimonialism", 219
pemuda, radical youth, 138–39, 147, 163
People's Council (Volksraad), 31, 82–83, 117, 131, 308
people's militia, 82
People's Security Army, *see* TKR
people's sovereignty (*kedaulatan rakyat*), 136, 139
Perhimpunan Indonesia (PI), 40, 47
Perjuangan Kita (*Our Struggle*), booklet, 140

Permesta rebellion, 240
Persatuan Perjuangan (United Struggle), 145
Pertamina, 271, 292
Peta, 103–4, 107, 110, 130, 131, 167, 214, 234
Petition of 50, 315
Pintokopurnomo, 84
PIR (Partai Indonesia Raya), 189, 208
PKI (Partai Komunis Indonesia), 2, 31, 147, 157–59, 193, 198, 218, 221, 223, 239–42, 245–46, 249, 253, 260, 263–64, 269, 307, 320
  Amir Syarifuddin, as member of, 157
  members massacred, 243, 244
PKN (Pakempalan Kawulo Ngayogyakarta), 32–35, 121, 150, 239
PKS (Pakempalan Kawula Surokarto), 35
PNI (Partai Nasionalis Indonesia), 33, 218–19, 221–24, 242, 325
political biography, 9
political contract, 69–70, 72–73, 100
political triumvirates, 246–47, 279–81
Pol Pot, 16
postmodern theory, 10, 12, 24
power typologies, 314–15
PPKI (Panitya Persiapan Kemerdekaan Indonesia), 133
Prabukusumo, 84
Prabuningrat, Prince, 44, 55, 58, 93, 103, 161, 175, 180, 189–90, 200, 205
  see also Tinggarto
"presidential" cabinet, 156
"President for Life", 259, 269
pricing policy, 274–75, 282
private enterprise, potential of, 256
priyayi class, 112
PRN (Partai Rakyat Nasional), 221

Projodiningrat, 176
Provisional People's Consultative Congress, see MPRS
PRRI (Pemerintah Revolusioner Republik Indonesia), 240, 324
PSI (Partai Sosialis Indonesia), 218–19, 221, 225–26, 229, 239
"psycho-biography", 9
Pujokusumo, Prince, 200
"pure Javanese", 112
Puruboyo, Haryo, 28–30, 48, 51–53, 55, 69, 91, 104, 116, 118, 120, 131, 133, 161, 182, 186, 205
Putera, the, 98, 111–12, 122, 125

R
racial superiority, 102
Radius Prawiro, 242, 248–49, 254, 266, 286
Raffles, Stamford, 63–64
Raisulngaskari, Prince, 44, 46
  see also Bintoro
Rajiman Wediodiningrat, Raden, 116, 133
Ranneft, Meyer, 47
RAPWI (Organization for the Recovery of Allied Prisoners of War and Internees), 139
Ratna Sari Dewi, 258
Ratu Adil (Just King), 29, 35
Ratulangie, Sam, 151
Ratu Pembayun, 48
recession, 279
Red Cross, 95, 140
Regional Indonesian National Committee, see KNID
regionalism, 2
Reid, Anthony, 23, 89, 130, 327
Renville agreement, 144, 156, 174, 193
Repelita (Rencana Pembangunan Lima Tahun), 284

Index

republicanism, and democracy, 136
Republican radio, 143
Republic of Indonesia currency, *see* ORI
Republic of Indonesia Private Staff, *see* SPRI
Republic of the United States of Indonesia, *see* RIS
Reserve Officer Corps, 131
revisionism, 19
Revolutionary Council, 245
Revolution, period of, 6, 15, 35, 36, 68, 72, 78, 105, 111, 113, 115, 122, 141, 152, 161, 191, 196–98, 215, 221, 227, 253, 270, 293, 294, 320, 324
"revolution", concept of, 23
rice economy, 253, 281–82
rice rationing, 105–6, 109–10
RIS (Republik Indonesia Serikat), 144, 196, 213–15
Roepi (Roekoen Pelajar Indonesia), 46–47
Roeslan Abdulgani, 195, 243, 266
Roestam Effendi, 48
Romme, Professor, 180
romusha programme, 107–10, 120
Round Table Conference, 191, 211, 217, 222
Royal Dutch Shell, 46
RMS (Republic of the South Moluccas), 216, 222
Rum, Mohammad, 187
Rum–van Royen agreement, 191–92
Russell, Bertrand, 21

S

Said, Edward, 42
Said, Raden Mas, 63
Saleh Afiff, 248
Saleh, Mohammad, 142, 144, 147–48 born, 167
Salim, Emil, 248–49, 281, 283, 298
Salim, Haji Agus, 116, 208, 320, 323
Sarbini, 248, 276–77, 298
Sarekat Islam, 31
Sarwo Edhie, 290
Sassen, Colonies Minister, 177, 191
Sato, Colonel, 103, 107, 259
Sayuti Melik, 116
Schama, Simon, 13
Schrieke, B.J.O., 56, 67
Schrieke, J.J., 41, 45, 56
scorched earth policy, 97, 174
"secret cabinet", 202, 247
Sedya Tama, daily, 169
Seinendan (army youth auxiliary), 110
Selosumarjan, 75, 106, 109, 112, 119–20, 129, 132, 138, 141–42, 161–62, 242–43, 248, 250, 263, 276, 288, 328–29
Semaun, 241
September 30, Movement, 243–45, 264, 269, 286
Serangan Umum, *see* General Offensive
Setiajit, 157
"Seven Up", group, 242
Sewaka, 218, 238
"shadow government", 271
Short Declaration (korte verklaring), 69
Shunkichiro, Miyoshi, 100
Sidik Joyosukarto, 218–19
Simatupang, Colonel, 174, 191, 195, 214, 219–20, 222, 228, 231, 233–34, 323
Sim Ki Ay, 199, 209
Sinar Matahari, newspaper, 139
Singapore, fall of, 95
Social Affairs Department, 176
"social revolution", 149
"sociography", 15

"sociological exoticism", 71
Soejatno Kartodirdjo, 125, 148
"solidarity-makers", 5, 113, 219, 221, 256
Solo Special Region, 159
"Some Observations on Early Asian Trade", thesis, 42
Somutyokan (Patih equivalent), 101
Sonobudoyo museum, 68
Soumokil, 216, 231
Spoor, General Simon Hendrik, 154, 165, 180, 181, 188, 191, 206, 209
SPRI (Staf Pribadi Republik Indonesia), 276
Sri Bintang Pamungkas, 315
SSKAD (Sekolah Staf dan Komando Angkatan Darat), 249
State Apparatus Supervising Board, *see* Bapekan
Stedelijk Gymnasium, 38
Stikker, Foreign Minister, 178
Stok, E.M., 47, 91, 175, 182, 189, 208, 318
Strachey, Lytton, 8, 13
Student Organisation for the Advancement of Indonesian Culture, *see* SVIK
Subadio Sastrosatomo, 218
Subandrio, 216, 240–41, 251, 261
subgenres of biography, 10
succession, in Java, 66–67
Sudarisman Purwokusumo, 152, 169–70
Sudarpo Sastrosatomo, 85, 218
Sudarsono, R., 139, 148
Sudirman, 143, 148, 158, 183, 191, 193, 195, 197, 199, 206, 211, 227, 323
sugar industry, 34, 63, 107, 127, 150
Sugih Arto, 242, 254
Sugiyono, Lt Col, 264
Suharto, 1, 3–4, 16, 20–21, 68, 107, 111, 146, 176, 181, 183–84, 193, 198, 210, 216, 226, 231, 233, 243–54, 257, 259, 261, 266, 269–73, 275, 280, 288, 294, 296–97, 305, 308–11, 313, 315, 320, 322, 326–28
  Acting President, as, 276–79
  Javanese leader, as, 317–19
  parentage, 291–92, 302
  President, as, 281–87
  rift with Hamengku Buwono IX, 289–93
Suharto, Tien, 290, 301
Sujarwo Condronegoro, 49
Sujatmoko, 207, 218, 248, 258, 265
Sujono Humardhani, 277, 328
Sukadari, 40
Sukardan, 242
Sukarno, 1, 3, 16, 18, 21, 33, 51, 69, 98, 108–9, 112–13, 116, 118, 135, 137, 144–48, 150–51, 158–59, 162, 173–74, 177–80, 189–200, 216, 218, 220–22, 224–36, 239–47, 249–54, 257–61, 263, 265–66, 269, 272, 275, 280, 283, 288, 297, 308–11, 313, 316, 320, 322–23, 326, 328
  Javanese leader, as, 317–19
  President, as, 133–34
"Sukarno debt", 284
Sukarno, Fatmawati, 201
Sukawati, 144, 216
Sukiman Wiryosanjoyo, 97, 116, 118, 131, 158, 217–20, 225
Sultan Agung, 63, 65–66, 135, 180, 316
Sultan, under the Dutch, 82–84
Sumarlin, Johannes, 248
Sumarsono, 171
Sumitro Joyohadikusumo, 229, 248, 280, 283, 290, 295, 299, 303
Sumodiningrat, *see* Kartodipuro
Sunan Giri, tomb of, 112
Sunan of Solo, 30, 32, 35–36, 50, 63–64, 70, 79, 83, 96, 99–101, 117,

Index

120–21, 131, 147–48, 159–60, 296, 321
see also Pakubuwono II, III, X, XI and XII
Sungkono, 158, 171, 195, 211
"Supersemar", see 11 March Order (Supersemar)
Supreme Advisory Council (DPA), 106, 159
Supreme Council, see Bale Agung
Supreme Operations Command, see KOTI
Surabaya, battle of, 142
Surono, General, 242, 292
Suryaningprang, Prince, 182, 200, 205
Suryo Guritno, Raden Mas, 101, 131, 158–59
Suryoamijoyo of Solo, Prince, 35, 116, 125, 147
Suryobronto, Prince, 200
Suryodilogo, Prince, 48, 111
Suryodiningrat, 30, 34, 51, 112, 121
Suryosuparto, R.M., 131
Susilo Bambang Yudhoyono, 84, 293
"suspension of arms", 192, 211
Sutarjo, 47, 82–84, 165
Sutoko, 236
Suwarto, Colonel, 246, 248, 264
SVIK (Student Organisation for the Advancement of Indonesian Culture), 46–47
Syafruddin Prawiranegara, 173, 299
Syahrir, Sutan, 97, 122, 140, 142–45, 147, 150, 152–53, 173, 178, 197, 218–19, 226, 292, 319, 323
  kidnapped, 148, 221
Syarif Hamid Alkadri, see Hamid II, Sultan
Syarif Kasim of Siak, Sultan, 136
Syech Maulana Malik Ibrahim, tomb of, 112
syndicalism, 146

T

Tahta untuk Rakyat, 198, 320
Taman Siswa educational organization, 30, 133
Tan Ling Jie, 157
Tan Malaka, 145, 147–48, 152, 157, 168, 199, 211, 323, 329
Taylor, A.J.P., 2
Tempo, 96
Tentara Rakyat Mataram (Mataram People's Army), 142
Thamrin, 82
Time-Life organization, 280
Times of Indonesia, 226
Tinggarto, Prince, 36–37, 39–40, 44, 46
  see also Prabuningrat
TKR (Tentara Keamanan Rakyat), 143, 145
TNI (Tentara Nasional Indonesia), 143, 151, 169, 174, 176, 181–84, 187, 190–92, 194–96, 210–11, 213, 215–16, 233
Tojo, Prime Minister, 101, 114, 119
"Tokyo Club" meeting, 273
"Tommy" Suharto (Mandala Putra Suharto), 329
Townsend, Lucy, 21
Tridgell, Susan, 11, 15, 21
TRI (Tentara Rakyat Indonesia), 143
Tun Razak, 259

U

UN Good Offices Commission, 145, 156, 173
Union of Subjects of Surakarta, see PKS
Union of Subjects of Yogyakarta, see PKN
United Nations Commission for Indonesia (UNCI), 182, 188, 194, 205

see also UN Good Offices Commission (UNGOC)
United States of Indonesia, see RIS
United Struggle (Persatuan Perjuangan), 145
universality of history, 306
University of Indonesia, 246, 249
UN Security Council, 175, 178, 183, 187
Untung, Colonel, 243
UN (United Nations), 258–59
Urip Sumoharjo, 154–55
Utrecht University, 41

V

van de Plas, Charles, 104, 143
van Langen, Colonel, 175, 180, 208
van Leur, J.C., 41–43, 67
van Marseveen, Minister for Overseas Territories, 182
van Mook, Hubertus, 71, 80, 144, 154, 177, 222
van Starkenborgh Stachouwer, Tjarda, 83
van Vreeden, Buurman, 177, 181
"village restoration", 43
VOC (Dutch East Indies company), 63, 66
Volksraad (People's Council), 31, 82–83, 117, 131, 308
von Vollenhoven, C., 41, 80

W

war economy, 120
"War of Independence", 23
Warouw, Lt Col, 227–28
Watson, C.W., 320
Westerling, Raymond "Turk", 213–14, 222, 231–33
West Sumatra, revolts in, 32
"whispering campaign", 204
Wijoyo Nitisastro, 246, 248–49, 265, 271, 276–77, 280–81, 283, 286, 298–99, 315, 324
Wilhelmina, Queen, 29, 48
Wilopo, 217–20, 225–26, 228, 235, 238, 265
wisik, concept of, 65, 87, 318, 328
"working cabinet", 283
World Bank, 258, 273–74, 283
World War I, 31, 49, 82
Wulangreh, text, 66

Y

Yamauchi, Resident, 103
Yamin, Mohammed, 116, 118, 148, 218, 221, 225, 323
Yap Thiam Hien, 315
Yogyakarta
  "capital of the Revolution", 145
  Central Government move to, 144–50
  defenceless, against Japanese, 96
  Dutch attack on, 173–99
  Dutch capture of, 2
  developments after the war, 118–20
  economic and social situation, 61–63
  history, 63
  ideology of principality, 64–67
  Japanese regulations in, 105–6
  law on "Specialness" of, 132, 163, 321–22
  local reforms in, 152–53
  population, 61–62, 168
Yogyakarta City Council, 152
Yogyakarta dynasty, 51
Yogya Kembali monument, 291
Yoshigawa, S., 100, 125
Young Man Luther, biography, 9
Youth Pledge, 33
youth welfare, 262
Yudhistira, King, 206

Z

Zoetmulder, P.J., 41

The Yogyakarta palace entrance on the main square in Yogyakarta.
J Monfries

The symbol of the Yogyakarta Sultanate. The letters in Javanese script are "HB", for Hamengku Buwono. Yogyakarta palace.

Hamengku Buwono VIII and Dorojatun's mother, probably around 1918. Public domain.

Hamengku Buwono VIII and his sons in the 1920s. Dorojatun is on the left at front. Public domain.

The Hoogere Burger School (Public High School) building in Haarlem, where Dorojatun studied for four years. The inscription "Hoogere Burger School anno 1906" can be read over the arch. The building was converted to apartments after the school closed.
J Monfries.

Wilheminastraat 7, Haarlem, in the next street, where Dorojatun lived with the Broekman family 1930–34.
J Monfries.

HBS-B certificate awarded to Tinggarto (later Prabuningrat), Haarlem, mid-1934. Dorojatun would have received a similar certificate before going on to Leiden University.
KRT Jatiningrat.

Kloksteeg 8A, Leiden, where Dorojatun stayed from 1935 to 1937. The forbidding inscription in English over the threshold was probably not there during his time. J Monfries.

J.J. Schrieke, Dorojatun's teacher on colonial law. Parliamentary Documentation Centre, Leiden University.

Dorojatun (not looking at camera) and Tinggarto (closest to camera) at a student event in October 1935, their second year at Leiden. KRT Jatiningrat.

Dorojatun and Tinggarto with a group from Java attending the wedding of Princess Juliana, January 1937. The demure young woman in the centre is the famously beautiful Princess Nurul of Solo ("Gusti Nurul"), at one time mentioned as a possible wife for Dorojatun. KRT Jatiningrat.

Dorojatun with several members of the same group. He has his hands on the shoulders of his cousin Hertog. The woman in the picture is the Ratu Pembayun (the equivalent title would be Princess Royal). KRT Jatiningrat.

Bas-relief at kraton portraying HBIX and Governor Lucien Adam negotiating the political contract. J Monfries.

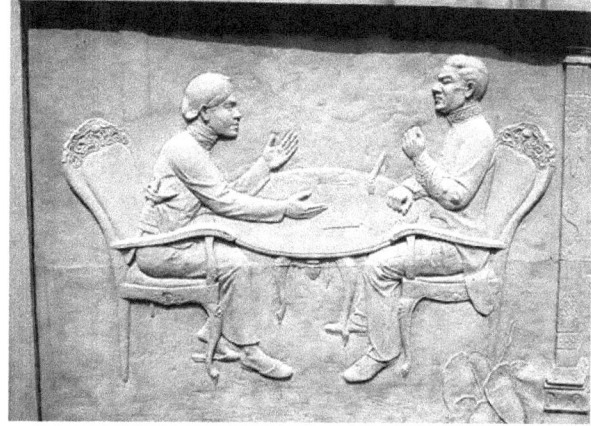

HBIX and Governor Lucien Adam at the coronation, April 1940.
R.D.S. Sumardi.

Mangunturtangkil Pavilion in the kraton where Hamengku Buwono was enthroned in 1940. J Monfries.

Official photograph of the newly installed HBIX. Public domain.

HBIX and Governor Adam inspecting an aircraft named "Winston Churchill", probably after the outbreak of the Pacific War (late 1941 or early 1942). R.D.S. Sumardi.

A view of the Selokan Mataram canal built in the Japanese period, Sleman. J Monfries.

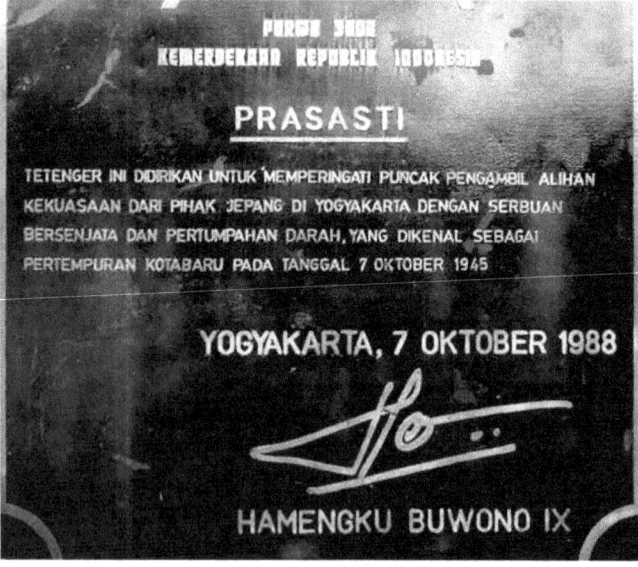

Kotabaru Monument inscription commemorating the attack on Kempeitai headquarters, October 1945. J Monfries. Translation of inscription: "This monument was built to commemorate the culmination of the struggle to wrest power from Japan in Yogyakarta through armed attack and bloodshed, known as the battle of Kotabaru, 7 October 1945 (sgd) Hamengku Buwono IX". The monument was consecrated in October 1988, thus probably being the last official action by HBIX before his death later that month.

HBIX and Sutan Syahrir during the revolution (1946?), probably not long after HBIX had joined the Syahrir Government. Public domain.

HBIX awarded rank of honorary general, 1947. Yogyakarta Regional Archives.

HBIX at a KTN meeting (Three Nations Commission, precursor to the UN Good Offices Commission), probably 1946. Sultan Hamid II on left of picture. Yogyakarta Regional Archives.

Hamengku Buwono IX Museum in the kraton. This is the furniture, transferred from its original location (Prabuningrat's residence), around which HBIX and Suharto planned the General Offensive of 1 March 1949. J Monfries.

Suharto's General Offensive Monument, Malioboro St. The panel shows Suharto planning the attack with his troops.
J Monfries.

Next panel – Suharto meeting the Sultan. The panels are of course in the wrong order. Suharto met HBIX before the attack, not after.
J Monfries.

HBIX and Pakualam caucusing on 1 March 1949 during the General Offensive. Yogyakarta Regional Archives.

Bas-relief at kraton portraying (1) HBIX defying General Meyer after the General Offensive on 1 March 1949; (2) HBIX and Suharto planning the attack. HBIX's openly angry posture in Panel 1 does not accord with his normal behaviour. J Monfries

HBIX and Sukarno on Sukarno's return from Bangka, April 1949. Yogyakarta Regional Archives.

HBIX shakes hands with Hatta on the latter's return with Sukarno from Bangka, April 1949. Yogyakarta Regional Archives.

HBIX and Suharto in 1949. The caption reads "Lt Col Suharto, as Commander of Wehrkreise (Military District) III, reports to Sultan Hamengku Buwono that his forces are ready to enter Jogjakarta, 29 June 1949". Source unknown.

Lt.Kol. Suharto sebagai Kom.W.K.III (D.I.Yogyakarta) melaporkan kepada Sri Sultan Hamengku Buwono, bahwa pasukan telah siap masuk Yogyakarta tgl. 29/6/1949.

HBIX signs transfer of sovereignty document, Jakarta, December 1949. Source unknown.

HBIX escorting Ali Sastroamijoyo (later Prime Minister) on a visit to Yogyakarta, in 1949. Just before this, Ali had been a member of the Indonesian delegation at the Round Table Conference in The Hague. Yogyakarta Regional Archives.

HBIX on an incognito visit to Beringharjo market, Yogyakarta, 1950. Yogyakarta Regional Archives.

HBIX and the Pakualam at a Regional Election Committee (PPD) meeting, 1956. Yogyakarta Regional Archives.

HBIX at a social occasion in the 1950s. The long-serving mayor of Yogyakarta, Purwokusumo, is visible at the centre rear. KRT Jatiningrat.

HBIX's first four wives — from left, Ciptomurti (third wife), Pintokopurnomo (first), Windyaningrum (second), Hastungkoro (fourth wife), in the 1950s. Source unknown.

HBIX and General Nasution saluting at an unknown ceremony in 1959, alongside then Col Suharto (with moustache). Yogyakarta Regional Archives.

HBIX speaking at a Trikora ceremony also attended by Sukarno, 1963 (original caption describes HBIX inaccurately as Defence Minister). Yogyakarta Regional Archives.

Funeral of Sutan Syahrir 1966 from left, Adam Malik, Johannes Leimena, Hatta, HBIX, Suharto. The wide publicity given to the state funeral of one of Sukarno's strongest political foes, in the middle of the crucial year of 1966, was used as an implied rebuke to Sukarno. © Indonesian National Library (also thanks to Leimena Institute).

New York Times advertisement, 17 January 1969, where Hamengku Buwono announces that Indonesia is open for business. Indonesian Government.

HBIX and two of his sons in the 1980s. From left — unknown, Prince Prabukusumo, Prince Hadikusumo (now deceased), HBIX. HH Prince Prabukusumo.

Front cover of *Tahta untuk Rakyat*, festschrift for HBIX, 1982.
© Kompas Gramedia.

HBIX in old age, 1980s.
Source unknown.

Entrance to the royal tombs at Imogiri, probably photographed in the 1930s. Yogyakarta Regional Archives.

HBIX's bier is taken to Imogiri accompanied by huge crowds, 7 October 1988. Yogyakarta Regional Archives.

Hamengku Buwono X taking the oath as Governor of Yogyakarta Special Region, 3 October 1998, after the death of Acting Governor Pakualam VIII. Yogyakarta Regional Archives.

www.ingramcontent.com/pod-product-compliance
Lightning Source LLC
Chambersburg PA
CBHW071228290426
44108CB00013B/1333